THE IDEAS OF
HENRY LUCE

THE IDEAS OF HENRY LUCE

EDITED WITH
AN INTRODUCTION BY

JOHN K. JESSUP

ATHENEUM
NEW YORK
1969

ACKNOWLEDGMENT

In preparing this book I have had help from many of Henry R. Luce's friends, relatives and former colleagues, too many to list. I am particularly indebted to Clare Boothe Luce, Mrs. Maurice T. Moore, Henry Luce III, Eric Hodgins, Hedley Donovan, Ralph Graves, Eleanor Schwartz, Mary Phinney, Betty Morris and all those associated with the preparation of Robert T. Elson's book, *Time Inc.: The Intimate History of a Publishing Enterprise, 1923–1941* (Atheneum, 1968). But I alone am responsible for any editorial errors of fact or judgment in what follows.   J.K.J.

CONTENTS

3   THE RULE OF LAW   151

4   EAST AND WEST   189

5   THE BUSINESSMAN AND HIS SYSTEM   216

9   AMONG FRIENDS   375

THE IDEAS OF
HENRY LUCE

INTRODUCTION
A LOOK AT LUCE'S MIND

T HE PURPOSE of this volume is to exhibit the mind of Henry Robinson Luce in his own words. His professional achievements as a publisher and journalist are described in the corporate history called *Time Inc.*, by Robert Elson, of which Volume I was published last year. There will no doubt be more than one attempt at a personal biography. The present volume has the different aim of letting Luce tell what he thought he was up to and why—not only as a journalist but as a man of many interests and beliefs and as a citizen of a fast-changing world. His was an unusually self-knowing mind whose great quickness and subtlety rarely trapped him in any form of self-deceit. He could and did change his mind about many things, but he had a coherent and responsible set of central convictions that changed remarkably little and that he was at great pains to communicate to others. Fair-minded students of Luce will want to take his own statements as the *prima facie* version, though not the whole story, of his life's purpose and meaning. Hence this book.

"Most of what I know . . . and much of what I think," wrote Luce in 1961, "has been expressed in some millions of words in TIME, LIFE, FORTUNE," mixed with "the continuous reportorial efforts of hundreds of colleagues." But, he added, "On various occasions, usually in the form of a speech, I express my views on major matters in my own idiom." These speeches, some 235 of which exist in print or typescript, are the chief source material of this volume. Luce was also a voluminous writer of letters, reporter's notes and office memoranda; he wrote more than a score of signed articles for his own and a few other magazines; he left behind the unfinished rough draft of a book about his involvement with American political men and events. All these records have been culled or consulted for the present volume, but the speeches make up the bulk of it. They have here been selected and arranged with a view to defining not only the range of Luce's serious interests but also the messages he mainly wanted to get across.

While at Yale he wrote his parents that he intended to be a journalist, but only "because the one thing I want to do is to be an orator, but no such profession now exists for the preacher must also be a pastor, the lecturer an examiner, and the public orator a political committee man." By the age of five in China, having heard a great many sermons, he was delivering some of his own to the neighbors' children or anyone else who would listen. At school in Chefoo he found debating "the best fun you ever saw"; at Hotchkiss and at Yale he not only debated but competed eagerly for oratory prizes, his crowning victory being Yale's DeForest prize in 1920. He was all the more competitive at public speaking because it did not come easily to him; he was handicapped by an early stammer that even in his forties made him sound, to at least one hearer, "like a jammed machine gun." Like Churchill, who was not a born but a self-made orator, Luce cultivated the art, and with the same assiduous passion that fired his journalism—the desire to inform, to awaken, to edify, to persuade. He worked hard on the content of his prepared speeches, and even late in life could be found rehearsing the next one before a mirror. He often sought advice on them from his family or colleagues, and sometimes accepted another's sentence or suggestion, but he used no ghosts; every speech was thought out and usually handwritten by him, and said what he wanted to say. Long practice gradually made him, if not a great orator, certainly a skilled and arresting platform performer who sometimes lost but usually held his audience.

The purpose of this book, however, is not to prove Luce's eloquence but to let him make his points. The selections are, accordingly, with a few exceptions, shortened or excerpted from their originals. Cuts are so many that it would have been pedantic to indicate them by the usual dots. Also not indicated are the few words supplied by the editor (for transitions or grammar, never for substance) and a few corrections of obvious mistakes. Like all journalists, Luce wanted above all to be read, and the present editor's rule has been to make that as easy as possible without violating Luce's meaning.

Luce would use the same speech, or with a few variations, on more than one audience, and he repeated his major themes many times in different words. He also frequently combined several favorite themes in the same speech, so that their classification into the nine chapters of this book is in many cases rather arbitrary. Luce believed above all in the unity of truth and in the relatedness of all branches of knowledge. He moved easily in a single speech from theology to history to politics to economics and a lot of other subjects. *De omni re scibili et quibusdam aliis* *—that early TIME slogan was the inventory of Luce's mind. It was not the systematic mind of a librarian, but neither was it a jumble. He organized his knowledge under various tentatively but contentiously held hypotheses plus a few more basic beliefs that he took on faith.

He was a better educated man than most of his contemporaries, partly because of his muscular and enthusiastic approach to learning; partly, no doubt, as he believed, because of the head start he got in the bracing climate of the school at Chefoo (page 378). At twelve he was translating verses from the Latin New Testament into French. At thirteen he was writing a long epic poem on "the missionary's sacrifices and rewards" and an essay on capital punishment. At fourteen he "had a long talk with Thornton Wilder † about Darwinism. He says it is quite the thing in the U.S." At fourteen also he first toured Europe by himself. He rode easily and with honors through the Hotchkiss and Yale curricula while carrying a heavy extracurricular load (and, at Hotchkiss, the menial chores of a scholarship boy). The pace of his education is indicated by this letter home from Hotchkiss after recovering from the mumps: "If I can get down to New York for the weekend, see a good show, hear two or three good sermons, get some good hours in the library and several square meals I'll be satisfied." Or this one from Yale: "Lunch with Laski ‡ yesterday was more interesting than ever. . . . It finally came to Einstein's theories. . . . Strange—it seems that what Dr. Berkeley worked out philosophi-

* Concerning everything knowable and various other things besides.
† Thornton Wilder, the American novelist and playwright, was a classmate of Luce's at Chefoo as well as at Yale.
‡ Harold Laski, the English political scientist and socialist, taught at Yale in 1919–20.

cally, the scientist has now proved. And *Sartor Resartus* is fact. Fortunately for me—a long avowed transcendentalist—it seems that I can stand on Einstein's ground and say, 'I told you so!' " Or this from Oxford, while doing postgraduate work in modern history: "I am doing my Greek Testament very seriously. . . . One pauses over phrases that one knew too well."

He had a scholar's interests but instead chose journalism because, as he reckoned at eighteen, he could "by that way come nearest to the heart of the world" and also because "it means that my interests must include everything from Beethoven to Labor Strikes." The nature of his profession excluded a concentrated erudition in any one field; but he remained all his life a steady reader in many fields, especially popular fiction, theology, history and political philosophy. Had he specialized, it would probably have been in history, in which his father had "wanted me to be learned."

As a recorder of current events, Luce was always aware of their wider historical framework. It was his sense of history also that made him so future-oriented and led him into occasional flyers in prophecy. An Air Force general visiting Maxwell Field, where Luce had been Chairman of the Board of Visitors at the Air University, found in his bedside table "a well-worn Bible" with Luce's bookplate in it and an old note in Luce's handwriting: "Write the things which thou hast seen, and the things which are, and the things which shall be hereafter" (Revelation 1–19).

His feeling for the continuity of history and for abstract ideas made him eager to impose order on the chaos of the world's daily happenings. "Our main business," he once told some colleagues at Time Inc., "is with the phenomenon, the event, the concrete, the particular man, here and now. But all of that makes no sense without the other. It is not our business to discover great new truths or teach great old truths. But unless we pay attention to the great truths, new and old, we will not do justice to reporting the phenomena."

A key word in that admonition is "attention." As his longtime colleague Max Ways pointed out in FORTUNE (April 1967), Luce's innate curiosity was less important than the fact that he was "perhaps the most attentive man of his time." His attentiveness, moreover, was "a carefully cultivated quality . . . a work of intellect, art and will," which he was therefore able to communicate by example to the journalists who came to work for him. "His magazines compelled attention because he and his companions paid attention," said Ways. Nobody could read as attentively—not speedily, just attentively—as Harry Luce. And as Dr. David H. C. Read remarked in his sensitive eulogy, "He listened, too, with an intensity you could almost hear."

In that eulogy, delivered at the Madison Avenue Presbyterian Church on March 3, 1967, Dr. Read listed some of the complexities and seeming contradictions in his friend and parishioner's personality. Luce, he said, was "an idealist who made his judgments with utter realism; a man with his roots in the world unseen who joyfully plunged into the arena of the world we know . . . a man of unlimited imagination who reveled in hard facts; one who could be gruff with the mighty and relaxed with little children . . . an intellectual who yet became the world's greatest popularizer of philosophy and art; a thinker who could see all sides of a question and yet make a quick and implacable decision." He was also a very successful businessman and a great editor, two functions that most journalists believe to be in conflict. Another conflict, as Luce said himself, was between his emulation of saints and heroes and his desire to be a "regular guy." He was extremely sophisticated on many subjects but undentably naive on others; he never pretended to knowledge he did not have, not even by the negative pretense of silence; his incessant questioning of received opinions was part of his genius as an editor. He was a loyal heir of Western (especially British) civilization and its values who was nevertheless an equal partisan of Asia and a prophet *contra* Kipling that East and West would meet. He was a Christian of innate humility whose favorite hero of legend was nevertheless the man who defied the gods, Prometheus. He was thoroughly aware of these and other conflicts in himself, and his reconciliation of them is not only a recurrent theme of these speeches, but the key to his wholeness, or what in a college essay he called "the integrity of the mind." The reconciliation usually had an American accent, as several chapters in this volume will show.

Luce was a man of strong and earthy emotions, and these made his presence always electric even though he usually kept his temper under strict control. "I am biased in favor of God, the Republican party, and free enterprise," he said in a testy moment; he was also for country and for Yale. But his prejudices, though he had a complete set, are not a very good clue to the real hierarchy of his values. He could be more accurately described, in descending order of importance, as in faith a Protestant Christian, in loyalty an unusually patriotic American, in politics a liberal and independent Republican, in occupation a journalist and a free enterpriser, in temperament a yea-sayer, in sentiment a Yale man. The balance of this freehand introductory sketch is an effort to fill out this framework and to point up the evidence of Luce's own words.

The Mellow Calvinist

Said Dr. Read, in the eulogy mentioned above: "Henry Luce was, above all else, a man of faith. That faith was not a vague quality of humanistic hope. . . . It was a quite specific faith in the sovereign God and Creator through Jesus Christ His Son. . . . As a child he learned the answer to the question, What is the chief end of man? To glorify God and enjoy Him forever. And this he sought to interpret in the dedication of his own gifts, in the life of his nation, and in his understanding of the modern world."

But the Presbyterian creed in which Luce was brought up did not set the bounds of his religious imagination. His was, as Dr. Read said, a "mellow Calvinism." He had learned it from his parents, an unusual pair of devout but intellectual Presbyterian missionaries who asked for, and believed that they often received, divine guidance in the decisions of their busy lives as bringers of Western education to China. Henry Winters Luce (1868–1941) was a sunny, energetic, but very independent evangelist who bridged the generation of 19th-century fundamentalist missionaries with the later ecumenical breed who measured their success less in terms of sectarian conversions than in practical human steps toward the moral unity of the world. He helped to found, expand or finance several of the leading Christian universities in China, meanwhile conveying his own open-ended religious zeal to his four children.

"With respect to religion there are three classes of people: the religious rationalizers, the irreligious rationalizers and the religiously inquisitive," quotes H. W. Luce's biographer, B. A. Garside, adding that "Luce belonged preeminently in the third of these classes." So did his elder son. Henry R. Luce was serious but not slavish in his churchgoing and private devotions. For many years, when Sunday was a working day at TIME, he got to church irregularly or not at all. He never forsook, but neither did he feel confined by, his Presbyterian creed. "It is a terrible thing," he once wrote, "to have to act always in accordance with your principles"—and when he found this too terrible, he was more likely to trust in the mercy of God than to fear His wrath.

An instructive comparison has been drawn between Luce's Calvinism and that of his older friend Max Aitken, Lord Beaverbrook, who came from a more fundamentalist Presbyterian background in Canada than Luce's in China. Beaverbrook was a rigorous predestinarian who believed that he himself was damned and who acted in the belief. He could praise God in bouts of devout hymn-singing, but not by mending his ways. Luce liked Beaverbrook enormously but also reserved for him an adjective he seldom used: wicked. Unlike Beaverbrook's, Luce's sins were never defiant. Unlike Beaverbrook, Luce felt that works as well as faith and election had some bearing on personal salvation. As a missionary's son and a born teacher, Luce felt something like contempt for Beaverbrook's cynical claim that his sole purpose as a journalist was "power—power—and more power!" Yet when these friends parleyed, in New York or London or on the Côte d'Azur, they spent as much time discussing the Westminster Confession as they did on journalism or politics.

It was not only with fellow Calvinists that Luce liked to argue theology. He did so with Reinhold Niebuhr, the neo-orthodox pessimist; with Arnold Toynbee, the quasi-Christian philosopher of history; with John Courtney Murray, the liberal American Jesuit; with Gerald Heard, the mystical syncretist; with William Ernest Hocking, the "God-intoxicated" philosopher; with Charles Malik, the Christian-Arab-philosopher-statesman; with his pastors George Buttrick and David Read; with colleagues at Time Inc.; with his family; with many others. He did not nurse his beliefs in private, but subjected them repeatedly to argumentative exposure. Like the civilized man defined by Justice Holmes, he was always able to question his own first principles; but he was equally able to reassert or redefine them when he felt the questions had been met. He saw no virtue in leaving everything suspended in doubt. "O Lord, I believe—help Thou my unbelief"—he said that more than once. Because he took the question of God seriously, his sharp but sometimes crabwise distinctions could puzzle the uninitiated.

"Ambivalence" was one of his favorite words, but he was in constant struggle to avoid its application to himself. He could disdain the naiveté of the young "God-is-dead" theologians while retaining great respect for the serious subtleties of their chief source of inspiration, Paul Tillich ("God is the ground of our being"). He was as much interested in Tillich's efforts to modernize the idea of God as he was secure in his own God-centered cosmogony.

John Courtney Murray made a curious point in reflecting on his Protestant friend's "astonishing and all but unclassifiable" mind. It was that many of the serious thinkers to whom Luce was most attracted—Hocking, Toynbee, Tillich, Heard and later Pierre Teilhard de Chardin—were all what Murray called "gnostics." By this Murray did not mean that they were followers of the second-century Christian heresy. He meant that they were all semi-mystic followers of personal paths to truth who put more of their puzzled faith in intuition than in revelation or authority. "Poor indeed is the unmystical philosophy," wrote Luce in college, and he never ceased to believe in the possibility of private visions of God. Yet he could not himself be called a gnostic. His own religion was less mystical than historical, rooted in time and place.

It was rooted in Palestine in the first three decades A.D. This historical event, as Luce saw it, was the high point of God's intervention in human affairs that began with Creation, picked up speed with Abraham, left signs for the eye of faith in every century, and will make its purpose fully clear at the end of the world. Luce's providential view of history remained intact against the arguments of his more learned and less certain friends.

He was the pioneer in introducing Toynbee's great *A Study of History* to the American mass audience (in LIFE in 1948). Although he later cooled toward Toynbee's political views, Toynbee exemplified the strong teleological sense that Luce admired in his "gnostics." It was their common vision of a spiritual evolution of mankind, of a new and more reverent Idea of Progress, that stirred Luce. Teilhard de Chardin was the last, his appeal being that of a distinguished scientist as well as an ordained Christian. Man could collaborate with God in his own evolution toward higher stages of life on earth, toward an approximation of the City of Man to the City of God! Although this notion aroused Luce's skeptical and Calvinist realism about the disabling burden of Original Sin, probably no contemporary vision appealed more than

Teilhard's to Luce's longing for a modern prophet for "a world come of age," a scientific model of Christian hope.

But such a hope is not a promise, and the long term is not the short. Meanwhile, as Luce often said, there was the "day by day, week by week, year by year" problem for the Christian of serving more immediate goals and preventing human life from getting any worse. Christianity was to Luce a two-dimensional religion, its believers "stretched between earth and heaven," duty-bound to improve man's lot on earth as well as to contemplate eternity. His father, like so many missionaries of the period, early discovered that the Bible could not be read or heard on empty stomachs. At Hotchkiss Luce even thought of becoming a businessman in China —"some big economic movement—railroads, mining, wholesale farming, 5 and 10-cent stores, news syndicates"—because "before the people as a whole become alive to the 'higher things' they must get their noses off the economic grindstone." Luce has been called "the very embodiment of Max Weber's Protestant ethic," as though he believed with Victorian prelates that "God is in league with riches." He had no such illusion, but neither did he believe that poverty was a source of spiritual strength. When a conscientious young writer rather fatuously chided him for paying his employees so well, Luce replied, "Do you want to be poor? I was poor once and I saw no merit in it, if you can honestly avoid it."

Luce was also concerned with the old question of whether the Church of God should give priority to making good men or making a good society. He was forever trying to correct an overemphasis on either of these duties. His sympathy for the unequal condition of the American Negro long antedated the civil-rights revolution; he put in a conscientious year as fund-raising chairman of the Urban League in 1947. He established in his father's memory a unique chair at Union Theological Seminary for visiting professorships and fellowships. His last great philanthropic effort was to help raise $50 million for the United Presbyterian Church, even though his own pet project, a National Church and Center in Washington, was for a time eliminated from the drive's objectives. He readily criticized his own church's stand, and that of organized Protestantism, on social questions. He was all for "the social gospel" except when it led its advocates into what he regarded as unrealism, as when the World Council of Churches went anti-anti-Communist or when Union Theological professors proclaimed that a social revolution was necessary to approach Christian goals on earth. He particularly resented this kind of dogmatism in churchmen who knew less about politics and economics than he.

In his personal relations, Luce's Christian beliefs were most manifest in his prowess at turning the other cheek to adversaries, in his loyal devotion to friends and family, and in his manifold and usually secret acts of private charity. His most obviously Calvinistic trait was not self-denial but an industrious jealousy of the clock. He hated any careless use of time, including small talk. Even in his last years of semiretirement he rationed his hours. In Rome in 1949, he and Time Inc. Vice President Allen Grover spent an exhausting day on Luce's always tight schedule, winding up with a grueling three-hour session in Luce's suite with the editor of *L'Osservatore Romano*. The interview ended toward 6 P.M., the guest left, and the interpreter fainted on the floor from fatigue. Next thing Grover knew, Luce was saying, "Al! We have two hours until dinner. What shall we do with them?"

"*I Consider Myself a Liberal*"

"The art of government is a very great art," wrote Luce in 1934, taking care not to call it a "science." He deplored the change in pedagogical fashion that turned "political philosophy," which he had studied at Yale, into "political science," implying its infiltration by those academic upstarts, the sociologists, and their spurious claims to exactitude. He often quoted Cardinal Manning's dictum that politics is a branch of morals, and he could sniff out the hidden philosophical premise behind any political generalization. Confronted for the first time by an axiom of Justice Holmes— "continuity with the past is only a necessity and not a duty"—he smiled in brief admiration and pointed out: "You could turn that around. Leaving the past behind is also not a duty."

His jumpy and elliptical style of discourse concealed the strong frame of Aristotelian logic in his mind. In political argument he seldom appealed to general principles. He held that "any doctrine can be carried too far," and once warned his editors that "devotion to principle need not cause us to be trapped in the dilemmas of moral absolutes." He favored Socratic methods and liked to withhold a part of his mind as long as possible, sometimes even from himself. Rather than end an argument by invoking a principle, he would continue it until his adversary would defeat—or preferably enlighten—himself in his own terms, not Luce's. This could be puzzling to many intent on figuring out "what Luce really thinks."

In the book he was writing at his death, Luce partially dropped this wary pose and indulged an elder's right to be didactic. He had a thesis: that U.S. foreign policy thrives when guided by traditional American principles and fails when it neglects them. It was a thesis that could be illustrated but not proved. But he left no doubt about what he meant by "traditional American principles," or why he thought America should stick to them. They were liberty under law; self-government by responsible and self-governing citizens; the reign of reason in argument and of constitutionally chosen majorities in power.

Luce also believed that society needs an aristocracy—one of worth, not birth or money. This need was a theme of some of his earliest speeches and even before he founded FORTUNE he was tentatively hoping that the American businessman might grow into an aristocratic role, since "those who have a sizable stake in the country ought, therefore, to yield to no other class in either the degree or the intelligence of their patriotism." As late as 1961, when Professor Philip Phenix of Columbia Teachers College published his treatise called *Education and the Common Good*, Luce was one of the few editors to notice—and applaud—its proposition that America should become a "democracy of worth" instead of a "democracy of desire." John Gardner had made a similar point in a LIFE article in 1960 that contained seeds of his later book called *Excellence* ("Can we be equal and excellent too?"). But much as Luce loved excellence, he sensed that the idea was not quite consonant with the American mood of the 1950s and 1960s, when so many of democracy's "desires" were being whetted by partial satisfaction. Mellowing in his later years, he stopped preaching his belief in aristocracy except indirectly—by singling out examples of excellence for journalistic treatment.

The emphasis of his political views changed with the changing trend of events. In the 1930s he scarcely made a speech without quoting Ortega y Gasset's rather pessimistic but prophetic *The Revolt of the Masses*. In the more resolute and self-confident American mood that followed Pearl Harbor, Luce's favorite quotations were from Whitehead, in which he emphasized the difficult choices facing a potentially great world civilization. Still later he rediscovered Whitman's hymns to "the democratic-republican principle" and quoted them repeatedly on the enlarging horizons of its destiny. Thus the curve of Luce's political thought, along a pessimism-optimism spectrum, moved steadily toward optimism, and his later speeches are those of a shameless yea-sayer.

Yet even in his Ortega y Gasset days, yea-saying was the clue to his temperament. He loved to don the mantle of Old Testament prophets but he almost always wound up expounding a New Testament faith and hope. An exception was a speech in Montclair, New Jersey, in 1937 (page 101), but there his audience was a bunch of complacent Yale and Wall Street types whom he felt duty-bound to jar.

Although he never ceased to "consider myself a liberal," Luce was intensely conscious of the tentative and fragile nature of "the American experiment" (as he often called it) in free self-government. Like most of the Founding Fathers, whom he admired extravagantly, he believed that governments were a badge of original sin and that if men were angels, no government would be necessary. One of the tenderest spots in his tough mind was for anarchists, whose love of liberty he shared and whose faith in human goodness he would have liked to share, but could not. His theology told him that only a world ruled by Christian love—i.e., the City of God—could dispense with the brutal hierarchies of order-keeping among men; and his political philosophy told him that constitutionalism and the rule of law were the surest way to maximize personal liberty, the highest political good, and minimize the role of coercion in a system of order.

"We do not say," he wrote in 1945, "that it is our duty to establish moral or other Utopias; indeed, we know that men are incapable of doing any such thing. What we say is that it is the God-given duty of men to organize human societies—not as ants organize them but with reflective thought and imaginative foresight. We must, that is, here and now, do the best we can, knowing that our best will be deeply tainted with error and corruption." When in 1966 the Saigon government announced a constitutional convention, Luce called it "one of the most exciting occasions in recent human events" and hoped that "every 'political scientist' in this country would test his wits" by the opportunity to contribute to the new Vietnamese constitution. "It would be interesting to see Walter Lippmann put himself to this test," he added. For his own magazines, "there may be a chance here to go beyond reporting and incite a number of Americans to think."

The possible flaw in American democracy, Luce feared, was its "one great assumption" that a "vigorous sense of right and wrong" would persist among men. Liberty means responsibility. To make a free democracy work, most citizens would have to govern themselves not by fear of the police, but by conscience. Democracy assumes that "there will exist strong moral sanctions broader and more compelling than the statute books." A democracy is therefore "a moral proposition" and its success depends on a common feeling that the laws, on the whole, are just or could be made so by legal means. The ideal of justice in American law, Luce felt, was symbolized by John Marshall's Blackstonian belief that the Constitution was to be interpreted by the light of the moral law of God's universe. In this way the laws would be kept in tune with the average citizen's conscience. Conscience played so crucial a role in Luce's system of political freedom that he did not believe a godless democracy would work. He applauded an obiter dictum of Justice Douglas' that "our institutions presuppose a Supreme Being" and deplored the Supreme Court's exaggerated reading of the First Amendment that ruled the Bible out of the public schools.

Although he did his homework in Marx, Lenin, Weber, the Christian Socialists, Sorel, Pareto, Burnham and other post-18th-century thinkers, Luce never encountered a body of political theory that he found as persuasive as the *Federalist Papers*. When Charles Beard wrote *The Republic* expounding such a view in 1943, Luce decreed that LIFE run a condensed version of the book in no less than ten installments. In 1949 he persuaded a rising young historian, A. Whitney Griswold, to present a similar thesis in FORTUNE. The article appeared in April 1950 and was about to go to press when Griswold, a dark horse, was named president of Yale. "A good editor is a lucky editor," said Luce.

Luce's own most famous venture in political prophecy, "The American Century" (page 105), was derived less from philosophic reasoning than from his gut feelings about power relationships and the state of the world in 1940–41. Today it reads like a series of commonplaces, since it has all come true; but it raised many hackles at the time and was widely misinterpreted as advocating a new American imperialism, much to Luce's distress. One critic called him "the Cecil Rhodes of journalism"; another said he showed contempt for "the rest of mankind." The critic who both-ered Luce most was the theologian Reinhold Niebuhr, who found an "egoistic corruption" in the very title. Luce greatly respected Niebuhr for his sensitivity to what God's purpose in human affairs might be; and having accepted his rebuke as far as the title was concerned, and having absorbed a book or two of Niebuhr's ser-mons on political morality, he wrote in 1946, "I know now about the pitfalls and heresies involved in 'The American Century.' I think I am no longer afraid to 'redefine' the American Century." Although he never rewrote the article as such, many of his subse-quent speeches were exercises in the refinement of its main themes.

There was indeed an occasional trace of jingoism in Luce's rhetoric, but not in the strictly logical and coherent case he made over and over again for "The American Proposition" and the corol-lary American mission in world history. Luce had much respect-able support for his belief that America has a historical mission. He inspired a series in LIFE in 1960 on the "National Purpose," to which both presidential candidates of that year contributed, and he would have been pleased but not surprised to find Senator Robert Kennedy reiterating the theme in his last speeches before his assassination.

Luce's own emphases on the various aspects of the American mission shifted somewhat over the years. In the 1930s he felt that liberty was a sufficient definition of our cause, but he always meant liberty under law and he later gave law equal billing. In the 1950s he did his best to make the promotion of world law a cornerstone of U.S. foreign policy, and nearly succeeded (page 187). Moreover, "The American Proposition" sometimes tried on borrowed gar-ments, as when FORTUNE advertised and almost endorsed Clar-ence Streit's *Union Now* in 1939. Luce shared Streit's belief in political freedom but felt cramped by the geographical limits of his plan to organize it in a federation of the established democracies. Luce took a global view of the American mission. When the first ("Dumbarton Oaks") proposals for a United Nations charter appeared in 1944, Luce studied them carefully, and a FORTUNE analysis by Luce and other editors made a number of suggestions for improving the draft, many of which were adopted at the San Francisco conference. But even the final U.N. charter never enlisted Luce's enthusiasm, since the veto made the U.N. a league of tempo-rary victors rather than the basis of a genuine system of world law. Yet he felt even less at home with the advocates of all-out world government, whose proposals he regarded as logical but premature.

He had no illusions about the obstacles on the road to a united world community. He had puzzled with Hocking, author of *Living Religions and a World Faith*, over how Christian ecumenism could ever come to terms with the world's other great religions. He had puzzled with F. S. C. Northrop (*The Meeting of East and West*) —and resumed the puzzling in his final speeches (Chapter 4)— over how to bridge the "profundities of difference" between Occident and Orient. He never proposed final answers to these mysteries. What he did feel, and never stopped feeling, was that America was ideally situated in time, space and inheritance to generate the answers.

"I wonder whether I will ever grow up and cease to be disappointed in what was intended to be so great and good a country," wrote Luce in 1946. But his frequent disappointments in America never added up to disillusion and were usually blamable on individuals. Not the least of these was Franklin Delano Roosevelt.

Luce's differences with F.D.R.'s domestic policies are reflected in Chapter 5. His differences with F.D.R.'s foreign policy between Munich and Pearl Harbor seemed more arbitrary but ran deeper. As a thorough internationalist, Luce gave both private and public support to almost everything Roosevelt did to resist Hitler. But he thought that Roosevelt did too little and that during the Great Debate between isolationists and interventionists, Roosevelt at best paltered with the isolationists (page 351). It was shameful, Luce felt, for America to let Pearl Harbor settle the issue instead of being led to its own moral decision about the war. His several visits to the White House during this period—F.D.R. made the mistake of calling him "Henry" (everyone on a genuine first-name basis called him Harry) and trying to charm him—left Luce either angry or bored. In 1944 he wrote, "Whatever Roosevelt may think now, he was in the 1930s the high priest of the isolationist-pacifism of that decade. . . . Who could have gone further in stultifying the power (physical) and the glory (spiritual) of America?"

Luce went to Chungking in the spring of 1941 and tried to repeat the visit after Pearl Harbor. Despite the approval of the War Department and General Marshall, a second trip was personally and permanently vetoed by F.D.R. From this Luce sadly concluded, "I think it is my duty to go on hating him." But he also concluded, well before F.D.R.'s death, that the President was "going to escape history"—i.e., he would be remembered as the courageous war leader of the Grosvenor Square statue rather than as the devious and unprincipled character Luce thought he knew. There was no bitterness in this conclusion; it was simply an observation about history. Luce never really hated anybody very long. His last epithet for F.D.R. (1964) was "the smiling wizard of democracy."

The public figure who disappointed Luce least, and for whom his admiration was almost unqualified, was Winston Churchill (Time's "Man of the Half-Century" in January 1950). Luce was an early friend of Indian independence and criticized Churchill's standpat colonial policy. He also thought Churchill was wrong to defer, during the war, any thoughts about postwar planning, a cause that Luce himself started work on soon after Pearl Harbor. But since Churchill was not an American and the torch of world leadership was passing to Americans, his shortcomings could be the more easily overlooked.

One of Luce's most frequent disappointments was the Republican party. As a boy he was a Bull Mooser, like his father, and T.R. remained a hero all his life. "Why could not God have saved Teddy for our times?" he would complain. The Republican party of Harding, Coolidge and Hoover left him cold, although he almost always voted for the Republican presidential ticket (an exception: 1928). He briefly considered running for the Senate in 1950 as a Connecticut Republican, but he was never as close to nor as trusted by the party leaders as his wife was. He acquiesced in the description of his magazines as "independent with Republican leanings." He never hesitated to contribute campaign funds to Democrats he admired, such as Stuart Symington.

Not until after 1942, when Life launched its editorial page, did Luce's political views become overtly and unmistakably reflected in his magazines. The effort to keep these nonpartisan and reportorially fair had reached a climax in 1940, when Life carried a signed "Statement from the Editor," calling the election "the most important American election since 1860" and declaring that he, Luce, would not knowingly shake hands or break bread with any citizen who failed to vote in it. Advice on how to vote, however, he conspicuously withheld. Yet Luce was personally very much committed to the cause of Wendell Willkie. It was one of the two campaigns (the other was in 1952) in which, he later reckoned, he not only had a personal commitment but "was influential in a small degree." Willkie and Eisenhower both appealed to him as potential modernizers of the Republican party, T.R.-style. Both were to disappoint him.

It was Russell Davenport, managing editor of FORTUNE, who soon after meeting Willkie quit his job and went to work for Willkie's candidacy. But Luce was early on the band wagon and wrote one or two major speeches for him during the campaign. TIME was often critical of Willkie's campaign tactics, but Luce thought his only serious error was the last-minute pitch to the antiwar vote, an appeal that F.D.R. could and forthwith did cancel with his own antiwar speech ("Your boys are not going to be sent into any foreign wars"). Luce's more serious differences with Willkie began in 1943. Willkie, now the author of *One World* and an active supporter of Roosevelt's war leadership, took to hounding out every sign and symptom of isolationism in the Republican party. Luce, who knew that serious isolationism had died at Pearl Harbor, felt that Willkie's scolding did nobody but F.D.R. any good. He said to Willkie, during one of their talks, "You can excommunicate 10 per cent of Republicans; in fact I'll allow you 20 per cent. But that's the limit, that's all." Willkie seemed to agree, but his tactics alienated friends of Dewey, Taft and even Alf Landon. He alienated so many Republicans that he was clobbered in the Wisconsin primary of 1944. He died before the election, and it was possible for his close friends to disagree on how they thought he would have voted that year. He was the kind of warm, intelligent, idealistic maverick that appealed strongly to Luce, but he was not enough of a Republican to succeed in the role he had been assigned in Luce's dreams for the party.

The Eisenhower attraction was less personal. By 1952, after twenty years of Democratic rule, Luce began to share a spreading apprehension that the two-party system was in danger. Analysis of the Democratic vote in certain areas seemed to validate the supposed Harry Hopkins formula ("Spend and spend, tax and tax, elect and elect") for a permanent Democratic lien on the White House. To disprove this cynical thesis, as Luce saw it, was more important than all other issues in 1952, and Eisenhower clearly had the best chance of insuring a Republican victory.

Luce was one of those who stopped to see Ike at NATO headquarters in early 1952 to encourage his candidacy. A LIFE editorial in March did the same. As the Republican convention drew near, Luce became more embattled on Ike's behalf—at the cost of a personal break with a close friend and classmate, David Ingalls, who was managing Senator Robert A. Taft's campaign. Just before the convention met, TIME appeared with an analysis of the polls and delegations showing that Ike could win and Taft could not. Reprints of other pro-Ike TIME stories were distributed to every delegate at Chicago.

Luce also helped Ike get elected. At a low point in the campaign, when the Scripps-Howard press complained that he was "running like a dry creek," Ike's most professional speech writer, Stanley High, appealed to Luce for help. He got the loan of two top Time Inc. men, Vice President C. D. Jackson (who had worked for Ike at SHAEF) and LIFE editor Emmet J. Hughes, who went to work supplying Ike with his best speeches and his best line ("I shall go to Korea").

Ike's first term, in Luce's opinion, held two real achievements. One was to stabilize the steadily increasing federal budget and at the same time guarantee a respectable posture of military defense. The other was to contest and badly damage, in world opinion, the Soviet Union's propaganda monopoly of the word "peace"—i.e., as Luce put it, Ike "shot down that phony Picasso dove." While John Foster Dulles committed the U.S. fully to waging the cold war, which Luce had taken very seriously since 1946, Eisenhower's magisterial benignity transcended the battle with such constructive proposals as atoms-for-peace and open-skies inspection. C. D. Jackson, by then a White House special assistant, coordinated the atoms-for-peace strategy. Dulles and Luce shared a mutual esteem cemented by their Presbyterianism. It was during Ike's first term that Luce came as close as he ever would to working for the U.S. Government: as consort to the U.S. Ambassador in Rome, 1953–56. In those years Luce divided his time between the Time & Life Building in New York and an office in Rome, where, while pretending to "pour the tea," he actually started what he called a "second career" as a student (and polemicist) in the world of Italian politics and business.

But Luce's personal agenda for the Eisenhower era included

several items that did not get as much White House attention as he thought they deserved. For one thing, Ike as a politician proved more skillful at protecting his own popularity than at imparting it to his party. He did little or nothing to modernize the Republican party or to recruit new blood. Ike "reaped where he had not sown," said Luce.

Luce also would have liked to see Ike wrest the cold-war initiative permanently from the Soviets by more fully identifying the American cause with a specific world cause or project, such as the promotion of world law. Dulles finally agreed on that one, but too late (page 187). Another such cause was a great expansion of world trade through lower tariffs, currency convertibility and more private investment. Luce made many speeches on this subject and C. D. Jackson did his best to give it a higher priority within the Administration. Time Inc. also sponsored two conferences of U.S. and foreign business leaders, at New Orleans in 1955 and at San Francisco in 1957, to promote a freer and wider investment market. The Eisenhower years saw quiet progress in this direction, but the conservatives and protectionists around Ike checked him from giving this cause the bold and dramatic American leadership Luce would have liked. Thus Ike, in the end, proved too cautious, as Willkie had been too incautious, to make Luce a happy Republican. The void left by T.R. in Luce's rather exacting pantheon was never filled.

Plenty of Fun and Profit

Luce's interest in world trade expansion was doubly motivated. It was part of his fervent internationalism, but it was also fired by his confidence in the American business system, which he saw as the engine in the "powerhouse" of the American Century. International business was the natural instrument, he felt, for the attempt to conquer poverty throughout the world in ways most congenial to the simultaneous development of free constitutional governments. This vision of the future placed quite a burden on the American businessman, whom Luce may have idealized somewhat as both an aristocrat and a revolutionary. If so, it cannot be said that Luce did not know what he was talking about. He knew by hard experience both the virtues and the defects, both the fun and the drudgery, of the American business system. He was a businessman before he became a full-time editor and, as the all-but-proprietary stockholder of Time Inc., he took a managerial role in all its major and many minor corporate decisions. If ever a rich man earned his fortune by hard work and attention to detail, it was Harry Luce.

To illustrate Luce's attentiveness, Max Ways tells the story of passing Selfridge's in London one day with Luce, who asked, "How's the store doing?" and added, "Poor Gordon Selfridge." "Why poor?" asked Ways, a new resident in London. Luce replied, "You mean you don't know what happened? The end of the story? Yankee boy came to London and showed the nation of shopkeepers how to keep shop. Built that great institution. Then he stopped paying attention. Got to playing around. Horses *and* women. He lost it. He lost the store. How can you pass here every day and not know that?"

Luce's attentiveness to business was wrapped in a genuine zest for it. To quote Ways further, "Luce liked business—liked to do it and liked to watch it. The marketplace neither terrified nor disgusted him. It was, of course, a place where you had to pay attention. Competition required that, the bankers required it, the customers required it. The market encouraged innovation and punished complacency. The market required and rewarded zest. That suited him—temperamentally, intellectually and morally."

Whether he really enjoyed the grubby details of business or not, Luce insisted on knowing about them. Unlike Gordon Selfridge, he never relaxed his attention, even after he had delegated most of the responsibility to others. He could and often did do every part of the job himself, from writing promotion letters and the annual report to adjusting wage scales and individual salaries, the latter guided by his strong belief in differential rewards and merit raises. The zest he took in his work can be sampled in the 1939 speech (page 45) called "How I Make My Living." It was still there over twenty years later (1961), when he addressed his Time Inc. executive family as follows:

"Tonight I pay my respects to the New Management—having in mind everyone in this room and scores of your juniors who are in new posts or newly confirmed in old ones. While there is no way of measuring these things, at the Harvard Business School or elsewhere, I would say that rarely in the history of organizations does it happen that so many right men are in the right spots as is now the case in Time Inc. Should I now, for modesty's sake, exclude myself from that sweeping encomium? Well, I don't. I include myself in!"

Luce's managerial style was sometimes cocky but never authoritarian. Indeed it could sometimes, especially in personnel juggling, be described as devious, or at least as somewhat mischievous; he occasionally seemed to take a private pleasure in causing trouble for his subordinates. He almost never gave commands or even seemed to make command decisions. Sometimes a new employee would ask how so informal, argumentative and unbusinesslike a man could maintain his authority over the high-powered collection of individuals he had gathered at Time Inc. John Shaw Billings, first managing editor of LIFE, had a short, true answer for that: Luce could think twice as fast as any other man in the shop. Luce operated on the assumption that freedom is the real source of efficiency; that people do their best work when implicitly invited to modify or enlarge their assignments. This principle produced no very clear table of organization, but it attracted and held some of the best business brains (as well as writing talent) in the country, notably Roy E. Larsen and Charles L. Stillman.

Such men were not only indispensable to Time Inc.'s financial success, but also shared the ceaseless dialogue that shaped Luce's thinking on editorial policy. W. A. Swanberg's life of Joseph Pulitzer argues that Pulitzer's two zeals, one for commercial success and one for journalistic truth, worked a conflict in the Pulitzer soul that made him a physical invalid. Luce, who was no kind of invalid, had those same two zeals; but when they produced a conflict he liked nothing better than to scrutinize, measure and resolve it. Not only was the advice of his business colleagues essential to the resolution, but they could also be a source of good editorial ideas.

The most notable example of a businessman's contribution to Time Inc. journalism is, of course, Roy Larsen's role in THE MARCH OF TIME, described in Elson's history. A lesser known example is Stillman's part in the change of FORTUNE's editorial attitude toward economic theory as it evolved from the 1930s to the postwar era. Luce never claimed a grasp of economic theory beyond the Manchester School, which left him dissatisfied and whose precepts he ignored whenever they conflicted with his liberal political principles. (Politics was superior to economics in his hierarchy of values and he even tried to reduce pure economics to its pre-industrial nomenclature of "political economy.") It was political, not economic, conviction that led him to espouse, well ahead of the pack, a federal responsibility for full employment as early as 1934 (page 225). It was Stillman who gave him the missing economic rationale for his hunch, by making the name of Keynes and compensatory fiscal policy respectable in Luce's and FORTUNE's editorial thinking. Early in the war Stillman, puzzled over the evident disjunction between unbalanced budgets and inflation, which was contrary to the economics he had learned at Yale, gave himself a stiff reading course in Keynes (and, more skeptically, in Alvin Hansen) at a time when most businessmen considered them socialists. He then explained the "new economics" in a brilliant office memorandum which became a basis for FORTUNE editorial policy from 1942 on, and which was one of those rivulets of informed opinion that led to the Employment Act of 1946. A federal full-employment policy was of course wholly compatible with—in fact it depended on—a vigorously expanding free-enterprise capitalism of the sort Luce (and Stillman) had been preaching for years. For a few years, especially under Truman, Luce nursed a Puritan scruple about the political morality (as against the economic wisdom) of abandoning the old guideline of the annually balanced federal budget; but the Keynesian logic to which Stillman had introduced him remained irreversible in Time Inc. policy.

Despite his zest for it and its central role in the international war on poverty which Luce foresaw, he knew that business was not the highest of human callings. Of Calvin Coolidge's axiom that "the business of America is business," he said, "I think I can improve on that: the business of business is America." One of his texts for informal speeches, especially to advertising salesmen, was the different roles of Martha and Mary in entertaining Christ at Bethany: Martha, who represented business, running errands and serving dinner, while Mary, who represented all higher arts and professions, sat in the house and anointed her Lord with costly spikenard. Mary, Luce allowed, had "the better part," but the salesmen as well as the editors who heard this speech—those at least who were not merely stupefied—somehow felt prouder of their jobs than before.

In 1938, Luce prepared to abandon his title of president of

Time Inc. and to assume that of editorial director. He had already made Ralph M. Ingersoll publisher of TIME. Wrote Luce, "If I give Ingersoll a job I prefer to have less of [vulgar money-making], it is partly because I have had so damned much of it, and not because I think it lacks imaginative values." He added, "I have had plenty of fun (and profit) as an entrepreneur, but from now on I intend to be a journalist."

The Journalist

At Yale once (so goes an old story in which there is probably some truth) Luce was hurrying, head down, across the campus between one extracurricular chore and another when Briton Hadden (who was to be cofounder of TIME) yelled at him, "Look out, Harry, or you'll drop the college!" Luce's sense of responsibility was indeed more serious than the boyish Hadden's, but it took him nearly a decade after Hadden's death in 1929 to institutionalize this sense of responsibility in the editorial policy of his magazines. As long as Luce was more entrepreneur than editor, TIME's editorial policy (in the words of its managing editor John S. Martin) "was to have no policy. It was mugwump." To which Luce added only that "it was on the side of truth against bunk."

Hadden was a journalist of facts and style; Luce's genius lay more in the spotting and measuring of trends. In the 1930s, in contrast with the feckless 1920s, trends were getting more serious and forcing editors to form opinions whether they wanted to or not. TIME, wrote Luce, must now "take its interpretative role more seriously." Was the Spanish civil war a rehearsal for Armageddon or not? Was Munich a mistake or just the consequence of past mistakes? There was a marked increase in editorial brow-furrowing. A series of policy committees were formed, mostly abortive, and Luce wrote one policy memorandum after another, many of them never sent. Ralph M. Ingersoll, an even more compulsive memo-writer than Luce, saw his opening and proposed a single touchstone for all editorial policy decisions: the objective truths and spirit of Science. Luce could not buy that as applied to journalism; but he was equally reluctant to formalize his own principles for the guidance of others.

Luce later called this "our first era of Responsibility-in-Crisis," in which the enemy was "indifferentism." The first big battleground was on FORTUNE, where the new managing editor, Russell Davenport, gradually came round to Luce's view that FORTUNE should take a more positive position in defense of the private-enterprise system, then at sea between left-wing attack and New Deal ambiguity. Davenport wrote a series of pathbreaking essays under the general head of "Business and Government," which were in effect the first editorials in any Time Inc. magazine. After his year with Willkie, Davenport returned to the Luce fold and launched the editorial page of LIFE, which ended the era of indifferentism as far as that magazine was concerned. In 1944 the LIFE editorial page first took sides in a national election. "At last we are committed," wrote Luce—committed, of course, not to the Republican party but to "an acceptance of direct involvement in politics," and in this instance to the election of Dewey. It was a commitment to something more than the capricious allotment of weekly orchids and scallions or deciding problems of taste of the "Hopkins' dandruff" variety.*

Immediately after Pearl Harbor, Luce set up a postwar planning department to work out long-term policy positions on major domestic and foreign issues, and its findings were published as supplements to FORTUNE and in shorter form in LIFE. Although Luce wrote few editorials himself, he was continuously involved in them, striving always to keep their positions as clear as possible.

As an editor, Luce was chary with both his praise and dispraise —"a hard-money man," as his longtime colleague Albert L. Furth called him—which made both his praise and his criticism the more effective when they came. He was not a niggler over small points. When taking charge of an issue of TIME, LIFE or FORTUNE, which he did whenever he felt out of touch, he would pass most of the stories without comment in order to concentrate on the few he considered truly important. "Vigor, not minuteness," said another old colleague, Eric Hodgins, "was the key to every editorial thing he did." And even when not directly editing, continued Hodgins (speaking as a former managing editor of FORTUNE), Luce "still had time for the two functions which he always performed superbly: the suggestion of story ideas and the contemplation of the

---

* A TIME report of a Washington function included a vignette of Harry Hopkins brushing dandruff from his shoulder. This became an intra-office symbol of gratuitous malice, or bad taste.

schedule. He would perform the first function best after he had been away for a while. He would come back with his pockets stuffed full of pieces of paper on which he would have written 'artichokes' or 'Belgian draft horses.' He wasn't asking that such articles be published; he was just calling attention to the potentialities.

"As to the contemplation of the schedule, Harry would cross-question you about every article. Once again, it was never a case of 'Do print this but Don't print that.' Harry merely wanted to be sure that the managing editor had a reason—preferably a good reason—for the inclusion of every article proposed. The quality of his control can best be exemplified by a cross-questioning he put me through once when I had scheduled a three-part series on the Radio Corporation of America. 'Why?' Harry wanted to know. 'What's the occasion? Have you got something special?' I said, 'No, Harry, I just thought it was time we looked at this behemoth again.' 'I don't see any point in it. I don't see any point unless you can cost David Sarnoff his job,' said the editor-in-chief. I confessed I had not been guided by so lofty an ambition, so I took the series off the schedule. These cross-questionings were always a little fearful but they were also always exciting."

Luce's views on journalism, its purposes and responsibilities, are made clear in the speeches in Chapter 1. Unlike many editors, he was unwilling to rest the case for a free press on the words of the First Amendment. He knew he was not living in James Madison's world and that the 20th century's trends toward collectivism would not forever exempt the press. In 1937 Luce wrote to Herbert Hoover: "In collectivist states, there is no room for the church or other agencies of conscience, of information or of morality—indeed they are precisely what the all-good and all-powerful state cannot tolerate. . . . How are you going to regulate a free press? And if you don't regulate it, I can see nothing to rely on except private conscience. And if you will rely to some extent on the private conscience of editor-publishers (hoping that the conscience of an Ochs will prevail over the conscience of a Hearst) why not rely also on the private conscience of bankers, manufacturers, educators, etc.?"

Later, Luce's concern for the political and moral justification of a free press led him to set up the Hutchins Commission, and his

surgical comments on its report (page 61) are a more sophisticated statement of his belief in the indivisibility of freedom. He
knew that a responsible press would require a somehow socialized
code of professional ethics, which explains the rather odd invitation
in his 1937 speech to advertisers (page 35), which was repeated
later in his McKinsey Lectures (1963). But he never saw a substitute for the conscience of the proprietor as the real source of
responsibility.

The role of the press in society, in Luce's view, was more than
political. It was an essential organ of self-government in fully
reporting public affairs, the *res publica*. But in mirroring all
aspects of man in society, and giving him "light and leading," it
also became essential to the development of the fullest possibilities
of an American civilization—"the first modern, technological, prosperous, reverent and democratic civilization," as Luce put his
hopes for it. This was the reason for the virtually unlimited charter
of LIFE's subject matter, as set forth in the famous prospectus
Luce wrote. And despite the circulation-oriented circumstances of
SPORTS ILLUSTRATED's birth, that magazine was justified in
Luce's mind on the grounds that it could improve the quality of
Americans' increasing leisure.

Luce believed that men are responsible for history as well as
vice versa. One former colleague thought the "sovereign purpose"
of his life was "to make some difference to history"; in any case,
Luce contributed his share, most conspicuously in and through
journalism. During his lifetime journalism all but completed its
change from a slightly disreputable craft to a well-paid and influential profession. Luce was proud of his part in turning the name of
journalist into "a good word." He was equally proud of his role in
raising the art of pictorial journalism to new heights, first in
FORTUNE and THE MARCH OF TIME movies, later in LIFE: for to
make people aware of their own civilizational possibilities meant
they must be shown as well as told. The explosive growth of
American democracy in numbers, literacy and affluence required
above all a rapidly improving means of communication if Ortega's
"triumph of mass-man" was to be turned instead into what Luce
called "the triumph of masses of men." Luce's magazines gave
this emergent mass democracy a clearer image of itself and a
broader set of common referents. Probably Americans as a people

are more conscious of their possibilities and purposes today than if Luce had not lived.

At Home in the Universe

"I confess I am something of a square," said Luce, who nevertheless immersed himself in everything contemporary, including the theater. He once asked the playwright Edward Albee, "Why don't you write a play about someone I can admire—someone like Paul Hoffman?" He was well aware that Albee was the wrong man to answer that question, which is why he asked him. His sense of humor ran to wit and irony rather than comedy; he smiled oftener than he laughed and he never told (nor liked to hear) blue jokes. His recreations were mainly tennis, golf, bridge, detective stories and jigsaw puzzles. He had no great manual skills and could barely drive a car. He had a good appetite for all the physical pleasures, including occasionally good food, though he normally took meals as a mere fuel stop and occasion for conversation. His only overindulgence was cigarettes; he was told to give them up after his first heart attack (1958), but didn't, although occasionally counseling younger colleagues to do so.

Luce's wealth and power, though they did not take him by surprise, came to him mainly as unsought byproducts of his real quest, which (as his successor as editor-in-chief, Hedley Donovan, put it) was that of "discovering everything he could about everything that mattered, and sharing his discoveries with the widest possible audiences." His subtle, probing, restless mind, so full of surprising facts and novel correlations, could question everybody and everything, including his own loyalties. Yet these remained intact, as illustrated by his speech on Yale (page 383). In 1965 he said to a young mother, "Please explain to me this identity problem of the young. It's one thing about them I can't understand. When I got out of Yale, I, like most of my classmates, knew exactly who I was, where I came from and even what I was going to become." He was himself the old-fashioned kind of Yale man described by Santayana in one of Luce's favorite quotations about Yale—"where American traditions are vigorous, American instincts are unchecked, and young men are trained and made eager for the keen struggles of American life."

Luce was also raised on John Bunyan and his ultimate metaphor for Americans-in-history, as for the human race, was that of a people on a pilgrimage. He once pointed out (page 298) that none of the monsters and obstacles on the path of Christian's progress represented the kind of social and political problems that preoccupy 20th-century man (and preoccupied Luce). They were instead all personal problems of sin and doubt, the kind that were virtually disappearing from the American vocabulary in Luce's lifetime. But they never disappeared from his conscience. As Dr. Read said in his eulogy, "While he enjoyed the dissection of sermons and theological debate, he also liked to be told . . . told of the duties of the Christian faith."

When Luce's second wife was converted to the Roman Catholic Church, some of his family and Presbyterian friends were seriously worried that Luce might become a convert too. But as he said himself, "An ample road to salvation was marked out for me in childhood," and his wife's Catholicism probably intensified rather than threatened his own interest in Presbyterianism. He often went with her to Catholic services as well as to his own. As his father had been an early ecumenist when the word meant Protestant unity, so the Luces were early ecumenists in the sense that emerged from the Second Vatican Council in 1965. Their creedal differences were a subject of discourse rather than a source of discord. They transferred their large South Carolina estate, Mepkin, to the Trappist order for a monastery, and Luce by his own request was buried there.

As a boy Luce had practiced the piano, but he later wrote, "I enjoy music, but because I have never made any, its real appreciation is to me barred." Luce's esthetic sense had other blind spots, such as the ballet and abstract painting; but it was masterly as a sense of timing and the general fitness of things. One of his most graceful achievements was the way he got offstage. He began preparing for retirement in 1959, turned his editorial responsibilities over to Hedley Donovan in 1964, left Time Inc. in excellent running order, and enjoyed three years of personal peace without any suspension of intellectual activity or interests. "Everything in the world is strange and marvelous to well-open eyes," said Ortega. Luce's eyes were well open to the end. Luce's father had said that the purpose of education was "to make a man feel at home in the universe." Luce did.

In his youth Luce wrote poetry, some of which stands up well today. He loved to quote poetry, though seldom anything later than Tennyson, and he sometimes got it wrong. A particular lapse was his repeated use in speeches of the phrase "beneath the wandering moon." He may have been quoting some unknown poet, but it is fairly certain that he had in mind the words Shakespeare gave to Cleopatra after Antony's death. He should now be straightened out, because the true version says what so many of his friends felt when Luce died:

> *The odds is gone*
> *And there is nothing left remarkable*
> *Beneath the visiting moon.*

JOHN K. JESSUP

1

JOURNALISM

Luce, said T. S. Matthews, onetime managing editor of TIME, *"was defensive about journalism." Said Luce, "There is nothing defensive about defending a thesis." In fact, he defended several theses about journalism, depending on whether it was seen as a business, a craft, a profession, an art or a political pillar of a free society. He was a by-no-means-uncritical defender of the press, as these selections show. His lifelong concern was to improve it, and he made at least four major contributions to that end.*

The first was the invention (with Hadden) of the newsmagazine, passionately educational but not didactic, its purpose "to keep educated people well informed." The second was to get the press involved in reporting and judging the previously veiled and neglected world of American business. (This theme is more fully developed in Chapter 5.) His third major contribution was so to broaden the range and enlarge the definition of news as necessarily to raise the intellectual standards of the reporter, writer and editor —and thereby also to raise their status and income. Luce was at the center of the changes that turned the Front Page *newspaperman of the 1920s into the professional journalist of today.*

His fourth great contribution was to pictorial journalism, both with FORTUNE *and* LIFE. *Whether or not the photograph was, as he claimed, "the most important instrument of journalism . . . since the printing press," Luce did more than any other man of his time to make of it "an instrument of significant journalism" and a vehicle of good news as well as bad (Number 3 below). Finally, he contributed to journalism a high example of proprietary con-*

*science and personal responsibility as part of the new professional-
ism. His own sense of responsibility included a mission: that the
press should help create a great American civilization.*

*One night in his senior year at Yale, when he was already
determined to be a journalist, Luce was at a meeting of "an
undergraduate club" (almost certainly Skull and Bones). As he
himself often told it, "An old grad seeks me out. He is Amos Wilder, father of my classmate Thornton Wilder. Old Amos is perhaps
the most brilliant man on the New Haven campus and certainly the
most overpoweringly eloquent. He sits me down in a corner and begins to speak with a deep earnestness. Presently there are tears in
his eyes. He is saying, 'Harry, don't. Don't go into journalism. It
will turn you into a cynic.' Amos Wilder had been a longtime newspaper editor himself. 'Don't,' he says, 'I beg of you. It will corrupt
and corrode you. It will turn your wine into vinegar. You will lose
your soul.' So he spoke for nearly an hour, but I went on my
way—but never forgetting those words.*

"Now to the extent that I have *become corrupted and corroded,
I cannot blame it on journalism. Partly because I had good luck
and had no cause to become sour and cynical about my profession.
But partly, I think, because the climate of journalism changed."*

---

1   THE PRESS AS A BUSINESS

---

*In the first of two Bromley Lectures at Yale, April 21,
1930, Luce developed his theme that the press was
better off for having become a business, albeit a recent
and a peculiar business. This lecture was reprinted by
the* Saturday Review of Literature *in 1931 after the New
York* Worlds *(*Morning, Evening *and* Sunday*) were
sold to the Scripps-Howard chain for $5 million.*

The press has only recently become a business. It is fundamentally different from any other business, but it is nevertheless a
business. For a century or more the press was roughly 1 per cent

learning and literature and 99 per cent patronage, blackmail,
vituperation, knight-errantry, hacks, bums, pomposity, starved
poets, statistics, adulation, fraud, idealism, politics, pieties. The
press was animated by every motive, from the basest to the noblest,
except the simple desire to discover and tell what happened. In the
latter half of the last century, some papers began to make real
money. But, only a decade or two ago, well after the great fortunes
of Bennett, Pulitzer, Medill, Northcliffe, Hearst and others had
been wrested from it, the press was not regarded as a business to
be taken too seriously. Whereas you might pay $8 million or more
for a tin-tack business that was making $1 million a year, you
would hesitate to pay $3 million or $4 million for a newspaper that
was making the same amount. In the case of small-town papers, the
physical equipment and the accessory job-printing business were
still regarded as of more definite value than the apparent profit-
making abilities of the paper.

Especially in the last decade has all this been changed. Big
newspapers have actually been bought and sold for fairly big
money. Before the stock-market crash, Mr. Ochs's New York
Times was casually referred to as worth $100 million. The Chi-
cago *Tribune* may make $10 million a year. Papers in towns of
50,000 or 100,000 population are valued at half a million, a
million, two million—figures that would have appeared fantastic to
their owners a mere decade ago.

The change was principally due to the fact that newspapers
could make good and *regular* profits provided they satisfied enough
readers. This sounds terribly obvious. However obvious, it was
revolutionary, as are most of the great facts that make modern
civilization. For the first time, it became possible for the press to
make money simply by satisfying public taste. There are nobler
motives, there are baser; here, at least, was an honest motive and it
drove out the others. Crookedness remained and of course remains.
Since the money comes only indirectly from the pleased public and
directly from the advertiser, many publishers live principally to
please the advertiser. But so tremendous has been the growth in
advertising, and so intense has become the competition for public
attention, that a publisher who has got his public can be sure of
getting enough advertising. The advertiser wants the eye of the
public, not the ear of the editor.

It is broadly true that since the press became a business it has become free. The press is by no means without its scandals, but when it comes to controlling the press, the truth is that the job of controlling the production of motorcars or oil or wheat is child's play compared with a venture to control the production of news. Now, obviously, I do not mean that all publishers are Unbound Prometheuses, noble, free and brave. But I do mean that they are quite as free as college professors, and quite as brave as politicians, or that at any rate there is nothing in the circumstances within which they operate to prevent them from so being. For the press is managed by those who own it and, in many cases, by those who love it. If this be a condition tending toward virtue, which I believe it is, the press ranks very close in freedom to a university like Harvard or Yale and, I suspect, ranks higher than some state universities.

Divorced from advertising, journalism might by now have developed higher professional standards; it might have provided that moral leadership the lack of which is so apparent in current civilization; its insights might have been keener, its wits sharper. But there is no evidence to support any such proposition. What has actually occurred is the creation of a press that in range and accuracy of news and in variety of entertainment was undreamed of thirty years ago.

---

2 ADDRESS TO THE COMMISSARS

This high-level pitch to the American Association of Advertising Agencies was delivered at White Sulphur Springs, West Virginia, April 30, 1937. Luce's bold demand for $100 million in advertising for LIFE *was well oversubscribed. But his riskier invitation to advertisers to become "ethical and cultural" critics (page 41) as well as subsidizers of the press never, perhaps fortunately, achieved a contractual formulation. He returned to the theme in 1963, but still in a vague and general*

way. Some advertisers and agencies were impressed by
his plea for support of "the true standards of journalism,"
but others continued to apply the cold-blooded test of
slide-rule circulation figures.

I stand before you because you are the only court in the land to whom I am accountable for the sum total of my acts as an editor and a publisher.

There are other courts and law-enforcement agencies standing guard over my behavior both as an individual and as the head of a profit-seeking corporation. But as an editor and publisher, as the senior partner* of a group of editors and publishers, I operate in a world so free that its only explicit law is that there shall be no law. Ours is the only business in America whose behavior the Senate of the United States would not yet dare investigate. This is the great freedom which remains. This is the Freedom of the Press.

But irresponsible as it may be in law, and objectionable as it may be, this lawless Fourth Estate is still not mere anarchy. Then what unwritten laws does it obey, what moons control its tides and eddies? The answer presumably is that the press obeys but one law, the law of 19th-century democratic laissez-faire economic determinism—or, more simply, that the press shall give the public what the public wants.

Many years ago I read a speech by the publisher of a big newspaper. He said his business was to give the public what it wants. Comparing himself to a great manufacturer, he glowingly described how he transformed the forests of Canada into an acceptable breakfast-table accessory. And then, comparing himself to a department-store owner, he presented his paper as a varied display of features—although he did not, as I recall, suggest that they were assorted bargains in scandal and crime.

Let us briefly examine this theory that it is the proper business of the editor-publisher to give the public what it wants. Under even the most elementary ethical analysis, it is false as a standard of behavior for the editor-publisher. For at least three reasons.

In the first place, the analogy between a department-store owner and a publisher is rendered false by the fact that the merchant and the publisher are dealing in entirely different kinds of goods. What the American public wants from the American merchant consists

---

* Luce often so referred to himself, though Time Inc. was never legally a partnership. He was the senior officer of a corporation.

very largely of what the public needs—since 90 per cent of the articles of commerce are the necessities or the near-necessities of life. The *merchant* who skillfully and ably gives the public what it wants is to a very large extent giving it what it needs. The *publisher* who gives the public what it wants has no reason to believe that he is doing any such thing.

In the second place, while the public may be duped by bad merchandise, it is far better able to judge of the practical quality of merchandise than of the spiritual value of its reading matter. It is one thing to be duped. It is quite another thing to be both duped and doped.

In the third place, even before the New Deal, it was the will of the people that the merchant should be largely controlled by rules of behavior roughly summarized as common honesty. But it is still the will of the people that practically no controls should be imposed upon the editor-publisher.

Surely such freedom, unrestrained by any definable rules of honesty or by any simple test of utility, is intolerable without some corresponding duty.

Nevertheless, the department-store theory of publishing, the give-the-public-what-it-wants theory, is the prevailing theory of publishing today. This is due to the interlocking of two great circumstances—to the interlocking of the great doctrine of Freedom of the Press with the extraordinary development of advertising. Let us see how this came about and consider its consequences.

There is one ideal which the American press has sought to maintain through forty years of expanding industry and advertising —the ideal of separation of powers—separation of the editorial department from the advertising department in order to avoid the evils of a kept press. And this ideal has been achieved to a remarkable degree. The day when the big advertiser could keep his wife's social triumphs in the paper and his daughter's scandals out of the paper was never characteristic of the American press. Venality of a minor sort does exist, but all the ordinary *Brass Check* * kind of indictment is pretty much beside the point. By and large the system worked and the philosophy worked. The American editor and the American advertiser established a concordat. The editor

* In *The Brass Check* (1920) muckraker Upton Sinclair accused the press of prostitution, claiming that journalism was in thrall to industrial autocracy. The title derives from a brothel coin, used for a prostitute's services.

said to the advertiser: You must not interfere with my sacred functions. The advertiser said: No, certainly not. On the contrary, if you, Mr. Editor, give the people, the great American people, what they want, I will support you; if you do not, I will not subsidize you. Now in a democratic country, what could be fairer than that? It is of the very essence of democracy. Big Business will not subsidize a press which is not the people's press. On the contrary, it will pour its resources into the press which most nearly pleases the people. And having established this constitutionally impeccable concordat, the businessman, with the applause of all good liberals, absolves himself from all responsibility for the American press.

But though the system and the philosophy worked, there was nevertheless a flaw. They worked too well! They substituted, for the old danger of a kept press, the new danger of the Press-that-gives-the-people-what-they-want. The inevitable operation of the system was to hold out enormous financial reward to the editor-publisher who had the knack of pleasing the people and who was content to be showman and tout. That situation was and is dangerous.

The first and principal danger of the Press-that-gives-the-people-what-they-want is the obvious danger that there is no significant restraint on vulgarity, sensationalism and even incitement to criminality. The second danger, which is more characteristic and perhaps even more insidiously deleterious to public taste and morals, is the fact that there is in this situation an enormous financial incentive to publish twaddle—yards and yards of mediocrity, acres of bad fiction and triviality, square miles of journalistic tripe.

In 1922, in the jazz age, the plans for publishing a weekly called TIME were submitted to a great Sunday editor * in New York. Desiring to be helpfully dissuasive, he explained that the American people did not desire to be informed, they desired only to be amused. No entertainers, we were downhearted. But like others before and since, we intended to publish or bust. The answer of course is that part of the public wants to be informed and part of the public wants to be amused, and all of the public wants to be both informed and amused. The public, that is, wants everything —everything from a bottle of beer to the hope of immortality. No editor-publisher is under any necessity to give it one rather than

* John O'Hara Cosgrave of the New York *World*.

the other. With such variety of taste to be served, the editor-publisher who describes himself as a panderer may be accurately defining himself but he is not thereby defining the limits of the Fourth Estate.

These two dangers—the danger of sensationalism and the danger of mediocrity—are inherent in the Press-that-gives-the-people-what-they-want. But there is another and a greater danger: the danger that such a press will not give the people what they must have—what they will perish without.

The present crisis in world affairs is a crisis in journalism. Fundamentally the reason why the modern dictatorships are unspeakable is not merely because of their murders and their concentration camps and their treason trials. Men can fight that kind of tyranny. The reason why they are unspeakable is that they corrupt the mind from within. They suppress the truth. They lead men by lies and fraud to desire and acquiesce in their own enslavement. And how is this corruption brought about? *By the destruction of journalism.* In more than half of Europe, journalism has been destroyed; in the other half it is mostly venal or emasculated.

This is the true poison of our time. And its only antidote is truth. And not only truth in a laboratory, but truth in the ears of the people. Unless the facts, the significant facts, the difficult, complicated facts of industry and finance and politics are put before the people, the people cannot govern themselves in an industrial society.

Insofar as the Press-that-gives-the-people-what-they-want is a press which does not give the people their political daily bread—their essential and necessary information—it is an unsuccessful press. And you and I must share the responsibility.

Let me give a specific example of how this responsibility works, both negatively and positively, and of how it rests mainly on the editor-publisher, but also on the advertiser.

There ought to be in this country and in this time an outstanding magazine of science.* Several weeks ago an intimate friend of one of my partners brought to him the prospectus of such a magazine and asked him to get my advice on the project and perhaps the help of Time Inc. as a publishing organization. My reply was that the idea of a great magazine of science was excel-

---

* Ten years later this need was filled when two Life editors, Gerard Piel and Dennis Flanagan, together with Donald Miller, bought out the old and ailing *Scientific American* and rejuvenated it (1947).

lent, that the prospectus seemed eminently sound, that in my allegedly expert opinion it had the possibilities of a great success. *But*, I added—just as every floor of a skyscraper is said to cost one life, so every important magazine costs nervous indigestion for at least ten people, and just at the moment we of Time Inc. had no viscera to spare.

Now, a year ago we had or fancied we had some viscera to spare. What did we choose to do? We chose to create a magazine called LIFE. This magazine, as you know, has published pictures of corpses, of nudes, of snakes, of the rear of a hippopotamus and a lecture on How a Wife Should Undress. It has been an enormous success. Evidently it is what the public wants more than it has ever wanted any product of ink and paper.

Nevertheless, I confront you with a question. It is, of course, not basically a question of whether we should have published one magazine or another—I have suggested the alternative merely to point the moral. The question is: Should we publish LIFE? And this is not a question only for my partners to decide. We have decided. We like LIFE. We believe it to be immensely important. We intend to be proud of it. We propose to put into it all the wisdom and understanding of which we are capable. Just as with THE MARCH OF TIME we have put significant journalism into the movie palaces of the land, so we propose to make of the unrespected photograph an instrument of significant journalism. We have decided. But it is also for you to decide. It is a question for each and every one of you to decide in your heart and in your mind, because each of you is deciding it in the pocketbook of your client. I said that I stand before you as before a court. Your court is also the Appropriations Committee of the American press: you are the Commissars, you exist as an alternative to the People's Commissariat of Public Enlightenment. Here today I make application not for a few incidental pennies; I ask that you shall appropriate over the next ten critical years no less than $100 million for the publication of a magazine called LIFE. You cannot escape a reply to this question. We will not let you. We will keep hammering persistently on your doors, asking for the money week after week. You will either give it to us, or you will not. If you do, there will be LIFE. If you do not, there will be no LIFE.

This illustration will serve to establish the extraordinary position in which the advertisers of America find themselves today. They are inextricably involved with the ethical and cultural standards of the American press.

And since that is the case, it is impossible to exaggerate the historic importance of their position. It is not too much to say that the fate of Western civilization can be influenced by the individual and collective behavior of American Advertisers in the next ten years.

Can we, in all conscience, leave the situation as it stands? Dare we continue the existing concordat between editor and advertiser? Or must we abolish the *supremacy* of the doctrine "Give the public what it wants" and insist that the advertiser, together with the editor-publisher, shall assume some burden of ethical and cultural responsibility for the press?

This question depends upon the answers to two other questions. First, can the public save itself? Can the masses save themselves from the barbarous dominion of the mass mind? If you have a complete, unqualified, irrational faith in the common man in the new revolutionary world, then you will believe in giving the public what it wants and whatever it wants and more of it—in education, in law, in goods and chattels, in art, in morals, and in all these things at once in the press. It was an advertising man, Bruce Barton, who made me read Ortega y Gasset's thesis on the mass mind [*The Revolt of the Masses*, 1932]. It begins by making you face the great new physical reality in society—crowds. Not merely Hitler's crowds, or Mussolini's, or Stalin's, or Hirohito's, but the crowds on American beaches, the crowds in the movies—the even vaster crowds you advertisers yearn for—mass circulation. These crowds, he says, will destroy civilization. But what about Thomas Jefferson, you may say, and all those who have lived and died in the fullness of a democratic faith? Alas, it is never possible for an honest mind to rest easily in a dead man's faith. There is always a difference. And one great difference between Thomas Jefferson and us is a difference in the press. Thomas Jefferson said that if he had to choose between government without newspapers or newspapers without government, he would choose newspapers without government. Well, today we have got government, gigantic government, and we will have to like it and probably Mr. Jefferson would have to like it. And in the second place we have got advertising and with it a Press-that-gives-the-people-what-they-want. Now Mr. Jefferson had neither of these. The press he knew was in many respects a dirty blackguardy press, but it consisted characteristically of crusading editors whanging away at the people, not to please them, but to persuade them, to argue with them, to debate before them the burning issues of the day. Mr. Jefferson's press was a heated political debate: it was not comic strips and baseball and Hollywood and elaborate criminology. It was not even an informative press—it had no such obligation as we have to inform. And above all, it was not, as our modern press is, the dominant mental and psychological environment of the people. No—the differences are so vast that if Mr. Jefferson were here today, seeing our crowds and our press, he would do some original thinking and state his democratic faith in new terms both of hope and duty.

But finally, the question I have raised depends upon whether it matters. Does it matter?

As to this, a man must first of all speak for himself. Here, then, I confess myself and say to you that, for me, it matters. And, next, a man must speak for his friends—for it is a lifeless faith which does not grow by the friends it is making. For my partners, therefore, and my friends and for those whom I know by their work—I say that for all of them it matters. We believe that never in the long history of Western civilization was the purely informative function of journalism more important than it is today. Our proudest boast will always be that we have fearlessly, eagerly and effectively transmitted significant information—not from one archive to another, but from the boisterous news fronts of the world into the minds of living and literate and free people. But we also believe that, vital and even sacred though this informative function is, it is not enough. It is not peculiarly the mission of the press to exorcise the Doubt which is conquering the Western world or to discover and rediscover standards of faith and excellence by which men may live. But if there is such a mission in the world—and we still say there is—then not only is the press its most powerful instrument, but, reluctant though we are to say it, the mission can succeed in large measure only in and through and with the press. That is what we believe. For whatever there may be in the conduct of our publications which denies this belief, we ask not your indulgence but your judgment.

Does it matter?

The American press is today, by all comparative standards, excellent. Its excellence arises from the fact that to so many of its leaders and workers it does matter. For however correct may be my analysis of the deadening effect of the doctrine "Give the public what it wants," the human truth is that journalists are still something other than efficiency engineers or buyers for cosmetic counters. For this we have to thank not only the tough individual souls of men, but the cultural tradition of our race. Not only the impulse, but the inner duty to see, to know, to tell, to teach, to create order and to protest against order when it denies conscience and liberty—this has been the dynamic of the Western world, and when it does not reveal itself in men of art or genius, it is the bee that buzzes in the ear of a journalist.

In thirty or forty years the advertising agency has created the art and technique of advertising. It has taught the manufacturers how to advertise. Perhaps now, in a new sense, and not solely in the profit sense, the individual advertising counselor must be prepared to offer to the advertiser advice as to how he can advertise *without* jeopardizing the true standards of journalism.

When he takes himself seriously as a critic of the press, and when he makes his client take him seriously, and when he makes the journalist view his criticism with respect rather than annoyance —then the advertising counselor will also think seriously of the nature of his own copy—in print and on the radio, which is the new press for which he is not indirectly but directly responsible.

This kind of advice will be difficult advice to offer. These are difficult judgments to make. They are precisely the judgments which in this critical decade every journalist will have to make. Not to lessen our responsibility, but, on the contrary, to announce a fuller acceptance of it, I invite you to become our severest critic as you have been our dearest friend.

3   THE PHOTOGRAPH AND GOOD NEWS

Luce's interest in photography long antedated LIFE; *he discovered Margaret Bourke-White, for example, when he was founding* FORTUNE. *In a speech before the Institute of Human Relations at Williamstown, Massa-*

chusetts, September 2, 1937, Luce repeated much of his White Sulphur speech (Number 2, above) but also included the following salute to the photograph.

I was recently amazed to see that the author of a book on Freedom of the Press devoted a great amount of space to the scandal that the scandals of advertisers are sometimes kept out of the press. The real point at issue there is whether a capitalist-controlled press withholds from the people the knowledge that many capitalists lead scandalous lives. Well, of course, if there is one fact about our society which is shouted daily to the people of America it is that rich folk get into trouble with chorines or gigolos, steal each other's wives and husbands, indulge in orgies, and are otherwise licentious. So, suppose one more scandal of one more rich man is suppressed? What of it? Not that I defend the suppression, and not that I would ever enjoy being in a position where I was party to any such suppression. But what of it? On the relevant issue of whether the press has presented a fair picture to the public of an aspect of American life, the criticism should be turned around. For if there *are* a number of rich or solvent people who live reasonably decent lives, never get more than moderately drunk and are not sexual monsters—then *that* is the fact which the capitalist-controlled press has failed to establish.

One of the inherent evils in journalism is that evil makes big news and good makes little or no news. Now to me the most exciting discovery which we have stumbled into, as other experimental editors have also stumbled, is the extraordinary power of the photograph to dramatize and lend fresh interest, news interest, to the good, which, for present purposes, I may define as the normal and calm as distinct from that which is disruptive or fantastic.

A few weeks ago LIFE published a picture essay on wheat—I mean wheat, growing and being happily harvested. The article had nothing to do with any frantic row in Congress over a farm bill, nothing to do with the horrors of drought and dying cattle. And it was the lead article and ran for nine pages. Now can you imagine any non-photographic magazine, intended to interest millions of readers, daring to devote its first nine pages to a descriptive contemplation of the fruitful and normal and quiet labors of farms and horses and harvesters and the wheat itself ripening beneath the sun? And yet it is precisely that kind of thing which LIFE is doing.

True, we make great efforts to keep close to the news in the conventional sense of the word—but the photographic angle on the news is just as apt to be dramatization of the pleasant as it is of the unpleasant proceedings of the human race.

The photograph is the most important instrument of journalism which has been developed since the printing press. The photograph, far from being the degradation of journalism, turns out to be an extraordinary instrument for correcting that really inherent evil in journalism which is its unbalance between the good news and the bad.

4 HOW I MAKE MY LIVING

This refreshing exercise in candor was delivered to the Stamford, Connecticut, Women's Club on January 4, 1939. The Luces were then living nearby in Greenwich.

I am going to make a speech about my business, a company called Time Incorporated. I have declined previous invitations to indulge myself in this manner. It has seemed hopeless to condense into one short hour, and for a group of strangers, a subject which leaves me puzzled and baffled after ten or twelve hours of more or less active cogitation 300 days in the year.

But I know why I feel the urge to talk about my business on this occasion. It is because you are my neighbors and it is my profound belief that people have a human right and human need to know about their neighbors' business and equally to have their business known of and by their neighbors.

For modern life, with its hurried impersonality and crowded loneliness, has brought forth no substitute for the social checks and balances of the small community. They are not the checks and balances of constitutional or even common law. They are the checks and balances born of day-to-day human relationships. Even today in a Vermont village it is difficult, say, for the supervisor of the poor to play politics with relief. The neighbors find out and find out quickly and he faces public opinion in the form of direct social pressure on himself and his family. Something of the same is true of the businessman employer. If he mistreats his labor, or if he is sharp or unfair to a fellow townsman, his crime is at least compounded by many an eyewitness. God knows, the social morality of the horse-and-buggy days was in many respects nothing much to boast about. But while we have made large gains in social law in our industrial civilization, it may well be feared that we are losing the habits of private virtue and personal responsibility one to another, without which social law cannot long endure.

Many people who live here do their work in the big city. Most of those who work in the big city are occupied in businesses or professions which are nationwide or even worldwide in their ramifications. It is fine that we live in an age of such wide horizons. But it is a matter of life and death that we should remain human and not become robots. To workers in the vastly ramified affairs centering in the big city, Stamford-Greenwich offers a chance to live, in part at least, the life of a good neighbor. Even more than that, the local community should assert its human right to know something of what its members are up to in the big city. Sometimes it should give neighborly encouragement. And sometimes it should pronounce that sternest of all judgments—a neighbor's disapproval or contempt. And so I desire to present myself to you and to make up for lost time by a rough outline of what I think my business is.

Time Inc. is a corporation owned by stockholders. The majority of the stock is owned by officers and employees of the company and their families. We are in business to make money, and we are proud of the fact that we have fairly consistently done so.

How does a magazine business make money? It is understood that magazines and newspapers make money out of advertising, but it is very little understood how this is done. Now one thing nearly every businessman will say about his business is: "My business is different." One way our business differs is that the economy of our magazines is based on a high revenue direct from our subscribers and newsstand customers. And because our revenue from our readers is so much higher than the norm in the magazine business, it is just as true to say that our profits come from our readers as to say that they come from our advertisers.

Thus, our revenues from advertising encourage us, entice us and even obligate us to spend a great deal of money in constant efforts to improve our products, and improved magazines in turn bring in more money from more readers. But it is still theoretically true that with severe economies the magazine TIME could break even with almost no advertising at all.

Now, I do not wish to be misleading. We are extremely interested in selling all the advertising space we can, and we are proud of the fact that in a fiercely competitive business our publications have proved themselves to be successful advertising media. But, in the case of our business, at least, it is a mistake to think of a magazine as an organism which feeds exclusively on the advertiser's dollar. In looking for dollars, our magazines are primarily looking for the reader's dollar. We think this is good business. We also think, more importantly, that this is good journalism. It is good journalism because it makes our magazines stand or fall on the judgment of their readers—a continuous judgment rendered by thousands or millions of readers on that most sensitive secret voting machine, the private cash register.

No two magazines, even considered merely as businesses, are exactly alike any more than any two people are—not even when they are in the same family. So, if I am going to use our business as a case history of the publishing business, it is necessary to narrow the field and choose one particular magazine. Let us take LIFE. LIFE is the only one of our magazines which is in what is called the mass field. LIFE has over two million paid circulation and is read by ten million people or more.

Now, first of all, in accordance with our policy of insisting upon a relatively high revenue from readers, LIFE is priced at 10 cents a copy and not 5 cents. The subscription price, even at bargain-counter rates, is $3.50, not $1 or even lower as is the case with some mass magazines. The result of this high price policy is that readers of LIFE pay nearly $10 million a year for this magazine. That is already a pretty good test of whether this is a magazine which the sovereign American people want, and, you may say, it is already a lot of money to publish a magazine with. It is not enough, however, to pay the bills. Despite its high price, LIFE requires substantial advertising revenue to make ends meet. Now on what basis is this advertising sought and sold? A page in LIFE costs $5,700. One-eighth of a page costs $800. But neither of these is the basic price ticket. The basic price ticket is $2.85 for one page in exactly 1,000 copies. For each unit of 1,000, the price of $2.85 a page is a normal accepted price ticket. Multiply $2.85 by 2,000 and you have $5,700.*

Now this does not mean that advertisers are standing around with bulging pockets ready to pay $2.85 to anyone who likes publishing magazines and has one or more of these units for sale. The question of why some magazines—of whatever circulation—get advertising and why some don't would lead one deep into a jungle of advertising theory. In any case, when through a magnificent display of statistics and other elaborate rituals of pure reason, LIFE has sold a page of advertising for $5,700, that amount is by no means all available to pay the bills our readers left unpaid. In the first place, nearly $1,000 is removed by a gentleman called the advertising agent, some examples of whom reside in this neighborhood. He is the gentleman who writes the ads, playing, even in a streamlined mass-production world, with the variables of human nature. But after the advertising agent has taken his fee, there are still other expenses to be paid out of the advertiser's check. For one thing, we have to print his advertisement. In LIFE, it will cost to print that one advertisement upwards of $2,000 for more paper, more engravings, more ink, bigger presses and more men working on them. And then the advertisement has to be carried around to every city and hamlet in the nation and for that Postmaster General Jim Farley and the other public carriers will demand, just for that one extra page, several hundred dollars. All together Mr. Farley's bill to LIFE, and mostly for carrying around the advertisements, comes pretty close to $2 million a year. Besides all this, one is not likely to get an advertisement without a salesman—and the salesman has other functions besides plying his customers with Scotch whisky and American Beauties. Indeed, the sales organization of a modern magazine is a continuous consumer's research bureau and makes a good many pragmatic inquiries into the mystery of distributing the wealth.

Nevertheless, having paid off the advertising agent, the paper manufacturers, the printer, Uncle Sam Farley, the salesman, the

---

* The analogous figures for LIFE as of January 1969 are: single copy, 40 cents; LIFE readers paid $50 million; cost of one-page black-and-white advertisement, $42,500; one-eighth page, $6,750; page rate or "basic price ticket," $5 per 1,000 copies, or, per reader, $1.15.

market-research man, and half a dozen taxes, and having provided
something for a dubious character named General Administration,
there remains a sizable piece of that $5,700 which can go to make
up the deficit for the editorial side of the magazine. Call it $2,000.
Then if LIFE sells, during the course of one year, 1,000 pages, our
gross profit from advertising is 1,000 times $2,000, or $2 million.

Now you may recall that I said that LIFE's readers pay $10
million a year for their copies of LIFE. All of that doesn't come to
us—there are newsstand vendors who have to make a living, and
there are various other costs which have to be charged against the
revenue from readers. But suppose that what we get out of it—and
we get most of it—fails by exactly $2 million to pay the basic costs
of making the magazine. Then, you see, if we have sold 1,000
pages of advertising, and if we go and pick up the gross selling
profit of $2 million on the complicated transaction, then we have
just made ends meet. And in that case, it would be said that LIFE
breaks even with 1,000 pages of advertising—or an average of
about twenty pages in an issue. Actually, I do not know exactly how
many pages LIFE needs, because we are not as technical about cost
accounting as we might be, and even if I did know, I wouldn't tell
you, because perhaps it is still best that some shred of mystery
should remain even between neighbors. Up to that point there is no
profit. Beyond that point each advertising page may be expected to
yield a considerable net profit to the publisher—at least we planned
it that way, and it ought to turn out that way provided the
unforeseen does not occur, and especially provided there has mirac-
ulously been no mistake in our arithmetic. The gross profits from
advertising do not pay for the magazine—they make up for an
insufficient revenue from readers, but they would never make up
for a complete lack of revenue from LIFE's readers. LIFE seeks
both the reader's dollar and the advertiser's, but if either one of
these is a better or more important dollar than the other, it is,
without any doubt, the reader's dollar that calls the tune.

Now a word about that final end figure—the net profit. In nearly
all capitalistic enterprises, the net profit is an awfully long way
away from where you began. That is why perhaps, in epochs of
more enterprising capitalism, people spoke of business vision—a
good businessman was a man who could see a profit far off, and an
enterprising man was a man who imagined he could see it, and
actually most men who built businesses were probably those who

simply said—hell, there must be a profit in this somewhere; let's go.

There is no kind of business which has to wait longer for its profits than a magazine or newspaper. Thousands and millions of transactions must be made over a long period of time before profits accrue to the owner. And all during that time—and while all the materials are being paid for in cash and while all the laborers in the vineyard are being paid, and while readers are profiting, presumably, from what they read and advertisers from what they advertise—through all that time, the newspaper or magazine is exposed on all sides to all the sudden or subtle changes in the atmosphere of public taste or public need. If it survives this ordeal of continuous daily or weekly traffic, then it is entitled to write upon its books an asset which is proudly described as Good Will. On the books, it is usually valued at $1. Stockholders sometimes value the Good Will of one magazine or of one newspaper at millions of dollars—for that Good Will, if it exists, represents the ability to make a profit. Editors and publishers have sometimes valued it at something more than their lives—for that Good Will represents the confidence which has been placed in them by a large group of people over a long period of time.

LIFE is an example of this long, long trail of profit. The total sum the stockholders have so far lost in the publication of LIFE amounts to nearly $5 million. What is there to show for it? We own no vast printing plant, no paper mills. We rent space in what the Rockefellers politely call the Time & Life Building. We have a little furniture. There is almost nothing * to show for it—and yet everyone concerned with LIFE is very pleased. The owners are pleased because their calculations persuade them that now the break-even point, of which I have spoken, has been passed and profits begin. It will take a number of years to make back that $5 million. I calculate that before LIFE's profits exceed the losses, something like 500 million copies of LIFE will have to be produced, distributed and avidly consumed by a number of people several times greater than the entire population of the globe. That

* Not true today. As of January 1969 Time Inc. had sixty-three wholly owned subsidiaries, including Eastex Inc., manufacturers of paper and paperboard; Printing Developments Inc., printing research and equipment; five television stations and four timber corporations. Long a tenant of Rockefeller Center, Time Inc. in 1960 moved into the present Time & Life Building, in which it shares ownership with Rockefeller Center.

will take us past a good many political crises at home and abroad, past a good many changes in ladies' millinery, past a good many hairs on a good many editors' heads. As journalists, we see hardly further ahead than next week's issue; as publishers, believing in our journalism, we imagine, and we hope not vainly, that we will be doing business at the same old stand after many winters and many springs have come and gone.

This is the economics. And now what about the dynamics? Time Inc. operates five publishing businesses known to various publics as the magazines TIME, FORTUNE, ARCHITECTURAL FORUM, LIFE and the monthly cinema, THE MARCH OF TIME.* To what precise degree any or all of them are driven by the profit motive it is impossible for me or anyone else to say. But one thing I can say, and that is that the profit motive was not in the slightest degree responsible for bringing any of our publications into existence. Each one of them was something radically new in its field, an adventure in informative journalism. To be sure, financial calculations were carefully made—all of the calculations proving to be wrong by wide margins. The calculations were justification of a long-shot risk and made no pretense of being estimates of probable outcomes. I do not know intimately the origins and growth of other newspapers and magazines, but I believe a wide generalization could be drawn—namely, that most and perhaps nearly all successful publications have had behind them motives which far outweighed the motive of profit.

These motives are many and various. Let us call one of them the motive of journalism. Why does anyone want to be a journalist? One has only to talk to any decent educated person who is not a journalist to realize how uncommon, how little understood, is the motive of journalism for its own sake. Even a good many of its practitioners regard it as at best a queer, and at worst an improper, occupation. One of the most fashionable attitudes among newspapermen is, or used to be, a bitter cynicism as to the degrading nature of their business. Then again, thousands of men have gone into journalism "because," as they explain to their friends, "it is such good experience." Others are would-be novelists who loudly

---

* THE MARCH OF TIME gave its first radio broadcast in 1931, became a cinema in 1935 and ceased operations in 1951. ARCHITECTURAL FORUM was acquired by Time Inc. in 1932 and started a sister magazine, HOUSE AND HOME, in 1952, but Time Inc. divested itself of both magazines in 1964. SPORTS ILLUSTRATED was launched in 1954.

disdain the fustian by which they eat. And yet another mark of the journalist is that peculiar thing—a nose for news. In my youth, I often heard that a nose for news was something you either had or you didn't have. That worried me a great deal because I wanted to be a journalist, but yet had no inner conviction that there was anything really distinctive about my proboscis. The doubt stayed with me for many years until one day, when somebody again said "nose for news," I realized how many people I had encountered who obviously didn't have it, and I promptly became convinced I had it. But I still don't know what it is.

George Jean Nathan * once undertook to annoy me and succeeded instantly. He announced that all editors are frustrated novelists—he knew because he had tried to be both. If having been one of the men of my college era who never even began the composition of a novel is refutation of Mr. Nathan's slur, I can offer that refutation. But I am now inclined to think that there is some truth in that Nathanism. Journalism is indeed a form of self-expression. But it is a new form, a very particular form. I will not call journalism art—though with a little courage, I might do so, remembering there was once some doubt as to whether the novel was properly an art form. But I should like to liken journalism to art for the sake of expressing the idea that there is a spirit alive today, and especially in America, which may be called Journalism-for-the-sake-of-Journalism. In its motivation, this spirit is akin to that compulsion and satisfaction in expressing oneself by giving shape to stone; there are men today who can only be satisfied if they can give the shape of coherency and accuracy and truth to at least some fragments of human events.

But this cult of journalism is not only a cult of self-expression. It also demands an audience. It needs to say something *to* somebody. It needs, that is, to teach. And again it parallels the motives of art. For after several decades of art-for-art's-sake, we are beginning to understand once again that it is only a small art which is confidential and that great art or greatly attempted art is that which carries a message to many beleaguered hearts. Archibald MacLeish has expressed this brilliantly in his dictum that poetry must once again become the art of public speech, and not merely of private

* Nathan (1882–1958) was cofounder with H. L. Mencken of the *American Mercury* and author of many reviews and books on the theater.

speech. Journalism-for-Journalism's-sake is the need to express one-self effectively to others in the widest perspective of Truth.

To round up a mass of confused and conflicting facts in some stinking back alley or in a clean-swept marble-tiled Foreign Office and to make a clean, coherent narrative out of either a murder or a peace treaty—to cope somehow with the million little chaoses of raw news and make some sense out of them which shall be true and accurate at least for the split second on the screen of time—that for some men is the greatest of satisfactions, the fullest kind of self-expression.

The thing about our company which may best explain its nature, its merits and its defects is this—that there are few journalistic organizations in the world which are so exclusively devoted to information-for-information's-sake. We are in the business of keeping certain people widely and variously well informed about the time of man in which they live, and thereby perhaps helping them and ourselves a little to understand where we stand between the mud and the stars. And why are we given a continuing franchise to do this work which gives us such deep satisfaction? Mainly because so many people derive such deep satisfaction from being thus well informed.

Not long ago, we subjected the question to an elaborate inquiry. And it turned out that the plain, average readers of TIME were notably better informed than any other categories of people which could be devised for purposes of a comparative test. We were glad that it was so. Indeed if it had not been so, our faces would have been red with an embarrassment which perhaps only a group hara-kiri could have relieved.

But there is one other test of our journalism and of all contemporary journalism in free countries. If people of all classes are far better informed than they used to be, then why is it that we seem to be making just as much of a mess of our world as ever our ancestors made in the days of their unenlightenment? I will leave the question with you—as perhaps the ultimate indictment of journalism and of a great deal else in the modern world. But leaving it with you, I also take it with me—for in it lies the doubt which too faithfully assails every responsible journalist. I will say only this— that just as the answer to the failure and befuddlements of democracy is more democracy, not less, so perhaps the answer to the unfruitfulness of journalism is more journalism, not less. And by more journalism I do not mean more of the same, but rather that journalism must enlarge its field, it must probe deeper, it must and will find a way to deal with those matters which lie most deeply in the nature and will and conscience of men and will make of them great matters, not private whisperings but great public arguments. There are more things in heaven and earth, O Journalist, than are included in your philosophy—or in your craftsmanship.

5   CAUSES, CAUSES!

This vignette of a prewar day at the office is from Luce's speech to a convention of LIFE *advertising salesmen at Buckwood Inn, Shawnee-on-the-Delaware, Pennsylvania, May 27, 1939. For about two years Luce had been trying to lead his magazines out of what he called their "era of indifferentism," and the question of how and when to take strong editorial positions was very much on his mind.*

There is a popular urge to characterize journals by the causes which they espouse. What causes, then, in the modern world are important to Time Inc.? Every cause in the world which has power to command the wills of men. Every hour of every day, streams of people come to our offices pleading causes. There are at least 100 people in the Time & Life Building, and probably 200 or 300 people, who have at least one cause pleaded before them every day. Every cause to which any of us are indifferent suffers thereby. Every cause which arouses our interest gains thereby. Of all the pleaders I see only a small fraction. But here are the causes I can hear in one day.

The Belgian Ambassador comes to see me. He is a charming gentleman. He wishes to point out that there is an idea brewing to appease Germany by giving her the Belgian Congo. Why, he

asks, should Belgium be the goat?—although of course he didn't
use just that language. And Belgium, he says, has done a very
fine job in the Congo. Won't I please send an expert reporter
to the Congo to make plain the good news about Belgian rule?
When the Ambassador has departed with all felicitations, I get a
telephone call about the Museum of Modern Art. Won't I please
put Nelson Rockefeller * on TIME's cover? In my mail are two
special personal invitations for LIFE to Come to a Party—each a
worthy cause. After the necessary personal acknowledgment I
route them down to join the thirty-six other invitations to a party
which LIFE has received that same day—most of them "causes" of
one sort or another. The next letter is from a high-ranking Republican leader asking me to please play down the Taft-Bricker ri-
valry † in Ohio because this will do the Republican party no good.
Before I have figured out how to reply tactfully to that letter, two
very chic ladies come in to talk about birth control. They recall that
TIME was one of the earliest, perhaps the very first, forthright reporter of the cause of birth control, and that FORTUNE's article ‡ on contraceptives was a milestone in their cause. They
want me to blast hell out of the New York World's Fair because
some "sinister" influences have sabotaged their show. Comes then a
telegram from a very kindly old gentleman, one of my father's
dearest friends, a bishop now turned Buchmanite. Here is the
telegram:

> YOU HAVE GONE TOO FAR YOU ARE ALIENATING THE BET-
> TER ELEMENT AMONG YOUR SUBSCRIBERS AND HINDERING
> INSTEAD OF SUPPORTING THE CONSTRUCTIVE FORCES OF
> THE NATION AT A TIME WHEN OUR CIVILIZATION IS
> THREATENED WITH COLLAPSE STOP IF NO REVERSAL OF
> POLICY OUR CONNECTIONS MUST BE SEVERED PLEASE PASS
> ON THIS MESSAGE TO YOUR FATHER

Buchmanites have spent hours trying to convert TIME editors.
Alas, if Buchmanism is the voice of God, the editors of TIME will,
I fear, have a hard time getting past the pearly gates. Comes then a

* Rockefeller had just been elected president of the museum and had not
yet entered politics.
† A TIME story, May 15, 1939, had just described Senator Robert Taft
and Governor John Bricker of Ohio as rivals for the next Republican
presidential nomination.
‡ February 1938.

brilliant Italian journalist to tell me that the American press has completely misrepresented the facts of Europe. But he doesn't want me to do anything. It is too late, he says. There will be war—and he expects to die. I could go on and on with this kind of illustration. Picture it this way: I could easily spend a full ten-hour day, six days a week, doing nothing except listening to the pleading of the causes of mankind.

What is Time Inc. to do? Obviously, to determine the merits of even a tenth part of these causes would impose upon us a task which by comparison would make the job of the Supreme Court of the United States look like the recess hour of a kindergarten or teatime in an old ladies' sewing circle. Consider the brains on the Supreme Court—the brilliant Frankfurter, the phenomenal Douglas, the mighty Stone, the unshakable Butler and, towering above them all, Charles Evans Hughes. Suppose they should all get fired and we could hire them all and set them up on the twenty-sixth floor as the Super Brain Trust of Time Inc. Well, now that I mention it, I think that would be a hell of a good idea—and maybe we'll get around to doing something like that someday. It's fun to think of Dave Cort or John Billings,* two hours before LIFE is going to press with its lead article, picking up the phone and saying: "Hughes? Oh, hey, Charlie, what do we do with Queen Elizabeth, give her the big hand, the razz gentle or the bum's rush?" And not so funny either, since on one kind of treatment or another may depend the balance of power in Europe and therefore the future of the white race.

Confronted with the phantasmagorical task of pronouncing, and pronouncing *now*, moral and scientific judgments on every conceivable problem, the modern journalist has often taken refuge under the claim of impartiality or just news-for-news'-sake. One of the most amazing reputations in the history of journalism has been TIME's reputation for impartiality. It arises not only from people saying it is impartial, but even more from the fact that people are always saying, so very bitterly, that it is not impartial. TIME is attacked with equal or slightly varying bitterness for being pro and con the same thing. What is most of all amazing about this reputation is that never, at least with my knowledge and consent, did TIME ever claim impartiality. TIME's charter is that TIME will

* Cort was then foreign-news editor of LIFE; Billings was managing editor.

tell—will tell the truth about what happened, the truth as it sees it. Impartiality is often an impediment to truth. TIME will not allow the stuffed dummy of impartiality to stand in the way of telling the truth as it sees it.

6   PARADOX OF ORGANIZATION

Luce rejoiced in the creative tension of seemingly irrec-oncilable purposes. In this speech to the staff at a dinner celebrating TIME's *twentieth anniversary in New York, March 11, 1943, he found such a tension in the Time Inc. organization itself.*

In these days of war, all of us are profoundly aware of that archetype of organization—an army. The making of a great army reminds us of some virtues which in civilian life we sometimes neglect—the virtues of loyalty, of discipline and self-discipline, of responsibility, and, when the need comes, the supreme virtues of courage and selflessness.

But, of course, the army is only one type of organization. There are many types. Now what I want to say to you may seem to be and perhaps is a colossal exaggeration. I want to say to you that *our* organization which we attempt in Time Inc. is as impossible an organization as anyone could conceive of. *Credo quia impossibile.* We believe in it *because* it is impossible.

Now what do I mean by the impossibility of this organization, the impossibility of that which exists?

I mean that we insist upon having in this organization seemingly irreconcilable virtues. Let us take our examples from purely human characteristics. We require in this organization many people who are more or less temperamental. I sometimes wonder whether the much-advertised opera troupes actually contain half as many temperamentalists as are to be found, wandering more or less at their own pleasure, in and out of the Time & Life Building.

We try not to give people bonuses for temperaments, but the truth is, of course, that we'd be a hell of a dead place without all our big and little prima donnas. But then at the same time we need an awful lot of just plain sanity—efficient, methodical and reliable people—fortunately we have more of them than of the temperamentalists. But the point is that we absolutely need both—and both these kinds of people have to work in close harness with each other. In terms of organization, we have to be efficient, we have to organize our work to precision of split seconds—just as our printing presses are machined to one one-thousandth of an inch. At this moment four million copies of the next issue of LIFE are scattered all over the country: each of them is exactly where it was planned that it should be—at this precise moment. To make that possible, thousands of people who work with us and for us had to do just what they were supposed to do, just when they were supposed to do it. General Somervell's * logistics require no greater precision. But at the same time, in doing this work, we had to allow the fullest possible play for imagination to function freely, for thinkers to think, for phrases to be found, words to be made magical, for ideas to incubate and develop—bright little ideas, and big ideas. Our organization must provide for individuals to do what only individuals can do.

Just as there were no journalistic precedents for TIME, so also there was no precedent for the kind of organization we required. Take the editorial department of TIME, THE WEEKLY NEWS-MAGAZINE—it looks nothing at all like a newspaper city room, much less like a high-class magazine "sanctum." Nor do we anywhere have a front office—a countinghouse—like the one I worked in at the Springfield [Massachusetts] *Republican*—at $8 a week and fifty or sixty hours a week.† Even our titles we had to invent. The word "researcher" is now a nationwide symbol of serious endeavor. I wonder if I dare reveal the fact that that title was originally conceived as a private jest, Hadden and I having once done "research" for a drinking club called the Yale Professors? Little did we realize that in our private jest we were inaugurating a new order of female priesthood, the modern vestal virgins whom

* Brehon Somervell was commanding general of the Army Service Forces during World War II.
† This was Luce's first job, in the summer of 1916.

levitous writers cajole in vain, and managing editors learn humbly to appease.

In describing what we strive for, we can only make use of other types of organizations. There is, for example, the university. Like the university, we seek to serve Truth, and must therefore maintain something akin to academic freedom. Like the university, we are in the teaching business. And even so, though we never see more than a tiny fraction of our students, our organization must fit not only ourselves, but most of all must fit our students. Or, again, consider the medical profession. Notable in that profession are the standards of professional conduct—the sacred oath of Hippocrates, to which each doctor must be true. We wish we could establish absolute standards for the profession of journalism. Many have been the attempts to do so—but journalism is something of a wild and unruly youth, not easily bridled by rule and oath. Should we then frankly adopt the carefree anarchy of Bohemia—for anarchy is also a type of organization—or perhaps pattern ourselves after the furious craziness of Broadway? Indeed, we need a touch of show business in our business. In show business, they say it takes four flops to make one wow. Perhaps we don't have enough flops.

And finally, of course, there is the obvious type of organization —the business organization. Needless to say, from that type of organization we have borrowed much—with some success. We are, for instance, a corporation. I remember when Hadden and I first discovered we had to incorporate. The whole thing seemed an elaborate waste of time—the lawyer's papers, the long formalities.

Well, business organizations have suffered a good deal of verbal abuse, but I would find it hard to exaggerate the enormous virtues which reside in the business type of organization. To mention only a few, there is the matter of strict accountability. Every dollar— yes, every last penny—must be exactly accounted for. And expenses must be accounted for against income. Where expenses exceed income—no words will get us out of it, no pious frauds, no glittering generalities. Bankruptcy knows no alibis. But beyond such obvious virtues, this, the business type of organization, has served us well because it has enabled us to exercise at least a rough justice in assigning to each man and woman an appropriate reward for service in our common enterprise. A few months ago I was talking to a philosopher about justice and he chided me for speaking of "rough justice." He said justice is an absolute; there is perfect justice or none. Well, so it may be among the philosophers, but in the practical affairs of men, we know we can go a long way toward mutual happiness if we are continuously and sincerely devoted to rendering a rough justice between us.

And in our own case a business type of organization has helped us to combine community of work with private freedom. Each of us does his work, draws his pay—and his private life is his own. Now actually each of us has a stake in the so-called private life of every other. This might argue that, for our vitally important work, we should have a highly paternalistic type of organization—watching over the welfare and conduct of each of us. The highly efficient Japanese textile mills keep their girls locked up in model dormitories, where they are carefully educated for wifehood and motherhood. Shall we, dear ladies, follow that thoughtful example? Such a notion is, of course, to us only more ridiculous than it is offensive. It is the business type of organization in a free society which enables us to exercise the maximum concern for your individual welfare combined with the maximum respect for your freedom as an individual.

These, then, are some random reflections on the problem of organization. Of course, the secret of successful organization lies in its purpose. Organization is only the body which without the soul of purpose is dead, and our purpose, of course, is journalism. And what is journalism? That is another speech, ten other speeches. Journalism for us means an unlimited interest in the whole of human life. *De omni re scibili et quibusdam aliis*—we'll never settle for anything less! We'll ride the trail of all things known and, taking our place with the gremlins in the stratosphere, we'll also peer over the cloud banks into the vistas of what is yet to be known.

But I would not let the celebration of a journalistic anniversary pass without at least one definition of journalism, however brief. And for this I choose one written by Eric Hodgins * in which he proves himself, I think, to be a master of the profession which he defines. He says: "Journalism is the conveyance of information from here to there; with accuracy, insight and dispatch, and in a manner that Truth is served and that the rightness of things is

* Hodgins, previously managing editor and publisher of FORTUNE, was then editorial vice president of Time Inc.

slowly if not immediately made evident." And as you reflect on that definition, it will be apparent how great a cause has bound us together in the past and binds us now.

7 CRITIQUE OF A COMMISSION

In the early 1940s Luce induced his friend Robert Hutchins, Chancellor of the University of Chicago, to assemble a committee of thinkers to study the philosophical foundations of the freedom of the press. With a grant of $200,000 from Time Inc. *and $15,000 from the* Encyclopaedia Britannica, *the "Commission on Freedom of the Press" spent four years preparing a 15,000-word report that was published by* Fortune *in April 1947 and, with supplements, as a book. An accompanying editorial expressed* Fortune's *disappointment in the superficiality of the report, which raised more questions than it answered and made only one mild legislative recommendation (that retraction be made a punishment for libel). Luce was even more critical of the semifinal draft submitted to him; he called it "philosophically uninteresting" and sent a long commentary to Hutchins before its final (not very substantial) revision. William Schlamm, a* Fortune *editor who had been working on a project for a new Time Inc. cultural monthly (never published), drafted parts of this commentary, but Luce signed it and wrote most of it. Excerpts:*

The Report asserts that "the development of the press as an instrument of mass communication has greatly decreased the proportion of the people who can express their opinions and ideas through the press."

I find in the report no documentation of this assertion. I think the Commission is under obligation to specify exactly when and where a larger proportion of the people had what ability to express their ideas through the press.

If it attempted to make such a specification, the Commission would find that it is involved in no easy quantitative calculation but in some very subtle equations which could be written only with the aid of great historical imagination.

If the proposition is true, it is of course of basic importance. I believe it is just not so.

My suspicion is that the Commission has allowed itself to make this assertion solely on the basis of the relative number of daily newspapers to the whole population. That would be to overlook the *access* of the members of the community to the columns of the press. I submit the following points of actuality:

1. *The Interview.* A common technique of the contemporary newspaper is the "interview." It permits tens of thousands of people to have their say (usually of little value) in printer's ink. Everybody gets interviewed from the new president of the Elks Club to the schoolteacher who has returned from a holiday tour of the Grand Canyon.

2. *The Press Agent* (including Eddie Bernays and the no less skillful Morris Ernst *). Mr. Bernays says in effect that any cause you want to get developed in the press he will develop. For a fee, of course.

3. *The Prescriptive Right in the Press.* The Commission does not seem to have realized to what extent the American community has achieved what may be called a prescriptive right to the use of the columns of the local newspapers. Every charity drive, for example, has or feels it has a right to a certain amount of space in the newspapers—even without fee paid to a press agent. Every institution in the town has a right to a certain amount of attention in the newspaper—one might say that even the whorehouses have a right to periodical advertisement. Churches, schools, basketball teams, art galleries, bowling alleys, sewing circles, sororities—they all have their "right" to space.

I am not at all sure that I like this development of prescriptive right. But there it is—and it is a very considerable access to the

* Edward L. Bernays, a nephew of Sigmund Freud, was a pioneer in the public-relations business. Ernst, the civil-liberties lawyer, has been an aggressive publicist for his own causes.

press. And it includes the "expression of opinion and ideas"—the most important idea of the manager of the basketball team being, probably, that basketball should be attended to.

4. *The Vicarious Expression.* A vast quantity of newspaper space is given to such things as "advice to the lovelorn" and "household hints," in which the opinion and ideas of the common man and common woman are, with enormous repetition, vicariously expressed. It may be a fault of modern life that too much of the participation in life is "vicarious." But the point here is that in the "lonely hearts" or "household hints" columns, the dominant motive is to express what the common man wants expressed.

5. *Variety of "Opinion and Ideas" in the Same Newspaper.* It is a cliché to say that 75 per cent of the press was against Roosevelt. Was it? In what sense? The two most powerful and widely circulated political columnists during the Roosevelt period were probably (1) Winchell and (2) Pearson—both brilliant pro-Roosevelt propagandists. Eleanor Roosevelt was a third.

6. *The Infinite Number of "Little" Publications.* There are tens of thousands of publications, periodical or occasional, put out by tens of thousands of organizations in the country—high schools, Rotary Clubs, art galleries, etc., etc.

The Commission has evidently been dazzled by the "bigness" of a big newspaper. If it nostalgically imagines some happier time when more people could "express their ideas and opinions through the press" I can only think that the Commission must be dreaming of the days of Benjamin Franklin's hand press. In that case, the Commission forgets that any young or old Franklin today can, with relatively *less* effort in the field of finance, go to a job printer and get several thousand copies printed of whatever he wishes to contribute to human thought. And young or old Franklins can—and thousands of them do—every day or week.

The Commission has also overlooked the well-established and by no means little publications of Organized Labor. Why some of the great unions have not used a few of their millions of dollars—and their presumably automatic patronage—to establish a few "regular" newspapers, like the London *Daily Herald*,* I frankly don't know. I presume they are well enough satisfied to "operate" on the existing press without losing their right to feel persecuted. But in

* Founded in 1912 as a strike sheet, the *Herald* was 49 per cent owned by the Trades Union Congress when it ceased publication in 1964.

any case, the fact is that practically all unions have papers—and some of them, like the Newspaper Guild paper, are very hotly opinionated.

7. *The Radio.* Twenty-five years ago there were some who thought the radio would supplant the newspaper press. Instead of that, newspaper circulations have enormously increased. But at the same time, thousands of new openings have been created by radio for untold thousands of people to talk their sense or nonsense to their fellowmen. Something like $400 million of advertising goes to support this added vehicle for the proliferation of tongues.

8. *Who Can't Say His Say?* Wouldn't it be truer to say that in our day even anybody with *nothing* to say has no difficulty in getting it published? The Commission owes us the recital of a single case in which (in our lifetime) anybody with anything to say did *not* get it published. In exchange we could supply the Commission with any number of case histories of people who, in the Commission's golden dream days, had indeed no chance to reach their fellowmen with an occasionally meritorious idea. The real trouble lies, as we all know only too well, in the infuriating inflation of unnecessarily articulated words. The crisis consists in the cheapening *easiness* with which anybody, anybody *at all*, can break into print (or over the air or on the screen). If the Commission had subpoenaed Willi Schlamm, he could have told them about his personal experience during the last eighteen months; how, in preparing a magazine of quality and ideas, he had to cajole, bribe, push and pull to get "the best minds" to present *any* ideas— entirely on their own terms, with editorial noninterference guaranteed. *He has not encountered a single idea that has been waiting for an opportunity to be expressed.*

The Draft Report proceeds to a doctrine of an "accountable press." But, with what seems to me the most appalling lack of even high-school logic, the Draft Report fails to state: Who is accountable? And to whom? And for what?

I think that the Commission should be in a position to answer these questions.

For, first of all, the Commission can say: "As to *who* is responsible—obviously the publisher or the publisher and editor." This statement of the obvious will prove to be, believe me, a very startling statement. See what it does. First of all, it relieves Mr. Eddie Bernays and the Chancellor of the University of Chicago of much of *their* responsibility for the wisdom or folly which they are well able to insert into the mass press. It does not relieve them of their own responsibility for their own words. But it relieves them, to a considerable extent, of the responsibility for having their words spread throughout the mind of the masses. To the extent that Mr. Bernays and the Chancellor are relieved of responsibility, the poor publisher, who may hitherto have felt little or no responsibility for the utterances of his distinguished fellow citizens, suddenly finds himself saddled with the weight of a great burden. And, be assured, he will protest. But I think the Commission can make its case. "Yes," it can say to the publisher, "you indubitably are the man. For you do have the power to kill Dr. Hutchins' premature recommendations of world government—or haven't you? For you have the power, if you would be on the *qui vive*, to confound the machinations of Mr. Bernays—or haven't you? That lengthy statement advocating Free Love signed by a fine collection of churchmen and educators—you don't *have* to print that, Mr. Publisher—or do you?"

Yes, by this gambit, the Commission could put the publisher right on the griddle! Roy Howard and Willie Hearst and Henry Luce—and also Mr. Joe Doaks, the local realtor who owns the Four Corners *Gazette*—they are the men! They have the legal power! We have discovered *who* is responsible.

Having discovered *who* is responsible, we can then go on to *what who* is responsible for. The Commission says he is responsible for providing a "service adequate to the needs of society." At this point I am going to be—at least I am intending to be—very constructive.

The Commission claimed to include within its survey not only a mass of magazines which have nothing to do with "news" or "public affairs," but also the radio and the movies, only a small part of whose produce concerns what is commonly understood to be "public affairs." I think the Commission was right to do so. It was right to do so because the daily newspaper itself has come to give more and more of its space and emphasis to matters like comic strips, which, however important they may actually be in the development of the mind of America, are not commonly thought of as being in the field of "public" affairs.

But having included this whole mass of stuff, the Commission forgot to take pains to distinguish in its judgment between it and the stuff concerning "public affairs" in the traditional sense. The press, if it is involved in "a service adequate to the needs of society," is involved in two quite distinct services. The one service I will call the news and "adequate" discussion of the news and of public affairs. The other service is, in a word, the service of Culture.

Here I think we really have something. What is new about the press, what was certainly undreamed of by John Milton and hardly dreamed of by J. S. Mill, is that the press, going far beyond "news intelligence" or political argument, has become a very considerable part of the mental and psychological environment of the mass of people. The villagers dancing about the maypole in Milton's day were hardly at all *directly* affected by the press. And the denizens of the slums of Mill's day hardly more so. But today nearly every American's mind—*and soul*—is directly and daily affected by the press. And it is affected not simply in the department of "public affairs," but in all its departments of imagination and sentiment.

So-o-o—what is the "service adequate to the needs of society" which is required? Two services. A service first (by traditional seniority) of news and comment on "public affairs." And second, a service of culture, a service of food for the imagination and the feelings and sensitivities of millions of people. At this point, Messrs. Howard, Hearst, Luce & Doaks would certainly, if they know what's good for them now or in the life hereafter, ask to be relieved at once of the positions into which they have got themselves. But the Commission will allow them no such easy retirement. What the Commission will do for them is to give them a candid judgment, as clear as possible, as to just how badly they are doing. And I believe the Commission would give judgment along some such lines as these:

> As to the service of news and public discussion, the press is not doing too bad a job. The main facts about current happenings the press does disseminate widely and with pretty fair accuracy. During the seventeen days of the coal strike in November-December 1946, most of the people in the U.S. knew pretty much all there was to know. In foreign news, the press does not do as good a job. The situation in China gets hopelessly lost from factual view and is left almost entirely to

propagandists (most of whom are left-wingers). But to bring China—or Brazil or Italy—into focus requires essentially more journalistic skill, and the Commission hopes the skills will increase.

The press also provides a wide variety of opinion. The press has to be careful about a certain tendency to "overload" the opinion along the line of its owners' convictions or prejudices but this is not too serious for, in general, the facts speak more loudly than their opinions.

But now, second, as to the service to Culture—*there* is something to which the press must really give a great deal more thought. American culture is not in a healthy state—or is it? The divorce rate is appalling and rising. Juvenile delinquency is appalling. The labor relations of our country are anything but happy. Creativity in the arts is very low. The press is deeply involved in all this.

At this point, I think the Commission is bound to say two things:

First, it is bound to give some brief appraisal of the state of health of the American Culture. Second, it is bound to say that obviously the whole of the responsibility for any lack of health does not lie with the press. For obviously there are schools and there are universities and there are college professors and there are churches and there is the law and there are judges and there are poets or those who claim to be poets and there are, even at this late date, fathers and mothers. In fact the total responsibility of the press for the state of U.S. culture may turn out to be considerably less than 50 per cent! So the Commission should, in a snappy paragraph, pay its respects to the schools and the universities and the churches and the law and the poets and the Elks and the Eisenhowers and the fathers and the mothers. And having apportioned a fair share of responsibilities on these other more senior institutions, the Commission should then wag a very professional finger at the press, pointing out that, by reason of technological circumstances and their own excessive enterprise, the press has muscled in on the great domain of Faith and Order. For which cause, the publishers and editors stand in peculiar peril of damnation.

Thus I have indicated, largely on your own showing, how great is the *what* that the *whos* are responsible for.

The final question is: to *whom* are the *whos* responsible for the very great *what* they are now involved in? And here, I think, the Commission must not be afraid to announce the greatest and most exciting discovery and rediscovery man ever makes: man is responsible to his Creator—or isn't he? I cannot read the Report without believing that that is what the Commission believes. Then let it say so—candidly and without fear.

To make the affirmation in this case is not to commit a breach of manners by mentioning religion when nobody asked you to. For it is necessary to the argument. And I will explain why.

A man is responsible to his Creator. But it is the sound instinct of mankind not to assert individuality in such morally egoistic terms as those proclaimed by Ralph Waldo Emerson. That is to say, in as many instances as possible, a man seeks to "institutionalize" his conscience—to exchange the loneliness of his own moral responsibility for a communal morality. In fact, it may be said that civilization consists in the "institutionalizing" or "communalizing" of conscience. In this there is, of course, always a great peril—the peril that a man seeking to save his soul through the community will lose it. And in a "good society" there will always be plenty of protest against convention, against excessive "order," against the monarch, against the mob and against amorality masking as manners and custom.

Nevertheless, it is a constructive instinct that bids us "institutionalize" whatever can be suitably institutionalized. Of this we may take the law and the legal profession as an example. Here in our Anglo-Saxon or Roman tradition is a prime instance of institutionalization—almost unknown to the Chinese. The lawyer's conscience as lawyer is so well taken care of by the law itself, its rules and practices, and by the Bar Association that the lawyer has to exercise only a minimum of individual moral choice in the practice of his profession.

Now the point is that of all institutions or quasi-institutions, the press is the least susceptible to having its conscience "institutionalized." And this is why in the quotation you so admirably choose, John Adams said that the "regulation of the press is the most difficult, dangerous and important problem."

My argument is this: In order to establish the moral responsibility of the press, you must first disclose a doctrine of the moral responsibility of individual men. The problem then is how to shift some part of individual responsibility in the case of the press to a more general group responsibility (professional, governmental or social). But you cannot go far enough along these lines to "solve" the problem of the press. That is to say, the individual responsibility not only of these laughably big publishers, but of every mother's son who is near a typesetting machine, continues to be inescapable and great. Keeping always in mind the inescapable individual responsibility, everyone of any moral sensibility whatever would wish to see how we can achieve a more institutionalized or communal responsibility.

And this brings us to the Commission's conclusions. They are not very exciting. They are not very radical. The Commission was not inspired to come up with apocryphal proposals. But the exciting thing is, precisely, that all that can be recommended is so unexciting. The position of the Commission is, then, something like this: These recommendations are all that we can find that you can properly do to give the press a moral relation to society; how vastly important it is, then, that about all that can properly be done should actually be done. Editors, for example, have long since set themselves a code * of ethics and no one can enforce it except the editors themselves; but in twenty years the editors have done nothing to enforce their own code. How dangerous, how very dangerous is such neglect!

I have given the Commission credit for believing in individual moral responsibility. But it is certainly not clear whether the Commission believes in responsibility to God or only to Society. And I suppose the Commission is divided on this point and did not wish to admit such a scandal of disagreement among wise men.

But, gentlemen, we look to you for the Truth as you see it. We will not accept from you any common currency of ambiguity.

If you can all agree on a doctrine of moral responsibility to something called Society—without having to press the question of God to a conclusion—you are entitled to do so for the sake of public easement and convenience. But then state your doctrine clearly. Why am I responsible to Society? And who is Society? And where is it?

---

* The American Society of Newspaper Editors adopted such a code in 1923, but it had little influence.

8   OBJECTIVITY

Luce had many tussles over TIME'S *reputation for "impartiality" and "objectivity" (page 56). The following excerpt is from his remarks at a dinner of* TIME *editors in New York, November 14, 1952.*

Ten years ago, I was initiated into a little cult of those who had discovered Arnold Toynbee. I liked his way of looking at things—so utterly different from all thinking then current. But then, five or six years later, when Toynbee became famous, I knew that I disagreed with him on one point, the critical point for now. Toynbee regarded America as simply a peripheral part of European civilization. I regard America as a special dispensation—under Providence—and I said so. My spiritual pastors shake their heads about this view of mine. They say it tends to idolatry—to idolatry of nation. I knew well the dangers of that sin. But I say we must have courage to face objective facts under Providence.

Objective facts? Yes, we are *for* objectivity. That will surprise you and confuse you. The confusion is my fault, and I'm here to explain and to get it straight.

We are for objectivity because there is objective truth, truth in the universal, scientific truth, moral truth, which is quite independent of what anyone of us or all of us think at any given time. Majorities do not make truth. Intellectual fashions do not make truth. Individual prophets come nearer to it—Amos or John the Baptist or Walt Whitman. We are not prophets, not intuitive seers —yet it's a bad editor who doesn't see a couple of jumps ahead. Mainly, we seek objective truth by ceaseless search for facts, by analysis and by making fact analyses come to life by the deepest understanding we can achieve of human nature and destiny.

What is the objectivity we are against? The alleged journalistic objectivity?

The term "journalistic objectivity" has two very different meanings. The older meaning implies merely a tone of voice. It is detached, nondidactic, unemotional. Lawyers' summations of evidence are frequently highly objective in *tone*. TIME and almost all other journals use this tone when they feel like it. It is strictly a literary instrument and only involves morals when it is carried so far that it *deliberately conceals* the fact that the writer has come to a conclusion and organized his material to fit it.

The second meaning of journalistic objectivity is a claim that a writer presents facts without applying any "value judgments" whatever to them. *That* is a modern usage and that is strictly a phony. That I had to renounce—and denounce. When we say "the hell with objectivity," this is what we are talking about. It is both theoretically and practically impossible to select, recognize or organize facts without using value judgments. This does not mean that value judgments are a necessary evil which must be held to the minimum. Quite the contrary. It means that 75 per cent of the business of recognizing, selecting and organizing facts is having correct value judgments.

We are happy to record fact as fact—out of sheer curiosity and exuberance—without always necessarily stopping to give it a value judgment or saying what it "means." For the journalist, the value judgment "Gee whiz" is plenty—for a great deal of what he puts out.

But we also seek the Truth in all fields—in the field of esthetics, in art and literature where "there is no disputing about taste." Oh, yes, there is. In a time of world crisis we seek it in politics, economics, in social arrangements—in philosophy, above all in the meaning of human life. We assert by faith one proposition: that life does have a meaning. We also acknowledge that the full meaning of human life touches the mysterious, even the mystical, because the Truth, the full Truth about the human adventure, will forever elude our finite intelligence, however clever.

The whole editorial staff of TIME is joined together in the search for Truth—and not with any perpetual escape clause that the Truth, though sought, can never be found. Some Truth we can know, we do know, because Truth is Truth, because it *is* objective.

9   JOURNALISM AND RESPONSIBILITY

*In this lecture to the School of Journalism at the Univer-
sity of Oregon at Eugene, February 20, 1953, Luce
gave one of the fullest expositions of his doctrine that
the proprietors of the press are responsible for the truth
of what they print.*

So far as I can recall, this is the first time in fourteen years that
I have made a public speech about journalism. How can such reti-
cence be explained—since this is a subject I am supposed to know
about. Part of the explanation lies right there. A pretty good definition of a journalist is someone who knows a little about everything and not very much about anything. Thus for a journalist to
talk about journalism is in some strange way unjournalistic. We
are better off when we are whooping up a murder story, never
having been a murderer or a murderee, or settling the affairs of the
world, never having settled any of them.

But there is a more personal reason. The basic pattern of
American journalism is the daily newspaper—the daily local newspaper. I am not a newspaperman. That is a title of great glory in
this country. I tried my best to earn it by inventing the word
newsmagazine. And very generously, our friends in the newspaper
profession have accorded to me and to my colleagues a sort of
second-class—or out-of-town—membership in their club. Not
being a full member of the club, I hesitate to make the "let's take
our hair down" speech; yet not being a complete outsider, I cannot
pretend not to know just where the slot machines are or how they
are rigged.

But there is yet another and a deeper reason for my reluctance to
talk on this subject. I do not know any problem in journalism
which can be usefully isolated from the profoundest and ultimate
questions of man's fate. One could perhaps except purely technical

problems from this sweeping generalization—such a problem as typography. But I would scarcely exclude even this. Take for example the contrast between the screaming eight-column, red-ink banner headlines of the New York *Journal-American*, a paper I read avidly (when I read it), and the chaste headlines of Roy Roberts' Kansas City *Star*. The contrast in typography between the *Journal* and the *Star* is a contrast in character. And character is destiny—both for a nation and for its press.

But if I seem to prove too much from typography, let me give you a better illustration of how journalistic problems are inextricable from ultimate problems. Surely you will all agree that the first canon of journalism is to tell the truth. Does the American press tell the truth? That raises a deeper question: Are the American people capable of receiving the truth? And that raises still a deeper question yet; it was asked by Pontius Pilate in Jerusalem: What is truth?

Recently the press of New York City has been engaged in what we are asked to believe is a great battle for freedom of the press.* Let's take a quick look at it. For a couple of weeks there has been going on in New York City a court trial involving prostitution. The advance ballyhoo for this prostitution trial was provided daily on the front page for a month, sharing honors with the new Eisenhower Administration. The public was promised dirtier dirt than they could get in any smut book—and all for a nickel, and all in the respectable form of a newspaper—and, less readably, in a newsmagazine.

Then the judge closed the courtroom. Then the outrage of the gentlemen of the press was beautiful to behold. In the skyscrapers of New York, John Milton and Thomas Jefferson lived again in the righteous indignation of a thousand newsmen.

Did the judge do wrong? Maybe he did. Was the principle of freedom of the press imperiled? Maybe it was. Some of my colleagues seemed to think so, and I had no brief to argue *contra*. The action of the judge was also condemned by the eminent New York *Times*, and the *Times* had nothing to gain from privileged dirt. But even if the New York *Times* was right and the judge was

---

* The sensational trial of the "margarine heir," Minot Frazier (Mickey) Jelke 3rd, accused of procuring and living off the earnings of prostitutes, became even more of a sensation when Judge Francis L. Valente barred press and public from the courtroom.

wrong, I am sure that all of you will confess with me a feeling of humiliation and shame that our profession is so obviously inspired by such ambiguous motives, and that the freedom we so uncritically demand is so often nothing more than the freedom to pander. If we pander to sensuality that is bad enough. But there may be even greater danger in the fact that freedom of the press is also freedom to pander to ignorance, to mediocrity, to group passions and prejudices, to hatred and meanness, to pander to all that is unlovely in democracy.

My confession—*mea culpa*—and my apology are done. I still do not see how any of the problems of journalism are to be solved in terms of journalism itself, but at least for a while I shall try to be a lecturer on journalism.

I choose the question of the monopoly newspaper. What I have in mind is a city of 100,000 or more population with a one-ownership press.

Is the monopoly newspaper good or bad? It certainly doesn't *sound* good. But my friend John Cowles of Minneapolis has made the case for it, and you are undoubtedly familiar with his thesis.* I am inclined to accept it. You recall the Victorian lady who in a moment of wide-eyed inspiration said: "I accept the universe." In learning of which, Thomas Carlyle exclaimed, "By God! She'd better." So I accept the monopoly newspaper because it exists and, in the nature of things, is going to continue to exist. What do I mean by the nature of things? I mean the nature of the modern newspaper.

The argument against the monopoly newspaper is that it deprives the community of differing presentations of news and opinion. Like so many highbrow discussions about newspapers, this one is fine, except that it ignores the actual nature of a newspaper. Does anyone feel strongly that a city ought to have several newspapers in order to offer the community a greater variety of comic strips, breakfast menus and cheesecake? One paper hotly vegetarian and another a strict adherent of the gospel according to Gayelord Hauser? † We believe in competition as a principle.

---

* John Cowles and his brother Gardner owned monopoly newspapers in Minneapolis and Des Moines. In a speech in May 1951, John Cowles said that noncompetitive dailies in general "have a deeper feeling of responsibility because they are alone in their field."

† Food faddist Hauser's book *Look Younger, Live Longer* created such a demand for blackstrap molasses that FORTUNE ran a story about it in January 1952.

But competition is not an unmixed blessing. And here again the press is peculiar—unbridled competition may lead to even worse results in the press than it did in the past in the marketplace. It is very doubtful whether inter-newspaper competition makes for the best presentation of serious news. One of John Cowles's most telling points is that a monopoly newspaper can afford not to go off half-cocked, not to balloon a trivial little three-hour scoop into apocalyptic sensation. A monopoly newspaper can afford to be accurate and responsible; a competitive paper often cannot. Cowles knows what he's talking about—and so do you. A monopoly newspaper might even be able to afford to cut a prostitution story down to its actual importance.

The typical American newspaper, in addition to being a medium of entertainment, is also a public service, by which I mean, in this context, nothing more glorious than a public utility.

Some years ago when a little magazine called TIME had attained a big circulation, a friend of mine came back to New York after a three months' trip across the country. He reported to me that TIME had an extraordinarily good standing throughout the country. I was as pleased as he was surprised. But then he gave me a solemn warning. He said that from now on TIME must never say anything, in substance or in manner, which was not in accord with the broad consensus of public opinion and public taste. "You see," he said, with warm enthusiasm, "you see, they expect you to be a public utility." And I said: "I'll be damned if I'll be a public utility." Now I have the highest respect for electric-light companies and department stores and I think that one of the finest developments in all human civilization is that business in America has achieved a public-utility aspect. Nevertheless, when I was a young man yearning to get into this business of journalism, it was not with the idea of becoming a public utility. I had my ideals and my selfish hopes—and anyone of you who has printer's ink in his veins knows pretty well what both were. We are flattered to be called public servants. But public utilities? Oh God, not that!

And yet that is the role which, in this great age of America, God has laid on us—and especially on newspaper editors and reporters. You, and to some extent even a maverick like me, have to be public utilities. In local-newspaper terms, you have to give publicity to all the "good" things in town. Every high-school tiddlywinks game must be recorded—or you will be accused of discrimination. You are a public utility. So why not also a monopoly? To be sure, you are not beholden to a public-utilities commission. No, you are subject only to the vested interest of every pressure group in town.

There is one more thing to be said about the monopoly newspaper. The head man—the owner-publisher-editor with his enormous responsibilities—presides not only over the presentation of the news, upon which democratic government depends; he presides also, in his way, over the housewife and her menus, over the school system, over the city government, choosing whether or not to send his reporters after it and expose and root out crime and corruption. Answer in many cases: Why rock the boat?

What do I suggest should be done about it? I can offer no suggestion except *personal, individual responsibility—and more responsibility.*

But when responsibility is exercised in human affairs, it is usually taken for granted that there is some reasonably clear charter to go with it. The doctor has his code—and his license. The soldier, even the four-star general, has his assignment. The businessman has his balance sheet. What about the journalist? Well, you cannot write an effective code for journalism—in a free country. At least it has never been done yet.*

I say you can't. But I also feel constrained to say, we must. Experience says we can't. But every age, that is every generation of journalism, must try. And this, I think, is the age of American journalism in which we may succeed if we try.

I start off with the traditional proposition that the main concern of journalism is public affairs. The Latin phrase is useful here—*res publica*—from which we get our word "republic." The main concern of journalism—and the *only* justification for freedom of the press—is *res publica*—the reporting and discussion of those matters which bear clearly and directly on the business of the Republic. Someone may say that in the modern world everything is the business of the Republic. While that may be true in some sense, if it is applied to politics, it becomes totalitarian. Religion is basic to our Republic, but it is not the business of our Republic. Gossip is universally human, but it is not the business of our Republic except as we corrupt our thought by making it so. So by *res publica* I mean essentially political affairs—those matters which are to be dealt with by the political organs of a free society. The primary function of journalism is to tell as many of the citizens as possible,

* See footnote on page 69.

as effectively as possible, what the *res publica* are, and what the *rational* debate on those subjects is.

From this, it seems to me there is a clear moral corollary which every newspaper owner—and every honest reporter and city editor —can apply. Am I giving my readers the best account of public affairs I possibly can? My right to entertain my readers with murder stories or comic strips, and to profit from that entertainment, is only justified provided I have laid before them a reasonably full and rational and sober account of the current problems of the Republic.

The second function of the press is to present to its readers a recognizable picture of their environment. We Americans, more than other peoples, need continuously to know who we are, where we are. We are not a fixed people, formed long ago in loyalty to a crown or to a river valley. We create ourselves as a nation as we go along. We have in common some fixed stars—and let us never lose sight of them: liberty and justice for all, and God, the author of liberty. But as Thornton Wilder says, "Americans are still engaged in inventing what it is to be an American." * So, like the people of the covered-wagon train, we need to know where we are, what is going on up ahead, and what is behind and around us. Above all we need to know who we are, pilgrims of what hope?

I suggest that responsibility should be applied in this field, too. I would liken it to an artistic responsibility rather than to a political responsibility. Are your reporters and writers giving a truly sensitive account of life in your community? Do they tell how people have fun on Saturday night or worship on Sunday—or work on Monday, and live every day with their hopes and aspirations—and their awful banalities? Here and there across the country there are reporters who do. But why doesn't every newspaper develop at least two or three writers who will really report "our town," lovingly, tenderly, truly? Are they afraid—or just lazy? I leave the question with you.

A third function of journalism, notably in America, is to respond to the American desire for self-improvement. This function needs little elaboration—it might simply be called education—education in nearly everything from geography quiz games to interior decoration. But one warning is perhaps timely. It is said with

* From an interview with Wilder for TIME's cover story, January 12, 1953.

regard to our enormous development of advertising that Americans
are becoming materialistic, not so much because of any subversive
philosophy as because their attention is more and more being
focused on physical things, deodorants, pills, iceboxes, gadgets,
things. I am not persuaded that this fear warrants the abolition of
advertising—a subject on which I have a slight bias; but I do
suggest that since the physical and superficial side of life is so
heavily covered in our advertising pages—and on TV—we ought to
be all the more concerned that in our editorial columns Americans
should find the material of self-improvement in the realm of the
mind, in the intellectual virtues. Neither religion nor common
sense suggests any reason to apologize for a high standard of
living, for good food, good wine, good houses, good health. The
only danger is that having gained all these things the soul may be
starved. "It needs must be that offense cometh, but woe be unto
him by whom the offense cometh." That, it always seems to me,
was said in the first century as a direct warning to 20th-century
American editors.

Fourth and finally, the function of journalism is to be a vessel
of Truth. What is Truth? This is indeed the question of every age,
but it is especially the question of this age because we scarcely
recognize it. We thought we had the problem of Truth fixed—let
anybody say what he liked—"I write as *I* please"—let everybody
teach and preach as he liked—and somehow Truth would prevail in
a cacophony of competition, in a wonderful Donnybrook Fair of
rowdy argument. However it is that Truth prevails (and in the
agony of centuries it does prevail), that is not the way—or at any
rate not the only way.

What is Truth? In our America, no supreme court of wise men,
no platonic philosopher-kings are going to promulgate any official
creed or philosophy. So—it is up to you and me, individually,
personally, to face up to this ultimate question and answer it as
honestly as we can in every day's work. This is what crusading or
serious editors do—and there are many of them in our America.
Yet if one were to pick the greatest flaw in the conventions of
American journalism today, it might be found to lie in the elaborate schemes for evading the personal responsibility of all journalists, and especially of owner-publisher-editors.

Mr. Arthur Robb, of *Editor & Publisher*, recently said: "I do
not believe any newspaper would keep a reporter or editor who was

as careless with the truth, who dealt with rumor and personalities as many columnists do." If an owner-publisher is seriously responsible for every word in his newspaper, he ought not to publish any columnist whose basic integrity he doubts—or with whose *basic* philosophy he disagrees. That is not the fashionable doctrine. The fashionable and convenient and profitable doctrine is that, in order to amuse the reader or in order "to give the readers various viewpoints," the owner-publisher has the right, even the duty, to print what personally he deplores or detests. In my view that is a childish evasion of a man's responsibility. It is worse than that: it is cynicism at the heart of American life.

The Miltonian conception * of Truth prevailing in open combat with error did not, I think, have the modern press in mind. For Milton, surely, had in mind individual men speaking honestly their own truth—or their own lies. The Miltonian doctrine does not apply to a situation where one man feels justified in being the profitable vehicle of another man's lies or another man's distortions.

The owner-editor cannot honorably evade his personal confrontation with every aspect of truth in every aspect of his paper. This sense of personal responsibility should be and can be shared with every member of the staff. Every reporter and subeditor should know that he is expected to be a man of intellectual integrity and that his honest coping with truth, in every department of the paper, will be respected. There is plenty of room for wide differences of opinion and taste—under a roof supported by a few pillars of conviction. But these differences should never be evaded. When basic differences of conviction are made clear, then men who wish to be both honorable and free will part company. We are called to be the servants of Truth: let us serve it together when we can, and separately when we must.

In order to bring my remarks into a field of focus, let me consider the responsibility of an editor in and toward the cold war. I regard an editor's responsibility in the cold war as being in fact far greater than his responsibility in a hot war. You really did not need the press—much—to win World War II. We all tried to help, and of course some sort of communication was necessary. When a soldier brought me a copy of TIME which had been read by twenty

---

* "Let [Truth] and Falsehood grapple: who ever knew Truth put to the worse in a free and open encounter?"—*Areopagitica.*

of his buddies while fighting hip-deep in a swamp in New Guinea, a copy that was smeared with jungle mud and illegible—I thought we had helped a little. But—they would have fought anyway and Rosie the Riveter would have riveted—after Pearl Harbor.

However, all the qualities of command of President Eisenhower and all the thoughtful brilliance of John Foster Dulles will not win the cold war—without us journalists. We have to understand this war in all its places and in all its phases—geographically in Europe, in the Far East, in the Middle East, and categorically in terms of weapons, money and men. It demands all the brains and time and energy we have. For the facts and the analyses have to be presented to the American people so that they may support not obvious decisions of necessity but difficult decisions of choice.

This means a presentation of the *res publica*—vivid, interesting, effective. The farmer must see far beyond farm prices to the whole of the *res publica*. The businessman must see far beyond a tariff advantage to the whole of the *res publica*. The college professor must see far beyond his cherished life in the academic shades to the whole of the *res publica*. And it means making your paper and mine, to the very best of our fallible abilities, vessels of truth. For this is a war of principle, of depth of principle.

I have not yet mentioned Senator McCarthy,* who has achieved the distinction of being the central character in all discussions of journalism. There is one challenge which can effectively be made to Senator McCarthy, who claims to be a Christian. That challenge is the challenge of charity. Freedom—academic freedom and every other freedom—depends on one thing: that we trust each other, and since no one of us is wholly trustworthy, it implies another thing, that our constant judgments of each other shall be made not sentimentally but with charity. With malice toward none, with charity toward all—let every college professor and every editor put *that* challenge to Senator McCarthy.

But we cannot put that challenge to him, except as we put it to ourselves. Does this mean we cannot win the cold war without achieving such a degree of moral responsibility as the world has never yet seen? Yes, something like that. For this is a greater age, a far greater age, than any which was ever seen beneath the

---

* In 1953, Joseph McCarthy of Wisconsin (1909–57) was at the height of his notoriety as chairman of the Senate Permanent Subcommittee on Investigations, airing charges of "subversive activities" in government.

wandering moon. Much has been given to us, much, much more of everything, much more liberty, than ever man had before. And more will be required of us.

Fallible, torn by our conflicting desires and interests, we cannot possibly succeed of and by ourselves. You see, the problem of journalism cannot be solved, cannot even be stated in terms of itself. Journalism can only succeed and freedom can be justified only by constant and humble appeal to the Light which lightens our darkness, to the Power which has set within us all a conscience and a prayer.

10   A DEFINITION OF *TIME*

To celebrate its fortieth anniversary, TIME *invited almost everyone who had been on the magazine's cover to a dinner at the Waldorf-Astoria in New York, March 4, 1963. Luce's address was chiefly an exposition of "The American Proposition" (see Chapters 2 and 3); the following excerpt was its framework for the occasion.*

I want to speak to you tonight about what TIME believes, about what TIME stands for. Ordinarily TIME is not thought of in these terms. It is not a crusading paper. It has no editorial page. To be sure, TIME makes judgments—in nearly every paragraph—sometimes with quite a sting. But TIME is not thought of as being primarily concerned with a basic philosophy of life and politics.

And yet this is what I want to talk about tonight because this is the story of the inner life of TIME, THE WEEKLY NEWSMAGAZINE. This is, if you like, the *inside* story of TIME.

TIME may often seem to be arbitrary—and perhaps actually is—arbitrary, whimsical, even, as they used to say, flippant. And yet through all the huge tapestry of 20th-century history which TIME has woven, there is a clear pattern of belief, a pattern which has become clearer and stronger with the years. TIME believes.

What does it believe? As my offering to this family birthday party, I am going to try to tell you, in my way.

This is by no means the first time that a spokesman for TIME has set forth its articles of belief. In our first prospectus, with the prudent modesty of youth, we announced certain "prejudices." Then, thirty years later, in 1953, we celebrated our birthday by publishing a brilliant essay by Max Ways. Speaking for TIME, Ways said that whereas in 1923 we confessed to "prejudices," in 1953, we stated convictions. Those convictions were fashioned in the fiery furnace of events—and also by intense and sometimes bitter arguments and also by ten-beer bull sessions among scores of editors, reporters and researchers of TIME, in New York and in bistros all over the world.

Last year Hedley Donovan * gave a talk on the editorial philosophy of Time Inc. The first point, he said, is that all our editorial employees are philosophers themselves. We have 1,200 editorial employees, so that makes 1,200 philosophers—and we have plenty on the publishing side, too.

Let me quote at some length from Donovan:

"These 1,200 men and women I am talking about—editors, writers, researchers, photographers, artists—are people who care very strongly about the subjects they are writing about, or researching or editing about, or making pictures of. They care very strongly about these magazines that their work goes into. They are concerned people, engaged people. They are highly individualistic and opinionated people, contentious people. And you might say that the key to the editorial philosophy of Time Inc. is that it takes people of just this sort to create magazines of the excellence we are striving for."

Donovan continues: "Now I know you will not misunderstand me—I am not trying to pretend that our editorial policies are settled by democratic plebiscite. Sooner or later in the editorial process there has to be somebody with the authority to say Yes or No. I think it is one of the highest arts of the TIME editor to know when that point has come for the Yes or No. Sometimes this fellow can get away with saying Maybe, but not as a rule. You've all heard that old journalistic cliché—it serves a lot of people as a substitute for thinking—that 'the truth probably lies somewhere in between.' Well, these editorial philosophers under the Time Inc.

---

* At the time of this speech Donovan was editorial director of Time Inc. He succeeded Luce as editor-in-chief in May 1964.

roof are mainly people who see the truth as being here, or over there—*not* somewhere in between, and not sliding around all over the place. They know what they think, and they expect their editors to know what *they* think. The editor also has to know when to turn off the debate and get the story to press. He and his staff are philosophers under a discipline—the discipline of deadlines."

Emerson said that a man—every man—bears beliefs as a tree bears apples. So belief is common to the stupid oaf, the silly woman and the murderous paranoiac as well as to the saint and the hero. Thank God, then, for the skeptic, the cynic, the caustic critic who hacks down the rotten apples and the tasteless ones. Yet when all the work of cynic and critic has been done, what is there more magnificently human than that a man should stand and say, "I believe." Surely there is nothing more remarkable under the wandering moon. Except one thing—namely, that many men should stand together saying, with heart and mind: "*We* believe."

For a good many decades now there has been worry about the quality of belief in the Western world. Some while ago I heard a story about André Malraux. He was at a White House culture dinner given, I think, in his honor. There he encountered a cleric in Roman collar. This is what Malraux is said to have said to the cleric: "I am a man of my age. I am therefore an agnostic. But I do not believe that an agnostic civilization can survive."

The problem of belief or faith is not entirely a question of believing in certain truths that are not mechanically verifiable. It is also, at any given time in history, a question of vision. "Where there is no vision, the people perish." There must be a vision of how to live an individual life, and also a vision of how the nation is to live, and in our day, of the whole world. If we do not see clearly how the whole world of man is to be fashioned and shaped, we may indeed be forgiven—at least momentarily—for the challenge is so immense, and so utterly without precedent.

And yet if you do believe—if you believe in any serious sense in things like freedom, justice, democracy, human dignity—you cannot evade the challenge of trying to figure out how these virtues may be made operative around the globe.

What, then, does TIME now believe? TIME's conception of human nature—what is man?—and TIME's value judgments run though all the fields of endeavor and all the categories of human aspirations and speculations.

TIME believes that human life is tragic and triumphant and also comic but never, as Sartre proclaims, absurd. Tonight I shall focus on just one category—political philosophy—one category of human existence in one unique time and place—the United States. My specific subject is the American Proposition.

By the American Proposition we mean the total political philosophy of the Declaration of Independence, of the Constitution, and of its evolution in the history of the United States to the present day. The whole of the American Proposition has been epitomized by FORTUNE in this formula: "The American Proposition consists of a word, a tendency and a method. The word is liberty. The tendency is equality. The method is constitutionalism." That is the core and essence of what TIME believes.

How well has TIME served the American Proposition? And one way to answer that question is to ask another: How well is the United States living up to its historic faith? I give you my answer quickly: since TIME's last birthday party, our twentieth, in the midst of the first truly global war, the United States has been doing well, very well.

We used to say that TIME is the most important magazine in America—in the world. We no longer indulge in that kind of boasting, but it is obvious that TIME is very important in the life of this country since several millions of our most capable citizens have a firm date with TIME each week for their most comprehensive and serious consideration of public affairs—the *res publica* of the republic. If, therefore, the country were in a sorry and shameful state, we would have to bear a share of the blame. And if, on the contrary, the republic is strong, we can drink our birthday toast in at least a moment of reflected glory.

11   THE FORTUNATE ONES

Luce gave the McKinsey Lectures at the Columbia University Business School on April 24, May 1 and May 8, 1963. He was chosen because Time Inc. had shown a special capacity to do what business generally needed to

do—attract and keep more intelligent and creative peo-
ple. In his first lecture, from which the following is an
excerpt, Luce gave evidence that people liked to work at
Time Inc. because of the "fun and excitement" of the
place and also because of their freedom to assume a
"proprietary interest in what we do and how we do it."
Ironically, the Charlie Mohr of this speech later quit
Time Inc. in a dispute over the magazine's handling of
his coverage of the Vietnam war.

Winter before last I had occasion to go to India for three weeks. For most of my time there I was in the company of one of our younger correspondents, Charlie Mohr. I got well acquainted with him and his wife, who besides keeping house and raising children in very difficult circumstances is writing a novel. In the hours we were together, in airplanes and in Calcutta traffic jams and in late-evening bull sessions with perhaps a bevy of other correspondents present—what did Charlie and I talk about? Well, pretty much everything, including food, sex and money. But mostly it was India, India, India—even food, sex and money were *sub specie Indiatis.*

Charlie Mohr was then thirty-one. He was born in Loup City, Nebraska, population 1,415. He worked as a roustabout on a Mississippi River boat and as a Steinbeckian migrant in the California vineyards. Then he went to the University of Nebraska, while he put in a forty-hour week as a reporter on the Lincoln *Star.* He had a passion to be a journalist. And that's what he is—and how—and that's the point. Before he went to India he was our White House correspondent. That gave him nearly three years of daily, almost hourly, observation of Eisenhower. And he went with Eisenhower thousands and thousands of miles all over the world.* I knew him, of course, as one of our young staffers covering the White House. But now I really got to know him in India. And what did I find? A man for whom there are not half enough hours in the day. India is his beat—450 million people, yes, and 3,500 years of history. Every day Charlie Mohr is convening with cabinet ministers or army generals or business tycoons, unless he has decided to take three days off and tramp through a dozen faraway villages. All the problems of India are his—the hopes, the frustrations, serious

* In the last years of his Administration, President Eisenhower traveled to Mexico, Europe, the Middle East and the Far East.

enough to make anyone weep, and every day something funny is happening on the way to the Indian forum. Nights—some nights— he's at home with his wife or maybe a small group of other journalists or an expert economist. And what do they talk about, argue about, even fight about? India, India, India. But not always economics or politics. You see, Mohr is a hunter—he was out to get a tiger-hunter's tiger. Not content with an occasional tiger-shoot with a maharaja, Mohr spent his own money to rent a hunting preserve—for a day or two at a time. India, India, India—from tigers to tycoons.

Have I conveyed something of the fun and excitement of Charlie Mohr's job? Isn't it romantic and glamorous? Yes, but it is definitely not indicated for everybody. It is a back-breaking, mind-breaking job—and some have even called it soul-searing. Only one man in a thousand is called to be a journalist. But the man who is called thinks of himself as one of the fortunate ones of this earth.

2

POLITICS AND PATRIOTISM

Luce's earliest recorded political remark was in a letter to his family from school in Chefoo when he was thirteen: "My sympathies are entirely with the revolutionaries [of 1911] so long as they have worthy men to place in power. . . . There are reports that the constitutionalists will be less tolerant than the Manchu Dynasty, but what grounds are they based on? I long to get a glimpse of the Shanghai papers."

And a few weeks later: "A revolution cannot make out of rascals, patriots, or out of the ignorant, wise. However, this revolution sends a ray of hope down China's broadening future."

Other political reflections of an American boy in China:

"Conservatism, though in some cases beneficial, is generally speaking the world's greatest evil."

"To my utter contempt of American citizens here in Chefoo, the Fourth of July passed without note to sound the glories of our day. Has patriotism fallen to this degraded state? Is there no spark left to show our ancient glory?"

From Hotchkiss, a letter to his father finds him relating politics to religion: "I wrote rather a hot oration on Christian Democracy, inspired by your letter, as to the foundation of America's leadership of the world at the close of the European war. The elocution master said he had not a criticism to make. . . . He told one fellow that the only fellow who could sling the religious bull without appearing foolish was Luce."

And in another letter, from Chicago during summer vacation, he ponders the link between politics and morality: "Mrs. McCormick and I spent the afternoon discussing the export of munitions . . . puzzling subject. Law and indeed justice seem to side with exportation. Morality would seem to favor embargo. But true justice must be moral . . . hence I am led unwillingly to favor export of arms."

At Yale he took pride in the fact that he and his fellow editors of the News "have played a major part in changing the spirit of Yale. There is now no college in the country more thoroughly and intensely patriotic—and intelligently!"

These early letters illustrate, as does his DeForest Oration (Number 1 below), what were to remain the chief political preoccupations of Luce's life. One was his classical view of the interconnectedness of politics and other human concerns. He saw politics as a branch of morals, just as morals is a branch of religion; but he also saw politics as central to problems of business and economics, work and leisure, peace and progress and civilization.

Luce's other chief preoccupation was the United States of America and its role in world history. His most famous paper, "The American Century" (Number 6 below), was preceded by four speeches rehearsing its theme, and followed by others further developing his view that the American role in history has been providential, purposeful and wholly distinguishable from that of its parental European civilization. "The American Proposition," as he called this body of doctrine, is spelled out especially in speeches Number 7, 8, 10 and 11 of this chapter; see also Chapter 3.

Luce himself pointed out (page 377) that patriotism is likely to come early and intensely to an American raised abroad, especially if your parents (like his) take care to teach you the facts about your country. Because he had no American hometown or regional loyalties, Luce's mental image of America was more than usually abstract or idealized—an image of the whole country, its ruling concepts and past achievements, rather than a place on the map. As a corollary, he took its shortcomings all the harder. As a student of history, Luce knew he had ample evidence for his belief in the unique purpose and special mission of America, and good company in it. He was also aware of the comparable claims of other nations (e.g., France's mission civilisatrice and Britain's service to the rule of law) without regarding them as rivals or obstacles to his claim that the 20th was "The American Century." In any case, his

patriotism was associated not only with his pride in saying civis
Americanus sum, *but with his dreams for the uniting of all nations
and cultures in a global City of Man. The next stages of this
mission would be the spreading rule of law and the meeting of East
and West in "the dawn of world history"—themes large enough
for separate chapters (3 and 4).*

1   WHEN WE SAY "AMERICA"

*Luce's prize-winning DeForest Oration in his senior
year at Yale was delivered in Lampson Lyceum, April
26, 1920. It foreshadowed not only his dissatisfaction
with American foreign policy but also other themes of
"The American Century."*

A great part of the content of the word "American" today is
history. And the glory of it shall never pass away. But when we
say "America" today we connote power. We hold the purse strings
of the world. Having enough ourselves to eat and to be clothed
withal, we sell in the markets of every nation. The huge wheels
and pistons which at all hours are astir like the quick breathing of
giants, the great fires which never sleep, the long rooms where
hour by hour the hands of men and women are ceaselessly at work,
testify to a national strength which hitherto the world has never
seen. America is power, and it sits astride the globe. But is our
greatness merely for the sake of greatness? Are we big to no
purpose? Is our strength void of quality? Has our force no
direction?

The test of the character of a modern nation is in its foreign
relations. Because of our history we have escaped the curse of
imperialism. We do not thirst for domination. But the last few
years give good cause to fear that we have escaped the sin of
Prussia only at the expense of believing nothing. Does America
believe in anything? Is there aught that she will fight for except

her existence? For three years, 1914 to 1917, there was in the world a moral challenge, but because we believed in nothing we could not answer it. To say that we fought for principle is ridiculous. Some of our noblest did; but as a nation we fought only when the last average American feared that one nation should conquer Europe and thereafter threaten our own existence. Is there, then, any policy for which we will fight?

But when we say "America" twenty years from now, may it be that that great name will signify throughout the world at least two things: first, that American interests shall be respected, American citizens entitled to trade and to live in every corner of the globe; second, that America may be counted upon to do her share in the solution of every international difficulty, that she will be the great friend of the lame, the halt and the blind among nations, the comrade of all nations that struggle to rise to higher planes of social and political organization, and withal the implacable and the *immediate* foe of whatever nation shall offer to disturb the peace of the world. If this shall be, then the America of this century shall have glory and honor. If this shall be, hers will be adventure more brilliant than Eldorado, hers a moral and ethical altitude unapproached by Puritan, a democracy broader in its influence than we have ever dreamed, an aristocracy of an incomparable nobility.

2   LET IT DIE

The title of this essay by Luce in the Saturday Review of Literature, *October 27, 1928, meant that the U.S. Constitution was obsolete and should be replaced by a new one. The Constitution was being technically nullified by the nonobservance of Prohibition, but was made even more obsolete, Luce felt, by Hoover's implied promise that Republicans could guarantee prosperity, a function for which the Constitution as then interpreted had failed to equip the federal government. This article was less than prophetic in the short run, since Prohibition was repealed five years later and the heavens did fall upon prosperity, however "intolerable to the American people." But in the longer run the Depression, which Luce elsewhere called a trauma in the American experience comparable to that of the Civil War, was to effect changes in American life and law comparable to those brought about by the Civil War amendments.*

We are faced with the fact that for the second time in our history a great part (possibly even a majority) of the American people have a grievance against the Constitution, and that this grievance is vociferous, and that there is no demonstrable prospect of relief.

It is difficult to believe that anything short of revolution can revoke the 18th Amendment within thirty years. The Mormons of Utah plus the 77,000 inhabitants of Nevada plus the Solid South can alone keep the Amendment where it is.

I suggest that the *system of government as set forth in the Constitution* is fundamentally unsuited to modern America. It will appear that in dealing with Prohibition we must deal ultimately with the whole structure of American government, and that an era of inevitable nullification may close with an attempt to match the new social order with a new form of government.

First, as everyone knows, States' Rights as a principle of U.S. government is little more than a memory.

Second, the federal government having assumed, by tacit consent, a great deal more power than even the "loose constructionists" ever dreamed of, it naturally follows that the President is a much more powerful officer than he was intended to be. That he should pretty well control the destinies of Nicaragua, without even the advice and consent of Congress, is a consummation which not even Bryce, the realist, could have been expected to predict.

Third, there is the matter of reapportionment. Of course it would be impossible for the people of the United States so consistently to nullify the spirit of the Constitution without occasionally nullifying its very letter. According to the Constitution, seats in Congress ought to be reapportioned among the various states on the basis of the 1920 census. Although President Coolidge was unlucky in his contests with Congress, he could certainly have forced through a reapportionment bill had he cared to. Perhaps he thought that since it should have been done during Harding's Administration, the whole matter might just as well wait for a new decade. In any case, each and every act passed by Congress and signed by President Coolidge would seem to lack some degree of constitutionality since they are not passed by a Congress elected in accordance with the Constitution.

Fourth, Negroes complain that the ballot box is not always easily accessible. This situation may be acquiring the prestige of old age, but is an instance, nevertheless, of nullification.

Fifth, finally, among what might be called fundamental concepts of American government, consider the almost total disrepute into which the Bill of Rights has come. "The right of the people to be secure in their persons, houses, papers . . . against unreasonable searches" is rendered meaningless when a policeman can walk into homes on mere suspicion of gin; or when a telephone conversation may be tapped by federal officers, or when any man's papers can be exhaustively snooped at by Income Tax officials upon the slightest excuse.

These instances of nullification go to the very heart of the *system of government* which, as embodied in the Constitution, we are taught to revere.

The Constitution was made for a country almost totally agricultural, for people whose garments and amusements were made in the home. It was made for people who had great distrust for a central government, but who also were able to know their representatives personally; and among whom politics was, at the very least, a major and continuing diversion. The Constitution was made for people who were intensely individualistic, and yet who, state by state, were bound together by a supraconstitutional allegiance to a common morality. The present contrast to all this need not be labored; it is discernible in any movie house anywhere any night.

That there is no present outcry against the Constitution is due, not so much to the perspicacity of the Founding Fathers as to the heroism of the Supreme Court. The floods of necessity, which have long since burst the dikes of the Constitution, have never quite been able to overwhelm the Mountains of Interpretation, from which nine heroes have repeatedly proclaimed that since it has not exhausted their cunning, necessity is still subject to their law.

But that people are content with the Constitution is due, even more than to the Court, to their docility and to the moribund condition of their political consciences, which is a direct result of the inappropriateness of the political system, and, of course, above all, to prosperity.

The Constitution does not, as is commonly supposed, say anything about life, liberty or the pursuit of happiness. That trinity, together with the now generally abhorred notion of the equality of man, was conceived by Thomas Jefferson in a heated and probably libelous attack on George III of England, which we call the Declaration of Independence. But if the most universal conception of the purpose of our government is that it is to secure the right to life, liberty and the pursuit of happiness, be it noted that the right to the pursuit of happiness is not the same as guaranteed happiness. If the popular equivalent for happiness is prosperity, be it noted that a government which endeavors to ensure the *right* to the *pursuit* of prosperity is radically different from a government which endeavors to ensure *prosperity*.

But now no party can successfully invite the suffrages of the people unless it practically guarantees prosperity to every man, woman and moron. Any candidate for the presidency who promises to make prosperity his principal concern is promising to do something for which his office is not constitutionally equipped. The Preamble to the Constitution does indeed mention "general welfare," but it was never intended that the President should be, literally or figuratively, the general manager of what President Coolidge so carelessly calls the "biggest business on earth." It is not recalled, for example, that George Washington ever alluded to himself as the bailiff of the biggest farm on earth.

The Constitution was a great and masterful collection of compromises. But this prosperity-versus-politics dilemma is utterly unimagined by the Constitution. Indeed, the Constitution is entirely on the side of politics. The Constitution presupposes the ideal of *stat justitia ruat coelum* [let justice prevail though the heavens fall]. The simple fact is that the idea of the heavens' falling upon prosperity is intolerable to the American people. And since that is a fact, it is equally a fact that the Constitution, even with any amount of distorted interpretation, is unsuited to the present needs and temperament of the American people. And since *that* is a fact, it is equally a fact that nullification has been and is inevitable.

To suggest the problem is to suggest the solution. If the Constitution of 1789 is unsuitable, and if, on the whole, it is desirable to have a Constitution, the alternative is a new constitution. Many a conservative may indeed shiver at the thought of stirring up the animals by the excitement of a constitutional convention. This is because new constitutions are associated with upheavals. But many a profounder conservative will perceive the wisdom of making a new constitution in a time of peace and plenty.

3   ARISTOCRACY AND MOTIVES

This speech illustrates the elitist undertone that surfaced from time to time in Luce's political thinking. It showed again in 1934, when, having read Pareto, he devoted a special issue of FORTUNE *to Mussolini's Italy and therein wrote a passing tribute to the Fascist revival of "certain ancient virtues . . . Discipline, Duty, Courage, Glory, Sacrifice." The following speech also asserts the hope that is more fully developed in Chapter 5: that in becoming more professionalized, American business would become the source of an American aristocracy. It was delivered to the Fortnightly Club in Chicago, November 28, 1930.*

Dean Wicks * of Princeton was making a speech at the opening of the current endowment campaign for the Northfield Schools— schools, as you may know, founded by Dwight L. Moody † for boys and girls who are financially unable to go to Exeter or Groton or Foxcroft. In the course of his speech he formulated a slogan. He said: "These are schools for boys and girls who have more *purpose*

* Robert Russell Wicks (1882–1963), for many years Dean of the Chapel at Princeton.
† American evangelist (1837–99) and pioneer of the Y.M.C.A.

than money." I wish that Dean Wicks were here tonight. For I would like to ask him *what* purpose, what kinds of purposes, do these Northfielders have? I would ask him to specify, to particularize, to be precise in his definitions of the purposes which are available to purposeful youths in modern America. And if he could define, and if he felt that these were purposes which could give ample significance to the lives of the ablest men of the coming generation—then I could cheerfully cancel my present remarks.

For what I have to say tonight concerns the inadequacy of motive in modern life. I wish to remind you of the intimate connection between motive and aristocracy, and finally to suggest that America today is the most amazing example in history of a civilization in search of an aristocratic principle.

For the first time in the world's history we have a nation of 120 million people who have enough to live *on*, and for the first time in the world's history the best of those 120 million cannot find enough to live *for*.

Dean Wicks's Northfielders have more purpose than money, but that isn't saying much because they haven't much money. What I want to talk about is the young man who has or will presently earn a fair amount of money, and I want to ask how it is possible for him to have more purpose than money.

Now what are the motives which have given significance to the lives of superior people? First, there is a group of motives such as art for art's sake, or truth for truth's sake, or goodness for goodness' sake. Happily these motives seem to be eternal and universal. But unhappily, as *dominant* motives, they are as rare as they are invaluable to humanity. All of us respond to them in some degree. But not yet are these the motives that men live by. They remain the currency of life only for the genius and for the hypocrite.

We are speaking of men of greater-than-average but not consummate ability, and we inquire what motives in the past have given direction and significance to their lives. Roughly, these motives can be divided into two groups. There is, first, the motive of honor and glory. And, second, there is the motive of a cause which is believed to be completely meritorious. Actuated by the first were all the conquerors of the world. Actuated by the second were all the martyrs. While for purposes of illustration we must refer to them, let it be understood plainly that our concern is not with the towering figures of history. We are discussing not Napoleon. We are discussing the marshal's baton which he placed in 10,000 if not a million soldiers' knapsacks. We are discussing not his generals of genius. We are discussing the little ribbon of his Legion of Honor. From this point of view let your mind roam across the chapters of occidental history. Are any of the motives which created the Western world available today for the ablest seniors at Harvard or Yale or the University of Chicago, who have fifty years of America before them?

In terms of specific careers, America has eliminated the motive of glory to be achieved by the sword. Peace, we say, has her victories no less than war. Has it? That is precisely what we are wondering. Now if this country had indeed an imperial policy, all would be quite different. Were we set upon conquering, if not the world, then at least the Western Hemisphere, the entire tempo of American life would be different. If conquest were our united national ambition, we would find a way of honor not only for Caesars but for centurions, and before every energetic Harvard man there could glitter the star of a proconsulship. How ridiculous this sounds. Yet to all the poets from Homer to Tennyson it would be astounding that it should sound ridiculous. And consider only yesterday the Germany of Bismarck. The German Empire was built on the motives implicit in a military hierarchy. Honor was honor indeed when it proceeded from an emperor's throne, and it motivated not only the military but even the professors and village aldermen, as witness the unpronounceable titles that every good German pronounces with his name as frequently as possible.

At the war's end there fell not only Germany and Austria and Russia but also Aristocracy. The Kaiser is exiled from Germany and the aristocratic principle is exiled from almost all the world. But, unlike the Kaiser, it will return. Where? How? And especially, will it emerge again in America? Not until now has the aristocratic principle been necessary to American life. For there is a direct substitute for aristocracy, and that is pioneering. As long as men can move laterally they need not move vertically. But when they must move upward or nowhere, then that movement must be on some ladder of aristocracy, however curiously it may be constructed. America's lateral days are over. For the young men today it is upward or nowhere. And, looking upward, they see little except the making of money.

But a ladder of aristocracy need not be one of swords. China has had her hierarchy of scholars, Rome and Scotland and New England their theocracies. France had her court of Louis XIV. And, better known to us, there was England's late great parliamentary era extending from Chatham to Balfour. But note that, whether the prize was for swordsmanship or oratory, and whether the prize was more often obtained by guile than by merit, the prize was always given by the state. So, today, where the state is dominant in the eyes of the people, you find the most articulate attempts to revitalize the principle of aristocracy. You find it notably successful in Italy, a state reborn by virtue of Fascist symbols and Fascist rank. Reduce Fascist rank to a level of democracy and you have destroyed *Fascismo*.

Now the simple fact is that, in America, honor from the state is so uncertain of achievement, and is in any case so lightly esteemed, that a career of public service is regarded as almost quixotic. While any man here would take a gilt-edge nomination to the Senate, few would fight for it, and no one would accept an election to Congress.* And as for telling your son just out of Harvard Law that he can achieve immemorial honor for his family by becoming a fighting young Assistant District Attorney and sending some gunman to the gallows—you would rather pay indefinitely his bills as a Paris art student. And, under the circumstances, I am sure I would, too.

But while the state has been about the only fountainhead of honor with which we are familiar, it is not, of course, the only dynamo of motive. Apart from the state in war or peace, there is another group of motives which can be summarized by one word: a cause. The perfect examples were of course the early crusades. Now causes or crusades have been of every conceivable variety, touched always with the sublime or the ridiculous or both. But the greatest of all causes, tested by its power to supply complete adequacy of motive, has been the cause of religion. Take religious folk in action like Innocent III and Wycliffe and Joan of Arc and St. Catherine of Siena and St. Ignatius of Loyola and Calvin and Mather and Moody. Of Thomas Becket it was said, "He was burning with zeal for justice, but whether altogether according to wisdom, God knows." Doubts they may have had but never Doubt. They found indeed great purpose in life.

* Luce was to outgrow this disdain for Congress; he took pride in his wife's membership in it (1943–47).

Now it is obvious that there is no cause in this nation today whose attractive power can be compared even for a moment to the cause of supernatural religion in past ages. Nor do I urge that there should be. Our purpose is simply to establish an all-important difference between our age and all its historic past. Where was the motivation of talent in times past?

Largely in the state and in religion. From the state, honor. From religion, a cause to magnify any office. The dual motives of career: aggrandizement and sacrifices. Opposites nearly always confused —supreme sacrifice in the state and vicious aggrandizement in religion. Motives inextricably confused. But always motives, available and sufficient.

Can the magic of these motives be reinvoked in different form and with different words? There are some, notably Walter Lippmann,* who intrigue us with their forecast of a new religion —a religion of decency and self-discipline and philosophical nobility. The great difficulty with this sort of religion is exactly what we are talking about tonight. It lacks motivation for any except the born philosopher. In Lippmann's morality, intelligence and not emotion shall rule. No one will quarrel with that. No, and no one is going to quarrel *for* it. Nondogmatic, it is also noncompetitive. It supplies neither rapture nor mission.

But you may say that, quite apart from any religion, there are noble causes. And so, indeed, there are. There is health and the conquest of disease. There is popular education—for in a democracy we must educate our masters. There is the abolition of poverty. The fact that our society is making what can only be described as magnificent progress along the whole line of humanitarianism may indicate that we no longer need any spurs to prick the sides of our ambition. This is a fashionable notion. Nice young men state it nicely as they board ship for Oxford. I am reluctant to dismiss this notion, but I must dismiss it. For, however altruistic people may now be, it is still naive to assume that altruism can be the dominating motive in the lives of a majority of able and energetic men.

So we come back to the motive of honor. I have suggested that, in whatever varying systems, the nature of honor has always in the past been identified with some principle of aristocracy and that, for the most part, it has been identified with the state. It is difficult to

* His *A Preface to Morals* appeared in 1929.

imagine the reintroduction of a vital aristocratic principle into the American state in the coming decades. Does this, then, mean that our best young men can look forward to nothing except making money and having fun? If I answered yes, that is exactly what it means, I would have, I think, the weight of evidence on my side. But I do not know the answer. And in any case I would desire to offer you some reasons for answering no, some reasons for believing that we may offer the best youth of the land something besides money and pleasure for their future.

If the aristocratic principle is unlikely to return to this country via the state, is there a possibility that we may evolve an aristocracy not of the state? I believe there is one remote conceivable possibility—namely, that the aristocratic principle may be re-created in America through what has always marched under the nicely middle-class name of business. There are four reasons for this possibility. In the first place, business is what we believe in more than any other agency of society. Second, business actually is what the best young men are going into. The whole point of this speech is that they are going into it with something less of spirit and enthusiasm than actuated their peers in the days of military or ecclesiastical glory. But they are going into it. Third, business will never be run on a democratic basis. Business need not be auto-cratic. But certainly business must be aristocratic. There must be a top and, if possible, the best men must get there. Fourth, and finally, business includes within itself a majority of the "causes" in which contemporarily we have at least some little faith—the cause of science, the cause of health, the cause of an efficient distribution of wealth, and even the cause of peace.

But in addition to the purely logical reasons for the possibility of an aristocracy there are bits of evidence that this development is actually in process. In the first place, business is slowly losing its self-consciousness. As long as it remains secretive and half-ashamed, it can produce no aristocracy. Its ever vaster organization gives it a public character and, similarly, it is rapidly assuming public responsibility for the public weal. Furthermore, the very complexity of modern business tends to make ability more impor-tant than luck. Again, in this connection, we are beginning to distinguish a little between a man's importance *to* business and the amount of money he gets *out of* business. The head of a great corporation may be a comparatively poor man and yet be held in higher esteem than his richest stockholder. This kind of discrimination must increase manyfold if we are to escape the disaster of a plutocracy and discover the true merits of aristocracy. Finally, from among many other bits of evidence we might assemble, it is to be noted that American Society with a capital S, no longer having great European courts for its ultimate sanction, is less and less inclined to deny that such dubious foundation as it has is a business foundation.

I have not said that an aristocracy is emerging. I wish I could. I have said that America is a civilization in search of an aristocracy. During the past century we have had good reason to grow up in the belief that aristocracies were deadening, if not decadent things. And so indeed they were—that is, some of the actual aristocracies were in their later manifestations, but there was nothing dead about the aristocratic principle. Let me quote from the man who made the Queen of England Empress of India. "It is not true," said Disraeli, "that England is governed by an aristocracy . . . England is governed by an aristocratic principle. The aristocracy of England absorbs all aristocracies, and receives every man in every order and every class who defers to the principle of our society, which is to aspire and to excel." There you have it. America has its limited aristocracies or rather its insignificant snobberies, its ruling cliques at large universities, in small-town churches, in Wall Street. But what we lack and what we look for is an aristocratic principle to support an aristocracy which, as Disraeli says, can absorb all our insignificant snobberies and, above all, give purpose to the lives of those whose nature it is to aspire and to excel.

Never was aristocracy more in disgrace than when it was necessary for royal Bourbons to flee by night to Varennes. It was about that time that Edmund Burke produced his great apologia for the aristocratic principle. Granting all the obvious evils in any system, he saw, as clearly as he had previously foreseen the independence of America, that a nation without an aristocracy is a nation all belly and no head. Let me conclude with an extract from this matchless genius in national morality:

> To be bred in a place of estimation; to be taught to respect oneself; to look early to public opinion; to stand upon such elevated ground as to be enabled to take a large view of the

widespread and infinitely diversified combinations of men and affairs in a large society; to have leisure to read, to reflect, to converse; to be taught to despise danger in the pursuit of honor and duty; to have cultivated an habitual regard to commutative justice—these are the circumstances of men that form what I should call a national aristocracy without which there is no nation.

4　IN A JAM

Luce was awarded his "Y in Life" in 1937 at the annual postseason party Nick Roberts, a professional Yale man, gave the Yale football team at his barn in Montclair, New Jersey. Delighted at a chance to shock his complacent friends, Luce delivered a blast (December 4, 1937) that was partially reported in the Herald Tribune *and in* The New Yorker *and gave him a briefly embarrassing reputation for pessimism.*

What I have to say is that this big world you and I are living in —this world right now—is a lousy, cockeyed world and a hell of a dangerous place to be in.

Full of good cheer as we are tonight, cushioned as we are by friendship and friendliness on all sides, it may well seem ungracious and even stupid of me to invite you to join in a bitter complaint against our fate.

There was a show on Broadway several years ago called *Merrily We Roll Along.** One brilliant critic summarized the play somewhat as follows: the hero is the most "fashionable" playwright in America. He has just produced another smash hit and is celebrating the opening on his palatial Long Island estate. He has dozens of friends, a beautiful new mistress, a yacht waiting to take them on a

* By George S. Kaufman and Moss Hart, 1934.

moonlight spin. He is surrounded by caviar, champagne and brilliant conversation. Now the problem which the rest of the play grapples with is this: how did the s.o.b. get into such a jam?

I'm going to recite a little on the proposition that we are in a jam. And I'm going to do this because, in my opinion, we Americans are entirely too cheerful. We may do a lot of squawking because the stock market goes down. And we may view the New Deal with the greatest and most solemn alarm. But we don't realize that we as a people are only about two jumps ahead of the Sheriff of Destruction.

War, modern war, the kind of war that destroys civilization, is in the world. In my time, Yale was turned into a military training camp. I think the chances are at least fifty-fifty that Yale will again be turned into a military camp within ten years. And if we build another Memorial Hall, there will be more than 212 names in it. They try to tell us that the European war scare exists mostly in America. The truth of the matter is that right now the gentlemen of England are trying to make up their minds whether they will let Germany grab Austria and Czechoslovakia—or whether they won't. War? Let alone the general threat, the place is already agreed upon—and only the time remains for gods and dictators to decide. So much for Europe. What is even a clearer fact is that you are going to have war in Asia from now until you get sick of watching it. War in Europe, war in Asia—and we stay out?

Well, let's stay home. What happens here? We've had nearly ten years of hard times. And is there anyone in this room who can stand up and tell us just when we get out of the hard times and stay out for longer than it takes to turn around and spit? Take politics. A hundred years ago, we had plenty of bad politics, but we had a system, a new system, a new idea which we believed in and which we dreamed of perfecting. What political ideals are valid now? Who here will stand up and show us how, ten, twenty, or fifty years from now, we will have a system of politics of which we can be proud, a system which breeds statesmen and in which statecraft may operate?

The new morality—a sentimental amorality—is far more likely to be developed in Hollywood than in Yale. Yale has spoken for 200 years of leadership in church and state. But in the years to come, what chance is there that the ideals of Yale will be anything more than a mewling protest against the roar of vulgarity?

And there are other facts. If you think that biology is deeper than ethics and that psychiatry is deeper than religion—then go deeper into biology and psychiatry. Harvard's great Dr. Hooton * has just recently pronounced biological doom on the human race unless, by some instant miracle, we can be persuaded to take our genes and chromosomes firmly in hand. And one of the greatest facts, which we hardly ever think of, is that today there is more insanity or near insanity than ever before in history. What are the statistics—something like one out of every twenty-two Americans may expect to spend part of his life in a bughouse. And God knows how many nitwits are at large in high places.

What does it all add up to? Is it not this—that man is passing very swiftly into a new phase of existence, based upon technology, which is based upon man's staggering mental achievements in the past—and the great question is whether we can adjust ourselves, physically, psychologically, morally and spiritually to a new kind of life on this planet? I have spoken of facts. What I have indicated is, of course, only the barest sketching of a scaffolding on which thousands of facts could be hung. And the sum total of all these facts could easily add up to the degradation of mankind.

* Earnest A. Hooton (1887–1954), the anthropologist, had suggested a "biological purge" to restore civilized man's fitness to survive.

---

5 AMERICA AND ARMAGEDDON

During the Sitzkrieg *of September 1939–April 1940, Luce's championship of the Allied cause was outspoken within Time Inc., but more cautious in public. After the fall of Norway, Denmark, and the Low Countries (he witnessed the invasion of Belgium) the threat to America became far more imminent and Luce made his views public immediately on his return from Europe. He spoke for national unity over a coast-to-coast network and published an article in* LIFE, *June 3, 1940, from which the following is taken.*

America is now confronted by a greater challenge to its survival as a land of liberty than any it has had to face in eighty years.

When I sailed for Europe in April, the American people were not willing to face the challenge. I believe they are willing to face it now.

The events of the last few weeks have shocked the American people. But these events were not things which happened by accident. They were not events like earthquake or famine or plague or fire. These were acts of men—long and carefully planned. They were planned with cunning and efficiency and implacable purpose. These events were an inevitable climax of the history of the last few years. But they are only one climax. Greater climaxes, of good or evil, are yet to come, and soon. The final defeat of Great Britain and France would be another climax, the immensity of which even now defies the imagination. If Great Britain and France fail, we know that we and we only among the great powers are left to defend the democratic faith throughout the world. We may never fight side by side, comrades-in-arms of France and Britain. But we know now that, fundamentally, their struggle is our struggle.

We have to take action. First we have to arm ourselves. We have to prepare ourselves to meet force with force—to meet force with *superior* force. That is a colossal job. The second thing we have to do is to make up our minds what we are willing to fight for. That for us, as for all free peoples, is an even harder job.

Our government has the constitutional duty of deciding exactly where and when and how the United States shall fight. But our government cannot and will not decide what we the people are willing to fight *for*. Only when our government knows what we the people are willing to fight for—only then can our government face the world with an intelligent and resolute policy.

In the end the great decision has to be made in the heart and in the private conscience of each and every American citizen. It is a responsibility which is altogether personal. You cannot escape it. I cannot escape it. It is the greatest responsibility which will ever come to us as citizens of the America we love. I have made my decision as to what I am prepared to fight for with everything I have and am, and as one citizen to another I will tell you as best I can how I have decided.

What I am willing to fight for is, of course, America; but not America as a geologic mass, not for its mountains and plains and rivers, greatly though I love them and much though they have concerned me. The America I want to fight for is the America of freedom and justice, the America which has stood throughout the world for the hope of progress in the democratic way of life and for faith in the ultimate brotherhood of man. America belongs to us, the lucky 130 million people who are living here today. But not entirely. A little of America belongs to every man and woman everywhere who has had faith in democracy and hope in a world of peace and justice. We the living, who control the destiny of America today, are the heirs of a great inheritance from men who lived and from men who died to make men free. What they meant by America is what I would wish to mean by America. And for that America I am willing to fight.

If something like this is the answer which will be given in the coming weeks and months by the American people, then I for one am completely willing to trust our leaders, whoever they may be at any time, in the White House, in the State Department and in Congress, to decide exactly where and when and how the American people shall take their stand at Armageddon.

6   THE AMERICAN CENTURY

This famous essay was written when the mood of the American people was at once strongly anti-Hitler and isolationist. When it was published in LIFE, *February 17, 1941, it produced a heavy demand for reprints; an attack from many liberal quarters such as the* Nation, *then edited by Freda Kirchwey, on Luce's "new brand of imperialism"; and a speech by Henry Wallace prophesying "The Century of the Common Man." Wallace and Luce exchanged much correspondence on their differences and retained great respect for each other. But Luce was puzzled and distressed by what he thought were misinterpretations of "The American Century" (see page 15).*

We Americans are unhappy. We are not happy about America. We are not happy about ourselves in relation to America. We are nervous—or gloomy—or apathetic.

As we look out at the rest of the world we are confused; we don't know what to do. "Aid to Britain short of war" is typical of halfway hopes and halfway measures.

As we look toward the future—our own future and the future of other nations—we are filled with foreboding. The future doesn't seem to hold anything for us except conflict, disruption, war.

There is a striking contrast between our state of mind and that of the British people. On September 3, 1939, the first day of the war in England, Winston Churchill had this to say: "Outside, the storms of war may blow and the lands may be lashed with the fury of its gales, but in our own hearts this Sunday morning there is peace."

Since Mr. Churchill spoke those words the Luftwaffe has made havoc of British cities, driven the population underground, frightened children from their sleep, and imposed on everyone a nervous strain as great as any that people have ever endured.

Yet close observers agree that when Mr. Churchill spoke of peace in the hearts of the British people he was not indulging in idle oratory. The British people are profoundly calm. There seems to be a complete absence of nervousness. It seems as if all the neuroses of modern life had vanished from England.

In the beginning the British Government made elaborate preparations for an increase in mental breakdowns. But these have actually declined. There have been fewer than a dozen breakdowns reported in London since the air raids began.

The British are calm in their spirit, not because they have nothing to worry about, but because they are fighting for their lives. They have made that decision. And they have no further choice. All their mistakes of the past twenty years, all the stupidities and failures that they have shared with the rest of the democratic world, are now of the past. They can forget them because they are faced with a supreme task—defending, yard by yard, their island home.

With us it is different. We do not have to face any attack tomorrow or the next day. Yet we are faced with something almost as difficult. We are faced with great decisions.

We know how lucky we are compared to all the rest of mankind. At least two-thirds of us are just plain rich compared to all the rest of the human family—rich in food, rich in clothes, rich in entertainment and amusement, rich in leisure, rich.

And yet we also know that the sickness of the world is also our sickness. We, too, have miserably failed to solve the problems of our epoch. And nowhere in the world have men's failures been so little excusable as in the United States of America. Nowhere has the contrast been so great between the reasonable hopes of our age and the actual facts of failure and frustration. And so now all our failures and mistakes hover like birds of ill omen over the White House, over the Capitol dome, and over this printed page. Naturally, we have no peace.

But, even beyond this necessity for living with our own misdeeds, there is another reason why there is no peace in our hearts. It is that we have not been honest with ourselves.

In this whole matter of War and Peace, especially, we have been at various times and in various ways false to ourselves, false to each other, false to the facts of history and false to the future.

In this self-deceit our political leaders of all shades of opinion are deeply implicated. Yet we cannot shove the blame off on them. If our leaders have deceived us it is mainly because we ourselves have insisted on being deceived. Their deceitfulness has resulted from our own moral and intellectual confusion. In this confusion, our educators and churchmen and scientists are deeply implicated.

Journalists, too, of course, are implicated. But if Americans are confused it is not for lack of accurate and pertinent information. The American people are by far the best-informed people in the history of the world.

The trouble is not with the facts. The trouble is that clear and honest inferences have not been drawn from the facts. The day-to-day present is clear. The issues of tomorrow are befogged.

There is one fundamental issue which faces America as it faces no other nation. It is an issue peculiar to America and peculiar to America in the 20th century—now. It is deeper even than the immediate issue of war. If America meets it correctly, then, despite hosts of dangers and difficulties, we can look forward and move forward to a future worthy of men, with peace in our hearts.

If we dodge the issue, we shall flounder for ten or twenty or thirty bitter years in a chartless and meaningless series of disasters.

The purpose of this article is to state that issue, and its solution, as candidly and as completely as possible. But first of all, let us be completely candid about where we are and how we got there.

Where are we? We are *in* the war. All this talk about whether this or that might or might not get us into the war is wasted effort. We are, for a fact, *in* the war.

If there's one place we Americans did not want to be, it was *in* the war. We didn't want much to be in any kind of war but, if there was one kind of war we most of all didn't want to be in, it was a European war. Yet, we're in a war, as vicious and bad a war as ever struck this planet, and, along with being worldwide, a European war.

Of course, we are not technically at war, we are not painfully at war, and we may never have to experience the full hell that war can be. Nevertheless, the simple statement stands: we are *in* the war. The irony is that Hitler knows it—and most Americans don't. It may or may not be an advantage to continue diplomatic relations with Germany. But the fact that a German embassy still flourishes in Washington beautifully illustrates the whole mass of deceits and self-deceits in which we have been living.

Perhaps the best way to show ourselves that we are in the war is to consider how we can get out of it. Practically, there's only one way to get out of it, and that is by a German victory over England. If England should surrender soon, Germany and America would not start fighting the next day. So we would be out of the war. For a while. Except that Japan might then attack in the South Seas and the Philippines. We could abandon the Philippines, abandon Australia and New Zealand, withdraw to Hawaii. And wait. We would be out of the war.

We say we don't want to be in the war. We also say we want England to win. We want Hitler stopped—more than we want to stay out of the war. So, at the moment, we're in.

Now that we are in this war, how did we get in? We got in on the basis of defense. Even that very word, defense, has been full of deceit and self-deceit.

To the average American the plain meaning of the word "defense" is defense of American territory—and without much concern for the Philippines. Is our national policy today limited to the defense of the American homeland by whatever means may seem wise? It is not. We are *not* in a war to defend American territory. We are in a war to defend and even to promote, encourage and incite so-called democratic principles throughout the world. The average American begins to realize now that that's the kind of war he's in. And he's halfway for it. But he wonders how he ever got there, since a year ago he had not the slightest intention of getting into any such thing. Well, he can see now how he got there. He got there via "defense."

Behind the doubts in the American mind there were and are two different picture-patterns. One of them, stressing the appalling consequences of the fall of England, leads us to a war of intervention. As a plain matter of the defense of American territory, is that picture necessarily true? It is not *necessarily* true. For the other picture is roughly this: while it would be much better for us if Hitler were severely checked, nevertheless, regardless of what happens in Europe, it would be entirely possible for us to organize a defense of the northern part of the Western Hemisphere so that this country could not be successfully attacked. You are familiar with that picture. Is it true or false? No man is qualified to state categorically that it is false. If the entire rest of the world came under the organized domination of evil tyrants, it is quite possible to imagine that this country could make itself such a tough nut to crack that not all the tyrants in the world would care to come against us. And of course there would always be a better than even chance that, like the great Queen Elizabeth, we could play one tyrant off against another. Or, like an infinitely mightier Switzerland, we could live discreetly and dangerously in the midst of enemies. No man can say that that picture of America as an impregnable armed camp is false. No man can honestly say that as a pure matter of defense—defense of our homeland—it is necessary to get into or be in this war.

The question before us, then, is not *primarily* one of necessity and survival. It is a question of choice and calculation. The true questions are: Do we *want* to be in this war? Do we *prefer* to be in it? And, if so, for what?

We are in this war. We can see how we got into it in terms of defense. Now why do we object so strongly to being in it?

There are lots of reasons. First, there is the profound and almost universal aversion to all war—to killing and being killed. But the reason which needs closest inspection, since it is one peculiar to this war and never felt about any previous war, is the fear that, if we get into this war, it will be the end of our constitutional democracy. We are all acquainted with the fearful forecast—that some form of dictatorship is required to fight a modern war, that we will certainly go bankrupt, that in the process of war and its aftermath our economy will be largely socialized, that the politicians now in office will seize complete power and never yield it up, and that what with the whole trend toward collectivism, we shall end up in such a total national socialism that any faint semblances of our constitutional American democracy will be totally unrecognizable.

We start into this war with huge government debt, a vast bureaucracy and a whole generation of young people trained to look to the government as the source of all life. The party in power is the one which for long years has been most sympathetic to all manner of socialist doctrines and collectivist trends. The President of the United States has continually reached for more and more power, and he owes his continuation in office today largely to the coming of the war. Thus, the fear that the United States will be driven to a national socialism, as a result of cataclysmic circumstances and contrary to the free will of the American people, is an entirely justifiable fear.

So there's the mess—to date. Much more could be said in amplification, in qualification and in argument. But, however elaborately they might be stated, the sum of the facts about our present position brings us to this point—that the paramount question of this immediate moment is not whether we get into war, but how do we win it?

If we are in a war, then it is no little advantage to be aware of the fact. And once we admit to ourselves we are in a war, there is no shadow of doubt that we Americans will be determined to win it —cost what it may in life or treasure.

Whether or not we declare war, whether or not we send expeditionary forces abroad, whether or not we go bankrupt in the process—all these tremendous considerations are matters of strategy and management and are secondary to the overwhelming importance of winning the war.

Having now, with candor, explained our position, it is time to consider, to better purpose than would have been possible before, the larger issue which confronts us. Stated most simply, and in general terms, that issue is: What are we fighting for?

Each of us stands ready to give our life, our wealth and all our hope of personal happiness, to make sure that America shall not lose any war she is engaged in. But we would like to know what war we are trying to win—and what we are supposed to win when we win it?

This questioning reflects our truest instincts as Americans. But more than that. Our urgent desire to give this war its proper name has a desperate practical importance. If we know what we are fighting for, then we can drive confidently toward a victorious conclusion and, what's more, have at least an even chance of establishing a workable Peace.

Furthermore—and this is an extraordinary and profoundly historical fact which deserves to be examined in detail—America and only America can effectively state the war aims of this war.

Almost every expert will agree that Britain cannot win complete victory—cannot even, in the common saying, "stop Hitler"—without American help. Therefore, even if Britain should from time to time announce war aims, the American people are continually in the position of effectively approving or not approving those aims. On the contrary, if America were to announce war aims, Great Britain would almost certainly accept them. And the entire world, including Adolf Hitler, would accept them as the gauge of this battle.

Americans have a feeling that in any collaboration with Great Britain we are somehow playing Britain's game and not our own. Whatever sense there may have been in this notion in the past, today it is an ignorant and foolish conception of the situation. In any sort of partnership with the British Empire, Great Britain is perfectly willing that the United States of America should assume the role of senior partner. This has been true for a long time. Among serious Englishmen, the chief complaint against America (and incidentally their best alibi for themselves) has really amounted to this—that America has refused to rise to the opportunities of leadership in the world.

Consider this recent statement of the London *Economist:*

"If any permanent closer association of Britain and the United States is achieved, an island people of less than 50 millions cannot expect to be the senior partner. . . . The center of gravity and the ultimate decision must increasingly lie in America. We cannot resent this historical development. We may rather feel proud that the cycle of dependence, enmity and independence is coming full circle into a new interdependence."

We Americans no longer have the *alibi* that we cannot have things the way we want them so far as Great Britain is concerned. With due regard for the varying problems of the members of the British Commonwealth, what we want will be okay with them.

This holds true even for that inspiring proposal called Union Now—a proposal, made by an American, that Britain and the United States should create a new and larger federal union of peoples. That may not be the right approach to our problem. But no thoughtful American has done his duty by the United States of America until he has read and pondered Clarence Streit's book presenting that proposal.

The big, important point to be made here is simply that the complete opportunity of leadership is *ours*. Like most great creative opportunities, it is an opportunity enveloped in stupendous difficulties and dangers. If we don't want it, if we refuse to take it, the responsibility of refusal is also ours, and ours alone.

Admittedly, the future of the world cannot be settled all in one piece. It is stupid to try to blueprint the future as you blueprint an engine or as you draw up a constitution for a sorority. But if our trouble is that we don't know what we are fighting for, then it's up to us to figure it out. Don't expect some other country to tell us. Stop this Nazi propaganda about fighting somebody else's war. We fight no wars except our wars. "Arsenal of Democracy"? We may prove to be that. But today we must be the arsenal of America and of the friends and allies of America.

Friends and allies of America? Who are they, and for what? This is for us to tell them.

But how can we tell them? And how can we tell ourselves for what purposes we seek allies and for what purposes we fight? Are we going to fight for dear old Danzig or dear old Dong Dang? Are we going to decide the boundaries of Uritania? Or, if we cannot state war aims in terms of vastly distant geography, shall we use some big words like "democracy" and "freedom" and "justice"? Yes, we can use the big words. The President has already used them. And perhaps we had better get used to using them again. Maybe they do mean something—about the future as well as the past.

Some amongst us are likely to be dying for them—on the fields and in the skies of battle. Either that, or the words themselves and what they mean die with us—in our beds.

But is there nothing between the absurd sound of distant cities and the brassy trumpeting of majestic words? Do we have to choose between the hard realism of Dong Dang and the vague idealism of democracy? And if so, whose Dong Dang and whose democracy? Is there not something a little more practically satisfying that we can get our teeth into? Is there no sort of understandable program? A program which would be clearly good for America, which would make sense for America—and which at the same time might have the blessing of the goddess of democracy and even help somehow to fix up this bothersome matter of Dong Dang?

Is there none such? There is. And so we now come squarely and closely face to face with the issue which Americans hate most to face. It is that old, old issue with those old, old battered labels—the issue of isolationism versus internationalism.

We detest both words. We spit them at each other with the fury of hissing geese. We duck and dodge them.

Let us face that issue squarely now. If we face it squarely now—and if in facing it we take full and fearless account of the realities of our age—then we shall open the way, not necessarily to peace in our daily lives but to peace in our hearts.

In the field of national policy, the fundamental trouble with Americans has been, and is, that whereas their nation became in the 20th century the most powerful and the most vital nation in the world, nevertheless Americans were unable to accommodate themselves spiritually and practically to that fact. Hence they have failed to play their part as a world power—a failure which has had disastrous consequences for themselves and for all mankind. And the cure is this: to accept wholeheartedly our duty and our opportunity as the most powerful and vital nation in the world and in consequence to exert upon the world the full impact of our influence, for such purposes as we see fit and by such means as we see fit.

"For such purposes as we see fit" leaves entirely open the question of what our purposes may be or how we may appropriately achieve them. Emphatically our only alternative to isolationism is not to undertake to police the whole world nor to impose democratic institutions on all mankind including the Dalai Lama and the good shepherds of Tibet.

America cannot be responsible for the good behavior of the

entire world. But America is responsible, to herself as well as to history, for the world environment in which she lives. Nothing can so vitally affect America's environment as America's own influence upon it, and therefore if America's environment is unfavorable to the growth of American life, then America has nobody to blame so deeply as she must blame herself.

In its failure to grasp this relationship between America and America's environment lies the moral and practical bankruptcy of any and all forms of isolationism. It is most unfortunate that this virus of isolationist sterility has so deeply infected an influential section of the Republican party. For until the Republican party can develop a vital philosophy and program for America's initiative and activity as a world power, it will continue to cut itself off from any useful participation in this hour of history. And its participation is deeply needed for the shaping of the future of America and of the world.

But politically speaking, it is an equally serious fact that for seven years Franklin Roosevelt was, for all practical purposes, a complete isolationist. He was more of an isolationist than Herbert Hoover or Calvin Coolidge. The fact that Franklin Roosevelt has recently emerged as an emergency world leader should not obscure the fact that for seven years his policies ran absolutely counter to any possibility of effective American leadership in international cooperation. There is, of course, a justification which can be made for the President's first two terms. It can be said, with reason, that great social reforms were necessary in order to bring democracy up to date in the greatest of democracies. But the fact is that Franklin Roosevelt failed to make American democracy work successfully on a narrow, materialistic and nationalistic basis. And under Franklin Roosevelt we ourselves have failed to make democracy work successfully. Our only chance now to make it work is in terms of a vital international economy and in terms of an international moral order.

This objective is Franklin Roosevelt's great opportunity to justify his first two terms and to go down in history as the greatest rather than the last of American Presidents. Our job is to help in every way we can, for our sake and our children's sake, to ensure that Franklin Roosevelt shall be justly hailed as America's greatest President.

Without our help he cannot be our greatest President. With our help he can and will be. Under him and with his leadership we can make isolationism as dead an issue as slavery, and we can make a truly *American* internationalism something as natural to us in our time as the airplane or the radio.

In 1919 we had a golden opportunity, an opportunity unprecedented in all history, to assume the leadership of the world—a golden opportunity handed to us on the proverbial silver platter. We did not understand that opportunity. Wilson mishandled it. We rejected it. The opportunity persisted. We bungled it in the 1920s and in the confusions of the 1930s we killed it.

To lead the world would never have been an easy task. To revive the hope of that lost opportunity makes the task now infinitely harder than it would have been before. Nevertheless, with the help of all of us, Roosevelt must succeed where Wilson failed.

Consider the 20th century. It is our century. It is ours not only in the sense that we happen to live in it but ours also because it is America's first century as a dominant power in the world. So far, this century of ours has been a profound and tragic disappointment. No other century has been so big with promise for human progress and happiness. And in no one century have so many men and women and children suffered such pain and anguish and bitter death.

It is a baffling and difficult and paradoxical century. No doubt all centuries were paradoxical to those who had to cope with them. But, like everything else, our paradoxes today are bigger and better than ever. Yes, better as well as bigger—inherently better. We have poverty and starvation—but only in the midst of plenty. We have the biggest wars in the midst of the most widespread, the deepest and the most articulate hatred of war in all history. We have tyrannies and dictatorships—but only when democratic idealism, once regarded as the dubious eccentricity of a colonial nation, is the faith of a huge majority of the people of the world.

And ours is also a revolutionary century. The paradoxes make it inevitably revolutionary. Revolutionary, of course, in science and in industry. And also revolutionary, as a corollary, in politics and the structure of society. But to say that a revolution is in progress is not to say that the men with either the craziest ideas or the angriest ideas or the most plausible ideas are going to come out on top. The Revolution of 1776 was won and established by men most of whom appear to have been both gentlemen and men of common sense.

Clearly a revolutionary epoch signifies great changes, great adjustments. And this is only one reason why it is really so foolish for people to worry about our "constitutional democracy" without worrying or, better, thinking hard about the world revolution. For only as we go out to meet and solve for our time the problems of the world revolution can we know how to re-establish our constitutional democracy for another fifty or 100 years.

This 20th century is baffling, difficult, paradoxical, revolutionary. But by now, at the cost of much pain and many hopes deferred, we know a good deal about it. And we ought to accommodate our outlook to this knowledge so dearly bought. For example, any true conception of our world of the 20th century must surely include a vivid awareness of at least these four propositions:

First: our world of two billion human beings is for the first time in history one world, fundamentally indivisible.

Second: modern man hates war, and feels intuitively that, in the present scale and frequency, it may even be fatal to his species.

Third: our world, again for the first time in human history, is capable of producing all the material needs of the entire human family.

Fourth: the world of the 20th century, if it is to come to life in any nobility of health and vigor, must be to a significant degree an American Century.

As to the first and second: in postulating the indivisibility of the contemporary world, one does not necessarily imagine that anything like a world state—a parliament of men—must be brought about in this century. Nor need we assume that war can be abolished. All that it is necessary to feel—and to feel deeply—is that terrific forces of magnetic attraction and repulsion will operate as between every large group of human beings on this planet. Large sections of the human family may be effectively organized into opposition to each other. Tyrannies may require a large amount of living space. But Freedom requires and will require far greater living space than Tyranny. Peace cannot endure unless it prevails over a very large part of the world. Justice will come near to losing all meaning in the minds of men unless Justice can have approximately the same fundamental meanings in many lands and among many peoples.

As to the third point—the promise of adequate production for all mankind, the "more abundant life"—be it noted that this is characteristically an American promise. It is a promise easily made, here and elsewhere, by demagogues and proponents of all manner of slick schemes and "planned economies." What we must insist on is that the abundant life is predicated on Freedom—on the Freedom which has created its possibility—on a vision of Freedom under Law. Without Freedom, there will be no abundant life. With Freedom, there can be.

And finally there is the belief—shared, let us remember, by most men living—that the 20th century must be to a significant degree an American Century. This knowledge calls us to action now.

What can we say and foresee about an American Century? It is meaningless merely to say that we reject isolationism and accept the logic of internationalism. What internationalism? Rome had a great internationalism. So had the Vatican and Genghis Khan and the Ottoman Turks and the Chinese emperors and 19th-century England. After the First World War, Lenin had one in mind. Today Hitler seems to have one in mind—one which appeals strongly to some American isolationists, whose opinion of Europe is so low that they would gladly hand it over to anyone who would guarantee to destroy it forever. But what internationalism have we Americans to offer?

Ours cannot come out of the vision of any one man. It must be the product of the imaginations of many men. It must be a sharing with all peoples of our Bill of Rights, our Declaration of Independence, our Constitution, our magnificent industrial products, our technical skills. It must be an internationalism of the people, by the people, and for the people.

In general, the issues which the American people champion revolve around their determination to make the society of men safe for the freedom, growth and increasing satisfaction of all individual men. Beside that resolve, the sneers, groans, catcalls, teeth-grinding, hisses and roars of the Nazi Propaganda Ministry are of small moment.

Once we cease to distract ourselves with lifeless arguments about isolationism, we shall be amazed to discover that there is already an immense American internationalism. American jazz, Hollywood movies, American slang, American machines and patented products are in fact the only things that every community in the world, from Zanzibar to Hamburg, recognizes in common. Blindly, unintentionally, accidentally and really in spite of ourselves, we are already a world power in all the trivial ways—in very human ways. But there is a great deal more than that. America is already the intellectual, scientific and artistic capital of the world. Americans—midwestern Americans—are today the least provincial people in the world. They have traveled the most and they know more about the world than the people of any other country. America's worldwide experience in commerce is also far greater than most of us realize.

Most important of all, we have that indefinable, unmistakable sign of leadership: prestige. And unlike the prestige of Rome or Genghis Khan or 19th-century England, American prestige throughout the world is faith in the good intentions as well as in the ultimate intelligence and ultimate strength of the whole American people. We have lost some of that prestige in the last few years. But most of it is still there.

As America enters dynamically upon the world scene, we need most of all to seek and to bring forth a vision of America as a world power which is authentically American and which can inspire us to live and work and fight with vigor and enthusiasm. And as we come now to the great test, it may yet turn out that, in all our trials and tribulations of spirit during the first part of this century, we as a people have been painfully apprehending the meaning of our time; and now, in this moment of testing, there may come clear at last the vision which will guide us to the authentic creation of the 20th century—our century.

Consider four areas of life and thought in which we may seek to realize such a vision:

First, the economic. It is for America and for America alone to determine whether a system of free economic enterprise—an economic order compatible with freedom and progress—shall or shall not prevail in this century. We know perfectly well that there is not the slightest chance of anything faintly resembling a free economic system prevailing in this country if it prevails nowhere else. What, then, does America have to decide? Some few decisions are quite simple. For example: we have to decide whether or not we shall have for ourselves and our friends freedom of the seas— the right to go with our ships and our oceangoing airplanes where we wish, when we wish and as we wish. The vision of America as the principal guarantor of the freedom of the seas, the vision of America as the dynamic leader of world trade, has within it the possibilities of such enormous human progress as to stagger the imagination. Let us not be staggered by it. Let us rise to its tremendous possibilities. Our thinking on world trade today is on ridiculously small terms. For example, we think of Asia as being worth only a few hundred million a year to us. Actually, in the decades to come, Asia will be worth to us exactly zero—or else it will be worth to us four, five, ten billion dollars a year. And the latter are the terms we must think in, or else confess a pitiful impotence.

Closely akin to the purely economic area, and yet quite different from it, there is the picture of an America which will send out through the world its technical and artistic skills. Engineers, scientists, doctors, movie men, makers of entertainment, developers of airlines, builders of roads, teachers, educators. Throughout the world, these skills, this training, this leadership are needed and will be eagerly welcomed, if only we have the imagination to see it and the sincerity and good will to create the world of the 20th century.

But now there is a third thing which our vision must immediately be concerned with. We must undertake now to be the Good Samaritan of the entire world.* It is the manifest duty of this country to undertake to feed all the people of the world who as a result of this worldwide collapse of civilization are hungry and destitute—all of them, that is, whom we can from time to time reach consistently with a very tough attitude toward all hostile governments. For every dollar we spend on armaments, we should spend at least a dime in a gigantic effort to feed the world—and all the world should know that we have dedicated ourselves to this task. Every farmer in America should be encouraged to produce all the crops he can, and all that we cannot eat—and perhaps some of us could eat less—should forthwith be dispatched to the four quarters of the globe as a free gift, administered by a humanitarian army of Americans, to every man, woman, and child on this earth who is really hungry.

But all this is not enough. All this will fail and none of it will happen unless our vision of America as a world power includes a passionate devotion to great American ideals. We have some things in this country which are infinitely precious and especially American—a love of freedom, a feeling for the equality of opportunity, a tradition of self-reliance and independence and also of

* Note that this proposal antedates the Marshall Plan and President Truman's "Point Four" by six years or more.

cooperation. In addition to ideals and notions which are especially American, we are the inheritors of all the great principles of Western civilization—above all Justice, the love of Truth, the ideal of Charity. The other day Herbert Hoover said that America was fast becoming the sanctuary of the ideals of civilization. For the moment it may be enough to be the sanctuary of these ideals. But not for long. It now becomes our time to be the powerhouse from which the ideals spread throughout the world and do their mysterious work of lifting the life of mankind from the level of the beasts to what the Psalmist called a little lower than the angels.

America as the dynamic center of ever-widening spheres of enterprise, America as the training center of the skillful servants of mankind, America as the Good Samaritan, really believing again that it is more blessed to give than to receive, and America as the powerhouse of the ideals of Freedom and Justice—out of these elements surely can be fashioned a vision of the 20th century to which we can and will devote ourselves in joy and gladness and vigor and enthusiasm.

Other nations can survive simply because they have endured so long—sometimes with more and sometimes with less significance. But this nation, conceived in adventure and dedicated to the progress of man—this nation cannot truly endure unless there courses strongly through its veins from Maine to California the blood of purpose and enterprise and high resolve.

Throughout the 17th century and the 18th century and the 19th century, this continent teemed with manifold projects and magnificent purposes. Above them all and weaving them all together into the most exciting flag of all the world and of all history was the triumphal purpose of freedom.

It is in this spirit that all of us are called, each to his own measure of capacity, and each in the widest horizon of his vision, to create the first great American Century.

7 OUR PURPOSE IS FREEDOM

*In this commencement address at Ohio State University
in Columbus, June 11, 1943, Luce stated his view of
the American purpose in its simplest form. Later he was
to qualify the definition of freedom by adding "and
order" or "under law"—and even to expand his conception of the American task to include the building of a
"civilization."*

Does the American nation exist for any particular purpose?
From among all the motivations of history, can we separate out one
clear purpose and say: for this purpose America is created, for this
purpose America lives?

It needs no laboring of history to prove that, in the first 150
years of its existence, this republic was thought to have a purpose.
The Declaration of Independence represented no mere nationalistic
revolt against an empire. It was a declaration of a purpose. Here
was something new in the world—a nation existing *for* a purpose.

Let me illustrate how unprecedented this proposition was *and is*.
Outside of America, the most notable example of an attempt to
found a state for a purpose was, perhaps, in England under Oliver
Cromwell. Stoutly the Ironsides proclaimed that they proposed to
establish in England "the new Jerusalem." But though Cromwelli-
ans represented a mighty force in England which persists to this
day, their messianic purpose was not suited to the prevailing
temper of England. Cromwellian England lasted only twenty years
and was followed by the gay restoration of Merry King Charles—
and the Ship of State finally got back on even keel again with
Queen Anne and John Churchill, Duke of Marlborough.

I make comparisons but they are not odious. For example, if a
balance sheet could be drawn, it would show, I suppose, that
civilization owes more to England than to the United States. Thus

I emphasize that I am speaking not of total good, I speak only of freedom. And even as to freedom itself, it may well be that not even yet has America contributed as much to the knowledge and practice of freedom as have the British Isles. Through the centuries since the Magna Carta, Englishmen have hammered out their liberties in the bold strokes of their temperament against the anvil of their proper interests. But the distinction I am drawing lies in this fact: that the British state was not thought to have, either under Queen Elizabeth or Queen Victoria, the one and supreme purpose—"to make men free."

Now Abe Lincoln did think that the American nation existed precisely and specially for that purpose. It was an extraordinary thought to think. It was more than a thought. In the minds of our fathers' fathers it was a fact. Is it still a fact? May we still believe it? Shall we make it a fact—which no power can ever again deny—either on this continent or throughout the world?

Before answering, we must take account of two contrary notions. One we might call the no-purpose theory and the other the all-purpose theory.

According to the no-purpose theory, the American nation has no particular mission; it probably never did have; anyway, from now on, America is to be no different from any other great state; it is simply to pursue its own best interests. This is a plausible view. It is the logical fruit of modern materialistic thought. It attracts men of ill will. It attracts, also, those who call themselves "realists" in the fashion of the day. History may prove it to be right. But I reject it. I want America to be different—always—to have a purpose—always until all men are free.

As for the all-purpose theory, it is in some ways more objectionable because more confusing and, therefore, dangerous. According to it, political freedom is okay but—it is not enough. According to the all-purpose theory, the mission of America should be nothing less—or hardly less—than the total elevation and benefaction of all mankind. This view of collective benevolence attracts many idealists. Many Americans, like myself, are reluctant to reject it. For in asserting that America has a mission, this view follows the great American tradition. While Americans realize that they have never entered into any compact with each other or with their forebears to provide well-being for all mankind, they may nevertheless contribute to the welfare of mankind in greater measure than any other nation in history. Let us pray we can meet the opportunity that lies ahead. But to say that it is the national purpose of this country to reform and elevate and support mankind is as false to ourselves as it is surely offensive to others. Not every mission is appropriate to the political state. To claim for it an unlimited mission to do good is to invite infinite confusion, ugly strife and, ultimately, disaster.

But political freedom *is* a uniquely appropriate mission of the political state. And the purpose to make men free is an abundantly adequate purpose. It is a purpose, an ideal, still far, far from fulfillment. The greatest battles of freedom, believe me, are still to be fought—even here, perhaps, in the land of the free.

In being persistently concerned about freedom, we will be what others *expect* Americans to be. A few days ago in North Africa, General Giraud * was asked: "What are we fighting for?" He replied: "As a Frenchman I say simply for the liberation of France. . . . But if I were an American I would say for the freedom of the world."

"If I were an American . . ." Shall we not, then, be still Americans?—and more than ever Americans in the clarity of our purpose to encourage and sustain, by all suitable means, a prevailing pattern of freedom throughout the world?

* Henri Giraud (1879–1949), a leader of Free French forces.

8 THE GREAT LIBERAL TRADITION

This speech, delivered when Senator Joseph McCarthy's anti-Communist fever was at its peak, was the commencement address at Temple University in Philadelphia, June 18, 1953. It may be considered the most carefully composed statement of the core of Luce's political philosophy.

A few weeks ago, I was taking a walk in Rome and found myself strolling along the banks of the Tiber. Partly to test out my first Italian lesson, I asked a middle-aged gentleman: "What is the name of this bridge?" "This," said he, "is Ponte Garibaldi." And then, his eyes lighting up, he continued: "And there is Ponte Mazzini and beyond the bend of the river, Ponte Cavour."

I thanked him and walked on, three names ringing like bells in my ears: Garibaldi, Mazzini, Cavour. It was a little startling. What were they doing here in ancient Rome? Of course, of course, they were the makers of Italy. Even so, I hadn't expected to meet them on that walk. You see, only a few minutes before, I had been in the Roman Forum of Julius Caesar and Caesar Augustus and Marcus Aurelius. And then on my way to the river, I had passed magnificent Renaissance palaces, one after the other. Right above me at that moment towered Castel Sant' Angelo, full of romantic and wicked stories of 1,800 years. And just beyond floated in its calm splendor the dome of St. Peter's. Classical Rome, Imperial Rome, Christian Rome, Renaissance Rome, and the Rome of a million living people all around me—all history seems piled on top of itself and intertwined in this Eternal City. And who in all this are Garibaldi, Mazzini and Cavour? They are, I reflected, the local heroes of the Great Liberal Tradition.

I mentioned this a few nights ago to a young friend and he gave me a very pained look. The liberal tradition didn't sound good to him. And perhaps it doesn't sound good to you. There is trouble today with the word "liberal." It has been taken for a ride in many a false philosophy. It has consorted with evil companions. It has mocked at God. Worst of all, it has got sick, anemic. And yet after we had talked about it a while, my young friend said to me: "Liberal—that's what everybody would *like* to be." Some of the older people here may feel, as I did, that that remark is deeply touching.

"Liberal is what everybody would like to be." Yes, of course. And why? Very simple; because we are all Americans. Even the reactionaries today call themselves the "true" liberals. False liberals, true liberals, it's quite confusing—and pathetic. Yes, if there's anything wrong with America today, it could be summed up in one symptom: that Americans don't quite know what it is to be liberal—joyously, thankfully, proudly liberal. For America—the whole of America—is the supreme embodiment of the Great Liberal Tradition and if, for as much as one generation, America forgets what it is to be liberal, then America will no longer be herself, but just one more stupid, fear-ridden empire ready to be carted away to the natural-history museum of human failure.

But what is the liberal tradition? I shall attempt presently a definition. One man's definition is unimportant, and in any case you will soon forget it. Next week or next year, when you find yourself in a good bull session, ask somebody—perhaps an older man—what is the liberal tradition. You will get all kinds of answers. It might interest you to keep on asking. And when you feel you have really found out what it is, then you will find what it is that *you* belong to. And you will find also that beyond your personal business of making a living and raising a family, this is what you have to live for.

America is the supreme embodiment of this tradition. Garibaldi wrote to Abraham Lincoln and spoke of our country as the "apostle of liberty, the harbinger of progress." A plain truth, which no 19th-century American would have wished to deny. America was the great magnetic hope and example, drawing to her all who wished to make Europe at last beautiful and free.

For it was not only Italy. Every country in Europe had its liberators and liberating movements. The 19th century is filled with attempts to crush liberal movements, and yet all the time liberty and progress swept on until, when Queen Victoria died in 1901, it was taken for granted that political liberty, international law and the more abundant life would be gradually established throughout the Western world and beyond.

But things went wrong, of course. Yes, they always do, and they have to be put right. Two terrible wars. Fascism, Communism—hundreds of books have been written to explain why, which we won't pretend to summarize this morning. Enough for us that, despite all the shattering catastrophes, a last great effort is being made to establish the liberal tradition—that is to say, political freedom, and equal justice, and freedom of thought and opinion, and common decency between men and men. It is a very close battle. The odds are, so far as anyone can see, about fifty-fifty.

Throughout Europe many good men are waging this battle. They wage the battle of liberty against the terror of the Communist armies. They wage it also against reaction, against rich and selfish men, against all the old rottenness built into the European systems which have not even yet been swept into the sewers of history. They wage it against apathy and, most frightening of all, cynicism.

The leader of this cause in Italy is Alcide De Gasperi.* Now it is extremely significant that De Gasperi is not only a Democrat but also a dedicated Christian. For if we were to pick out from all the books one basic thing that went wrong in the 19th century and after, it would be that, in Europe, the struggle for liberty was too often anti-religious and religion was too often anti-liberty. All that was for reasons which are quite foreign to our American experience and which it is almost impossible for Americans to understand. For, of course, from the days of George Washington to Dwight Eisenhower the natural American phrase is: "Liberty under God."

Europe struggles to establish a God-fearing liberty. But it can only succeed on one assumption—namely, that it can count on the strength and vitality of the Great Liberal Tradition in America. Is there any reason to doubt? Yes, there is; there are witch-hunts and book burnings, and if they are mostly figurative, they are still bad. And, as you well know, the loudest noises that issue from the Congress of the United States today are not always the voices of liberty. They are too often the voices of hate, of fear, of vulgarity.

But the Senators would not talk like that unless millions and millions of Americans responded to them. They speak to the worst in us and the worst in all of us responds.

I do not think that anyone of you in this hall today wishes to destroy liberty in America. But I do say, in America today, liberty is not loved sufficiently and the Great Liberal Tradition, the only true American tradition, is not honored and reverenced as it ought to be.

If we are to serve the liberal tradition, we must understand what it is. One is tempted to define it as the sum of everything good. For it is true that the liberal view of life does try to make room for all the best that has been, or can be, thought or done. But we must be more precise. The liberal tradition is made up of certain key elements, of which I would cite three:

First, the liberal tradition stands, obviously, for political liberty —that is, for government of the people, for the people, and *by* the people. Plato could not conceive of government-*by*-the-people. And Queen Elizabeth I, now so enthusiastically remembered, would have deemed the executioner's ax much too good for any heretic babbling about government-*by*-the-people. Are the people in fact too

* Premier, 1945–53, and leader of the Christian Democratic party.

dumb or too wicked to govern themselves? Much of history, including much recent history, would testify that they are. But the liberal
tradition says no—it says you and you are not too dumb or too
wicked to govern yourselves. How do you feel about it? If you feel
that you are fit to govern yourselves or at least fitter than any
tyrant in any guise, then, you see, you do belong to the liberal
tradition. And you will have to fight for what you belong to and
what belongs to you.

Second, the liberal tradition stands for reason. It holds that
since man is a reasoning animal, he has a duty to try his honest
best to be reasonable. But since every man is fallible, each of us
must respect the candid opinion of another. For this reason, the
liberal tradition emphasizes the spread of knowledge and of the art
of thinking which we call education, in order that all men may
know how to be more reasonable. Without the liberal tradition
there would be no Temple University—there would not be two
million American girls and boys in college and millions more in
high school.

Third, the liberal tradition emphasizes the application of the
moral conscience to the affairs of *this* world. You do not need
freedom or democracy to be a Christian; you can be a Christian
behind prison bars or facing the lions in the Roman Colosseum or
in the catacombs—indeed, it is in places like that where the greatest sanctity has shown itself. Religion, if it is at all serious, is
concerned with another world. The liberal tradition has a profound
reverence for all life and the mysteries by which our little worldly
lives are bounded, but it is this world, our world, the world of here
and now which must also be saved—be saved from injustice and
poverty and cruelty and ignorance and disease and all the horrors
with which most of the people who have ever lived have been
afflicted. The liberal tradition emphasizes the continuous application of the religious conscience to the affairs of *this* world.

Liberty, reason, conscience—these I suggest are the basic elements of the Great Liberal Tradition. And if these are the basic
elements, then it is surely self-evident that the whole American
experience is not only part of this tradition but that it is its supreme embodiment.

First, liberty is the purpose and heart of the whole American
experiment.

Second, reason is the mode and daily sanction of our government-by-debate. This truism would hardly have been worth stating in times past; it is worth stating now, when techniques of brainwashing oppose the claims of reason over the minds of men. Here in America, we have gone far toward developing a form of brainwashing. Its name is anti-Communism and it has become for millions of Americans a substitute for thinking.

Third, our system honors the claims of conscience; indeed, religion and morality are fundamental to our experiment with liberty, for it is only if the American citizen considers himself accountable to a higher power than his government that he can argue his right to govern himself among men. That is what we mean by "liberty under God." Europeans know about liberty and Europeans know about God, but many Europeans have had no experience of liberty under God. And many of them see little connection between the two. We know—or should know—their true connections. The American will never cease to ask with Thomas Jefferson: "Can the liberties of a nation be thought secure when we have removed their only firm basis, a conviction in the minds of the people that their liberties are the gift of God?"

Thus America embodies the liberal tradition. Small wonder that every American would like to feel himself a liberal, small wonder (as my young friend said) "that's what everybody would like to be." For in the sense we use it, it does not mean the opposite of conservative, nor is it measured by rate of forward motion alone. Many great Americans of *conservative* temperament have been bulwarks of our liberal tradition from George Washington to Dwight Eisenhower, from John Adams to Charles Evans Hughes and William Howard Taft and Senator Robert A. Taft. Whatever their views of human nature or social change, they were never neutral about liberty, nor deaf to reason, nor careless of conscience and truth.

America has taken a conservative turn; very well, that means that for a moment the principal responsibility rests with conservatives for maintaining the health and vigor of the great tradition. But it is also necessary that the self-styled liberals do their part. Just as conservatives like Senator Taft did essential work in combating the excesses of liberalism for fifteen years—and did it honorably—so now we require liberals to combat the excesses of bad conservatives. And they, too, should do their work honorably— and with some courage. Let them not be crybabies nor merely demagogues of another color. Let them, too, use the tools of argument and reason.

The work of the liberal tradition cannot be done by a single party or a single style of mind. It requires the combined work of thinkers like Mazzini, fighters like Garibaldi, negotiators like Cavour. It requires its poets, those "unacknowledged legislators of the world," as Shelley called them; it requires its men of practical wisdom in practical affairs. It requires all of us who understand and glory in the liberal tradition.

Are there enough of us? Do we care enough? This is a good question for you who have been called "the silent generation." The noise of the enemies of the liberal tradition is less alarming than the silence of its friends; for the noise has been heard before. Our liberal tradition has survived witch-hunts whose hunters were far more fanatical than those that plague us today. Our liberal tradition has been denied and betrayed repeatedly, from the anti-Catholic Know-Nothings of the 1850s to the Ku Klux Klan of the 1920s. This story is shameful but not new. It repeats itself but never triumphs. The contest is no different today from yesterday. The bigots are no more powerful and not armed with new weapons; the Bill of Rights is intact; there are no political prisoners in our jails. Then why are so many of the friends of the liberal tradition either cowed and silent, or noisy on false scents?

We are told that some liberals are afraid to speak up because they are afraid of losing their jobs or being ostracized because of errors of thinking in years past. Then I say to all older people here, let us all declare a spiritual amnesty for all errors of the past. For who among us has not erred in one way or another? Let us begin anew to seek truth truthfully and to cope in good faith with the massive practical problems of today. Let us do this for the sake of our children so that they may know what it is to think, to speak, to live as free men.

And to you young men and women I say, you must not allow yourselves to be disinherited from the Great Liberal Tradition— just because some of my generation made mistakes before you were born. Claim your inheritance. At least, know what it is before you throw it away. For the danger is not that the liberal tradition will be refuted; the danger is that it may be forgotten.

Your generation has one plausible excuse for ignoring the liberal tradition. Partly because of what human reason has wrought in our scientific laboratories, the terms of existence on this planet are changing very fast. Your own children will spend part of their active lives in the 21st century—whose physical horizons will probably be as different from ours as ours are from the Middle Ages. You therefore have reason to question the relevance of any message such as mine to your own futures.

But this uncertainty is also no new thing in human history, no newer than human bigotry or human lies. And as these have always yielded to courage and reason, so uncertainty has always yielded to faith. Whatever your environment may prove to be, the liberal tradition will still have its work to do.

It has much work to do now. There is one aspect of the liberal tradition which I have not mentioned. Although generous in valuing other traditions, it has always held that its own principles—liberty, reason and conscience—are universal principles, known or aspired to by all men in all times. Thus Mazzini, while striving to bring Italy to birth, at the same time dreamed of and worked for a united Europe. Thus the enormous force of Woodrow Wilson's speeches during World War I, which offered the hopes of the liberal tradition to the whole world.

Today we have in Europe an audience that needs and thirsts to know that some political principles are timeless and universal. We all need to know that *liberty, reason, conscience* are still the keys of American belief and behavior, that the American people as well as their President, the young as well as the old, the conservatives as well as the progressives, are still united within the Great Tradition and will not let it perish from the earth.

9   NATIONAL PURPOSE AND COLD WAR

Luce testified before Senator Henry Jackson's Subcommittee on National Policy Machinery on June 28, 1960. Khrushchev was then approaching the peak of his "adventurist" policy, brandishing nuclear weapons, threatening Berlin. The "National Purpose" series appearing in LIFE *that spring was later extended to include contributions by both presidential candidates.*

From your letter, Senator Jackson, I understand that the business of this committee is to consider how the government of the United States can be better organized to carry out the national purpose. The basic question concerns national purpose. Once it is clearly established what the national purpose is, then means to carry it out can be more readily devised, and men and resources can be dynamically mobilized.

The first question to me is as follows:

"Do we, as a people, now have a clear understanding and consensus about our national purpose?"

For some time there has been a growing demand for definitions of our national purpose. All kinds of study groups and committees, official and unofficial, have been formed to seek the answers. So far it has seemed that all this earnest talk and thought has produced no results. So it *seems*—but I do not believe that is strictly true. I believe that something very important has been going on in America, that some results are already visible, and that greater results will soon be evident. So the first part of my answer is: No, we as a people do not have a sufficiently clear consensus about our national purpose—*but* we are proceeding rapidly to get it.

What is the American national purpose? In my view, the United States was founded for a purpose and it can endure only so long as that purpose is its highest law. The founding purpose of the

United States was to make men free, and to enable them to be free and to preach the gospel of freedom to themselves and to all men. That purpose has withstood all manner of trial and tribulation, stress and strain. It is still our purpose. Our task now is to reassert that purpose by our own actions in our own time so it may continue in the lives of our children and their children through unimaginable changes in the circumstances of human life.

It is in relation to the cold war that our sense of national purpose can be most sharply defined and will be most profoundly tested.

What should be our purpose in the cold war? Very simple: we must win it, and the sooner the better.

LIFE has just concluded a series of nine articles on the national purpose. Each article made a valuable contribution to our present concern; perhaps the most specific statement on national purpose was made by General David Sarnoff. He said that we must decide to win the cold war. There must be, said General Sarnoff, "an unequivocal decision to fight the so-called cold war with a will and on a scale for complete victory." And furthermore, the news of this decision must be plainly told to the whole world.

A decision to win the cold war involves enormous risks. It involves, indeed, the greatest foreseeable risk of total war. The nearer we come to winning the cold war, the greater the risk of hot war. So long as we are only halfhearted about the cold war, there is no reason why Soviet Communism should turn to total war. But when they see they are losing the cold war, then Soviet Communism may face the choice of war or disintegration.

There are those who say that we should never present our enemies with so hard a choice. Perhaps they are right. Let us by all means agree that sound international politics includes the building of silver bridges for a beaten enemy, that it is not for men to demand unconditional surrender of the devil, and that the war aims of a civilized nation must be limited aims. Accordingly, let me suggest limited aims.

A minimum definition of victory in the cold war would be: to sever the state power of Russia and Red China from the mission of their present Communist rulers to Communize the world.

In other words, as Lincoln said about slavery, Communism must be so stopped from spreading that men can confidently foresee its withering away. That is a limited war aim. It would be quite a victory. Certainly it will not be achieved by our being only halfhearted about the cold war. It is quite a different aim from waiting like Micawber for a happier turn in human affairs. That course I believe would be in the highest degree irresponsible, and probably fatal to the U.S. and the cause for which it lives.

Our objective is to reduce the threat of organized Communism. If this is described as a negative aim, it is no less valid. Yet we all realize that you can't beat something with nothing. If we do not want Communist governments or Communist chaos to prevail, then what do we provide in its place?

This question challenges all of us and requires me today to attempt to state the positive national purpose of the United States in world affairs. Our national purpose must be to promote, by every honest means, the establishment of constitutional governments—that is, governments which respond to man's dream of freedom by giving him freedom under law. In 1917, President Wilson expressed this purpose by saying we must make the world safe for democracy. For me, that is still the best one-phrase definition of our national purpose. But I would add the correlative: that we must also make democracy safe for the world. Democracy becomes actual only when it exists in and through constitutional governments.

Experts seem to agree that many of the existing nations of the world are not ready or able to establish stable constitutional governments. Indeed, only a very few of the nations of the world have a background of history and tradition conducive to constitutional government. Most nations lack many other attributes, too. They lack current experience, they lack competent personnel, in many instances they are dangerously divided within themselves. All of this underlines the vastness and extraordinary difficulties of our task. The task nevertheless is there and we must undertake it—to promote and support constitutional governments.

10   THE AMERICAN PILGRIMAGE

Luce first began to preach the building of an American civilization in a speech to the American Institute of Architects in 1957 (page 273). Having coined for that occasion a phrase he liked—"the first modern, techno-logical, humane, prosperous and reverent civilization"— he continued to use it in other contexts, as in this speech to the Chicago Y.M.C.A., January 23, 1962.

"Character is destiny." The destiny of the United States depends on the character of its people. Yet the United States takes no official responsibility for shaping the character of Americans. The character of the people is left *to* the people, and *their* character shapes the government and the destiny of the nation.

The Y.M.C.A. is the oldest, the biggest, lay organization directly concerned with the character of the people. Thus the Y has been essential to the American system. For the American system has assumed, from the Founding Fathers on, that what the Y.M.C.A. has done would be done. The Founding Fathers made no provision in the Constitution for the training of citizens—either in the manner of Athens or of Sparta or of Rome. Just the opposite: the Founding Fathers rested the Constitution on the faith that good citizens would be made, generation after generation, by the help and guid-ance of free and responsible patriots.

I am told that at this moment the leaders of the Y here in Chicago and elsewhere are asking themselves the most searching questions about all their programs. The Y is trying to find a "new sense of direction." As one leader put it, "Today, goals and aims are far more elusive for the Y than they have been through all its history."

What is true of the Y is true of the whole American nation. The basic problem that today confronts all Americans transcends that of world Communism. What confronts us is nothing less than the meaning of human life.

One evening not long ago, six or seven of my editorial colleagues and I got into a bull session. It started out with the perfectly normal question, for editors: What are the American people interested in? After an hour or so, one of my senior colleagues got himself real wound up and declared that the American people are not interested in much of anything—except, of course, themselves and their personal causes and their trivial pleasures. The marvels of science? We've had them. Expanding prosperity? We take it for granted. And so on. But—as good dialogue should—this outburst provoked an eloquent, and I think a true, reply from a younger colleague. The young man's reply went something like this:

This has always been the country of easy answers. We have an easy slogan for practically everything. We're the country of the endless frontier, of the big sky, of manifest destiny, of unlimited resources, of go west, young man, of opportunity for all, of rags to riches, mass production, nothing to fear but fear itself, technical know-how, a chicken in every pot, gung ho and can do. For 200 years we've worked pretty hard and with great success, but we didn't have to think about it very much. Simple, clear-cut answers: lick the Indians, lick the British, lick the wilderness, lick the Germans and make the world safe for democracy, the Statue of Liberty offering to take on all the tired, the poor, the homeless and downtrodden and to cure them of fatigue, poverty and hunger.

Sure, we had problems, but they could always be solved by hard work, ingenuity and faith. What we didn't need were things like doubt, uncertainty, questioning, thought.

What we are seeing now, my young colleague proposed, is the end of the American daydream, or at least the end of the American lead-pipe cinch. We have achieved everything, conquered the continent, invented the incredible, disposed of fatigue, poverty and hunger. We have won all the marbles—and it just isn't enough. Further, the U.S. of A. knows or feels that it is not enough.

In many ways it would appear that we are coming apart at the seams: a scarcity of happy marriages, an abundance of delinquents and psychiatric patients, misery in the suburbs, chicanery in the marketplace, dismay on the liberal left, fanaticism on the far right. But these are the extreme manifestations of unrest. Meanwhile, in the vast middle of the U.S. of A., what is going on is a lot of soul-searching and wondering and worrying and *thinking*. America is thinking, groping, trying to understand and to come to grips with itself.

Now, the spirit my young colleague expresses is, I believe, the hopeful fact about our country. To be sure, in saying that America had been the country of easy faith, he was not doing justice to our forefathers—to the trials and tribulations they overcame, to the heartbreaks they endured and to their mighty works.

Nevertheless, he says something profoundly right about our present and our future. I will put it another way. We are a Pilgrim people. And we now are called upon to set forth on the greatest pilgrimage of all—to make our way, not to a new land, but to a new civilization. Everything we know, from the atom to the stars, the frightening power of our knowledge, the bewildering meditations of our hearts—everything calls us to leave our comfortable habitations which no longer comfort us, and to strike forth on a pilgrimage to a new civilization.

When I speak of civilization, I am speaking of something which Americans have not been primarily concerned to build. We have been primarily concerned to establish a form of government—government of the people, by the people and for the people. In this we have succeeded. We have been concerned that under this form of government people should have opportunity, and that people who could not meet the challenge of opportunity should be cared for with Christian compassion. But we have not been primarily concerned to build a structure of society which honors, above all, the transcendent value of the good, the true and the beautiful. So, I say, we are now called upon to create that society—to create on this continent the first modern civilization—the first modern, technological, humane, prosperous and reverent civilization.

The blueprints? Yes, they are coming out now in various forms, but especially in books from scholars who think and who also pray. They are not at all like the cries of the reformers thirty or forty years ago. They have little to say about economics, Marxian or otherwise. These new geographers of the new civilization are concerned with the quality of life, and their subject is apt to be education. One of the most notable books is *Education and the Common Good*, by Philip Phenix, professor of education at Teachers College, Columbia. And what is he saying? Professor Phenix speaks in terms of democracy. Very briefly, he says that what we have now in America is a democracy of desire, and we must transform this into a democracy of *worth*.

Democracy of desire means a place where everybody has a chance to go out and grab what he wants. And this is the dominant conception of democracy today—in all fields of life. This form of democracy is man-centered. Its emphasis is on acquisition, on efficient production for large-scale consumption.

The other type of democracy centers around devotion or loyalty to the good, the right, the true, the excellent. That is the democracy of worth. It is to reach that democracy of worth that we must leave our comfortable homes, our outworn values, and set forth on a massive pilgrimage.

Every human being needs goals and principles by which to direct his life and shape his conduct. When such principles are lacking, personal existence loses its zest and meaning, life seems stale and unprofitable, and personality decays. That is why we hear so much today about "frustration," about "futility" and a growing sense of the meaninglessness of life itself.

In the past, as wave after wave of immigrants came to Chicago from overseas or from the American countryside, the task of the Y.M.C.A. here was to put them on the path of opportunity where they would find meaning in their own achievements and acquisitions and, incidentally, in helping to build the America which we have built.

But now it is not enough to put a young man on the path of opportunity. He does not need our help much in relating himself to the democracy of desire; it lures and seduces him easily enough. He does need our help in relating himself to the vision of the democracy of worth.

There are signs all around us that this vision is beginning to take hold. Let me cite just a few examples. First, there is a new word: Excellence. The ideal of Excellence is making its way, like yeast, throughout American thought and feeling.

There is a new feeling for Nature. Somehow the feeling grows that Nature, our land, belongs to us—not merely as something to be exploited, but as something to be loved, and by love enjoyed. And what of our cities? Staggering problems here; but we begin to see that cities must have beauty and order, and that only by a yearning to give this beauty and order can we begin to get on top of the grim and grimy problems.

And—our new confrontation with leisure. The problem of leisure! What a newly odd phrase! In all the history of man, leisure has never been a problem except for the very few. Now it is every man's problem—or nearly. For where we have got to in American life, where we have wanted to get to, is the making not of an aristocratic culture but a democratic culture. That is why it is necessary now to speak of a democracy of worth—a mass culture of excellence. As Professor Phenix tells us, leisure, or recreation, for most Americans today, is "no longer on the margins of life; it is a major factor, if not *the* major one, in determining the tone and temper of mass culture."

To make the leisure hours meaningful—the billions of man-hours of leisure that loom ahead—that is the great new challenge to us all. To quote Jacques Maritain: "No leisure time will be enough for a man to experience the joys of knowledge, of art and poetry, of devotion to great human causes . . . of silently conversing with God." Can the Y help the coming generation to rejoice in its hours of leisure? If so, it will be helped in the most difficult part of our American pilgrimage.

---

11   PROVIDENCE IN THE COLONIES

In this address to the Society of Colonial Wars at Wayne, Pennsylvania, May 17, 1966, Luce gave his Providential view of history a new and special application.

Your summons to me required me to give myself a refresher course in colonial history. And in this course, however sketchy, two things struck me most forcibly. In the first place, I was struck by how thoroughly the colonies had already developed our fundamental ideas of government before the making of the Constitution in Philadelphia. Incidentally, I was struck by—or, may I say, vividly reminded of—the towering character of William Penn. His portrait hangs in the magnificent hall of Christ Church College, Oxford—in the company of Prime Ministers, Viceroys of India, Lord Chancellors and others, scientists and writers, whose names are writ in gold in the book of history. The other day, my editorial assistant, knowing that I love to boast of being a member of Christ Church, warned me about mentioning this in connection with William Penn, because, she said, he was expelled from Christ Church. I had forgotten that. I looked it up, wondering what intellectual or moral fault he had been guilty of. And what did it turn out to be? William Penn was fired because of his religious beliefs. He would not bow the knee to the ecclesiastical lords of the Anglican Church —and, of course, it followed that he established in this realm of Pennsylvania religious freedom and indeed freedom of speech in general. That is only one example of how the principles of the First Ten Amendments—our Bill of Rights—had been formulated, not only in theory but in practice, here on this American continent, even before the Founding Fathers were born.

The second thing that struck me in my recall of colonial history has, it seems to me, a pertinent message for us today. When we think of the colonists who left their homes and risked that dangerous passage of the ocean, we are apt to think mostly of their desire to escape from Europe—to get away from its injustices, its intolerances, its rigid class structures, its dynastic wars. What struck me even more forcibly than what the colonists left behind is what the colonists brought with them from Europe to the new land. And this in turn leads me to put before you tonight a theory of history. It is the Providential theory of history—best known perhaps as the doctrine of Providence. Now I suppose there is not a single historian in this country today who would risk his professional standing by interpreting history in terms of the doctrine of Providence.

Fortunately, he doesn't have to. For in our highly departmentalized system of scholarship, the doctrine of Providence comes under theology and the job of the historian is to record ideas, not to pronounce on them. But one thing all historians would agree on is that the doctrine of Providence—the Providential theory of history —was almost taken for granted by the leading men of the colonial period and after. Thus, for example, even as late as the Declaration of Independence, listen to these resounding lines—"with a firm reliance on the Protection of Divine Providence, we mutually pledge to each other our Lives, our Fortunes, and our sacred Honor."

The doctrine of Providence does not mean that anyone, however pious or learned, knows the intentions of Providence. The illusion that one does is the insidious danger of this doctrine. But for those who believe that God is the Lord of history—then it is fitting and proper to seek out the workings of what was called the hand of Providence.

I think I see the hand of Providence in the colonization of North America. Mine may be a gross misunderstanding of history. But let me offer the colonization of America as an example of the working of Providence and see how well it fits.

What seems to me to be most clearly Providential is that it occurred exactly when it did—most significantly between the death of Queen Elizabeth in 1603 and England's Glorious Revolution in 1688. That was exactly the time to bring to these shores all the greatness of Western civilization, to plant the seeds of that greatness here, to allow two centuries to pass for the maturing of those seeds, in fresh soil in new climate, so that our country would be ready, in a radically new age, both to defend and to enlarge the meaning of the West.

Let me recite, more or less at random, what the colonists were able to bring to this country—that is to say, what had been achieved in Europe. There had been the Elizabethan Age. The English language reached its height of glory, of which Shakespeare is the supreme artist. Then comes the reign of James I; we get the King James version of the Bible. And, furthermore, we get the King James Bible in print, printed! Shakespeare and the Bible —and also printing, which was essential to the political thought and to the general life of the colonies. In more sweeping terms, there had already occurred in Europe the Renaissance and the Reformation, those two great movements of the human mind and spirit. We may include in the Renaissance a recovery of the classical world—the glory that was Greece and the grandeur that was Rome. And the Reformation stands for a recovery of religion as a serious proposition—a view which the Renaissance had tended to undermine. The Reformation, for reasons on which historians largely agree, had consequences also for the political order, a tending, despite all theocracies, to constitutional government.

And now, if we take the little temporal step from 1603 to 1688, when early colonialism was in full tide, what do we find? We find that in England the divine right of kings is dead and gone; constitutional government, though heavily aristocratic, has been finally and irradicably established. We find also that the Thirty Years' War, that worst of the wars of religion, was long since finished and religious tolerance had set in, in practice, if not yet fully in principle.

Again it was in the 1600s that science really got going, its greatest name being Isaac Newton. You recall Newton's wondrous phrase about how he had only picked up a few pebbles on the shore of the infinite ocean of knowledge. There was the spirit of the pursuit of knowledge which so deeply characterized some of our colonies, especially New England and Pennsylvania. And there was another man who picked up quite a pebble on that shore—William Harvey, who, after all the centuries of human ignorance, discovered the circulation of the blood. And there were a number of others—like Halley of Halley's Comet and Boyle of Boyle's Law.

An inventory, then, of what the colonists brought to this new land would include, in terms of broad categories: technology— enough technology to cope with field and forest and to do business on the high seas; a middle class, with honest pride in itself, which even today is so lacking in most of the world; a love of learning and the spirit of science; language tuned to a perfection hardly to be excelled; serious religion, sometimes showing the face of fanaticism, but tending to combine piety with tolerance; and finally, among many other great matters, the fundamentals of human government.

Most of this has been expressed in a hymn usually sung at Yale commencements:

> *O God, beneath Thy guiding hand*
> > *Our exiled fathers crossed the sea;*
> *And when they trod the wintry strand,*
> > *With prayer and psalm they worshipped Thee.*

> *Laws, freedom, truth and faith in God*
> > *Came with these exiles o'er the waves;*
> *And, where their pilgrim feet have trod,*
> > *The God they trusted guards their graves.*

In that hymn is expressed the note of exile but also the realization of the enormous treasure the colonists brought with them.

And, of course, the idea of Providence.

But I must go a little further to fill out my suggestion of the Providential nature of the colonization of America.

Suppose it had occurred not in the 1600s and 1700s? Suppose it had happened in, say, the 12th or 13th century? Many of the things that I have cited could not have been in the precious cargo of the colonists. Perhaps the transference of feudalism, with all its beauties of cathedral and manorhouse, might have been enough. My imagination is not up to it. But what I can suggest with some assurance is that it was Providential that the colonization did not occur later than it did.

What happened to Europe after, say, 1750? Well, of course, Europe went on from strength to strength—it went on from the Age of Enlightenment to the Age of Empire. And of course during the 18th and 19th centuries there was close communication between Europe and America—thanks to the printing press, to the ever-faster sailing ship and to the steamboat. But I do not see any essential genetic mutations which would have been of great value to the founding of a new nation of Western civilization. And, on the contrary, I see in the mounting splendor of 18th- and 19th-century Europe a number of developments which we were happily spared. The burden of empire, for example. We are required today to assume worldwide responsibilities, but not in the sense of imperialism. And as an example of what we were happily spared, I would especially stress the French Revolution. In one brief word, there is all the difference in the world between the French and the American revolutions. Whatever may have been good in the heritage of Rousseau and the guillotine, the fact is that Europe suffered an ideological split from which it has hardly recovered. To be sure, the French Revolution proclaimed the rights of man, but it totally rejected the religious tradition of Europe, and was never able to achieve that balance between freedom and order upon which constitutional government must be based. Hence, the wild swings between democracy and tyrannies; hence, the ugly posture of class warfare, culminating in Karl Marx and Communism; hence, the powerful division, not so much between one religion and another, as between all religion and no religion. When Nietzsche said God is dead, he really meant it—unlike some of his recent plagiarists.

I am by no means saying that, by contrast, our forefathers on this continent pursued their prosperous course with sweetness and

light and amity. We, too, have had our moral shame, we have had
our tragedies, notably the Civil War. All I am saying is that when
our exiled fathers crossed the sea, they were able to bring with
them a more than sufficient cargo of intellectual and spiritual goods
for the making of a great nation of the West—in a new land, with a
fresh start. And I cannot think of much that could have been added
to the cargo, essentially, for the purpose of the creation of the
United States.

There is one more point about the nature of American colonization. Though the first immigrants were people of many kinds, they
had a sufficient unity of language and background so that the
formative institutions of the United States could be established to
make ready in the 19th century for the vast influx of other immigration—which, in the last 100 years, has so enriched our
country.

The early colonists were mainly English, but they rapidly became, before the revolution, Americans. As Stephen Vincent Benét
put it,

> *And those who came were resolved to be Englishmen,*
> *Gone to the world's end, but English every one,*
> *And they ate the white corn-kernels, parched in the sun*
> *And they knew it not, but they'd not be English again.*

Thus, in a sketchy manner, I present a case for the Providential
character of the making of this nation. If anyone wishes to reject
this vision of human affairs, he is entirely free to do so. Reason
alone cannot compel agreement. But what everyone must agree,
everyone who examines the record, is that the colonists themselves
deeply held this belief, this vision. You recall the moving speech in
which Benjamin Franklin said: "I have lived, Sir, a long time; and
the longer I live, the more convincing proofs I see of this Truth,
that God governs in the Affairs of Men." In 1786, George Washington, writing to a French diplomat, says: "The foundation of a
great empire is laid, and I please myself with a persuasion, that
Providence will not leave its work imperfect." Thomas Jefferson, a
deist, not a Christian, in his second inaugural, speaks of how God
"led our fathers, as Israel of old." And this faith continued far
into the 19th century. George Bancroft, the first famous historian
of our country, recounted, in several volumes, how the history of

America is really the story of the wonder-working of the hand of God in the American forest.

But what has this to do with us today? A philosopher has said that life can only be studied backward but must be lived forward. This sense of Providence has by now almost vanished in our secular society. The word itself is hopelessly old-fashioned. But suppose this sense, by whatever name, could be revived, what might be its meaning for us today?

The Providential theory of history is far from being a claim to, or a promise of, indefinite success, wealth and power. It is far from saying that, somehow or other, all will be well in the best of all possible worlds. But the doctrine of Providence does say something far more important than that. It says that there is a purpose in human history, that the story of man is not meaningless, not a tale told by an idiot. It says that there is a purpose in history, and it invites men and nations to share in the understanding and achievement of that purpose, age after age.

"Man proposes, but God disposes." Thus both individual men and nations are called upon to propose the best they know—to propose not merely lofty, vague ideals, but to propose the courses of action that are most likely to actualize the good in the reality of future history. That invitation and that obligation are directed today most pointedly to the United States.

---

12   THE PURSUIT OF SIGNIFICANCE

Under this title the College of Wooster at Wooster, Ohio, held a colloquium to celebrate its centennial. Luce contributed the following thoughts on recent U.S. history (December 12, 1966).

Recently a group of enthusiasts has proposed a way for men to overcome death and become immortal. The way is quite simply to have one's corpse frozen, put in a deep freeze and then reanimated years from now, when, of course, science will have become fantastically more capable than it is today. This group of enthusiasts is called the Life Extension Society and it publishes a newsletter called *Freeze-Wait-Reanimate*.

Dr. Joseph Sittler, the distinguished University of Chicago theologian, commented on this proposal. He called it "an exalted form of madness." And then, said Sittler: "Man is a profoundly historical being" and to extract him from his historical setting is to destroy him.

What does it mean to say in our time that man is a "profoundly historical being"?

I am going to try to answer that question tonight not by talking about history, but by reciting to you a summary of twenty-five years of our own American history. If ever history was made, it has been made in the last twenty-five years by the American people. My brief recital must of necessity be arbitrary, but I shall try to be as honest as an honest writer of headlines. And let us see whether events will speak for themselves as to meaning and purpose.

First, on December 7, 1941, the Japanese destroyed a large part of the American fleet in Pearl Harbor. That put an end to all vacillation on the part of the United States Government about full entry into World War II. We proceeded for the next four years to fight a war in nearly every part of the world as no nation had ever fought before. We fought in the jungles of New Guinea; we maintained roads through the mountain passes of Persia; we sent convoys into the Arctic Ocean. We fought in mid-Pacific two or three of the greatest naval battles ever fought. We became the supreme air power in the first massive warfare of the skies. We landed in North Africa and we mounted the most gigantic of logistical attacks on the continent of Europe. With the help of allies, we won the first truly global war.

Second, even before victory was entirely assured, we set ourselves to organizing postwar global peace. Most notably, this took the form of the United Nations. Excuse me now for a moment of parenthesis. Personally, I think we would have done better to take a little more time about the United Nations. I think it deserved four or five years of more careful deliberations. But, even if too impetuously, the United Nations Charter was written in San Francisco and ratified by the U.S. Senate by a vote of eighty-nine to two.

Third, besides the United Nations and its many subsidiaries, we took the lead in setting up a whole series of international economic organizations like the International Monetary Fund and the World Bank to finance world trade and capital investment in backward nations. These organizations have worked well, though after twenty years some changes may be due.

Fourth, in 1947, we created what history knows as the Marshall Plan. It was utterly without precedent in all human affairs. Along with the Marshall Plan, there came to be established the practice of foreign aid. I said the practice, not the principle. But much of the world considers it to be a principle, and currently India is berating us for not giving them enough. What is the principle involved? No one has defined it. But there it is—the established notion that the taxpayers of one country should, not by voluntary charity, but by government action, help poor countries to become less poor.

Fifth, we took, on the battleship *Missouri*, the total surrender of Japan, the only modern power in Asia.

Another parenthesis, please. I have been saying "we." I don't like to say "we" because, actually, everything I refer to was done not by an amorphous "we" but by individual men. You and I didn't die at Monte Cassino—soldiers with their own names, officers, sergeants, privates, died or were wounded there. Or, again, "we" didn't split the atom. Great scientists and their fellow workers did—with, of course, the help of our money. But "we" is what we commonly say, and perhaps it points to the fact that even the most useless of us is a "profoundly historical being."

So—we, led by General MacArthur, occupied Japan. I know of nothing in all history which surpasses the Japanese occupation for its combination of pragmatic success, generosity of purpose and beneficial consequences. The occupation was both complete and short, and Japan stands today a most prosperous nation and a democratic nation.

Sixth, after two or three years of reluctance, we accepted the necessity of having to see the world in terms of what we dubbed a cold war. The cold war, we now hope, is thawing—may even be an outmoded expression. But let us honor the resolution of President Harry Truman in putting into history the Truman Doctrine—he said we would defend Greece and Turkey against Communist aggression and subversion, and we did.

Greece and Turkey were barely saved before there came a

sudden attack by North Korea on South Korea. Overnight, President Truman promptly ordered American soldiers to fight. The President was backed up by an overwhelming majority of American politicians, press and people. That cost us 33,600 American lives.

Seventh, the American dedication to the defense of freedom was exhibited in action in a series of other places, notably, for example, the Berlin blockade of 1948–49.

Eighth, we took the lead in forming NATO and we have for seventeen years maintained the strongest military force on the continent of Europe.

Let me turn to a few domestic matters.

First, there was no postwar depression as gloomily predicted by liberal pessimists. On the contrary, we have, with a few minor interruptions, put on a performance of economic well-being far beyond the dreams of utopians. This has been not only a triumph of production—even more, it has been a miracle of distribution.

Second, our capacity to produce and distribute has led to what in other times would have been deemed arrogant madness. We have declared war on poverty.

Third, we pushed the progress of science and technology beyond the boldest extrapolations—and, of course, far beyond our collective comprehension.

Fourth, again because of our prosperity but also for other reasons, we trebled or quadrupled or whatever our educational establishment. Quality is harder to measure than quantity, but it seems safe to say that our educational standards, especially at the higher levels, far exceed anything known before.

Fifth, besides our concern for the eradication of poverty and the exaltation of education, we have undertaken to solve practically every identifiable ill that threatens well-being—not only all manner of disease, but also air pollution, water pollution and all that sort of thing.

Finally, for the moment, in 1954 the Supreme Court handed down the most important decision since *Marbury v. Madison*, demanding desegregation of schools. The Negro problem in America is unique in all the world; it would be hard to imagine any problem more heavily loaded with greater human difficulties. But this decade will be remembered as the decade in which we formed an irreversible determination to solve it.

So—there is my ten-minute history of the United States in the twenty-five years since Pearl Harbor. What have I left out? I have left out our failures—for example, in my opinion, our tragic failure to be more effective in helping China to achieve a destiny different from that which overtook it.

And what else? I have obviously left out our major history-making effort of the last two or three years—Vietnam. The returns are not in on that and, as the British used to say, it is a sticky wicket, but I believe that it will prove to be one of our most significant achievements. For two reasons: first, because it is likely to open up an era of progress for all Asia, and second, because it will establish a mutuality of interest between the West and the East—and a genuine dialogue as to the nature of man in the political order. One world, yes. This is a *kairos*—a fullness of time.

The theme of this centennial is Significance. It seems extremely difficult for modern men to establish significance in philosophical terms, in ontological terms or in creeds or, simply, in words. So I have attempted a different strategy. The name of that strategy is the proposition that Action Speaks Louder Than Words.

I have set forth before you some of the mighty acts of the United States in recent years. Whatever ambiguities these acts may contain, it seems to me to be impossible to look at this tapestry of mighty acts without seeing at once that it has, like any great work of art, a self-evident coherence. This panorama of American action, in war and in peace, displays not only dynamics but, even more important, a dynamic coherence.

Nevertheless, you are not satisfied, you are not convinced. Such is the nature of reflective man that he will not be content with facts, however compellingly they compose themselves. Actions speak louder than words—but there is another ancient rubric, namely, Ideas Have Consequences.

And so, to complete my argument from history, I must put before you the proposition that all these mighty acts of the United States had their origin and their long gestation in ideas. Brevity requires that I must condense all the ideas into one. The idea is the making of the United States.

For most of our history, the feeling was that the United States should set an example to the world. What essentially happened in the 20th century was that it was no longer enough for America to be an example; it became her destiny to throw in her lot with the destiny of all mankind. Ours is the first global age. The United

States is the leader in this first global age. Our leadership may fail —and certainly will not achieve any global utopia. We move into the life of the whole world with our virtues and defects. What can be said hopefully is this. As we move into enormously greater challenges than we have ever known before, we may hope that our virtues may be strengthened, our defects purged at least of provincialism, and our ideas clarified in the furnace of global reality.

Surely, here is significance on a scale of wondrous amplitude. And yet, I cannot close on a note of joy and thanksgiving—not yet.

Last April, the poet Richard Wilbur gave us an essay on poetry which, it seems to me, must be one of the finest essays ever written on that subject.

Toward the end he spoke with a tender poignancy of his difficulty in being both a poet and an American today. He said:

"It is also the desire of a poet to put his gift at the service of the people of his own time and place. And that is a happiness not easily come by in contemporary America."

He went on to say:

"When the poet addresses himself directly to our society these days, it is commonly in a spirit of reproach and even secession and seldom, indeed, in a spirit of celebration."

That bothers me very deeply, as I am sure it bothers you. It does not bother me in the sense of stirring up my conscience for, even without a poet's help, I can catalog the faults, the specific and even blatant faults which beset our nation—and for which each of us has his personal share of responsibility. What bothers me about the poet's testimony is that it leaves me at least partly baffled. Why is it that our America is unbeloved of poets? Why is it that Walt Whitman could celebrate America—and modern poets, no?

The very greatest poets have celebrated their societies—Virgil and Dante and Shakespeare and Milton—and that most delightful satirist, Alexander Pope. Any schoolboy knows that the civilizations these poets celebrated were not all glory and grandeur. To put it bluntly, in many respects they stank—stank at least as malodorously as ours with the odor of violence and treachery, with filth and disease and debauchery, and with poverty taken as the norm of life. And yet the greatest poets were the greatest celebrators of the achievements and aspirations and heroisms of their times and places.

Why not for us also? I do not know. This is a great sadness for us all—the sadness of the poets.

But that is not the last word. For my last word tonight, I turn to another of your centennial speakers—to your own Dr. Aileen Dunham. She is determined to lift up our hearts. And it is not by chance that she is an historian.

Dr. Dunham says that the prophets of gloom, and we may include the poets, have not caught up with the radically new conditions under which the life of men and nations must be lived now and hereafter. Conditions which have with them possibilities of disaster and equally of triumph.

"One of the ways we are failing today," says Dr. Dunham, "is a lack of will and imagination to conjure up visions of the future." Her vision is of a world where all men live creatively as brothers and where everyone accepts his responsibilities of citizenship according to his capacity. What is required of us is that we should "set for ourselves noble goals like the pursuit of creativity, truth or happiness."

Perhaps Dr. Dunham may accept an amendment to her inspiring prescription. I would say that what we need to do is not so much to conjure up new and nobler goals, for the noblest goals—for example, brotherhood—have long since taken lodgment in the hearts of men. What we need is to rejoice that these goals exist, and we need to have faith that, more than ever before, we can shape our country and our world in the likeness of these goals and visions.

"By faith, Abraham." So history began. By faith—so shall history continue to exemplify ever richer meanings of justice and of mercy, of liberty and fraternity.

3

THE RULE OF LAW

"My trouble is I think theories should fit facts and vice versa,"
said Luce. "They don't always, but I keep trying to make them."
A prime example of his tenacity in this line was his long involve-
ment in the World Peace Through Law movement, an account of
which will be found in speeches 5 and 7 below. Few laymen
develop such a deep interest in the law as Luce did. He started
from a cosmic theory that was also a religious conviction: that man
lives in a moral universe to whose natural laws all human law can
be and should be made more or less conformable. American consti-
tutional law having been originally based on this conviction, he felt
Americans have a special right and duty to promote world law.
This was the groundwork for his subsequent tussles with the state
of American jurisprudence (Numbers 1 and 3) and with more spe-
cific problems of domestic justice and international order.

Without these speeches, the American bar might never have
initiated the World Peace Through Law movement. Charles
Rhyne, for example, who became president of the American Bar
Association in 1957, ranks Luce's Hartford speech very high
for its influence on lawyers and once said that Luce "has done more
than any person to further world peace through law." Luce made
over twenty such speeches to lawyers and business groups between
1950 and 1965. One of his repeated themes was advocating the
repeal of the Connally Amendment, which was tacked onto the
1946 Senate resolution ratifying U.S. participation in the World
Court. This amendment reserves to the U.S. the right to decide

whether any dispute before the Court involving the U.S. is a do-mestic matter and hence outside the Court's jurisdiction. Wrote Luce: "This is bad law [since] no man can be the judge in his own case. But it is also bad foreign policy, with a built-in boomerang effect against American interests. Until the Connally Amendment is amended, our bad example will keep the Court in its present scandalous idleness and also frustrate any U.S. claims to be a champion of law in world affairs."

Luce's advocacy persuaded President Eisenhower to ask the Senate for repeal of the Connally Amendment, but without result. Presidents Kennedy and Johnson did little about it and the amend-ment still defaces U.S. policy (1969). It also marks a failure in Luce's lifelong effort to make the facts of politics conform to theories—but not for his lack of trying.

1   REVERSE MR. JUSTICE HOLMES

This speech was delivered in Dallas, April 19, 1951, at the opening of a new Legal Center at Southern Methodist University. It was reprinted in part in Fortune *that June. For how Luce came to write it, see page 179.*

For how Luce came to write it, see page 179.

We heard this morning able speeches on "The Law and Busi-ness," "The Law and Labor" and "The Law and Education." I propose to speak on "The Law and Everything." This may seem to be an unwarranted extension of my assignment, "The Press," but actually it is not, for the business of the press is everything— more or less.

The claim of right of the journalist to talk about everything is one which, I think, you are inclined to grant—with somewhat the same indulgence that kings of old granted it to the court jester. And indeed the modern journalist might be likened to the king's fool. If the fool be both conscientious and prudent, he will contrive both to tell the truth and to get paid for it. That perhaps is why we call it the newspaper game.

But even though journalism may have the right to talk about the law along with everything else, you will have noted that the press in fact says very little about the Law as Law. To be sure, we are not laggard in exploiting the field of criminal justice—lower case j. But the law itself enjoys an extraordinary immunity from public interest. And so do lawyers as lawyers. That's one way in which they are smarter than anybody else.

The American people are governed by lawyers—and they always have been. Thus in our gush of talk about politics and government we are speaking of lawyers—or ex-lawyers. But in modern times, there are very few lawyers whom even educated laymen know of *as lawyers*.

Fortunately for me, there is currently one lawyer who is known to movie fans—the late Mr. Justice Oliver Wendell Holmes.

As soon as I thought of him I knew that whatever I might have to say today could be said in terms of the towering figure of the Magnificent Yankee.

As a young man, I knew of Holmes as an immensely attractive figure and it seemed unthinkable not to concur in the liberal adoration of the old gentleman.

But then some while later, as our world was shaken by catastrophic events one after another, I began, like all of you, I'm sure, to try to look a little more deeply into the nature of things. And—along with many other matters—this involved taking another look at Holmes, especially as after his death the glorious myth grew and his name was placed on the high altars of our culture and enshrined in books, both popular and learned. And the more I looked at Oliver Wendell Holmes, the more troubled I became. And so, looking forward to being with you today, I thought I would try to define this trouble and to present it to you.

I discovered, of course, that the task of identifying the Holmes trouble has already been done, and far better than any layman could hope to do it. It has been done especially well by Harold McKinnon in the April 1950 issue of the American Bar Association *Journal*. He opens his article as follows:

> Two things about Justice Oliver Wendell Holmes need reconciliation. He had a very bad philosophy. Yet he ranks

among the greatest men of our time.

His philosophy was agnostic, materialistic, hopeless of the attainment of any ultimate truth, meaning or standard of value.

And my question to you is this—an honest question asking for an honest answer: Does it really matter that Holmes had a very bad philosophy?

The characteristic American answer would, I suppose, be: "No —if Holmes was a good man and did good, his philosophy doesn't matter—and anyway, it couldn't have been too bad." That would be the characteristic American answer—and the American having made that answer would feel unhappy about it, uneasy, worried, puzzled, wondering.

And this uneasy answer, I submit, indicates, as unmistakably as the finger of a clock, the point at which America has arrived: we have arrived at the point historically where we can no longer proceed with any health or happiness on the blithe assumption that it doesn't matter what any of us believe—or whether there is really anything to believe.

I submit to you today that we ought to believe what is true, and that the truth is that we live in a moral universe, that the laws of this country and of any country are invalid and will be in fact inoperative except as they conform to a moral order which is universal in time and space. Holmes held what I have just said is untrue, irrelevant and even dangerous.

I submit to you further that you as lawyers have one urgent task more important than all others—to reverse Mr. Justice Holmes— and to do so for the sake of the law itself, for the sake of the American people, and for the sake of our own individual peace of mind.

There is one great thing—among others—to be said for Mr. Holmes. He knew what he believed. Most of his disciples today don't. Do you?

What did Holmes believe? He believed, most importantly, that there is no ultimate truth anywhere to be believed in.

Since that was his clearly stated belief, some of his more melo-dramatic dicta which I shall quote are *not* out of the context of his general thought.

Holmes said: "I see no reason for attributing to man a significance different in kind from that which belongs to a baboon or to a grain of sand."

Holmes said that men have no natural rights and if a man will fight for what he calls his rights, so will a dog fight for a bone.

Holmes said: "Truth is the majority vote of that nation that can lick all the others."

Holmes said: "I believe that force . . . is the *ultima ratio*."

The "clear and present" labels of this philosophy are materialism, militarism, relativism, agnosticism and, in the most charming and civilized sense of the word, cynicism.

Such was the fully disclosed belief of this American hero. And note well, Holmes was essentially a *spiritual* hero—one who disclosed and revealed truth. Mr. Justice Frankfurter said that Holmes is Plato's "philosopher become king," and the late Mr. Justice Cardozo spoke of Holmes as "the great overlord of the law *and its philosophy.*"

And note well, again, that the fame and glory of Mr. Justice Holmes did not arise from his popularity with the common man. It was the elite who successfully promoted his canonization. It was not only the rising elite of the law; he appealed also to writers, artists, and nearly the whole of the academic world. Though he was skeptical about reform, he appealed to social reformers. The victorious liberals and their fellow travelers of the 1930s put his name—along with Jefferson's—on their banner, while neglecting or rejecting the names of Washington, Adams, Madison, Hamilton and Marshall. This fact cannot be dismissed as a mere aberration of children following a Pied Piper, nor the sudden insanity of Gadarene swine. The worship of Holmes was connected with much, perhaps most, of what was good in the recent past of our nation.

And here I should like to make full acknowledgment of the sympathetic view that can be taken of Holmes's philosophy. Certainly it has corollaries, especially as he drew them, that were attractive in the ancient Stoics and always will be. Courage, style, the love of learning and of excellence—we shall never have enough of these Holmesian qualities. Moreover, he used these qualities, along with his enormous vitality, to undertake a work in the world that needed doing in his time.

When I say his work needed doing, I venture into a field you know better than I. Holmes, I take it, was the elder prophet of the school of American legal realism which brought our 19th-century jurisprudence back into touch with the facts of life. He and his friends forced your profession to admit that other disciplines, such as Mr. Brandeis' sociology, had something to contribute to the perennial quest for justice; that the distribution of property, especially in a democracy, has some bearing on the right to it; and that even judges may be subject to bias and indigestion. Since these propositions were an open secret among all who sued in our courts or voted in our elections, it was well that they be brought to the attention of our "aristocrats of the robe." The Holmesians undertook this corrective work. They fought a long battle, which ended in 1937,* but from which the law has not recuperated yet, for in correcting one evil they created a worse—the undermining of the law itself.

Holmes's philosophy foreshadowed this disaster. Yet the only charge to be leveled at that philosophy is that it denies the immutability and unity of truth. Does it matter? Do we care?

It seems to me that it does and we do. I give you this observation as a journalist trying to discern the signs of the times—it seems to me that we as a nation have come to the point where the most immediately urgent questions are precisely those questions which are perennial and profound. Can we believe anything? What, then, do we believe? That, I think, is already the Number 1 question in America, outranking in historical priority even our fight against Soviet Russia.

I could not hope to persuade you that this assertion is true unless I could make an appeal to the pragmatism that lies close to the heart of every American. Why is it so urgent to settle *now* philosophic questions which will never finally be settled until Kingdom Come? Let me illustrate the pragmatic necessity by reminding you how Americans look—how *you* look—to people in Europe, in Asia, to people everywhere overseas. You do not look good. We do not look good. I think you know that. The picture they paint of us, you resent—and so do I. They say we are materialists—the spawn of a materialism preferable to that of Communism, but materialists

---

* In that year Franklin Roosevelt launched and lost his fight to "reform" the Supreme Court by enlarging its numbers and so unblocking its opposition to much New Deal legislation. In the same year Chief Justice Hughes defused the issue by leading the Court in a more flexible direction, notably in its upholding of the constitutionality of the National Labor Relations Board and the Social Security Acts. "A switch in time saved nine."

nevertheless. They say that we are only interested in gadgets—in motorcars, bathtubs, iceboxes, and TV. We rebut that description, and in part the rebuttal is accepted. Yes, we have many good qualities—"human" qualities—we are generous, openhearted, kindly, in a sort of tactless way, etc. But when all is said, America and the Americans still do not present an attractive picture to the world. Why? Because the people of the world do not feel that we stand for anything—nor for anything deeply and fundamentally relevant to the mighty drama of human destiny—with its eternal dialectic of tragedy and redemption.

And *do* we stand for something? How about the Law? Do we stand for the law? What law? Coming from where and going where? And with what relation to universal truth beyond the pragmatic boundaries of Texas politics? Now if you could give answers to these questions (with all humility in the face of an infinite universe and yet clear answers)—then the world would hear.

But who can give these answers? Could the Supreme Court? I tell you that the Supreme Court of the United States could win the worldwide battle for the minds of men by one humble affirmation that we and all men live in a moral universe. The Supreme Court could win this battle, but not without reversing Mr. Justice Holmes. Oh, they might not have to reverse a single one of his legal opinions. They would have to reverse simply his philosophy —his clear and beautiful and brave and mistaken notion of truth.

But you are still not convinced. If a nation lacks the understanding that comes from reason and faith; if a nation lacks faith, it cannot overnight achieve faith as an expedient means of avoiding disaster.

So, I say to you, this nation still has the faith. The faith is there beneath all the dreadful clutter and confusion of our noise. The faith is there; it needs only to be evoked.

As test case, let me present to you a statement of "The American Proposition"—in two brief paragraphs. For this statement I am indebted to my colleagues of FORTUNE.

"The essence of 'The American Proposition' can be understood only against the long religious history of mankind. . . . Freedom is real because man is created by God in the 'image' of God. Man carries within him something that the merely animal does not have, the divine spark, the 'image.' . . . The human individual thus has a special status with regard to all other things and beings on earth: he must live, and must be entitled to live, by the laws of God, not just by the laws and directives of men.

"According to 'The American Proposition,' this special status is couched in certain Rights. . . . These Rights are 'unalienable,' grounded in the universe itself, reflecting universal laws of nature: that is to say, they are natural, not merely political, Rights."

Between the general philosophy stated there and the general philosophy of Holmes there is no middle ground. A choice must be made.

In suggesting that the Supreme Court make solemn pronouncement of its choice, I am not being entirely whimsical. I realize I intrude upon your lawyers' instinct. You will say that philosophical utterances from the Court are at best mere obiter dicta. Look deeper. Look deeper.

This nation was founded upon a social contract expressed in those two paragraphs. That social contract has been breached and violated—its moral basis undermined by humanistic explanations. That social contract must be restored and made whole. Either that or you will have a totally different social contract, to which, gentlemen, many of you will *not* in conscience give your allegiance. I am suggesting today that the legal profession is challenged to find means to spread across the American sky the news that the law by which we seek to live, however imperfect a copy it may be, is nevertheless grounded in the Law of the Universe.

You may say that you cannot talk in the 20th century the language of the 18th or 13th. Very well—then restate "The American Proposition." You have only to believe that truth itself is great —so great that not all the physical laboratories and not all the books in all the libraries can obscure the radiance of what is forever true.

The secular order is conformable to the spiritual order when it accepts, in reason if not in faith, the moral basis of all things. In this social contract there is full liberty of conscience. Anyone can doubt anything. The believer is indebted to the doubter for constant reminder that truth is always greater than we think and the doubter is indebted to the believer for his very life and existence and partial sanity.

And now, gentlemen, if I have spoken extravagantly, I ask your indulgence and plead that if your profession is in want of anything, it is not in want of sobriety, caution, discretion, prudence; if it is in want of anything, it is in want of extravagance, enthusiasm, heroism, and these qualities I would willingly incite.

The sins and shortcomings of my vocation are serious; and they are also very apparent for all to see. The problems of the law are less visible to the casual citizen. Surely we agree that all of us—all professions, all Americans—are deep into the greatest crisis of our history and therefore all of us should strive to do all that we can to meet the profound challenge to all that is good. But your profession is many centuries senior to mine. Thus I accord to you the prior position in the great struggle for liberty and order—Liberty *under* Law. In my view, it is not the primary duty or competence of the press to discover and declare the standards of faith and excellence by which men and nations must live. But it is the duty of the press—and should be its most joyful duty—to be an honest broker between the great thinkers and prophets of truth and the mass of men. If in your so great and honored profession, there shall arise deeds of heroism—heroism of the mind and spirit—I pray that we of the press will not be far behind to note and to give thanks.

2 "THE AUSTINIAN RUT"

In this speech, delivered to an American Bar Association meeting in Yellowstone Park on June 17, 1952, Luce was still concerned with fundamental theories of jurisprudence rather than with practical embodiments of a world law policy. But his practical proposal for a Hoover-Truman Commission on Social Justice, though stillborn, was at least ingenious.

Man has always known intuitively that life is more than the law. He has rarely been willing to die for the law as such; he will lay down his life for a friend. And so it is that justice itself has been called a second-class virtue. Nevertheless, if there is ever again to be a tolerable peace, if hope is to win a decisive victory over despair in our times, then, I believe, the master instrument of our labors must be the law.

Obviously that requires a conception of law as something far greater than the mere accidental product of clashing interests and irrational psychologies. Therefore, I wish to raise with you today the question of the philosophy of law and of jurisprudence, because I believe this is the most urgent question of this period of American and of world history.

In preparing myself to confront you tonight, I came across an article by Professor Thomas A. Cowan in the Columbia *Law Review* entitled "A Report on the Status of Philosophy of Law in the United States." I quote now the opening sentence:

"The most striking observation which occurs to one reporting on . . . philosophy of law in the United States is that the subject matter of the report seems not to exist."

Gentlemen, that statement not only shocked me, it scared me. For that bit of type seemed to spell out the intellectual impotence of America at the height of its power.

Professor Cowan's report continued: "To the foreigner, American philosophers, apparently spurning all philosophical traditions, seem to be characterizable under only one all-inclusive 'ism,' namely, anarchism."

Is this the final American know-nothingism—compared to which all Ku Klux Klans and witch-burnings are scarcely more than childish aberrations? Do we have here, among the wise men of America, the last and final treason of the clerks? This might well be the plain reading of the books and the law reviews. But I come here nevertheless, in the greatest confidence, because you are here. This whole meeting has been inspired by your intent to vindicate and validate the law in principle and in spirit and in truth.

And thus you are giving, after so many centuries, a perfect illustration of the psyche of Anglo-Saxon and American law. For it is precisely at times of revolution and crisis that Anglo-American law rises to the challenge of ultimate questions. As one authority for this statement let me cite Professor Harold J. Berman of the Harvard Law School.

"Anglo-American law," he says, "despite its distrust of theory and its emphasis on the practical exigencies of the particular case, has produced jurisprudence in periods when its basic assumptions were threatened. . . . When revolutionary ideas were abroad in the 18th century—ideas which ultimately broke out in the French Revolution—William Blackstone wrote his *Commentaries on the Law of England*, which served both in England and America to restore the foundations of the common law and [to protect them against] the new rationalism."

That is how it happened that Abraham Lincoln knew two books —the Bible and Blackstone. Can you imagine a European rationalist saving the union? No, it took a lawyer with the Bible and Blackstone, reading each by the light of the other.

Professor Berman concludes: "In times of relative stability, it is customary to forget that the attempt to grasp and comprehend the totality, and to see the particulars in relation to that totality, is in fact part of the Anglo-American tradition. It is that part which is reserved for crises."

Well, gentlemen of the American bar—you have your crisis! You could hardly ask for a bigger one. This time Americans must vindicate the law.

What the world now needs, more than food or goods, is order. Healthy, durable, progressive order is the product of the law. The United States inherited a great legal tradition and achieved at its founding a reformulation of legal philosophy. This was characteristically a nation of law and it was derisively referred to as "a nation of lawyers." In one sense, in the actual formulation of rules of human relations, this American tradition still continues with great vigor. But at the philosophic level, American legal thought has been sterilized by a pragmatism which yields too easily to positivism. The essence of all positivistic theories is that there is no theory. It is a magical, not a rational, approach. If the American legal proposition is restated in its entirety, it will have to rediscover a basis more intellectually respectable than pragmatism.

In the last few decades we have incorporated a huge amount of social justice into our legal fabric. But we have no coherent—or generally received—philosophy of government and law to match our actual performance in this field. Here is a classic example of social facts outrunning social theory. This is a strong point for the pragmatist; he may well say, with pride, the less theory the better the practice. But it may also be a fact that pragmatism has come to the end of its rope.

In a recent issue of the University of Pennsylvania *Law Review*,

Dean Pound * argues that the rise of the Welfare State is undermining our traditional law concepts. He says: "Belief in the obligatory force of contracts and respect for the given word are going, if not gone." And further: "This one conspicuous human demand which in America was the one chiefly asserted and chiefly respected, namely, the claim to liberty . . . is almost disappearing."

Dean Pound's warning must be taken seriously. The serious response, it seems to me, is to develop a rational philosophy of social justice to match our great inheritance of the philosophy of liberty.

Let me illustrate the point by a fanciful proposal which you gentlemen might turn into fact. Half a year from now, we will have another ex-President of the United States—if we may take Mr. Truman's words at face value. Mr. Truman has told us he is going to do what he damn well pleases. I suggest that there is a really historic service Mr. Truman could render. Let him join with his fellow ex-President, Herbert Hoover, in a Hoover-Truman Commission on Social Justice.

My proposal is therefore that Messrs. Hoover and Truman should set themselves, with the aid of the best philosophers, theologians, sociologists, lawyers and other experts, to find and enunciate an area of agreement on the basic principles of social justice in American life and in relation to government.

There is a vast treasury of material waiting for the Hoover-Truman Commission. There is the vast literature of legal commentary on our actual social legislation of the last few decades. Despite philosophical anarchism, surely in all the best of this writing some fairly clear lines could be traced for an American philosophy of social justice.

Second, there are the papal encyclicals on social justice. They themselves are the distillation of decades of experience and responsible thinking in our industrial age. How much of modern Catholic theory can or cannot be incorporated into an American philosophy of law and government?

Third, there will be meeting in Evanston, Illinois, the World Council of Churches, symbolic of much ecumenical thinking on the problem of social justice.

I should also point with hope to that great new phenomenon—

* Roscoe Pound (1870–1964) had been dean of the Harvard Law School for twenty years.

the socially conscious business corporation. This year the National
Council of Churches begins publishing six volumes of its findings
on the ethics of our economic system. One of the things that
emerges from these studies is a clearer outline of a new rationale of
behavior for the business corporation. Behind it lie many years of
sincere if faltering steps by American business leaders to turn
American business management into a profession. Could it be that
business will become a profession only to find that law has become
a mere trade? It seems unthinkable. Yet to be in something more
than a trade, a lawyer must be something more than an honest
broker of rules and conflicts. The facts and needs of social welfare
have gone far beyond any existing rationale of justice and right;
they need a new framework of norms and values if they are to be
contained by law.

Out of the hard thinking and the human compassion of many
men over many years, the Hoover-Truman Commission could produce a philosophy of law and of government in relation to the needs
of social justice which should command wide and deep assent.

Let me then make the assumption that a great philosophy of law
will be achieved—and that, even now, we are moving toward it. I
should now like to show that, on that assumption, we can reasonably
hope to carry out our world task of leadership.

There are three reasons for this prognosis. They are: first, the
universality of the idea of universal law; second, the emphasis
today in most of the world on social justice; third, the fact that man
is a religious animal and the fact that law and religion are closely
related.

As to the first: the idea that ours is a universe of law (of moral,
not merely physical, law) is the most nearly universal idea to be
found in human history and among men today. The Roman jurist
Gaius gave it classic utterance: "Every human community," he
says, "that is regulated by laws and customs observes a system of
law which in part is peculiar to itself and in part is common to
mankind." It is our adventurous task today to seek in every tribe
and nation that part of their law which may be regarded as
common to mankind and by which therefore they will be willing to
be bound to us and with us under law.

Several years ago Professor Northrop of Yale pointed out how
Oriental thought is dominated by the ideal of harmony with nature
—a concept close to our traditional natural law. I once asked

Chiang Kai-shek to expound to me the inner meaning of the Chinese word for liberty or freedom. He replied that the Chinese character for freedom resembles the character for fish, and that he thought of freedom as being like a fish swimming in water—freely, according to its nature and in harmony with all Nature.

Now that is not our idea of freedom at all, but it is highly representative of Asian thought. We of the West may have a profounder insight into what Niebuhr calls the paradox of human freedom and justice—and of the impossibility of a perfect reconciliation of freedom and justice in human life. The Orient, hymning nature's harmony, is too prone to overlook its tooth and claw: nature must be conquered as well as obeyed. And nothing in nature is so obstreperous as human nature. But the point here is that we can find common ground with the deepest instincts of the Orient in terms of fundamental and pervasive law.

Second, the strongest urges and desires of Asians today are not toward liberty, personal liberty, in the 18th-century terms—or even in terms of 20th-century America. Freedom of speech, freedom of religion, freedom of enterprise—these have relatively less appeal in the East. The freedom Asians seek is primarily nationalist freedom—freedom from foreign rule or "exploitation." And, as part of that sort of freedom, what Asia mostly seeks is social justice.

Take India, for example. There is a strong view in India that the United States owes it to India to supply vast sums of money. Why do we owe billions to India? Simply because we are rich and they are poor. Astonishing theory—but maybe they are partly right. In any case, we ought to insist on a serious, logical—and public—discussion of this point. It would at least enlighten a lot of Americans. I think there would come out of it some solid mutual agreements on rights and obligations in the economic sphere.

Third, as to the relation of law and religion, most people in the world even today are religious. We Americans have a bizarre habit of ignoring this fact. Everywhere in the world there is in fact an intimate relation between religion and government, between religion and law (even in Soviet Russia, even in the U.S.A.). The relationship expresses itself in different ways. Many of the world's states do not hesitate to declare a certain religion to be the state religion. Sweden and Norway, for example, and some of the states of South America whose votes are so important to us in the U.N.

Or consider our good ally, Pakistan. Obviously, we cannot become as one with the sons of the Prophet in religious faith. But we can, both from our Roman and our Christian inheritance, acknowledge with them the supreme and sacred character of the law. Mohammed himself had an instinct for law and order which Dean Wigmore * called "almost Roman in its spirit." He quotes Mohammed's saying: "One jurist is more powerful against Satan than a thousand unlearned men with their prayers."

It would be a bold man—certainly an unfashionable man—who would say the same about our Western jurists today.

For a hundred years, the Western lawyer has been rigorously educated away from any notion that his calling had anything to do with power against Satan. The law became just another human institution to be analyzed logically. In terms of jurisprudence, this is called, I believe, "the Austinian rut." † As the rut deepened, the idea of a natural or universal law, and then even the idea of justice itself, got swallowed up in it. That is the situation of which Professor Cowan could say that the philosophy of law in the U.S. "seems not to exist."

In American society as now constituted, you, the lawyers, are in a unique position. You have always done most of the ruling in America, but now you are unique in another way. You are better qualified than any other group in American life to deal both with pragmatic particulars and with general ideas. You are in a unique position to respond to the greatest need of the age—you can mediate between the fierce claims of the pragmatic and the inescapable claims of the universal and eternal.

Soon after Hiroshima, Oswaldo Aranha ‡ of Brazil sent a phrase ringing through this country. He said: "The United States, which has disintegrated the atom, has the duty now to integrate the world." That's a rather tall order—which will not be fully accomplished before Judgment Day. But we do have a duty to move forward and to lead in that direction. We can do so by our native habits and predilections for liberty—and by a recovery and a recreation of a profound sense of the sacred and saving character of the law.

* John H. Wigmore (1863–1943), dean of Northwestern University Law School 1901–29, an authority on evidence, criminal law and international jurisprudence.
† John Austin, 19th-century English jurist, was the author of the influential *The Province of Jurisprudence Determined*, which drew a sharp distinction between law and morals.
‡ See Chapter 8, page 359.

3   THE PUBLIC PHILOSOPHY

Walter Lippmann gave this title to his book of 1955, in which he developed a theme he had first described in 1937 as "the abiding truth of the older liberalism"—the idea of a higher law above all positive law and political behavior. Lippmann argued that this public philosophy or "tradition of civility," akin to if not identical with the idea of natural law, had to be recaptured before Western civilization could regain its coherence. This was one phase of Lippmann's thought with which Luce could thoroughly agree. He used it in an address at St. Louis University, November 16, 1955, here excerpted:

In this year of 1955 we are all enormously indebted to Mr. Walter Lippmann for having reminted the phrase, the Public Philosophy. Mr. Lippmann surveys the events of his lifetime and is appalled by the decline of the power of the West. He finds that the cause of this appalling decline has been the progressive denial of the Public Philosophy. Today, he says, it has all but vanished from men's minds, and he wonders how it can rise again from the dead and rule again.

Mr. Lippmann writes as a pessimist, I speak as an optimist. One reason for my optimism is the very fact that Mr. Lippmann, our leading pundit, has written as he has. But there are other greater signs of the times and, with all grateful respect, I think Mr. Lippmann has neglected to read some of those signs. For today, the Public Philosophy flies at the masthead of our actual Public Policy.

President Eisenhower made a major address for the 200th anniversary of the birth of the greatest Chief Justice of the United States, John Marshall. In that speech is the plainest assertion of the Public Philosophy that any Chief of State has ever made in modern times. I quote a few key sentences:

1. The President said, "Our nation is ranged with those who seek attainment of human goals through a government of laws . . . Those laws are rooted in moral law, respecting a religious faith that man is created in the image of God."

2. The President said, "Eagerness to avoid war [can produce] agreement that injustices and wrongs of the present shall be perpetuated into the future. We must not participate in any such false agreement."

3. "We must be quick to understand another's viewpoint, honestly assumed. But we must never agree to injustice . . . well knowing that if we accept destruction of the principle of justice for all, we can no longer claim justice for ourselves as a matter of right."

That, it seems to me, is the clearest, plainest commitment ever made to the Public Philosophy, to the moral law, at the very summit of human affairs. The Public Philosophy now flies at the masthead of our Public Policy.

Is it an unrealistic policy? On the contrary, I believe it is the profoundest realism. For if the Public Philosophy means anything, it means something which is written somewhere in the hearts of all men—in their hearts and in their consciences. Even in Soviet Russia. As I have observed the modern world—the confused, half-crazy world—I have observed this: that whenever the United States stood up firmly for principle, an electric wave of encouragement ran around the world. Whenever the United States faltered, compromised with justice, put expediency above principle—when that happened, tens of millions were saddened and millions lapsed into cynicism. The strength of America is in the principles by which we exist as a nation.

4   PEACE IS THE WORK OF JUSTICE

*This speech in Hartford before the Connecticut Bar
Association, October 23, 1956, was given special timeli-
ness by the Hungarian and Suez crises, already in their
early stages. It was also the speech that Charles Rhyne
considered to have led most directly to the involvement
of the American Bar Association in the peace-through-
law movement, especially after Rhyne became A.B.A.
president the following year.*

I will make two speeches. The first of them takes two minutes—
and here it is:

I am told that when that famous citizen of Hartford, Mark
Twain, was asked to stipulate his full address, he answered: "My
name is Samuel Clemens and I reside at 351 Farmington Avenue,
in the city of Hartford, in the county of Hartford, in the state of
Connecticut, in the United States of America, in the World, in the
Solar System, in the Universe, in the Mind of God."

You will note that the first part of that stipulation is all very
legal—city, county, state, nation. But when you come to the world,
there is no longer a legal ring to it. There is nothing law-ful about
the world: it is a law-less place. When you get past the world, all
is again legal, for both scientists and theologians assure us that the
universe and the Mind of God manifest perfect law.

Gentlemen, the task of our generation is to make the world at
last a law-ful place—to make it at last a proper legal residence of
man. This is the task in which the legal profession must take the
lead.

That is my two-minute speech. My message is now delivered to
this distinguished company—and you are all respectfully excused
from hearing further argument.

However, for those who may feel that this banquet merits further digestion, I respectfully submit a somewhat more formal thesis:

In the decade since World War II, the government and people of the United States have exerted themselves mightily for peace. They seem to have utilized every conceivable means to this end, both human and divine. All except one. We have not made use of the law. In the words of Professor Hocking, "Such use as we have made of the law has been timorous, and unenterprising."

The people of the United States have prayed for peace—crowding their churches as never before. They have spent $50 billion of their national treasure to help foreign countries in the belief that economic progress would lead to peace. They have spent abroad other billions in private philanthropy. They have set up information and propaganda agencies in hundreds of cities. They have sent missionaries of foreign aid, dedicated people, to the remotest provinces of earth. They have developed and maintained fantastically powerful—and expensive—armament. *Si vis pacem para bellum.* They have fought a bitter war in Korea, sending their sons into battle and gaining no clear victory. They have maintained the most powerful army and air force in Europe. They have built bases in far-off lands. Their fleets patrol the seven seas.

Nevertheless, we have not achieved peace. Not in the proper meaning of the term—which is that peace should be the normative and expected state of affairs. The peace we have is precarious. It is continually subject to blackmail. It is not based on clear principle commonly accepted. Season after season we are faced by the distasteful choice between dubious war or partial surrender.

You will say perhaps that all this is in the nature of things in the 20th century. And I will agree; and in our minds there will be not only the untamed terror of the H-bomb; there are other equally explosive factors—such as democracy, and old peoples becoming new nations. Reminding ourselves of the immensities of the problem, we would agree further in giving gratitude and honor to our American statesmen for their pilotage of a free America through the narrows of disaster.

Yet this is not our goal. Our goal is a peace of deeper satisfaction. My thesis is that the law is the most effective and the most necessary means for that kind of peace. This proposition is true in reason and philosophy. The wisdom of the ages supports it. *Pax justitiae opus*—and justice is the work of the law. I shall respectfully assume that the philosophic truth of the relation of peace, justice and law is a basic conviction of all the members of this learned profession—and I shall be mainly concerned here to illuminate that truth by some pragmatic tests and proposals.

My argument rests on the proposal that the United States should give to the promotion of law an absolutely primary position in its relations with all mankind—with all nations, races and tribes, and ultimately with each individual soul that inhabits the globe. The phrase "peace-loving nation" is too easily used to confuse. The phrase "law-abiding nation" can be given clear, strong and decisive meaning.

There is a distinction to be made between law within a nation and international law. But this distinction should not be exaggerated. In urging the promotion of the use of the law, I shall be referring both to the law within nations and to the law between nations.

Understood in all its phases—from the smallest business transaction to the greatest negotiations at the summit of global politics— the law will prove to be the most effective means to peace for many reasons, but notably the following three:

First, it is through the appeal to the idea of law that the United States can most effectively bind itself to other nations and peoples in mutual respect.

Second, it is by insistence on the fundamental importance of law that the United States can most effectively challenge our enemies, however contemptuous they may seem of law and justice.

Third, it is through the law that the United States can harness together our vast military might and our political and ideal purposes.

As to the first point—that law is a binder between us and other nations—let me speak first of those nations that we consider our natural allies, our fellow members of Western civilization. What is the touchstone of this civilization? Some would argue that it is Christianity; others that it is the quest for liberty or the scientific method. But from the time of Solon in ancient Greece to the present, there is no stronger thread throughout the history of the West than its development of law. The secular history of the West is not just a series of wars and dynasties. It is also a series of great political decisions which have become the people's law. From Runnymede in 1215 to Connecticut's Charter Oak and on to

Philadelphia in 1787, from the Treaty of Westphalia to the latest decisions of our Supreme Court, law is the language on all the political milestones of Western progress.

"The king is under God and the law"—so was it in monarchic Britain, and so it is with our own king, the sovereign people. Even liberty, the most sacred word in the American vocabulary, is known to us as "liberty under law."

In politics, the greatest common denominator of human feeling and passion is the sense of injustice, which is the obverse of the desire for justice. It is our sense of injustice, therefore, which will make Americans most at home with other peoples. And whoever speaks of justice must inevitably think of law. Once the sense of injustice transcends a brutal desire for vengeance, it inevitably comes face to face with the oldest problems of law.

It is true that our Western legal systems are fundamentally different from those of Asia. Our Western legal systems have an objectivity and precision which are not in harmony with Oriental tradition. Yet it should be noted that today many Asian countries are acquiring, and feel the need of, more objectivity in their law. The basic point is that no people, no tribe, however backward, is ignorant of law. Every nation under the sun, whatever its culture or ideology, has law of some sort. If, therefore, we wish to promote the rule of law in the world, we should first inquire of every nation: Tell us, what is your law? Such an inquiry, if launched by the President of the United States and other leading statesmen, could generate throughout the globe a marvelous concern for law, and bestow on it in the minds of men the central role it actually occupies in our own society.

President Eisenhower electrified the world by his proposal for air inspection of armaments. What I am suggesting is that there should be initiated and continued forever an inspection of the law of each and every nation by each and every other nation. Thus we shall have made most vivid to all mankind the differences which exist between us all, and we shall discover the points where we can, and most need to, grow together in a common respect for law. And thus we shall undertake the glorious enterprise of building a *law-ful* world through a tradition which becomes increasingly the common law of the world.

My second argument is that it is by a persistent appeal to law that we can most effectively confound our enemies. The most sensational event of 1956, until the revolts in Poland and Hungary this past weekend, was the six-hour speech by Khrushchev at the Twentieth Communist Party Congress. Anyone who read the full text of that speech must have been struck by the fact that fully one-half of it was directed to law. More than anything else, Khrushchev was determined to show that Stalin had violated Soviet law. And that on the contrary he, Khrushchev, would respect the law. Even a tyranny requires law. However shameless a tyranny may be, it cannot long afford to be ashamed of its own law.

The Soviet empire today is full of troubles. Essentially the Kremlin problem is to base its rule to a greater degree on the consent of the governed—both within Russia and throughout the Soviet colonial empire. How to do this and yet retain their immoral and arbitrary power? That is their dilemma. Note, as a major example, their playing down of the secret police and the police state. They seek to give the appearance of the rule of law. And in politics, appearance is a large part of reality. If rulers feel that they must *appear* to be lawful, then to an extent they must *be* lawful. I do not wish to oversimplify, but there is a causal connection between the Khrushchev speech on law and the revolts in Poland and Hungary, which he ruled illegally.

My argument, then, is not merely that a great global inquiry into law would expose the evils of the Soviet system; my argument is that a general concern for law would further incite concern for law within the Soviet empire—and once that process began, we could expect in consequence either the last reactionary convulsion of tyranny or a gradual but profound transformation of the Soviet system. Either way, the challenge to be lawful confounds the evil in our enemies.

My third argument for giving the highest priority to law in world affairs is that it is through international law that we can harness our vast military might to the service of our political and ideal purposes.

Whenever the subject of world peace is seriously discussed, we encounter some such sweeping dictum as that the world will be ruled "either by the law of force or the force of law." Such a choice is unreal. You will always have force in the world—now more than ever before. And you will always have law in the world—we hope more and better. The problem is to get force and law together. What we really mean is that we seek the rule of law backed by force. As Pollock * said: "The sheriff and his posse lurk in the background of every rule of law."

Ultimately a vision of global peace requires a picture of world government, a government making world law and backing it by a monopoly of organized force. World government is not the business of our generation and none of us is likely to see it. I invite your passing attention to world government only for the sake of ultimate logic. The business of this American generation is to establish, through an ever-larger part of the world, a rule of law enforceable within that area and defensible against any barbarians who may choose to remain outside. That, as I see it, is our task during the next twenty years. We have barely started. Yet I believe the time has come when we must and will launch this enterprise on a global scale.

* Sir Frederick Pollock (1845–1937) was Justice Holmes's lifelong English correspondent and fellow jurist.

---

5 A BIG YEAR FOR THE LAW

The immediate background for this speech, made to the Indiana Bar Association at French Lick, September 20, 1957, was the meeting of the American Bar Association in London that summer. Although Anglo-American sentiment was at a low ebb as a result of the Suez war, this meeting was addressed by the Lord High Chancellor of England, by Sir Winston Churchill, by Chief Justice Earl Warren, by Attorney General Herbert Brownell and by other leaders of both the English and the American bar. Wrote Luce, "Somehow the speeches caught fire, oratory took on a touch of profundity. The Americans and British found—when the wounds of Suez were still smarting—what deeply united them, something which through all their history they had been fighting for—liberty under law."

A few weeks ago the new president of the American Bar Association, Mr. Charles S. Rhyne, returned from your historic meeting in London and gave clear and emphatic utterance to the meaning of his distinguished job as spokesman for the lawyers of America. President Rhyne said:

"A goal of the American Bar Association, vital to every citizen, is the development of the legal machinery to insure peace under law . . . To achieve such rule of law is the greatest challenge and the greatest obligation of the legal profession . . . That our predecessors have failed is no cause for dismay. We, faced with the dread possibility of atomic annihilation, dare not fail. I am sure we will . . . create the legal machinery which will end war forever."

President Rhyne goes on to say: "Our job as lawyers is not only to write the rules of law but to sell those rules to the people of the world."

Gentlemen, at this point I feel that I might say, with profound relief, that I have no more to say. If the lawyers of America are going to put their backs into this job, then an editor can return to his proper role of reporter and commentator. In recent years my friends have often asked me—why, if I feel so deeply about the law, why didn't I say more about it to the general public from my platform as an editor. Perhaps I should have—and certainly I will.* But hitherto my reason has been this. The constructive uses of the law are difficult for ordinary people to understand. Many people think of law as something static or negative or even repellent. They do not easily envision law as a civilizing force. It is necessary first of all that lawyers should believe in the civilizing power of the law—and carry a torch for it.

Now in 1957 that torch has been lighted. And what I will try to do today is to offer some conspicuous examples of how, in 1957, the course of history is compelling us to see in the law both our necessity and our hope.

The greatest single event for the advancement of the Law was the meeting of the American Bar Association in London. For one thing, it marked the restoration of the Anglo-American alliance. What is the real basis of this alliance? Its real basis is our common reverence for the law. We live by the law. We hold our freedom by

---

* TIME inaugurated a regular section of news about law in October 1963. Previous attempts to report this subject, also under Luce's prodding, had been made in TIME and FORTUNE.

the law. It is this to which the peoples of the English-speaking world come back, through all the twists and turns of our conflicting politics. If we really want the Anglo-American alliance to work, we must give it work to do. The work which America and Britain must do together is a work of law-making and of law-upholding.

A few months ago I received a letter on this subject from Prime Minister Robert Menzies of Australia, who wrote:

"We will no doubt see the idea of 'action according to the law' spread over the world as true self-government spreads. . . . Perhaps we do not always understand that the 'rule of law' and 'the rule of Parliament' can be separately stated in words, but are not easily separated in fact. They are Siamese Twins. Self-government is not only a political conception. It is also a legal conception. In short, I don't believe that there can be any form of Parliamentary self-government without a recognition of the rule of law."

These are truly words of wisdom. Bearing them in mind, let us remind ourselves of where the age-old struggle for self-government stands at the moment. Self-government is the most generally accepted form of government in the non-Communist world today. The idea of self-government has no serious rivals in the minds of men; it has only subverters.

The Communists would subvert it by design. The new nations of Asia and Africa, trying it for the first time, may subvert or lose it through incompetence or ignorance—ignorance of the fact that, as Menzies says, self-government is a legal as well as a political conception. The concept of Parliamentary government, spread throughout the world by the British, is impossible without the rule of law. The United States for its part has led in spreading the idea of government under a written Constitution with a Bill of Rights; this is even more inconceivable without the rule of law. Now, therefore, we must work together—Great Britain, the Commonwealth, the United States—to establish self-government more firmly by making clear that without the rule of law, self-government is a mockery and democracy is a delusion.

The London meeting reasserted, for all the world to hear, this indissoluble connection. And it went further! It also asserted that law must be the basis of proper relations *between* self-governing nations. Mr. Herbert Brownell, the Attorney General of the United States, said:

"Our greatest deficiency is that we have not yet applied our knowledge of how men may govern themselves by law to the determination of all disputes between countries . . . We must perfect a machinery for a settlement of international disputes—not occasionally but on a total basis—under a tribunal or system of tribunals which will command general confidence."

Also at that meeting there rose up Sir Winston Churchill himself, and he said:

"We have now reached the point where nations must contrive a system and practice to resolve their disputes and settle them peacefully."

Thus the chief law officer of the United States and the ranking statesman of the West took the lead, among many others, in saying that our chief business now must be to expand and vitalize the rule of law.

In Sir Winston's speech he politely but firmly expressed his dissatisfaction with the United Nations—a dissatisfaction which has been prevalent in Western Europe ever since the Suez war. Well, there is this to be said. The United Nations was flawed from birth by an inadequate legal conception. If the U.N. is to have any future, it must be gradually transformed by its own members into an instrument of justice as well as a focus of diplomacy. With all its faults, it is a binding agreement among its signatories, and for this reason alone a respect for law compels a respect for the words of the Charter. The U.S. was therefore profoundly right in opposing, under the Charter, the attack on Egypt. The British for their part showed their respect for solemn agreements by complying with the U.N. command. What a contrast with the case of Hungary, in which the Soviet Union flouted the U.N. Covenant and once again branded itself an outlaw.

This has been a big year for the law—at home as well as abroad. What made this a headline year was the extraordinary batch of decisions which the Supreme Court handed down in June. So let me say quickly that, to most of those headline decisions, I take strong and not very respectful exception. For example, I think the decision in the Jencks case * revealed a shallowness in the legal philosophy of the eminent Justices. The Court was concerned to

---

* The Court (for procedural reasons) ordered a new trial for union official Clinton Jencks, who had received a five-year jail sentence on conviction of filing a false non-Communist affidavit under the Taft-Hartley Act.

assert the rights of the individual; good, but it forgot that the law is also and equally responsible for the community as a whole—not only for the rights but for the very existence of the community. Nevertheless, whatever anyone thinks of the June decisions, they reminded us of how we as a nation live by the law.

In the last of the summer decisions, the Supreme Court acted with a splendid unanimity. That was the Girard case. You recall how the newspapers of the land reported what they chose to consider the shocking news that an American soldier in Japan was going to be tried in a Japanese court. Editors from coast to coast made the eagle scream. Well, eagle-screaming rarely does editors any harm. They profit by it. The only harm done by eagle-scream-ing is to America itself. Fortunately, all the demagogic uproar quieted down when the Supreme Court spoke.* That in itself is a tribute to the innate American respect for the rule of law. But the consequences of the Girard case were even greater. For it taught us what any high-school boy should have known, that we cannot have soldiers and bases and other enterprises all over the world without accommodating ourselves in some degree to the law of other nations. You can say, of course, that we can bring all our forces home and go isolationist. That, indeed, is exactly what the eagle-screaming headlines were trying to say. They were appealing to the latent isolationism that lies in most of us—as it does in most men everywhere. Nearly all of us wish at times that the world would just go away and leave us alone. But the American people overwhelmingly know that that is childish nonsense. We are deeply resolved to do our part in the world. To do that means getting on with other people—by law and through law.

The Girard case was important because it concerned the most troublesome problem in the free world today, namely, the problem of national sovereignty. The only way by which we can get any effective handle on this most troublesome problem is through the extension of the rule of law. One hundred nations or more now claim absolute sovereignty. Many of them cannot even meet the first test of sovereignty—namely, self-defense. The claim is there-fore not only immoral and idolatrous; it is also inherently absurd. This whole modern exaggeration of the idea of national sover-

* It found that the Japanese court had jurisdiction over Army Specialist 3/C William Girard under the terms of the U.S.-Japanese Status of Forces treaty.

eignty is a disease. It poisons world politics, it is the greatest bar to economic progress, and it threatens the collapse of capitalism. But what are you going to do about it? Especially as no nation is more touchy about sovereignty than the United States itself. The rule of law provides the answer. For civilized nations are willing to limit their sovereignty in one manner—namely, through prior agreements, freely and lawfully negotiated and solemnly sworn to. To make an honorable agreement dishonors no nation. This is the path of honor which the United States must make clear and wide through the jungle of pernicious nationalism.

6   LAW AND FOREIGN POLICY

In this address to the Missouri Bar Association in St. Louis, September 26, 1958, Luce expanded on his views on Holmes and also on why the U.S. is especially suited to lead a peace-through-law movement.

I should like to tell you how it happens that I am here tonight—a layman undertaking to speak to lawyers about the law. After World War I, I returned to Yale to finish my college course. Being a poor boy with no visible means of support except my wits—a dubious asset—it was natural that family and friends could think of no way for me to get on in the world except to be a lawyer. Accordingly, I spent a summer at summer law school. I took Criminal Law and the Law of Property. Reading the famous cases of trespass and murder in 17th-century England, I thoroughly enjoyed the pleadings—the who-done-its. But just as I can never figure out the answer to an Agatha Christie, so when I came to the judge's summary and verdict, I found that my best chance of being right was to flip a coin. Heads, John Doe is guilty; tails, Richard Roe is not guilty. I could follow the judge's logic, but I could not foresee it. Clearly, I had no aptitude for the law. So, for thirty years I paid no more attention to it than any other American. Some part of that period was spent industriously breaking the law of Prohibition—and possibly some other laws on which, I trust, the statute of limitations has long since run.

Then, in 1951, I was asked to come to Dallas to be one of twenty or thirty speakers at a convocation opening the Legal Center of Southern Methodist University. For some reason, I felt an urge to speak about law instead of about something I might be supposed to know something about. But what to say? I hadn't the least idea. A little research was indicated. And so over a weekend, I took out to the green hills of Connecticut some copies of the American Bar Association *Journal*. And there I came across a learned and documented attack on Justice Oliver Wendell Holmes. His memory had recently been enshrined in a biography and in a movie (*The Magnificent Yankee*). What could possibly be wrong with that hero of all liberal and enlightened men?

Well, when I found out what was wrong, I was shocked. Mr. Justice Holmes had said some things (page 152) that added up to an assault on everything I had learned at my mother's knee and everything I had discovered about the meaning of America. Obviously I had to read further, and the conclusion I came to could be crudely summarized as follows: that what had gone wrong with the world, and especially with our Western world, was essentially the same as what had gone wrong in the philosophy of Mr. Justice Holmes, a great, noble, humane, civilized American.

When Holmes was a young man in the 19th century there was in Europe a crazy philosopher whose name was Nietzsche and his most famous cry was "God is dead!" Nietzsche was a good prophet. The Western world has pretty well lived up to his prophecy. He foretold the Superman. The Superman of Science, who will know all things. The Superman of War, who will hold mankind in thrall. The Superman of Psychology and of Mass Politics, who will brainwash the children of Eve into obedient puppets. Now, today, many facts and forces of our world fit that picture. And we are seriously told that tomorrow all the facts and all mankind will conform to that picture—to the rule of Superman, uncontrolled by any fundamental principles or any higher law.

We are here tonight, free men and women dedicated to the law. We are here to deny that picture. We are here to say that it shall not happen, because that picture of tomorrow does not correspond to two truths. The first truth is that man is born subject to the laws of his own nature, fixed by God and not by the preferences of men. The second is that man is born free—free to oppose God's will or to seek it. He resolves this paradox and makes his freedom real and substantial by working out a relationship of liberty under law. Where liberty and law are seen as derived from the same source, a source beyond the power of any government, then liberty and law are compatible. Sophocles' sorrowing Antigone spoke for the West —but not for Justice Holmes or the prophet Nietzsche—when she defied the tyrant and appealed to the higher law:

> *It was not Zeus, I think, gave this decree,*
> *Nor Justice, dweller with the gods below,*
> *Who made appointment of such laws to men,*
> *Nor did I think your edicts were so strong*
> *That any mortal man could override*
> *The gods' unwritten and undying laws.*

The general political truth of our time is the tragic retrogression of this idea of law. In our lifetime, in view of the rapid rise in global complexities, what we have needed is more law with greater universality. Instead of which we have got relatively less international law, more fragmented and shockingly disregarded. The growth of law has not kept pace with the urgent need for it. So it should be no surprise that wherever freedom survives today it is in peril. Wherever order survives, it is insecure. This very night, St. Louis may literally cease to exist. There may not be a human being in this community alive tomorrow. It has been many a decade since *that* danger was a practical concern of practical men.

What can a practical man do about it? First, he can admit that the danger is real. Second, he can understand that our shameful peril is a result of the weakness of law throughout the world. Third, he can recognize that it is for us Americans not only to uphold what law there is; it is up to us to extend the rule of law in every direction, throughout the world.

Why us? How did we Americans get elected? Well, we have the tools of force in quantities to command the respect of those who respect only force. No other nation now has, or has any foreseeable chance of getting, enough of the tools of force to repel the enemies of law and freedom. That's one way we got elected, and that by itself would be enough to place upon us the responsibility.

But force alone will not do the job. What created the job in the first place was the mistaken notion that force is an adequate foundation for order. What needs to be added to force is its justification—the goal of creating the supremacy of law.

The main point I want to stress tonight is the meaning of law to the foreign policy of the United States. The advancement of the rule of law must be made the visible principle that guides all our diplomacy, all our relations with friends, with enemies and with neutrals. It must become the keystone of our foreign policy. The advancement of the rule of law is the cause which can give to our foreign policy intellectual coherence, dynamic purpose and brilliant clarity.

As a nation we have been a long time waking up to this fact. But we are waking up. In the last year, the rule of law has picked up momentum. Things have happened, all adding up to a worldwide forward movement of the law.

They tell me that not all lawyers are enthusiastic about the Rhyne-Malone crusade [the A.B.A.'s World Peace Through Law movement—pages 168 and 174]. They tell me that some think the Bar Association should confine itself to getting fatter fees for lawyers. Never having begrudged a good lawyer his good fee, I would answer the practical objection by pointing to a practical possibility. In twenty or thirty years, even without a great war, the world may be one in which no lawyers will make any fees, fat or lean. Lawyers are not universal. As Justice Cardozo pointed out, there are no utopias that reserve a place for lawyers. Nor do lawyers flourish in dictatorships nor in static civilizations, such as ancient China. Lawyers exist and earn fat fees in the fruitful tension represented by the phrase "freedom under law." So those who spurn the Rhyne-Malone crusade may need to think twice on purely practical grounds if they have any regard for their sons—or their junior partners. I want lawyers to survive. I want them to be part of the pattern of the future because without them there will be no liberty, and justice will have only the meaning that a mechanical monster may give it.

Eleven nations have accepted a United States invitation to consider how Antarctica may be placed under international control.* Next, outer space. This year saw the beginning of technical work

* A treaty was concluded in 1959 and ratified the following year by the U.S. Senate.

on how law should apply beyond the atmosphere. We can all see plainly enough that there must be a law of outer space. But is there any necessity for the supremacy of law in outer space that does not also logically apply to the more difficult problems of inner space? An ironic possibility appears. We may first establish a law of outer space and then work inward from the moon to make the earth a lawful dwelling place for man.

The one law which the world most urgently needs is a law to abolish atomic weapons and to enforce that abolition with a thoroughgoing inspection system. But suppose we got that one most-needed law. Suppose it stood alone in a sea of international anarchy. How long would it last unless we worked quickly and well to build out and down from it an ever-spreading edifice of law? Imagine an aggregation of men with no law. Then they get a law against murder. If you have a law against murder and no law against theft you are going to get a lot of homicide, some justified, some not. And if you have a law against theft and no private law defining and regulating the rights of property and contract you are going to get a lot of larceny.

The idea of the law is indivisible: no law stands alone. That is why the quest for a lawful world must not be confined to warding off those dangers which could do most spectacular damage. A humble fisheries treaty, made and kept within the spirit of a law beyond the power of any nation, contributes to a structure that may someday be capped by the effective outlawry of nuclear weapons.

I have said that one way this nation got elected to the responsibility for bringing order to the world was the fact of force. The enemy has it. The United States has it. If we do not oppose our force to the enemy's, who will?

But there is another way in which we got elected. We have been elected to this task because of the peculiar nature of the American nation. Uniquely among all the nations of the earth the United States is a nation formed by legal compact—a written constitution —designed for the stated purpose of securing liberty under law. Words by every President express our unique dependence on the concept of the paramountcy of law in all human affairs. Even among Anglo-Saxon nations, the United States is almost alone in retaining its devotion to the principles of judicial review of the legislative will. This devotion is now being tested more drastically than it has been tested for generations. There is ruthless criticism of our present Supreme Court, and even challenges of its right to the final word on what the Constitution means.

Yet I have seen no serious challenge of the principle that there *is* a final and binding meaning to our Constitution. I hear of no serious attempt to abolish our troubles with the theory that custom and comfort are higher norms than justice and law. If the Supreme Court were to abdicate tomorrow, this nation would by its very nature be erecting another ultimate spokesman of our sovereign Constitution and the supreme law of the land.

A brilliant Frenchman, Amaury de Riencourt, in his book *The Coming Caesars*, has forecast for the United States in the modern world a role comparable to that of Rome under the Caesars. I do not agree with his forecast. But his analysis of what we are and who we are is profound and mostly true. And especially brilliant is his chapter on the law. He says, "Americans may not always be law-abiding but they are, like the old Romans, more law-minded than any other nation." And why? Because, says Reincourt, "Freedom of the individual from arbitrary tyranny and the paramountcy of law are inseparable." That statement contains just about the whole truth of human politics.

When America makes the rule of law its Number 1 objective in world affairs—then and only then will American foreign policy express the character of this nation. The example of our country contributed mightily to the worldwide drive for national independence; it is up to us to see that that drive moves forward in orderly channels. The United States achieved a prosperity that stimulates men everywhere to demand more material things; it is up to us to see established the kind of order without which such hopes are illusions, doomed to end in bitterness and anger. We invented the atomic bomb; it is up to us to tame it.

The key is law. Not merely survival, which leaves us chained by fear, stolidly awaiting attack. Not self-interest, which cannot safely be pursued in a lawless world. Not a flabby idealism. The key is law, in all its manifestations and especially in its essence, the place where order and freedom meet.

7   THE STORY TO '65

Except on the issue of the Connally Amendment, Luce could take considerable satisfaction in the activities sparked by his speeches on World Peace Through Law. Here he reviews the record in a speech to the Shelby County Bar Association in Memphis, Tennessee, May 3, 1965.

There is an old adage that nothing can stop the triumph of an idea whose time has come. The advancement of the rule of law is an ancient idea whose time has come in many times and places and whose success has brought about most of what we know, historically, as civilizations or great societies. The age of Hammurabi, 2,000 years before Christ, might be cited as one example.

Now reasonable men like you or me, and especially lawyers, might have thought the time had come for a mighty resurgence of this idea—on a world scale—at the end of World War II, in the year 1945, in San Francisco, in the making of the United Nations, and in all efforts to make peace. But that did *not* happen. Instead, somehow, in and around 1945, the idea of the advancement of the rule of law got lost—very lost.

The United Nations was not essentially based on law or on the development of law. Quite the contrary, it was based on naked power—that is, on the Security Council. The assumption was that peace would be kept by five great nations voting unanimously, each of them having been supplied with an absolute and completely arbitrary veto.

One voice and only one strong voice was raised against this weird perversion. That was the voice of the late, great Senator Arthur Vandenberg. He was dismayed that the Dumbarton Oaks proposals—the blueprint for the United Nations—made almost no reference whatever to the basic concepts of justice and of law. On the Senate floor, Senator Vandenberg said: "I want a new dignity and a new authority for international law. I think America's self-interest requires it." And then Vandenberg went to San Francisco and, in one of the few serious battles against our Russian allies, managed to get into the Charter at least some reference to justice and to law.

Ten years later, two facts became apparent. One was that, however useful it might be, the United Nations was not the reliable highway toward peace—and principally because, by its very nature, it had made so little progress in developing standards of justice and methods of law. The second fact of 1955 was the enormous efforts which the United States had made and was making to maintain peace and to defend freedom—through the United Nations and, even more, outside the United Nations. But the United States, too, had almost totally neglected the development of international law.

And then something happened to cause us to try to overcome this extraordinary neglect: the meeting of the American Bar Association in London in 1957. In the year after London, A.B.A. President Charles Rhyne and scores of people like Dean Erwin Griswold of Harvard Law School and my old friend Dean Robert Storey of the Southwestern Legal Foundation got tremendously active. Here at home they set up local committees in nearly every state and county. And they traveled around the world interesting lawyers in all the free or neutralist countries.

Major regional conferences were organized—finally, for this period, a conference of more than 1,000 judges and lawyers from 105 countries, in Athens in 1963. I was there as an observer and it was a tremendous experience to see all those lawyers of every color and background with a great sense of having the law as a vital bond in common.

The week-long Athens conference consisted of a great deal more than oratory. As a layman, I was overwhelmed by the multitudinous technical subjects that were taken up. The largest part perhaps concerned business law. I have no doubt that the advancement of the rule of law in all business and economic matters would do more to increase the flow of world trade and raise the standards of living of the world than all the economic aid you could dream of.

It is estimated that there are about a million lawyers in the world. Nearly all of them have been contacted by your World

Peace Through Law committee. Thousands of them are dues-paying members of the movement. Many specific tasks have been undertaken, such as codification and compilation of all the vast amount of treaty law and other forms of international law which already exist.

There have been many other efforts of great importance. Very greatly to be admired is the International Commission of Jurists, which first met in West Berlin in 1952. Since then, it has made a splendid contribution. Its 45,000 members of the bar from some sixty nations have issued carefully documented protests against the violation of human rights in Hungary, South Africa, Tibet, Angola, Cyprus, Latin America—a whole library full of lawyers' briefs in support of liberty.

Here in the United States, Duke University's World Rule of Law Center, under Arthur Larson, deserves special mention for tackling the huge job of codifying what is being done to promote the rule of law. Many other of our finest universities have dramatically built up their studies of international law. And I must also amend what I said earlier about the United Nations. Despite the fact that it has so far failed to elevate the general importance of the rule of law, its many agencies have worked hard to find new lawful means of dealing with many matters such as space, aviation, communications, and even the ancient law of the seas.

Then, we must take note of the European Common Market—itself a creature of law, of *international* law. Its own court has handed down more than 1,000 judgments, virtually all of which have been accepted by the states involved. In fact, it has been said that never before has there been so much study of international law and never before so much international law made and, to great extent, adhered to.

The European Common Market reminds us that not all development of law needs to be global in character. There can be regional systems of law with regional courts. The Organization of American States is very much in point tonight.* We may be grateful that it exists; we would be even happier if it were more effective.

But one stark question remains. What has been done by the governments of the world, by the political leaders of the world, to advance the rule of law as a basic concept and as applicable to

* The U.S. had that day asked other O.A.S. members to send troops to help end the civil war in the Dominican Republic.

serious conflicts? The answer is—almost nothing. And why is that? Again, I shall answer from my own personal experience.

We go back to 1958, when John Foster Dulles was Secretary of State and when this movement began to get under way. At first it seemed that Foster Dulles didn't think there was much pay-dirt in it. At one point, I asked if I might have an hour of his time. At the appointed time, I entered his office and he began to expound to me the current headline crisis—I think it was Syria that was making the trouble of the moment. I said to him: "Foster, I haven't come to see you to be briefed on Syria. I want to talk to you about the rule of law." With a barely concealed look of boredom, Secretary Dulles eased himself into a deep leather chair and patiently listened to my spiel. After a quarter of an hour I could sense that a million brain cells were beginning to click in Dulles' powerful mind. Soon he got out of his chair and began to pace the room. In the next three-quarters of an hour, I heard the most cogent case for the necessity of the advancement of the rule of law as a basic cardinal element of American foreign policy. Dulles' conclusion was that the United States needed the concept of law to give coherence to all aspects of our foreign policy. The United States could not proceed in its world mission with only military alliances, economic hand-outs and peace-loving clichés. A few months later, Secretary Dulles said just this in a major speech to the New York State Bar. Tragically, it was his last speech. A few weeks later Foster Dulles went to the hospital with his final illness.

That was a setback for our cause. We felt that President Eisenhower would not wish to embark on a new course in American foreign policy without the assurance and the help of the man he trusted so deeply—John Foster Dulles. However, in his State of the Union speech in 1959, President Eisenhower asked for the repeal of the Connally Amendment. He did so again in 1960. President Kennedy did not give it the high priority it requires.

Any talk by an American President or an American Senator about the rule of law is meaningless and even hypocritical—until we repeal the Connally Amendment. By the same token, the moment we repeal it, the United States can stand forth as a champion of law and of justice for all mankind.

As you know, five years ago, in 1960, the House of Delegates of the American Bar voted to repeal the Connally Amendment. By a close margin, to be sure; but by far the greater weight of distinction and authority was in the majority vote to repeal. But still there has been no debate in the Senate on this point. The reluctance to debate this matter seems to have something to do with sentiment for the late, beloved Senator Tom Connally of Texas. Perhaps only a Texan President can free us from that impediment to leadership.

The only good book written in favor of the Connally Amendment was written by another friend and neighbor of mine in Phoenix—Denison Kitchel, the closest adviser to Senator Barry Goldwater. *Too Grave a Risk* is the title of the book. What is the risk? The risk is that some dispute would arise which the World Court would decide to be under its jurisdiction, whereas we would regard it as strictly a United States domestic issue. I cannot, at this moment, rebut Kitchel *in toto* as I should like to, but there is one important point to make. Kitchel and others seem to think that the United States is the only country that deeply values its own sovereignty—its sovereign control of its own affairs. Nothing could be more mistaken. The fact of the modern world is that most countries are, if possible, just as sensitive about their sacred sovereignty as we are. The logical consequence and the actual fact therefore is that the World Court leans over backward to make sure that any given dispute is truly international in character. The World Court leans over backward in refusing to take jurisdiction of domestic issues.

Those of us who are devoted to the cause of world peace through the advancement of the rule of law believe that if the President and the Senate of the United States would make the advancement of the rule of law their *primary* aim, and would show America to all the peoples of the world as being the champion of this reasonable ideal—that would be the greatest thing the President could do to give coherence and hope and energizing power to the foreign policy of the United States.

4

EAST AND WEST

Luce's birth, boyhood and lifelong interest in China gave an Oriental accent to his public reputation and to part (though certainly not the major part) of his work and thought. He once classed himself with the "hopeless sentimentalists about China," but rejected any suggestion that this meant a divided loyalty to America. He disliked the nickname "Chink" at Hotchkiss and Yale and he winced at the tag of "China boy Luce" from columnists Westbrook Pegler and Walter Winchell. After the Korean war and the fading away of MacArthur, whose trans-Yalu policy he had personally favored, Luce began to take less interest in China, including Formosa. At Taichung he erected a beautiful chapel, designed by I. M. Pei, as a memorial to his father. It was dedicated November 2, 1963. But Luce did not see it until he stopped for his last visit to Formosa (and his old friends the Chiang Kai-sheks) on his way to the Tokyo Olympics in October 1964. In 1965, after many years' lapse, he resumed making speeches about Asia (Numbers 5 and 6 below) but it was now the whole of Asia and its future that preoccupied him rather than China alone.

The period of his most partisan involvement in Chinese affairs was 1937–48. Even before the Japanese attack in 1937 he favored personally, though not overtly in print, an embargo on U.S. scrap exports to Japan. By 1939 he even thought the U.S. "should have challenged with all our power the flagrantly illegal conquest of Manchuria in 1931." The war in China was largely neglected by the American press and public before Pearl Harbor, and a trip to

Chungking and the front lines which he and Clare Luce made in May 1941 (she called it an "escape into reality") gave them something of a scoop when they described it in LIFE *(June 30, 1941, page 344). This trip also gave him material for his most intense period of speechmaking, a period in which he sparked a $5-million fund-raising campaign—even writing to every* TIME *subscriber on his own letterhead: "If every* TIME *subscriber would give $5, we would complete a fund for China worthy of America."*

It was the cause of China that brought to a climax Luce's mounting differences with F.D.R. and the official conduct of the war. Luce was one of those who thought the China front should have a somewhat higher priority on lend-lease schedules than Roosevelt and Marshall, with their Hitler-first strategy, were willing to give it. These policy differences, though marginal in fact, were magnified in public argument to the point where Luce and his allies were called "Asia-firsters" and later "the China lobby."

The issue of aid to China grew desperate toward the end of the war against Japan, when the latent Chinese civil war revived. Luce believed the U.S. owed its wartime ally, Chiang's Republic of China, full military support in installing it as the legitimate government in Nanking, as the U.S. had restored de Gaulle in Paris. His correspondent in China, Theodore H. White, came to believe that Chiang's was not a viable government without a purge of the Kuomintang and even a coalition with the Communists. Luce and White quarreled on this issue in December 1944. But White's view of the Kuomintang had so much support in U.S. Army and diplomatic circles that Luce's pro-Chiang bias made enemies in China as well as at home. Knowing this, Luce felt obliged to advise his management executive committee "of the possible serious error of my policy in re China." Luce went on: "For myself—barring details of execution—I have not the slightest doubt that our policy has been right. . . . Nevertheless, it is, in some respects, a dangerous policy to pursue and I shall be glad to receive from any of you advice and counsel thereon." The committee did not ask him to change it.

The propaganda war between Mao Tse-tung's "agrarian reformers" and the Kuomintang, of which Americans were the chief targets, was already presaging the imminent civil war. To Far East correspondent William Gray, Luce cabled on August 16, 1945, what he called "a brief statement of our journalistic and editorial policy toward Chinese affairs":

"*(1) Our basic policy is to present the news in accurate nonpartisan and understandable manner. (2) We accept just as our government accepts Chiang as the head of the duly constituted and duly recognized China and loyal ally of America. (3) As between the liberal and reactionary forces loyal to Chiang, we favor the liberal. (4) We are not prepared to have any part whatever in any propagandistic efforts to overthrow the existing government of China. (5) We believe that it's always been and is at least as much to the interest of the U.S. to aid our ally Chiang as it was to aid our ally Stalin. (6) Finally, in accordance with the historic policy of the U.S. laid down by outstanding Secretaries of State from Hay to Hull, we believe that U.S. principles and interests will be best served by an independent China free of foreign domination of any sort. This is not sent to you for your guidance in reporting the news. It is sent to you simply as a sort of first-aid kit to help you in the fierce partisan and propagandistic battle which you may encounter in Asia.*"

A year before Chiang's flight from the mainland in 1949, Luce was still attempting to get him all-out U.S. support. Not only had he published a "last call" argument for U.S. intervention by William Bullitt in LIFE (October 13, 1947), but in January 1948 he personally lobbied high-placed friends like Under Secretary of State Robert Lovett and Senator Arthur Vandenberg. By then he was bitter and almost without hope. "The measure of the degradation of American policy in the Pacific," he wrote Vandenberg on January 12, "is the fact that a few guys like Judd * and me have to go about peddling a vital interest of the United States and a historic article of U.S. foreign policy as if it were some sort of bottled chop suey that we were trying to sneak through the Pure Food Laws. This was certainly not the case in the time of John Hay."

Dean Acheson asked for time to let the dust settle on the China tragedy and time did at least cool its passions. Teddy White and the Luces resumed their friendship in the 1950s. By 1965, Luce could write the analytical memoir about the fall of China that is Number 4 below.

* Dr. Walter Judd, who had been a medical missionary in China before the war, was a U.S. Congressman from Minnesota from 1943 to 1963.

1   THE CHINA COLLEGES

In 1941, Luce threw all his spare energies into the United China Appeal (later United China Relief), making fifteen speeches on the subject between December 1940, when he became a director of the Appeal, and Pearl Harbor. The following is from a speech in Boston, March 12, 1941.

One beautiful day, the summer before the war began, I found myself not far from the village in the French Alps where lived that extraordinarily intuitive female, Gertrude Stein. Never having seen her before, I was surprised to find how American the famous expatriate was—in her accent and in her detailed knowledge of American affairs. She did not know that I had any special interest in China, and we had been speaking not at all about China but only about the frustrations and failure of American life. You can then imagine my surprise when suddenly she announced: "The only way for America to save herself is for America to save China!" We shall not attempt today to justify any such extreme oracular utterance. But—who knows? At the moment it seems rather the other way around—it would seem that for four years, with infinite patience and fortitude, China had been helping to save America— while America slept. In any case, today every thoughtful American knows that somehow the Chinese people are enormously important to us and we to them.

May I tell you of just a few of the things which are represented in the United China Appeal? Among them are thirteen colleges and universities. These colleges are teaching while the bullets fly and the bombs fall, teaching chemistry and history and mathematics and art and music and philosophy. Will you let me speak of these colleges simply in a small autobiographical fragment?

I was born on the campus of the first Christian college in China. Certainly it was Christian, college it might be by courtesy, but it was not a campus. Two or three brick barracklike buildings narrowly enclosing a small sort of drill ground housed the first pioneers of Western learning in Cathay.

When the founder of that college, Calvin Mateer, sailed for China in the 1860s, he was 166 days on the water. In his first twenty or thirty years in the coastal town on the Shantung promontory, he saw cholera and other plagues sweep over the province a dozen times and carry with them tens of thousands of Chinese. Death took his colleagues and their wives and children, and so, when I was a boy, little American graveyards had long since begun to write their modest memories into the scroll of Chinese history. Many a time Mateer saw the blood of riot and civil war spilled in the streets of the cities and the smoke of the burning villages set afire by tortured ignorance and fed by despair and poverty and famine. Far away in the palaces of Peking the lords and ladies fingered the wine of courtesy. Far away in the drawing rooms of New York and Boston cultured people spoke of not interfering with the wise, beautiful old culture of China. But Calvin Mateer knew better. He knew the Chinese people as few Chinese emperors have ever known them. And he interfered—oh, profoundly he interfered. And for that interference, the true philosophers of modern China, men like Ambassador Hu Shih,* are today deeply grateful. The dose that Dr. Mateer began to inject into the old veins of China from his obscure corner of an obscure coastal town may have been a little severe. For the dose he offered them was the doctrine of grace on the one hand and the second law of thermodynamics on the other. The patient reacted strongly—and continues to react. Dr. Mateer's therapy may have been a little violent—and not perfectly suited to the patient—but it started a revolution which will never end until the Chinese people can look themselves in the face and look the world in the face and say without arrogance or apology: We Chinese people are as worthy of our time as the creative followers of Confucius and Mencius were of their time more than 2,000 years ago.

At the turn of the 20th century, when my father joined the infant faculty, he hastily brushed up on his physics, hastily forgot his Greek—and quickly discovered that the time had already come

---

* China's ambassador to the U.S. 1938–42.

to think in larger terms. So large were the terms that they were a little terrifying to some missionary folk. But not to Dr. Mateer. His long beard was steely gray now, but his great eyes could still look 100 years ahead. One of my earliest recollections is the excitement and argumentation about "moving the college." On the other side of the coastal hills, on the inland plain, a new campus was built—a real little campus this time with a tower in the middle, a star-gazing observatory in the corner, and, most wonderful of all, an athletic field. And they called it Shantung Christian *University*. How brave the name—University! Think of the meaning of that moment in 1904, when for the first time that word was heard among 50 million people. How valiant was the faith and hope and love which could fling out such a sign and symbol of truth over so vast a sea of immemorial ignorance and superstition and fear and poverty.

For ten years the university prospered and increasingly justified its title, all the while giving to the new Republic of China more than its share of leaders. There were not enough leaders to transform China over night, but enough to make that transformation someday inevitable. And then—but this was "after my time," to use an old-China-hand expression—Shantung University moved right to the center of the province—with an even bigger campus, and it became known as Chefoo University, with special emphasis given to its medical school.

By this time there were ten or twelve Christian universities in China. But one was missing—there was no outstanding institution in Peking, the cultural capital of old China. And so the last, and I think it can be said by generous agreement the greatest, task of university building in China was the creation of Yenching University at Peking. My father's part in this was largely that of the humble beggarman—he got the money. But there was one other phase of Yenching with which he was concerned, and I mention it here as deeply symbolic of the development of Chinese-American relations. It is the matter of architecture. Shantung University, like most foreign buildings in China, whether commercial or missionary, had been built in American style, a plain and to be sure useful and economical American style, but esthetically empty. This bothered my father—and one of his most cherished dreams came true when the architect, Henry Killam Murphy, worked out for Yenching a magnificent blending of American functionalism and gay, brilliant Chinese beauty. And this merging of the American into the Chinese was simply the outward and visible symbol of an inward and spiritual grace which all the American leaders of education in China have cultivated for years and years—namely, the desire that in the management of their institutions, Americans should become less and less and Chinese more and more. Today most of the colleges are mostly run by Chinese. If this be imperialism, make the most of it—and if this is imperialism, the Chinese would say: give us more.

As the conflict with Japan has dragged on year after year, these thirteen colleges have gone steadily ahead with their work in one place or another. Dormitories and classrooms have been crowded to the limit. Despite all the dangers and difficulties, both Chinese and Western staff members of the colleges have remained at their posts. Several of them have lost their lives as a result. They have stood before the Chinese people as a practical and indispensable symbol of the enduring friendship and understanding of the American people. The young men and women whom they are training in increasing numbers today will be the leaders of the new China.

2   FOUR MESSAGES FROM CHINA

When Luce and his wife made their visit to Chungking and the front lines in May 1941, there had been very few American reporters in China for two years. The trip gave Luce material for many more speeches for United China Relief. The following is from a speech in New York City, June 18.

I promised to bring you a message from China, from Generalissimo Chiang Kai-shek and Madame Chiang. Every moment in China has its message for America. Out of them all, I have chosen four. One from the Generalissimo, of course, and then one from a

Communist, one from a mud wall and one—well, one that concerns you most of all.

The message from the Generalissimo is all the more interesting because the words were spoken in the course of an earnest conversation, not made up for a message. We were talking very brass tacks. The Generalissimo, in his analytical manner, quiet, precise, intense, was dealing with military matters. At one point I asked him what he thought about the progress of the war in Europe, and, since we were talking brass tacks, I was expecting a shrewd judicial answer. And this is what he said: "The war in Europe is not merely a matter of relative firepower. This is a war of good against evil, of law against lawlessness, of humanity against tyranny. Therefore, it concerns every man. And, therefore, it cannot end until good has prevailed over evil."

Oversimplification? The Generalissimo's is a very subtle and complex mind. All the right on one side and all the wrong on the other? Oh no, the Generalissimo will tell you plenty that's wrong in China, lots of what's wrong with the British Empire—and even with America. But sometimes in the course of human events it is necessary for men to strike a balance, to make ultimate decisions, to act and never to turn back. Chiang Kai-shek has done just that. He is not asking our help as the price of his resistance. He has been fighting for four years, paying a stiff price in cash or goods for every bit of supplies from Russia or anywhere else. And whatever we do, he will go on fighting to the last bullet.

My second message is from a Communist. Having uttered that horrid word, I suppose I ought to report to you my findings on the Communist problem in China. That's easy. I found that the one form of American aid which Chiang Kai-shek has received in great abundance is advice on how to handle the Communists. This advice has been free of charge—gratis. The Gissimo is, I am sure, most grateful, and since the Chinese always wish to repay their debts, he may even look forward to repaying this debt to us with interest. For he is not unaware that we, too, have a Communist problem.

Fortunately for Chiang Kai-shek, some of the Chinese Communists love China better than Moscow. It is from one of these that I bring you a message. She was a Swedish girl who several years ago became devoted to the Chinese Communists—like some other left-wingers we know. At a small dinner given by Chou En-lai, the Communist leader, she said to me: "You know the remarkable

thing about China is that everyone who comes here becomes en-
chanted with the tremendous possibilities for achieving whatever it
is they want to achieve." And then she documented, "Take the
German military advisers. Two years ago they hated to leave—
they practically wept over their wine for days before departure.
They wanted to make armies, and the longer they stayed in China,
the more they became convinced of the perfectly beautiful, wonderful armies they could make in China. You see," she added, "it's
just the same—with soldiers, with businessmen, with missionaries,
with doctors, with Communists, with Fascists—anybody who
really wants to do something with and about people can do more of
it here than anywhere in the world."

Surely I do not need to add that this is true not because the
Chinese are suckers and pushovers, a soft, pliant mass of humanity, but just for the opposite reason—the Chinese are tough-
minded, intelligent, realistic—and added to all that now, is a vital
eagerness to build the new highroads of progress. The ideas, the
techniques, which will thrive in China are those which can meet the
test of material and spiritual reality.

What is spiritual reality? I bring you now a message from a
mud wall. It was a wall which screened the entrance to a small
ravine wherein was quartered a company of Chinese soldiers just a
few miles from the front lines. On the wall, in the form of a
diagram, was a complete outline of Sun Yat-sen's program for
China. It began with the simple necessities of food, shelter and
family. It moved on to other things—education, industry, national
defense. But what were the two words at the very end—at the
climax of the diagram—that's what I was most curious about. The
last two words were *ho jen*. And what does that mean? That means
universal brotherhood. And that's the message I bring you from
the mud wall.

And now, finally, I bring you a message that concerns us as
Americans most. I bring you a message from the A.E.F.—the first
A.E.F. of World War II—the American Expeditionary Force in
China. Is there one? Of course there is. There has always been one
in China, some five to ten thousand Americans of all kinds—educators, missionaries, businessmen, soldiers, diplomats—most of them
good, some of them not quite so good, but all of them working with
China, hoping with China and sharing with China an unshakable
faith in that great future when China will be a mighty force on the

side of peace and decency.

This A.E.F. stands higher in Chinese esteem today than ever before. And its numbers are growing. American experts are now on the Burma Road, resolved to double and quadruple its traffic. And now American aviators are enlisting with China—our first real heroes of the war, going out to back up the heroism which our A.E.F. has already shown out there in these terrible years. If any of you knows any of them personally, do not fail to write them. They feel very far away. They need, they have earned encouragement. But my job is to bring you a message from them. I do so in the words of Rewi Alley, the brave, tough organizer of the Industrial Cooperatives.* He happens to be a New Zealander but he is working with our A.E.F. Many of you know him, and America is much in his mind. His face, desperately earnest, is before me at this moment. His words are these: "If only they realized . . . if only Americans knew. . . ." I heard these words, these identical words, a hundred times. If only Americans knew what? If only Americans knew how tremendously much they could achieve in China today—if only they knew what colossal things could be done with only a little money, a little sympathy, a little courage.

* Thousands of small, mobile factory units known as Free China's "guerrilla industry."

---

3   CHINA'S POSTWAR DREAMS

After Pearl Harbor the U.S.-China alliance became official and the Chinese cause became a matter of lobbying for marginal increments of lend-lease in competition with the higher-priority European front. Luce's speeches on China accordingly shifted their emphasis to postwar prospects. The following is from a speech at Rochester, April 22, 1942. The Chinese longing for peace here described was to be a factor in the government's defeat by the Communists.

Most Americans may think China is fighting for survival. If so, they are just 100 per cent wrong. Survival of what? Survival of the China of the early 20th century—corrupt, disunited, humiliated, famine-cursed and plague-smitten? Oh, no. Survival of what? Of Confucius and dear old gentleman scholars with long fingernails and polite manners? Oh, no. To be sure, China is rediscovering Confucius, curiously assisted in that rediscovery by the light of Christianity. To be sure, Wisdom will always be in China the Prince of Virtues. But it is not for survival China fights—not the survival of the China of twenty years ago or of twenty centuries ago. China fights for a new and more excellent nation than ever inhabited the Flowery Kingdom—to re-establish in that nation the best of the past and to go on to greet a new sun shining upon a universal humanity from a universal heaven.

One summer's night ten years ago—which is only yesterday—I found myself in a garden in a small Chinese city near Peking. A Chinese professor sat talking to me about the English poets. In the moonlight the nine stories of a pagoda glistened. And I would have been well content that night to believe that we are only such stuff as dreams are made of. But this professor's dreams were not of gossamer: they were dreams of the triumph of the human spirit through sacrifice and death. He told me his hopes for China. Strange hopes they were. For he wished China to fight then, instantly. He wished China to fight in order to be defeated. He wished China to be driven back across the plains into the mountains, up the river and deeper into the mountains—back, back, until all that remained of China should be pure gold of the spirit, all dross burned away. And from that irreducible China would come, in God's time, a stronger and more excellent nation on the earth.

My friend of the moonlit garden has had his wish. The great agony has come to his people. Millions have died a brutal death, millions more have suffered torment. It is a terrible thing for a man to have wished all this for his country and his people—and to have had the wish come true. But happily for my friend—for the whole world—out of this death there has issued life. Everywhere in China today, life is bursting forth—fresh and strong and vigorous—life such as has not been seen in Asia in many centuries.

The poet, crying from the depths to his creator, writes: "Must Thy harvest-fields be dunged with rotten death?" In China today they understand that it must be so. When I asked a Chinese soldier why he was so sure of victory, he replied, "Because I am no longer afraid to die."

It is certain that the Chinese people have suffered. But unless we clearly understand why they suffer, our sympathy is not truly enlightened or aroused. There is a purpose in this struggle. The Chinese know what they want. They want to drive the Japanese out of China, of course. But that is not all they want. They have other and larger and quite definite aims and desires.

Most specifically, the Chinese people want to achieve some small part of the material welfare of this age of science and technology. They want it—and intend to have it soon. When Chiang Kai-shek was asked what he was going to do when the war ended, he said: "Build railroads." Their plans for the railroads are drawn. With modern transportation they will solve a basic fault in their agriculture—the specter of famine in one province while ruinous surpluses are piling up in another. Their plans are also drawn for hydroelectric power plants. And they want quantities of machinery—and the technical skill to go with it. In short, they want to lift, and lift again, their standard of living.

But they have other equally insistent purposes. They look for a great artistic and intellectual revival. They are eager for good government—local as well as national—in a land which has often shown a genius for government.

And most of all, there is a desire—seen in many practical manifestations—for the achievement of a moral integrity both personal and national. If it could ever be said of any people anywhere at any time, I think it can be said of the Chinese today: Blessed are they, for they hunger and thirst after righteousness.

This, then, is the pattern of victory: the deep desires of men formulated into a common resolution; a vast population of highly individualistic people united to the death; a citizen army accepting unfamiliar discipline and unspeakable hardship to fight for a government which can barely feed it and cannot give it arms to match its foes; a leader, consecrated to one aim, whom a skeptical people trusts as a child trusts his father in the moment of peril—this is the pattern of victory.

What, then, would be victory itself? Let me conjure this picture in fragmentary human terms. First of all, for millions of Chinese it means a return from exile to their homes. Chungking is a city of exiles. Thousands of men and women who compose the wartime government under bombs—they will be glad to have the bombs cease, but I think they will be even gladder to go home—one to the immemorial beauty of Peking, another to the lovely lakes of Hangchow, and another to the bustle of Shanghai. In a thousand cities and towns of China, a million little shops will open up again —each shop the joyous pride and care of its owner. Canton, today a ghost city of the dead, will hum again and victory may be sweetest of all in that city which has given so much to the creation of the Republic of China. In Nanking the government, finding much destroyed, will resume again the architecture of a capitol worthy of the republic. Everywhere schools and colleges will be bursting to overflow with young people more eager to learn than to fight. Around and endlessly beyond the cities, the greatest number of self-respecting farmers in the world will be able to do a day's work and get a night's sleep, free from their daily battle of Lexington. As people in town and country seek the benefits of their victory— better transportation, wider credit, more education—there will certainly be some confusion. But there will be joy and hope in that confusion.

A whole nation going back to its homes—each man belonging more than ever to his place because he won it by trial of battle. Yes, that would be victory.

But it is a greater victory than that. For the nation now ready to go back to its homes is a far greater nation than the nation which was driven from its homes with rape and carnage. Each man knows now that he is a part of something greater than himself. For he is a part of a nation which he himself has called into being.

4 HOW CHINA FELL

Luce's dreams—and those of so many Chinese—for post-war peace and prosperity in Asia began to die in 1946. The circumstances are recounted in the following chapter from the unfinished book which Luce was working

*on at the time of his death. Actually, Luce did not
abandon all hope for a free China until early 1948.*

Late in 1945, President Truman learned that Chiang Kai-shek
was having trouble in establishing the authority of his government
over China. So he telephoned the man whom he considered to be
the greatest of all living Americans—General George C. Marshall.
This great man was on his farm in Virginia, where he thought he
had retired from all active duty. Responding to the call of the
President, Marshall went to Washington and thence to Nanking,
the capital of China, with full power of attorney to act on the
Chinese scene.

Nearly a year later, in November, I and two of my editorial
colleagues were sent to Nanking in an Air Force plane by Stuart
Symington, a close friend of President Truman's and Secretary of
the Air Force. It provided me with just about the most fascinating
week of my life. On a dawn-to-midnight schedule, I saw nearly
everybody in Nanking. And when it was over, I knew the Marshall
mission had failed.

In order to have even the most elementary understanding of why
it failed, it is necessary to go back to August 14, 1945, the day the
war ended. The situation in China at war's end was extremely odd.
When the war ended on the battleship *Missouri*, Chiang Kai-shek
and his armies were in Chungking and in the Far West of China
(analogous, say, to Denver and the Rocky Mountains). The Japanese were in occupation of the whole of East China, from the cold
but fertile plains of Manchuria to the warm rice paddies of the
South. East China included the whole of the immense Yangtze
River Valley and nearly all the major cities such as Peking, Tien-
tsin, Nanking, Shanghai. It included most of the wealth and most
of what had been modernized in China. There were about one million Japanese soldiers. All the Japanese soldiers surrendered to
Chiang Kai-shek—that is to say, to his representatives, who had to
be flown to various centers to take the surrender, and to a few of
Chiang's guerrilla commanders, who had survived the eight years
of war.

This extremely odd * situation can perhaps be most vividly por-
trayed by briefly employing one of those "ifs" of history. *If the*

---

* The oddity lay in the fact that although Chiang's representatives took
the Japanese surrender, his troops were not in a position to control the
surrendered territory.

U.S. had not dropped the bomb on Hiroshima, the situation in China by the summer of 1946 would have been utterly different. For by then Chiang Kai-shek, accompanied by victorious armies, would have been in control of all of South China, of Shanghai and Nanking and all the Yangtze Valley.

Until Truman took his decision, the expectation had been that the weight of American military power would be transferred to the Pacific and then, in the spring of 1946, General MacArthur would lead a massive assault on Japan. This assault, it was calculated, might cost up to 200,000 American casualties and the avoidance of those casualties is the main justification for dropping the bomb.

Actually, however, Japan was literally tottering on its last legs. In May–June of 1945, on a tour of the Pacific theater, I spent a morning at Cavite in the Philippines with Admiral Frank Wagner in front of huge maps. Admiral Wagner was in charge of air search-and-patrol of all the East Asian seas and coasts. He showed me that in all those millions of square miles there was literally not a single target worth the powder to blow it up; there were only junks and mostly small ones at that.

Similarly, I dined one night with Admiral Radford * on the carrier *Yorktown* leading a task force from Ulithi to bomb Kyushu, the main southern island of Japan. Radford had invited me to be alone with him in a tiny room far up the superstructure of the *Yorktown*, where not a sound could be heard. Even so, it was in a whisper that he turned to me and said: "Luce, don't you think the war is over?" My reply, of course, was that he should know better than I. For his part, all he could say was that the few little revetments and rural bridges that he might find to bomb in Kyushu wouldn't begin to pay for the fuel he was burning on his task force.

When I got back home, I went straight to my friend Jim Forrestal.† I had hardly completed a sentence before Forrestal picked up the telephone and called Secretary of War Henry Stimson. Stimson having gone to Long Island for the weekend, Forrestal sent me to Under Secretary of State Grew.‡ Both

---

* Arthur Radford later became Chairman of the Joint Chiefs of Staff, 1953–57.

† James Forrestal (1892–1949), the first Secretary of Defense, was at that time Secretary of the Navy.

‡ Joseph Grew (1880–1965) had been Ambassador to Japan for ten years before Pearl Harbor.

Forrestal and Grew and others understood—or strongly hunched—that Japanese surrender could be obtained almost immediately—on one condition, which was that Japan should be allowed to retain the Emperor, which a few months later we did allow. Something was very wrong with the intergovernmental communications in the last months of Roosevelt and the early months of Truman. Just what it was is one of those things which can probably never be figured out by historians.

But let's get back to the illuminating "ifs." If the bomb had not been dropped and if the well-laid plans for the MacArthur invasion had been carried out—then, almost certainly, the following would have occurred on the mainland of China. In September–October of 1945 there would have been a major Chinese offensive, with American-trained Chinese divisions, leading out of the mountain fastness and down to Canton. It would have been successful. Then, during the winter, having regrouped around Canton, the Generalissimo would have marched north and taken the Yangtze Valley as he had done twenty years before. If the Japanese had then surrendered in the spring of 1946, Chiang Kai-shek would have been in a position to move armies up to Peking and Manchuria. He would still have had to face the Mao Tse-tung trouble. But he would have been in an infinitely better position to do so.

I am not saying that thereafter under the government of Chiang Kai-shek all would have come up roses. But Chiang would have had a chance—and I think he deserved that chance. One thing is sure, as I am in a position to testify—the great mass of the Chinese people were not yearning for land reform or anything else. They were deeply happy that the war was over, that the Japanese were out. What they wanted was normalcy. That mood might not have lasted for more than several years—indeed, it presumably would not have. But at war's end what they wanted was quite simply to plant their fields in peace, to go back to the shopkeeping they so much enjoy, to the pleasure of family and festivals.

All of that is what they didn't get. Instead, one consequence of the earlier-than-expected ending of the war was that Mao Tse-tung's Communists, who had conserved their guerrilla forces during the war and who were enclaved in places nearer the strategic north and east, now undertook to make the return to normalcy impossible. They set out to harass, sabotage and destroy the Nationalist government. This they did partly by shooting, but mainly by disrupting the economy by such simple means as tearing up railroad tracks.

So—General Marshall was dispatched to put things right. And in November 1946, I was flown out to see what progress was being made.

I knew many of the people in Nanking—people in government, educators, businessmen and others. I knew General Marshall and I knew very well the American Ambassador, the Reverend John Leighton Stuart, who had been a close friend of my father's. I also knew Chou En-lai. He was there, negotiating with Ambassador Stuart and General Marshall and, through them, with Chiang Kai-shek. I must record the utter confidence as well as the good humor with which Chou En-lai spoke to me. While he didn't say so in so many words, I had the chilling feeling that he expected soon to be in control of all China. At the end of my stay, I figured he was right.

There was one beautiful and memorable day. It was Chiang Kai-shek's birthday. Madame Chiang had arranged an outing. The party consisted of the Generalissimo and the Madame, General and Mrs. Marshall and myself and three or four aides. We traveled for about two hours on a private train to a large lake. There we boarded a houseboat and were served a delicious lunch. We came to an island on the top of which there was an old temple. On the terrace in front of the temple, looking out on the lake, there were steamer chairs. On one of them the Generalissimo stretched out for a nap in the warm November sunlight. The rest of us did likewise.

On the way home we had difficulty getting through the big lakeside city because by then it was known that the Generalissimo was there and the entire populace was in the streets cheering and almost mobbing him and his party.

Back on the train, the Chiang Kai-sheks retired to a compartment. I thought that General Marshall would proceed to tell me about the progress of his mission. But no—perhaps he didn't think it was the right place, but, in any case, what I got was a long and earnest exhortation on the necessity for universal military service in the U.S.

Back in Nanking in the evening, I went, as I did nearly every night after dinner, to have a chat with Ambassador Stuart. This night he was especially disturbed. He had been conferring with Chou En-lai and he said to me, in evident astonishment: "You know, Harry, these Communists don't *think* like Chinese." The significance of this remark was that Leighton Stuart was known, both favorably and critically, as one of the few Westerners who knew China so well that "he thinks like a Chinese."

The next day I had my two- or three-hour briefing from General Marshall. What Marshall was trying to do was essentially to get the Communists and the government together—that is, to form a coalition. This was nasty medicine for Chiang, whose government was the lawful government of China and who had been the loyal ally of the United States. And it was naive, for even if the Communists were to join a coalition they had no intention of settling for anything less than a complete conquest of China. The only alternative was to give full support to Chiang, including the use of American troops. That is what Ambassador Stuart favored. So we had the ironic situation of the man of God favoring military action, and the soldier unwilling to use the sword.

History says that the Communists took over mainland China in 1949. I have trouble remembering that date, because as far as I am concerned, the Communists had won in 1946, when the Marshall mission ended. The General went home after Christmas. The mission had been a tragedy for him and for China and for the cause of human freedom.

5 EVEN MORE IMPORTANT THAN COMMUNISM

Luce spoke or wrote little about China after 1948 until late 1965, when the clear need for a new U.S. policy toward Red China—a policy which Professor A. Doak Barnett called "containment without isolation"—inspired Luce's concern for a new "Transpacific Dialogue." That was his title for this speech to the Commonwealth Club of San Francisco, December 3, 1965.

> *East is East and West is West, and*
> *never the twain shall meet,*
> *Till Earth and Sky stand presently at*
> *God's great Judgment Seat.*

Some would say that Rudyard Kipling's dictum has been obsoleted by the events of the 20th century. I would say that East and West have just barely begun to meet. Whether a real meeting of the minds will occur remains very much to be seen. And so I venture to speak to you today about the two great halves into which mankind is really divided—the Orient and the Occident, divided by reason of thousands of years of quite separate history, resulting in profoundly different intellectual, ethical and political patterns of thought and feeling.

As for us Americans, a sweeping summary of our recent past and our future imperative might go as follows. In the first half of the 20th century we rejoined Europe, rescued it from its civil wars and became the leader of the West. In the second half of the 20th century, we will test our leadership of the world by whether or not we can do our part in bringing East and West together in basic mutual understandings, intellectual, ethical and political.

Twenty years ago, just after the war, Professor Northrop of Yale published his famous book, *The Meeting of East and West.* He began by saying:

> The most important ideological conflict confronting our world is the one rendered inescapable by the major event of our time—the meeting of East and West. Within the all-embracing and deep-going issues raised by this momentous occurrence the other ideological conflicts of our world are partial components.

I thoroughly agree that the East-West confrontation is even more important than the struggle with Communism. Communism becomes every day more irrelevant to the future of the world, both because of its economic incompetence and its absurd philosophy. Atomic-powered Russia is, of course, another matter. As a matter of power politics, Russia is still a formidable enemy. But, ideologically, the East-West problem remains, as Northrop said, the top priority, and I would add that it is within the East-West conflict that Communism remains a danger. Communism is still a danger in the Orient because of the intellectual and moral confusion caused by the breakdown of Asia's traditional thought patterns under the impact of the West. The West had a shattering effect on the Orient but was unable to be constructive, partly because the West itself was going through a period of revolutionary change and intellectual confusion and also because of the West's indifference to and ignorance of the mind and soul of Asia.

Today the prospects for dialogue between West and East are immensely better than they were only a short while ago. When I was at Yale there was only one course on Oriental history—it was a two-hour course and was attended by six students. The situation was hardly any better on the day of Pearl Harbor. At that time it would have been hard to find twenty Asian experts in the whole country. Today former Ambassador [to Thailand] Kenneth T. Young Jr., head of the Asia Society, counts at least 2,000 experts and says that number will be doubled in a few years. At a recent week-long visit with Yale undergraduates, I found in the course of casual conversation that hundreds of students are taking courses in Oriental history and philosophy, and quite a number of them are actually learning the Chinese language.

We also learn by experience, which often means bitter experience, which often means war. In mid-20th century, we engaged the Japanese in a death-grip struggle. We put on a magnificent performance in the occupation of Japan. We fought a dangerous and frustrating war with the Chinese in Korea, and meanwhile we took command of the Pacific Ocean—70 million square miles of it. And now again, we are getting acquainted with Orientals, friends and foes, in the cities and the treacherous jungles of Vietnam. The list of our recent discoveries and experiences in Asia is almost endless.

And, of course, our experience is not all grim. The tourist visiting Tokyo for the Olympics and making his way round to Hong Kong and Bangkok and Bombay finds much that is exotic, but he is perhaps even more impressed by how all the great cities of the world get to look more and more alike, with their skyscrapers, traffic jams and discothèques—and television in every hotel room. In the ordinary ways of life, in the adaptation of every sort of technology, the world seems to be becoming one worldwide civilization.

But all of this does not go to the heart of the matter. The heart of the matter is that we have hardly begun to plumb the profundities of differences which lie between West and East.

These fundamentals were set forth in Professor Northrop's book, at least a minor classic of philosophic analysis. Professor Northrop's conclusion is that the thought patterns of the West are logical and objective and those of the East are subjective and spiritual. This is sometimes called the theory of complementarity: that the East and the West complement each other. Put it very crudely, and the equation comes out that the West has half the truth and the East has the other half, and if you put the two together, then you have the whole truth about human nature and destiny. That view has long had a wide appeal. It was Northrop's genius to give it highest technical expression.

But I hold a contrary view. The view which I believe accords with the facts of our time has been best expressed by Bishop Stephen F. Bayne Jr., formerly of the State of Washington. In very summary terms, it would be as follows: at this point in history, the East has little if anything to say or to propose to the West. It is the West which must speak to the East out of our complex experience and faith. This does not mean that the future of mankind will be fashioned by the West. It does mean that the future of mankind will be fashioned by the response of the East to the West. The responsibility of the West is to know what it is it has to say, and to say it well—to give effective reasons for the faith that is in us.

The response of the East to the West is already obvious in many ways. The East is eager to acquire our technology. That is to say, the nations of the East want the obviously useful material end products of Western civilization. But what lies behind and beneath modern plumbing and the automobile and atomic energy? We might say that what lies behind our technology is the Renaissance, with its enthusiasm for the expansion of human power and happiness through knowledge. Actually, we must go much further back —to the miracle of Greece, with its extraordinary leap into the logic of mathematics and philosophic reason.

There is one story which perhaps better than any other illustrates the profound difference in the soul of the East and of the West. It is a Greek story, the myth of Prometheus—the story of the hero who defied the gods in order to bring fire to men. For that offense to Olympus, he was tied to a rock and for endless days had his liver torn out by a vulture.

Now there is no such story in the whole vast mass of Oriental myth. Weird and various as is the mythology of the East, there is nothing like this—for the idea of defying the gods is utterly repugnant to the East.

Prometheus stands for progress—onward and upward, from the dung heap to the stars! The Oriental idea is more nearly one of endless cycles of recurrence.

Prometheus stands for progress as in the conquest of nature. The classic Chinese idea is harmony—of man with nature. You can see this in a thousand paintings of the Sung dynasty. There amid romantic hills and rushing streams you will see, in some modest corner, the tiny figure of a man contemplating—it is the artist himself, placing himself *in* nature, not above nature or in contest with it, but harmoniously *in* it.

There are two important Oriental attitudes toward nature. One we have already described—the idea of harmony. The other attitude, notably Buddhist, is that all that is physical is an illusion. We might call it the wish to escape from nature and from all that we would call reality and they illusion.

Now these fundamental notions, expressed either in myth or in formal philosophy, obviously have their reflection in political ideas. And it is of political ideas that I wish especially to speak.

In Aspen, Colorado, this summer, Mortimer Adler * gave a notable paper on East-West, which he says he would have entitled "the yeast from the West" . . . except that an Indian economist beat him to it. Adler said that the first great invention of the Greeks was the *polis*, the city-state, from which we get our word politics. The invention of the *polis* involved two related inventions:

(1) The invention of the constitution and constitutional government; and

(2) the invention of the primary constitutional office, namely, the office of citizen.

The triple invention—the city, the constitution, the citizen—finds hardly any equivalents in Oriental concepts.

There is another thing which has developed in the West and not in the East. That, quite simply, is law. There were no lawyers in

* Director of the Institute for Philosophical Research and co-editor with Robert Hutchins of *Great Books of the Western World*.

India until the British came—and now there may be too many. There is not a single lawyer in China today—and there never was. They had magistrates in China—and now commissars.

Of course, every tribe and civilization is somehow governed—by tribal chiefs, by mandarins, by beneficent emperors or by commissars. The point simply is that government in the Orient has never been characterized by principles of law or by positive law under which all men are equal.

Will Durant says in his volume on Rome: "As Greece stands in history for freedom, so Rome stands for order; and as Greece bequeathed democracy and philosophy as the foundations of individual liberty, so Rome has left us its laws and its traditions of administration, as the bases of social order. To unite these diverse legacies . . . is the elemental task of statesmanship."

The diverse tendencies of which Durant speaks are freedom and order and it is in these terms that the politics of the West has been fought out and worked out—at painful cost but with considerable success. But these are not the terms which have patterned the politics of the Orient. And that is the heart of the matter.

What does the United States stand for? Surely we can agree on one rubric: we stand for liberty under law. And that, essentially, is what the West has to say to the East.

The East is in a truly revolutionary condition, seeking to become modern, seeking, that is, to become something radically different from what it has been. It is this painful quest for modernity which makes it the duty of the West to offer the best that it knows and has—not only in technology but, more important, to offer whatever we think we know of the universal goods of liberty and law.

The question still remains—what can actually be done about such a seemingly abstract and amorphous task?

Before I suggest an answer to that question let me tell you about one of the most heartrending experiences of my life. It was in November 1946, in Nanking, near the end of the Marshall mission to arrange matters in China—that truly tragic failure. I was on a somewhat special mission requiring me to see scores of people from Chiang Kai-shek and Chou En-lai and General Marshall on through the top echelons. In the midst of this overloaded schedule, I began to get telephone messages from Madame Dr. Wu, the distinguished president of the best women's college in China. I had neither time nor energy to return the calls, but they kept on coming. Finally I said okay, I'll call on Dr. Wu at noon tomorrow. I arrived at the beautiful campus and Dr. Wu hastened me into her inner sanctum. She spoke with highly controlled lucidity and a desperate urgency. She spoke of her girls—it was their first term at college after eight terrible years of war. She spoke of them and of her wide acquaintanceship in Nanking. And she said—my girls and all of us are in deep trouble. The basic trouble is that we have lost the old Chinese morality—call it Confucian—and we have not really assimilated the morality of the West—call it, if you will, Christianity. Now, said she, what you must do when you get back to America is to make the President send us a commission. A commission of what? Of economists? No. A commission of philosophers, of moral philosophers, in which she may have included sociologists and such. This commission must stay in China for a year, said Dr. Wu, and help us articulate a basic moral philosophy for the New China.

Naive, wasn't it? But Dr. Wu was a highly sophisticated person. Desperate, heartrending. I think I knew then that China was doomed to Communist tyranny.

Now let us jump back into 1965. And I cite again Kenneth T. Young Jr., a top expert and a man deeply concerned. He tells me of the rapidly disintegrating factors today in nearly all of Asia. And I think he would not exclude Japan despite all its apparent success. Ambassador Young calls for a total strategy for dealing with Asia. He says: "Perhaps a kind of intellectual Manhattan Project for Asia could pool all our brains and resources on strategic thinking to see if we can come up with a complete formulation of strategy in the next few years."

An intellectual Manhattan Project. I underscore the word "*intellectual*." Of course, Ambassador Young has all the concrete factors in mind—agricultural reform, economic development, etc. I am sure that, like me, he takes great hope from the fact that right now that remarkable American, Eugene Black,* is in Manila organizing the Asian Development Bank. But I am also sure that Ambassador Young means to include in his Manhattan Project the kind of fundamentals which I have tried to put before you today.

Let us imagine that the intellectual Manhattan Project is organ-

---

* Black was head of the International Bank for Reconstruction and Development, 1949–62.

ized. Let us suppose it includes political philosophers—or political scientists, as it is more fashionable to call them today—a rather silly fashion in my view, but let that pass. My question is this: Would these political scientists agree—would they basically agree on what is meant by liberty under law? Would they basically agree on the meaning of the West and of America? Would they basically agree on what it is that the West has to say to the East? Curiously, I think they would.

And if they didn't—if they really couldn't basically agree—then what? Well, then, that would be a sign that Western civilization approaches its end. *Der Untergang des Abendlandes* [the decline of the West]—at last! Europe faltered and America failed.

But I think they would agree, and I will tell you why I think so. However much American political scientists and kindred experts would disagree among themselves, their serious confrontation with the ideas of the East would reveal to them the essential and dynamic unity of the Western tradition—its unity and its validity.

President Kennedy, paraphrasing Wilson, said: "Let us make the world safe for diversity." By all means. That is part of the Western tradition. Diversity to seek truth because there is truth here and now—and on and on into infinity. Diversity to be an independent citizen because there is a city of which the citizen can and ought to be a self-respecting member. Diversity to speak freely because the West posits a universe of coherent dialogue—coherent and meaningful.

Indeed, it is perhaps only in a serious confrontation with the East that the West can rediscover, even recreate, a knowledge of itself. There is one other thing. In trying to explain itself to the East, the men of the West will not only rediscover the meaning of the West; they will also discover with more precision what, in the year 1965, is most lacking in the West—whatever that deficiency may be. Thus they—and we—will end up learning from the East.

The future of mankind depends on the response of the East to the West. And that depends on whether the West knows what it has to say.

6   TOWARD COMPATIBLE SYSTEMS

*The last speech of Luce's life was to students at the
University of California at Santa Barbara, February 1,
1967. A variant of Number 5, it included this view of
the political news from Saigon.*

An extraordinary happening has been going on in Saigon in the
last two or three months. A constitutional convention has been
writing a constitution. In speaking today of basic differences between Asia and the West, I call primary attention to this happening as something radically new in Asia. Both historically and
philosophically, the making of a constitution lies entirely outside
the thousands of years of Asian thought and experience. Until the
20th century, there was no constitution-making in Asia. In recent
decades there has been quite a lot—trial-and-error efforts with
more or less success.

In the Saigon constitution, there are two grand particulars
which are especially significant. There is a bill of rights, guaranteeing certain rights to individual citizens as against the state—
freedom of speech, freedom of religion, freedom from arbitrary arrest and so on. Nothing of this sort is anywhere to be found in the
Asian tradition. Also, the Saigon constitution establishes an independent judiciary, including a Supreme Court to pass on constitutional questions. Nothing resembling an independent judiciary is
in the Asian tradition.

I start with differences in political systems because I assume the
main mutual interest of Occidentals and Orientals is that we should
have peaceful relations and that what would be most highly conducive to peaceful relations would be a compatibility between our
systems of government. I say compatibility; by no means am I
saying identity, or even close similarity. It is desirable and necessary that nations and peoples should develop their own styles of

government and social behavior. But it is also desirable that there should be a recognizable degree of compatibility between the various systems by which the people of one world are to be governed or, better, to govern themselves.

In a prophetic repeal of Kipling's dictum about the non-meeting of East and West, the late, great philosopher William Ernest Hocking, in one of his last books, *The Coming World Civilization*, said: "We seem to stand on the threshold of a new thing, civilization in the singular." In many ways, this new thing would seem to be already here.

As part of going modern, each nation in Asia and in Africa wishes to establish its identity and never in history has there been such a search for identity as now characterizes most of the nations of the world. Nationalism is one expression of this search for identity—that is a Western concept. The West, having invented nationalism, now seeks to transcend it—or at any rate to moderate its claims. What is certainly true about the West is that we ourselves are going through a period of radical change. The gulf between us today and us tomorrow may be an even bigger gulf than the one between East and West. It is said of today's youth that the gulf between them and their parents is greater than previous gulfs between generations. Young people today must be prepared to find, twenty-five years from now, that the gulf between them and their children will be even greater.

Thus, as to East and West, the biggest truth is that all mankind is moving into a future world, whose shape and manner of life we can hardly imagine.

You may recall the refrain of that grim ballad of ten years ago about atomic war: "We'll all go together when we go." It is not simply a question of atomic war. An astonishing future lies predictably ahead. It is into that future that we all go together—or, at any rate, our children, children of the West and children of the East.

5

THE BUSINESSMAN AND HIS SYSTEM

Luce was a pioneer in making news of the semiprivate world of American business. In Time*'s early days, when Briton Hadden did more than his share of the editing, it fell to Luce to take most of the responsibility for the business side of the magazine, and he early developed a knowledge and curiosity about business that lasted his life. The* Time *Business & Finance section was also, in the 1920s, developing more news than the magazine had space to print, and this waste of material, together with Luce's personal interest in the subject, led to the launching of* Fortune *(1930), the business magazine which was very largely Luce's creation.*

Luce early developed theories about business and the business-man. They were based more on hunch and experience than on economics, a discipline he affected to dislike. Having come to know many businessmen, Luce admired some, felt contempt for others, saw good and bad in most, but cast the type in an idealized role. The businessman was to be a key agent, constituting a new aris-tocracy in fact, in Luce's dreams of a coming American civilization.

Luce began speaking in this vein in the Hoover era (page 99). The ensuing Depression, to be sure, proved a poor environment for the development of a loftier job description for tycoons, most of whom were then ready to settle for survival. But Luce persisted, alternating or combining several themes about business in speeches during four decades.

One theme was that modern business was worthy of a greater literature than the "antiquated imaginations" of writers and dram-

atists were giving it. Since these were failing to "create an image of the great businessman" which other businessmen could emulate, "it is evidently left for the journalist to disseminate a more precise and detailed account of what business is all about, and second to prod the indolent mind of Art" (so he said in a lecture in New Haven, April 22, 1930). That purpose, plus the doctrine that all business was affected with a public interest, was the essence of Luce's charter for FORTUNE.

A second theme of his speeches, especially during the Depression, was that the American businessman and the free-enterprise system, if permitted to, could create far higher levels of national income than the 1930s were seeing (Number 4). After World War II, Luce expanded this theme to a world stage (Numbers 7 and 8).

A third major theme was that the businessman belonged historically to the Great Liberal Tradition (page 123), which he had in fact helped create, and that he should rejoin that tradition as a political liberal instead of a conservative, being the real initiator of most social change. His Ohio Bankers Association speech (Number 4) was perhaps the high point of his effort to reconcile business and liberalism.

A fourth theme was that certain characteristics essential to a complex business civilization, notably simple honesty ("the promises men live by"), were badly needed in other spheres of society, notably politics. The businessman was also a natural carrier or agent of political freedom and was gradually becoming, via his expanding corporation, an agent of social welfare and justice (Numbers 9 and 10).

These were the main supporting arguments for Luce's concept of the businessman as aristocrat. Certainly in America, and to a growing extent in Europe, the businessman comes much closer to answering Luce's description, both in fact and in the popular mind, than he did when Luce began his crusade. The intense journalistic spotlight which TIME and FORTUNE turned on the previously curtained world of business was partly responsible for this change.

1   AN ADMONITION

*This excerpt is from a speech to businessmen in Roches-
ter, New York, in March 1928. Considering how long it
would take business—and the Republican party—to
emerge from the political doghouse the Depression and
the New Deal were later to build for them, Luce's
admonitions were prophetic.*

I instinctively share, with most Americans, an almost fantastic
faith in the industrial and commercial future of this country. I
share a temptation to vote for the man who would be most friendly
to what is known as big business. And, of course, it is nonsense,
cheap and rhetorical nonsense, to talk about divorcing business and
politics. You might as well talk about divorcing your heart and
your liver. But, gentlemen, every time politics does a favor for a
particular business, or for a particular class of business, a blow is
struck at the prosperity of this country. The voter who votes for his
business differs from the bribe-giver chiefly in that the bribe-giver
gets a better bargain. American business needs no favors. Let
politicians, great and small, make America politically and socially
safe for 120 million, for 150 million, for 200 million people to live
in; let politicians create a nation, free, proud and patriotic; let them
do that, and American business will owe them a debt which all the
oil companies in the world could not repay. Therefore, gentlemen,
don't vote for the quick profit; vote for the long investment.

Second, far from its being inevitable that business should be
tory in politics, it may be suggested that business ought naturally
to be liberal in politics. I use "tory" to mean any party anywhere
which fundamentally prefers what is to what may be. I use "liberal" as its opposite. Toryism resists change; its original basis was
land; land changes little from spring to spring. But business is the
great innovator. And business is the great believer. Business dis-

cards the good for the better, the best for the once impossible. Business, the believer, discovered credit, which Church and toryism had for centuries tried to outlaw. And with business came liberalism. It remodeled thrones, rewrote constitutions, altered, adapted, renovated, recreated. And what could not be renovated, it removed.

But of late, only within the last fifty years, business has been jockeyed, especially in America, into a defensive, suspicious, false tory position. Defensive, because business, the great innovator in all else, is popularly conceived of as opposing any and all political innovation. Suspicious, because typically its distrust of politicians is exceeded only by its contempt for them. False, because a tory businessman is as unnatural as a liberal Dalai Lama. You often hear, these days, that silly remark that the least government is the best government—silly because, like the intellectual concept of anarchy, it is utopian. It will come true in heaven, in which time and place it will be equally true that the best business is no business.

2   THE TYCOON

The word "tycoon," as a generic term for important businessmen, was introduced by TIME *in 1928, a transplant from its original meaning of "great lord" of feudal Japan. This speech, given by Luce in Rochester, New York, in June 1929, defines the type as it was then emerging and as he felt it would later develop.*

The Japanese tycoon is extinct. It is in our country that the tycoon has reappeared—quite different from the ancient Japanese and far more numerous.

Well, what is a tycoon? He is almost inevitably a rich man, though not necessarily worth more than a million. The electrical tycoonishness of Owen D. Young,* for example, bears no relation

* Young (1874–1962) was then chairman of General Electric Co.

to his wealth, and A.T.&T.'s Gifford * was a tycoon probably before he was a millionaire. And all very rich men are not tycoons. Vincent Astor, for example, can scarcely claim tycoonship. The financier becomes a tycoon when he takes a directing part in an industry or branch of commerce. Thus Arthur Curtiss James,† largest individual railroad stockholder in the U.S., might conceivably *not* be a tycoon, but, as a matter of fact, he is because his railroad empire takes him seriously.

You might suppose that such a conspicuous inhabitant of the globe had long since been annotated and described. Not so, however. The world's greatest reporter is Sinclair Lewis. His were the two greatest scoops of this generation—*Main Street* and *Babbitt*. Now he is just out with what might have been the greatest scoop of his career—for in his book *Dodsworth* he has sighted the tycoon. I said might have been. Mr. Lewis indeed spotted the tycoon, but he was too little familiar with the unseen world in which the tycoon lives to describe him comprehensively as he described George F. Babbitt. For, like all old-style reporters, Mr. Lewis knows practically nothing at all about Business with a capital B.

The American tycoon is not organized. This is something unique in history. *Here, for the first time, we find a civilization in which the most powerful men do not constitute themselves an order.* At first glance you might think that this was due to the individualism of this country. But everyone else in this country is organized except the men of power. The laborers are organized. The preachers, teachers, lawyers, doctors are organized. And no one is more proudly and joyfully organized than the average businessman. Within the next few months a thousand national conventions of various businesses will be held, and regional conventions will number nearer ten thousand. At each convention a tycoon or two will be in attendance, due object of curiosity and honor. But nowhere this year will there be a convention of tycoons. The press would screech with amazement and alarm if one were held.

The title "tycoon" has no moral significance and no intellectual significance. Provided he is within the law, a totally amoral person may be a tycoon. In fact, the legalities of business have been so important in our groping development that perhaps the surest way

* Walter Gifford (1885–1966) was the up-from-the-ranks president of the American Telephone & Telegraph Co.
† James (1887–1941) built an empire that included one-seventh of all U.S. railroad mileage.

to become a tycoon is to start out as a lawyer. Of course, to be a lawyer implies a certain minimum of moral rectitude. A lawyer, also, is not likely to proceed far without some intellectual equipment. A shining example of the lawyer-trained tycoon is the aforementioned Owen D. Young, who is perhaps the best prototype of the new tycoon. But, as we know, many is the tycoon who, outside of let us say his own oil business, is incapable of the simplest logical sequitur.

Now I should like to suggest that a great many factors are contributing to alter this situation and that possibly we will witness within this generation the real emergence of the tycoon as a recognizable member of an order, or at least of a category—the tycoon as public character. Let me list some of these factors.

First, there is the corporation. We have scarcely begun to see the effects of the organization of the wealth of society largely into and by corporations. However large may be personal wealth, corporate wealth will be larger, and most personal wealth will tend to become only something like a life interest in a small part of corporate earnings. Thus the tycoon becomes less and less the owner and more and more the semidetached or, at any rate, detachable manager. Thus he becomes less self-conscious. He does not have to feel that talking about his business is the same as talking about his own private account at the bank.

Second, there is not only the increase in the corporation, but the increase in size of the corporation. Along with this may be put the urge to merge. This, in turn, means that a few men will have the power to speak for an entire branch of our economic civilization. If they have the power to do so, it will soon follow that they will have the responsibility and obligation to do so.

Finally, business demands for its direction at the top greater and greater intellectual powers. Shrewdness is necessary, but it is less and less the shrewdness of the horse trader. Technology is necessary, but it is less and less the technology of the tinker. Personality, as in everything, is necessary, but it is less and less the personality of the apple-cheeked, doorbell-punching drummer, nor yet of the conscientiously boisterous, gin-supplying good fellow.

Now this glance over current tendencies familiar to all of us yields, I think, a forecast, however dim, of the coming tycoon.

He will be, typically, not a boor but what may be most briefly described as a gentleman. That is to say, he will owe his position not to inheritance of a vast fortune, nor to some freak of nature or luck. He will owe it largely, of course, to a genius adaptable to the needs of the age. But, aside from that, he will owe it to careful education and rigorous apprenticeship. This training is primarily useful in giving him a mind which works logically and quickly. But, as a by-product, this training will render him a cultivated citizen of the world. It is likely, therefore, that he will avoid the grosser crudities of the present industrial scene, and will at least be responsive to soundly artistic suggestion. The coming tycoon, furthermore, will have hundreds of acquaintances who speak much the same language as his own. Therefore, when he comes to select aides and provincial governors, he is likely to look to those of similar moral standards and mental processes. Tycoons will become less and less dissimilar as to background, taste and general deportment. So that in 1950, when an oil tycoon and a meat tycoon meet a cinema tycoon, they will recognize each other.

Nature, of course, never produces a perfect type. And among the new-style tycoons we will always see a recurrence of the old style. There will always be the romantic tale of the drug clerk in Kansas * who bet his first thousand dollars on just the right oil lease, and then had wit enough to make out of it the Sinclair Oil Co. There will still be the man who is powerful merely by reason of great inheritance, incredible luck, or a purely manipulatory shrewdness. But it is unmistakable that the tycoon is evolving into a type.

With respect to his public relations, the tycoon 1929 model cuts a ridiculous figure. In the dark ages of the last generation, when business was just emerging, some old sly banker told his press agent to say that he hated publicity. So, for thirty years, many a tycoon has felt it necessary to tell his press agent that he hated publicity. Then, too, the tycoon began to think it was infra dig to be too accessible to the press. So he got into an office behind five other offices and employed three secretaries to do nothing except to say that he didn't receive interviewers. Then, of course, so many tycoons made fools of themselves when they did run into the press that other tycoons thought it best not to risk any such dangerous encounter. So here you have had the tycoon of yesterday and even of today, a potent, forceful character, a master of many men, often

* Harry F. Sinclair (1876–1956), later to be the subject of a profile in FORTUNE (November 1932).

with great powers of imagination, and yet forced by his press complex to be kittenish as a Victorian subdeb or boorish as a lion sickening in captivity. And, of course, there's another reason. The outgoing style of tycoon very often had something to conceal. There was, perhaps, a deal thirty years ago which he doesn't want the press, by any chance, to stumble into. Or perhaps his father started the family fortune by stealing the kitchen sink. Or perhaps his maternal grandfather kept a saloon in St. Louis.

But the chief reason for the outgoing tycoon's press complex had been the Stygian ignorance of business which has almost universally characterized the press. The average reporter knows much more about astronomy than he does about industry. The reason this has been so is fundamentally that the public has never taken much interest in business as business. And the reason that is so is because business as the prime determinant of society began only day before yesterday. But now all this is changing, has changed. No group of stocks in Wall Street has made such a steep and unabating ascent in the last decade as has the news value of American business. This fundamental shift in public curiosity will radically alter the physiognomy of the tycoon as public character.

In order to serve the public, reporters will have to do fewer novels and more economics in their spare time. And perhaps we shall have to put on a few more clean collars so that the nice new clean tycoon will not find us so distasteful.

Confronted with a reporter who knows sufficiently well what he's talking about, the tycoon will have to know what *he's* talking about—which, of course, all genuine tycoons do.

Not only will the tycoon have to know what he's talking about but he'll have to learn how to say it, which very few tycoons do. The tycoon, in turn, will take in a few less leg shows and a little more literature.

A host of results will flow from the development of this business-press relationship. Many more tycoons—and not merely the picturesque ones like storyteller Schwab or baseballer Wrigley *
—will emerge as well-known characters. Being well known, they will be depositories of public trust. As such, they will constantly be called upon for advice and even for positions in local and national

* Charles M. Schwab (1862–1939) was the great steel salesman who helped J. P. Morgan found U.S. Steel and later headed Bethlehem Steel. William Wrigley Jr. (1861–1932) was the chewing-gum tycoon who owned the Chicago Cubs both as a hobby and as a business promotion.

government, and this will be thought to be good.

And so I give you the new tycoon, the newsworthy tycoon. Let him act. We watch.

---

3   LIBERALS, CONSERVATIVES AND LIBERTY

By the New Deal's second year, its impulsive unorthodoxy had alienated or alarmed not only Republican businessmen but many old-line Democrats, including two previous Democratic presidential candidates, John W. Davis and Alfred E. Smith. The latter joined the Du Ponts and other "economic royalists" (F. D. R.'s epithet for them) in supporting the American Liberty League, a propaganda organization claiming that Roosevelt had deserted the cause of liberty and had become a totalitarian dictator. This distortion of the case against Roosevelt boomeranged and helped him to his landslide victory in 1936. But Luce had a more precise and reasoned case against the New Deal—and another one against the conservatives. He spelled them out in this speech at Scranton, Pennsylvania, on April 19, 1934. The first of his "minimum principles" was a bold if crude anticipation of the full-employment policy to be made official in the Employment Act of 1946.

Since today an extensive, if not unlimited, authority is exercised by liberals, we are treated to the highly amusing spectacle of tories decked out in cap and bells crying one to another, "Liberty, give us Liberty." The echo of these cries appears in the press but it meets with little emotional response because the suspicion remains that the contemporary advocates of liberty are chiefly concerned with the perpetuation of their own privileges. The trouble with the conservatives in this country is that they have not had an idea since the Civil War.

I think we can define a series of *minimum* principles which the conservatives must acknowledge and under which they must develop some ideas of action before there can be any hope that our heritage of liberty can be conserved by the conservatives. I will name two of these principles—and vaguely suggest a third.

The first is that a livelihood must be guaranteed to every man. Less than a year ago I was talking with one of the keenest and finest bankers I know. He was scandalized by this proposal. The other day I asked one of the most famed men in the Republican party what he thought. He said: "Yes—it should be done as far as practicable." That, of course, completely dodged the issue. But in my own mind there is no doubt whatever that if either of these men could put aside all his acquired conceptions and with a fresh mind set out to discover what modern America is, he would come inescapably to the conclusion that America can and therefore must guarantee a livelihood to every man. And no qualifications. This does not mean that every man must be guaranteed any share whatever in the staggering quantity of desirable and the even more staggering quantity of undesirable luxuries which we can produce. We can begin by guaranteeing, if you like, a livelihood of comparative hardship, or at any rate of the greatest simplicity. But it must be a guarantee of livelihood. Nor is this really any new thing in our country. It has existed from the foundation and it is doubtful if our government would have existed throughout the 19th century had it not been possible for us to say, not only to our citizens but to millions every year across the seas, "There's a job for you here— come find it. It may be the back-breaking and soul-twisting job of plowing open the northern prairies. Or it may be a daily gamble against death in the rolling mills. But it's a job—no worse than your cousin has in southern Italy or Manchester, and you are free." In fifty years the freedom has become ironic and the job does not exist. But the job can exist. We know that. Therefore it must—and with it the beginnings, at last, of the New Freedom.

The second principle is that there must be a dwelling for every man, woman and child, and that it must conform to some minimum standard of decency. I think we must accept this principle for much the same reason as the first. When man could go out to Nebraska and dig himself a cave of mud and collect from the treeless countryside enough sticks to heat it with, he could say, "This is very bad. It is even worse than I had in Poland. *But I shall make progress* and meanwhile here it is and it is mine and you and the tax collector and the captains with stars on their breasts and destruction in their hearts can leave me alone." But today you cannot say to a man at the Bowery branch of the Y.M.C.A.—here's a ticket to Nebraska.

The third principle that I will only suggest is this: there must be developed a widely understood pattern for the reward of talent. Our first two principles concerned themselves with every man— with the vulgar, the moronic, the unpleasant specimens of humanity and with those who are as poor in spirit as in purse, but whom, for some reason beyond our comprehending, Jesus blessed. This third principle concerns itself with what, humanly speaking, is the superior man.

The greatest practical test of a nation's devotion to liberty is the extent to which it maintains the open door of opportunity. No country has met this test as splendidly as our own. It may have been a credit to our resources rather than to our spirit, but the result remains. Whether or not a boy has wanted to be a research scientist in chemistry, a bad novelist or a millionaire, that boy has had a better chance to achieve his dream if born in 19th-century America than if born at any other time in any other place. But it must be apparent that profound changes in our social organization make it more discouraging today than thirty years ago for the man who is trying to discover his path to the rainbow.

In the whirligig of time, it may very well be that the liberals having fought the battle of liberty for a thousand years, it will soon be the turn of the conservatives to defend her—even at the barricades. But liberty will not be defended except by those who love her. And the question which every conservative must ask himself is whether he loves liberty or only himself.

The future of liberty rests, for the moment, with the reigning liberals, and so it is to Washington that we now proceed.

I do not think the threat to liberty comes from any of the measures of the government or from all of them. Nor does it come from the principles of the New Deal, which are vague and essentially humanitarian. The threat comes from nothing more tangible than a flaw in the spirit of the New Deal, which I can most quickly describe as an animosity which may amount to hate. And what the New Deal hates or tends to hate is, in a word, Big Business.

One of the two real New Dealers to whom the President gave an ambassadorship is Professor Dodd.* Now Professor Dodd of Chicago said of Al Capone that after all he only copied the methods of Big Business. I say that is a damnable libel. But never mind my opinion. General Johnson † just the other day, after a better opportunity to see into Big Business than was ever given to any man, said: "Business is intrinsically straight." Now I submit that most Americans—certainly a vast number of them—would laugh appreciatively with Ambassador Dodd's wisecrack and would accuse General Johnson of an extravagant use of baloney.

The question I raise is this: Does the President laugh heartily with Ambassador Dodd—or does he sincerely agree with General Johnson? I hate Al Capone. Between righteous indignation and brutal hate there is a thin and wavering line. My hate could easily become, let us say, vindictive. Mr. President, do you hate Big Business as I hate Al Capone, and do you propose to teach the American people so to hate?—that is the question I raise.

What I hope is that the season of bitterness and muckraking is perhaps coming to a close. I hope that in the years to come we may reform, above all, our attitude of mind toward modern industry. On the one hand, modern industry is not a private affair governed by mysterious laws of supply and demand which only the witch doctors on their private yachts are capable of understanding. On the other hand, it is not a Machiavellian invention of a clique of capitalists. Modern industry, if we could only encompass it within our feeble imaginations, is the instrument by which it is given us to achieve in our lifetime nearly all that mankind has struggled for in centuries of blood and sweat and futility.

When we perceive this—then we will no longer tolerate any scheme for curbing modern industry. All schemes for the limitation of production, except the conservation of irreplaceable natural resources, will appear to be the most absolute nonsense. Schemes for distribution of unlimited production—ah yes, that is precisely what we must attempt, and with a faith which as yet does not exist in the conservative mind.

Let me say frankly and regretfully that I do not find within Big Business itself much inspiration for this task. But there is certain evidence that Big Business is ripe for inspiration. I do not ask that

* William E. Dodd (1869–1940), University of Chicago historian, was Roosevelt's Ambassador to Germany until 1937.

† Hugh S. Johnson (1882–1942), a general during World War I, headed the National Recovery Administration, 1933–34.

the President should become the inspired leader of the party of Big Business. There should be no such party. Parties should and will cut across Big Business as they do across other areas of life. But is it too much to ask that the President should lead Big Businessmen as he leads others by courage and hope as well as by fear?

---

4   CALCULABILITY OF ABUNDANCE

Before the Ohio Bankers Association in Cleveland, November 10, 1937, Luce further developed his ideas about liberty in an industrial age but also reinforced his case against the New Deal with a demand, to be echoed by Wendell Willkie in the 1940 presidential campaign, for greatly increased national production. "The calculability of abundance" was to become better known a quarter of a century later as "the revolution of rising expectations."

I suppose there will be little disagreement in this room that the business outlook is bad. I suppose we would all agree as to the diagnosis of the trouble. Is it not simply this—that the policies of a powerful President of the United States are based on the assumption that private capitalism will work, whereas in fact private capitalism is not working?

The President takes credit for the fact that the national income has risen from its low of $40 billion [in 1932] to some $65 billion this year. He referred the other day to a possible $100-billion income—which he said might occur "the Lord knows when." * Actually, this happy event does not depend upon the Lord God Jehovah, but rather upon the expectancy of productive expansion in an industrial society. Ten years ago, in 1928, the national income was $80 billion. After ten years, after the full swing of a long decade of peace, we ought to be hitting the trend line of

* It occurred in 1942.

expansion. A national income of $100 billion ought to be in reasonably plain view.

The smallness of our national production today is a national disgrace, a wicked disobedience of the ancient injunction to increase and multiply, a miserable failure to function as the intelligent, creative animals we pride ourselves on being.

Take our pathetic inability to build houses. The birds have nests; the foxes have holes; the beavers, I have no doubt, are as busy this year as ever; but whereas we are faced with the worst shortage of houses since the Pilgrims landed on Plymouth Rock, we seem less capable than the savages of Africa of building appropriate shelter for our mighty American tribe.

If private capitalism is not working—why is it not working? On that question, too, everyone here will agree. We know that private capitalism functions only under conditions of confidence and that today there is little confidence. Now perhaps private capitalism ought not to lack confidence in the President and his Administration. But capital is not always reasonable. You can lure it, coax it, seduce it and ruin it; you can manipulate it, regulate it and promote it—but there is a sense in which you cannot reason with it.

In the present case, however, there is good reason for distrust. Over the years Franklin Roosevelt has made most businessmen feel that he does not like business—that he does not like industrial enterprise. The dangerous fact is this: while basing all his policies on the assumption that private enterprise will work, he has based his political popularity on the implication that business is antisocial, unpatriotic, vulgar and corruptive.

Now what can be done about this situation? Many a businessman thinks that nothing can be done. If he is not really despondent, if he is not really desperate, it is because he clings to an optimistic faith in the American people, from whom he does not yet feel himself to have been expatriated.

But are we not involved, you and I, in something more than a mere cycle of business and politics? Is there any real reason to believe that a swing of the pendulum will bring us back to conditions of long-term business confidence and of industrial enterprise? All the evidence, it seems to me, whether you have regard to this country or to the entire world, indicates that we have come to a critical climax in the affairs of man; that the outcome is highly uncertain; and that the alternative is either a century of brilliant human accomplishment or a century of disaster and decay. I believe we have only one choice—either an altogether new high level of productivity or the bitter bread of social turmoil, war and scarcity.

To be specific, I have spoken of a national income of $100 billion. Let me speak of a national income of $150 billion or of $200 billion—and I do not mean the dollars of any man's caprice, but gold dollars or a sounder buying-power dollar if anyone can invent one.

Now, cautious and conservative as bankers ought properly to be, you know in your hearts that the potential productive capacity of modern industry is vastly greater than anything we have yet seen. Every businessman is sore—sore in his heart, because however hard he may be working, he knows that not only his own personal progress but the march of industry as a whole is throttled down to a halting half-speed.

Well, now, this vision of vaster productivity is also in the hearts of the people. The basic ideological change in the American mind is the *new doctrine of potential abundance*. One of the most amazing phenomena in recent times was the spread of Technocracy.* You recall the way it swept the country way back in 1932. The idea, you recall, was that if all the machines were put to work under the control of technicians, nobody would have to work very much and everyone would have $20,000 a year. A theory launched with no authority behind it, with almost no organization, with no program, it was hardly mentioned in either the press or on radio until suddenly it seemed to have millions of converts. Meanwhile, you have also had Huey Long with his promise to make every man a king on $5,000 a year; Father Coughlin, Upton Sinclair, Dr. Townsend † with his really very conservative promise of $200 a month—not to mention the rise of socialism in one form or another —all this, while the government was spending at a faster rate than the world has ever known.

Now, in my opinion, it would be a profound mistake to dismiss all this either as bad economics or as vicious demagogic nonsense.

---

* A nostrum whose chief prophet was engineer-economist Howard Scott and whose popularizers included Stuart Chase and Upton Sinclair.

† "Long, Coughlin, Sinclair (who was defeated when he ran for governor of California in 1934) and Townsend were figures in the New Deal era phenomenon described by historian Arthur Schlesinger Jr. as "the Rise of the Demagogues."

We are confronted here, not with a popular superstition, but with a popular intuition. The hope of greater abundance is soundly based, if not on experimental fact, at least upon reasonable calculation combined with popular intuition as to the genius of our times. And, all demagoguery to one side, this intuition is the dynamic in our actual social trends. The shorter-hour week, social security, price-pegging—the attitude that you may as well pay the bonus—WPA and TVA and Grand Coulee—all of them presuppose that Scarcity is no longer the common enemy of mankind and that much greater wealth can be turned out of the industrial spigot.

The businessman who feels and feels rightly that he is being thwarted, that he is being cheated of an opportunity to participate in a brilliant forward march of industry, the intelligent industrial worker who feels that there should be out of all this machinery and capital and genius a solid $2,000 a year for him, and the gullible old lady who feels that the skyscrapers of New York and the great mills of Pittsburgh and Cleveland and Chicago should somehow provide for her simple little wants—all these, as well as the theoretical socialist or the practical humanitarian whose soul is shocked by the spectacle of dire want in the midst of plenty—they are all responding in differing ways to a new thing in the world—and that new thing I call the calculability of abundance.

For this I believe is a new and valid thing in the world. In all the pre-industrial ages, and today in such a pre-industrial civilization as China, all human life has been organized around one basic equation. That equation is that one man by the sweat of his brow, and by the sweat of his wife and children from dawn to dusk, could just barely, barring acts of God, get himself enough to eat and to be clothed. That great equation on which the whole life of the world was organized has now been canceled. A thing called standard of living, which is a very different thing from the mere absence of starvation, is now calculable in the modern world. The reasonable calculability of abundance is, I believe, the gigantic new reality to which mankind is striving with such stupidity and heartbreaks to adjust itself.

If this is true, then obviously the nature of business during the rest of this century will be conditioned by how men choose to act on this premise and promise of industrial wealth. And with this as a base point, may I set in order, as I see them, some of the other major phenomena of our times?

The concept of abundance leads naturally to the idea of planned economy. It leads easily to every kind of crackpot scheme, but most dangerously it leads to planned economy. Since abundance is obviously *there*, but since it has not been arriving automatically and uninterruptedly, it was easy to believe that the fault lay with a few greedy and probably dishonest capitalists who were getting more than their share—and that anyway there must be a way to *plan* it so it would all come out according to the premise. The agency of planning must, of course, be supreme, which means the government. Now we have had a chance to learn something about planning in the last few years—a little from our own country, but a great deal more from the experience of other nations. And we know this, that when you start to plan one thing the plan doesn't seem to work unless you also plan the next thing. There is no halfway house for planned economy. The planning agency must have supreme power, and that supreme power tends to become universal. And we know something else. You cannot plan the economy of a nation unless you plan all parts of a national life—the nation's press, its amusements, its education, its diet, and even the tempo of its sexual activity.*

And we know something else. If you are going to have planning, you cannot have your plans changed every two or four years by a free-for-all election battle.

Planned economy is completely inconsistent with concepts of democracy and liberty. This is clearly stated by Benito Mussolini, perhaps the ablest manager a poor nation ever had. Fascism, says Mussolini, has stepped and will step again upon the more or less putrid corpse of liberty. What, then, is liberty, if it be not already dead?

The essential characteristic of political liberty has been identified with brilliant simplicity by Harold Laski. He said that if in any state there is a body of men who possess unlimited political power, those over whom they rule can never be free. The fact that the power may be held as a result of an election makes little difference. If any government holds the minimum amount of power which is requisite for planned economy, the people over whom that government rules can never be free. And thus we come to the great issue in the modern world. It is the issue of Planned Economy versus Freedom.

---

* For a less doctrinaire statement of Luce's views on the incompatibility of freedom and planning, see page 241.

Suppose it is urged that liberty bakes no bread for the mass of men. Suppose that liberty is weighed in the scale against the hope of an abundant life—and so it is today, everywhere. There is then one assumption we must accept. Given a choice between ice cream and cake on the one hand or liberty on the other, the mass of men of all classes, including businessmen, will choose ice cream and cake.

What then? Must we reconcile ourselves to planned economy and bury our sweet dream of freedom?

The answer, of course, is, that in the real world of fact and logic no such choice exists as that which seems to exist between abundance and liberty. The more abundant life may be problematical in a free society; it is utterly impossible in anything except a free society. And this is true for a very simple reason. The abundance which can be produced by an industrial society can be produced only by a very advanced degree of division of labor and by the most intricate and speedy exchange of the products of extreme division of labor. The economy of abundance is therefore so complicated, so intricate in its myriad relationships, so changing, so delicate and dynamic that it is incapable of being planned or directed by any conceivable human government.

Planned economy is not even theoretically possible except for nations which are both poor and bellicose. The minute you speak of abundance and peace and the pursuit of happiness you are dealing with so many millions of differing tastes, palates, hopes, ambitions, skills and aptitudes that the whole concept of planning becomes at once ridiculous.

Freedom is not therefore merely an abstract ideal for politicians to fling about on either side of the fence when it suits their purpose. Freedom is the necessary condition of high standards of living based on the division of labor working in vast markets responding to the creative genius of a dynamic technology. Freedom is therefore above all the business of businessmen. And this is true despite the unfortunate occurrence of the American Liberty League, and despite the association of liberty with an impenetrably tory attitude of businessmen of the past decades.

Political freedom was born out of the urgencies of modern trade and enterprise. It grew up rapidly and violently throughout the Industrial Revolution. And whether this century will be recorded as one of expansion or of contraction depends most of all upon whether political freedom can be preserved.

But freedom must not only be preserved; it must be expanded. It is here, I think, we will find the trouble we have got into. For fifty or sixty years before the New Deal, freedom under law had not been expanding; it had been contracting.

While, under conditions of essential political freedom, modern industry was putting on such a demonstration of rising standards of living as the world had never seen, the mass of men nevertheless felt cheated. And not without cause. They saw the growth of monopolies, great accumulations of wealth, high tariffs, public franchises for private profit and all manner of special privilege. Added to all this was a classic exhibition of corruption in local government. Blame the graft on the politicians, on the big Democratic city machines, but remember that a businessman's civilization tolerated it and paid for it. In short, the laws of a free society had not kept up with the rapidly changing conditions of industry, commerce, population and human life.

The Administration of Franklin Roosevelt is, therefore, not an accident. It is a climax. It has been of great and historic service in breaking through an appalling and scandalous neglect of the art of government. It has been the first concerted attempt to adjust the inequalities and to attack the accumulated evils of a system which businessmen were either afraid or too lazy to change. Mr. Roosevelt showed a splendid eagerness not only to relieve distress but also to practice once again the art of government.

The art of government is not the art of doing nothing. And the art of governing by laws and by policies which receive the assent of the governed is unfortunately more difficult than the art of governing by plans, by hirelings, by sycophants, by force and by fiat. The low esteem in which politics has been held by recent generations of Americans is in itself the measure of our failure to govern.

Through three brilliantly expanding centuries, political freedom developed side by side with the revolt of businessmen against arbitrary government, side by side with the demands of businessmen for an economy of free exchange under laws which warranted confidence over vast spaces and over long intervals of time. Though often checked or distorted by vested rights or conflicting interests, the cause of historic liberalism was thus the cause of business and intimately of every businessman. And it is more than ever so, today.

I would recommend that every businessman should forthwith

become a student of history, and particularly of the history of liberty. If we find ourselves today nearly destitute of capable political leaders, it is at least partly because we have neglected this. A body of businessmen literate in the history of liberty, and of their own calling, will provide breeding ground for leaders. And when American businessmen become the well-briefed advocates of the liberal state, they will also provide the greatest army of proselytizers the world has ever seen.

Second, I think that businessmen must accommodate themselves emotionally to pretty nearly the full degree of socialization which has recently taken place. I think that most of the New Deal's social legislation is justified as a makeshift catch-up on long decades when the processes of law lagged behind the requirements of industrial expansion. And now the time has come, I think, when the President must declare flatly and frankly for the only economic principles which he possesses—which are the principles of free capitalistic enterprise. If he has the courage to do that—and he is a man of courage—then business must take him at his word. The times are too critical for malice—on either side. It is now Franklin Roosevelt's task without delay to restore the long-term conditions of confidence which private capitalism requires. The hope of his ill-fed, ill-clad and ill-housed depends upon the vastly greater productivity of free capitalistic enterprise under law. He knows that. We know that.

And finally, no matter what the President does, we can render no greater service to the cause of business or the state than to mind our own business with more mind than we ever have before—with more efficiency, more ingenuity and more enthusiasm. I know that enthusiasm is hard to prescribe today. But if we cannot find it in the immediate conditions of our employment, I believe we can look for it and honestly find it in a cause which is greater than ourselves. The cause of freedom is your business and my business. As a journalist, I am in command of a small sector in the very front trenches of this battle of freedom. My mother didn't bring me up to be a soldier and I am not asking for any fight. But let me assure you that I and my colleagues—we are enlisted in this war: for life. And how do we propose to fight? First of all, by doing our job, as we in our private consciences see the job, in the most efficient, profit-making manner we know how.

Thus it is as a businessman as well as a journalist that I can say to you in all sincerity: acquaint yourself deeply with the cause of freedom and—make as much money as you can. The more money you make, the more efficient your business will probably be. Take full credit for all your achievements. Challenge every lie of collectivism. Call the cheap bluff of every politician who tries to pretend that *he* feeds the people. Be quick to cheer every honest politician of any party. Be utterly frank—you have nothing to hide.

Make money, be proud of it; make more money, be prouder of it. School yourself for the long battle of freedom in this century. Look forward to victory—and to the achievement of a more abundant life.

---

5   THE PROFIT MOTIVE

Luce had a keen sense of his audience and would rather surprise than flatter one he knew. At the Hotel Woodstock in New York City, on April 21, 1938, his father's friend, the global evangelist Dr. Sherwood Eddy, chaired a group of clerical and academic men who, under the name of The American Seminar, were about to make a nationwide social study of the U.S. Probably the last thing they expected or wanted to hear about was the profit motive.

Last week I was privileged to dine with a small group of Columbia and New York University professors who are especially interested in public opinion. As an alleged pessimist, I was amazed by their pessimism. Specifically with regard to freedom—freedoms of all sorts, academic freedom, religious freedom, freedom of the press, etc.—there was a feeling that there was really a very small chance that these freedoms would persist in this country ten years from now. As one of the professors saw the situation, it boiled down to this—that the 19th-century freedoms were bound up with laissez-faire capitalism, that laissez-faire capitalism is through, that even in this country the social pressures are getting too fierce, and that before long we should see the end of free capitalism and with it the end of other freedoms.

Something like that is, I suppose, the problem and the puzzle which, in the long view, interest us all more than any other. With your permission I would like to talk for a very few minutes about one important part of that puzzle, the profit motive.

Perhaps all I have to say comes down to this—that it is peculiarly necessary today to meet the issue of the profit motive clearly, and to be, after all the talk is done, either for it or against it. It is a hard choice. There is enormous temptation to weasel; to talk about "reasonable" profits; "fair" profits; to get out from under by saying that human rights must be placed above property rights, etc., etc. The profit motive is not a noble motive. It is not a gallant motive. You can't imagine going to war in the name of the profit motive. It is not artistic. It is not dignified. And yet it seems useful.

But there is another reason why I choose this subject. I suspect that more men in this room are capable of enjoying a symphony concert than are able to read a balance sheet or are able to hear in their ears the counterpoint between a balance sheet and a profit-and-loss statement. You are what Europeans would call intellectuals. It is my impression that of all the conspicuous phenomena in modern life the one that is least apt to be comprehended by intellectuals is the profit motive. And by comprehended I do not mean grasped simply as geometrical theorems may be learned by rote or dialectically comprehended. I mean comprehended as music is, or as football is comprehended by those who like football. I would like to press this analogy. Supposing that music were a vital issue in our democracy—and perhaps it should be, perhaps it is far more important than the profit motive. Well, it would then be most unfortunate if all the intellectuals turned out to be tone deaf. They would struggle with the problem of music—but would they ever comprehend it? If they all knew they were tone deaf, they would make great allowances for that fact. Now the intellectual does not like the profit motive. He is just not that kind of *homo sapiens*. But not for a minute will he acknowledge that he does not comprehend it. Being an intellectual, he can comprehend anything—or certainly anything so commonplace as profit used to be. To make his self-assurance complete, he calls business economics; he is far better read in economic theory than the businessman he meets; he is therefore certain he understands business better than the businessman. Actually, the intellectual is tone deaf to business. What matter? He has read economics.

Let me speak from my own experience. In the publications for which I accept responsibility when called upon to do so, we have the job of finding men to write on nearly every subject—and over the years by all odds the hardest job is to find men who can write well and who can also write about business. This problem presented itself to us acutely long before there was noise in the land about rightists and leftists. There are men who can read poetry and there are men who can read balance sheets. The men who can read poetry can write. The men who can read balance sheets can't write. That, happily with some exceptions, seems to be the general rule. The writing man is fundamentally just not interested in business. Now most writing men today are perhaps of the left. But if it is said that a writing man cannot write well about business, except to attack and ridicule it, because he is a leftist, I would say that it is quite as likely that he is a leftist because he cannot write about business.

Journalists are intellectuals of perhaps a low order, but I would say that what is true of journalists is true today of most intellectuals. Most intellectuals are against business, not really for intellectual reasons, but for a psychological reason—for the simple reason that everything about business which does not actively offend them bores them. So, in speaking frankly to a group of intellectuals tonight, who are starting out on sociological investigations of this country in this time, it has occurred to me that I could perhaps be of no better use than by cautioning you against a natural, and even per se a laudable, intellectual bias against business and the profit motive. If this is impertinent, I ask your pardon.

6   A THOUGHT FOR DETROIT

In a speech to the Detroit Economic Club on April 3, 1939, Luce made another effort to define a larger and more respected role for the businessman. In it he said: "The business of business is to take part in the creation of the Great Society," a phrase which, though first used as the title of a book by Graham Wallas in 1914, was to be made famous by Lyndon Johnson in 1964 (Number 10). In it Luce also said the following:

A devotion to liberty is of equal concern to all citizens of the republic, but it is inseparable from the concept of businessmen and business enterprise. For example—there is a certain amount of intolerance in this country today. In idle women or drugstore cowboys, a little intolerance may be pardoned. But not in a businessman! The businessman who for one moment condones or is party to intolerance may not be a knave, but he is certainly a fool. At whatever point liberty is challenged—in schools, in universities, in the press, in the church, in assembly—wherever liberty is challenged, let the businessman pick up the gage. For liberty is in good part his creation, and liberty is today the only charter which grants him the right to exist.

7   OPEN THAT DOOR

World War II demonstrated that U.S. industry was capable of even more incredible feats of production than Luce, Willkie and others had said it was. With the achievements he had to his credit, the businessman could feel more at home in American postwar politics than he had before Pearl Harbor. But he was now to be swept up in the new politics of the cold war and of world trade and development. Luce put the challenge to the American Association of Advertising Agencies in New York City on November 18, 1946. In the decade following this speech, U.S. business investment abroad was approximately to triple.

Back in 1943, the Republican party, under the leadership of Senator Vandenberg and Senator Taft, held a meeting at Mackinac, Michigan. That meeting produced an historic word: "participation." The Republican party promised fullhearted participation in the affairs of the world for the sake of world peace and world prosperity.*

If this country happened to be ruled by a dictatorship or a socialistic oligarchy, then it could still participate in world affairs, but its participation would be confined to participation by and through the government.

But "participation" has a special meaning for Americans. It means, in world affairs, participation by all kinds of Americans in their various lawful callings. It means participation by free and independent educators and journalists, by free and independent

---

* At that meeting the Republican Postwar Advisory Council, sensitive to the charge that Republicans were isolationist, unanimously approved "responsible participation by the United States . . . in cooperative organization among sovereign nations to prevent military aggression."

scientists and ministers of the Gospel—and by free and independent businessmen. And so I urge each and every one of you to participate actively in overseas business. If you are not regularly engaged in it, find some way to give part of your time to it. If you are a senior executive of a firm doing only a small part of its business abroad, plan to give an extra amount of attention to the smaller child.

Now this call is certainly not an invitation to enter into any easy and delightful green pastures. On the contrary, if you find business at home difficult, you will find business abroad more difficult. A businessman's lot isn't easy anywhere, but the businessman who goes abroad this year and next is in for aggravations and frustrations of a new and special kind. I shall mention two kinds, both political.

First, you must expect to be accused of all manner of wickedness, even, and especially, when you don't deserve it.

In many places, indeed in every place, someone will tell you, nastily, that you are not wanted. Molotov * has already told you that. He calls you dollar imperialists and expects you to cower in moral turpitude. He says you aren't wanted and gives the signal to all his stooges to say it behind your back, to your wife, your children, your friends, your pastor. Well, I can tell you the answer to that one. Don't believe it: it is a lie.

Everywhere in the world the people want the American businessman. And most of the governments want him too—even when, for the sake of their own particular demagogueries, they have to make noises to the contrary.

The peoples of the world are easily confused, but basically they *want* what the American businessman can bring. And they like the way he brings it.

Then there is a second difficulty. Many countries, especially in Europe, which are opposed to Communism have nevertheless rejected the idea of a return to free enterprise. Or at any rate they think they have. Now here we must distinguish between the uncompromisable issues of human liberty and the relativistic questions of economic system. Mr. Attlee and Mr. Bevin,† and millions

* Longtime Foreign Minister of the U.S.S.R.

† Clement Attlee (1883–1967) and Ernest Bevin (1881–1951) were then the Prime Minister and Foreign Minister of Britain's Labor Government.

with them, believe that you can have socialism *and* freedom. I don't. But I could be wrong—on that one. I'll believe it when I see it. Meanwhile Mr. Attlee and Mr. Bevin and their followers sincerely believe in civil liberties and that they will never allow their socialism to take on the monstrous wickedness of a police state. Meanwhile, also, the Attlee-Bevin socialists stand with us against tyranny in whatever form. Therefore we shall and must stand with them in opposition to tyranny and in defense of freedom and civil liberties.

So much for the fundamentals. Now, as to the matter of taste in economic arrangements, there is something else to be said. Whether or not Mr. Attlee would like to see America turn socialist, his urgent practical need is that American capitalism should be a huge success. A serious failure of our economy would be almost fatal to Britain. For several years, at least, the success of all European non-Communist socialisms depends on American capitalism. That is a simple paradox which had better be quite clearly understood.

There is much that our government can and must do to make it possible for the American businessman to make contact with an outside world that needs and wants him. But businessmen themselves must actually do most of the job. That is why it is so important that the policies the government lays down should be parallel with your own aims, and of a kind within which you can act.

The economist's prescription for world trade set forth by Under Secretary of State Will Clayton * is a good one, and it is to be hoped that every enlightened businessman will support the new reciprocal tariff cuts on which hearings are soon to begin. Everyone will favor this program who places the interest of his nation as a whole above that of any particular industry.

But mere tariff cuts, especially reciprocal cuts, are not a very searching answer to the economic problems ahead of us. We need creative ideas. The real job is no longer merely the 19th-century Trader Horn job of trading beads for ivory tusks. The real job is to stimulate the creation of wealth abroad, and to build up foreign countries to the point where we can trade freely with them at far higher levels of economic activity. The job is not just to jump

* William L. Clayton (1880–1966) was chief of foreign economic affairs in the State Department from 1944 to 1947 and a strong advocate of freer world trade and investment.

aboard an export-import boom; that's only part of it. The job is to participate in a worldwide capital expansion of a sort that will link our industries, our finances and our markets directly with every other country in the world.

The kind of participation I mean is new, but it already has its American models. I refer you to Westinghouse Electric International. When President William Knox of Westinghouse International surveyed the coming export boom, he gave it about three to five years. So he decided to start selling something for which the demand would not slack off so soon and which would generate its own means of payment. The product he is exporting, moreover, is one already favorably known throughout the world, requiring, I am sorry to say, no very costly advertising campaign to introduce it. But it is a product which will generate more advertising and more business of all kinds between America and other nations than anything else Westinghouse makes. The product is know-how.

Westinghouse has already negotiated deals with Mexico and China to help build factories in those countries. As part of the deal, Westinghouse is bringing 300 Chinese and 200 Mexicans to East Pittsburgh to teach them how to run those factories; 150 are there already. It sounds as if Westinghouse were deliberately dealing itself out of the Chinese and Mexican markets for electric waffle irons and 25-watt bulbs. Possibly, but Mr. Knox doubts it. And certainly he is not dealing himself out of his more important market for generators, transmission equipment and other high-technology installations. Nor is it his plan just to start these factories running and never look at them again. Westinghouse is obviously at the start of a long and mutually profitable association with the Mexican and Chinese markets. Its name and its men have gone into those countries to stay.*

And right there is one fundamental of true internationalism: "go to stay." The Committee for Economic Development has advised all foreign-traders to adopt this policy. It will be all too easy to skim the cream from this sellers' market and come home. But if our foreign trade is to do the most good, both in keeping us prosperous and keeping other countries friendly to us, it must be continuous. Go to stay.

All of us can think of other projects for exporting American

---

* The Chinese undertaking was brought to a halt by the Communist take-over in 1949, but the one in Mexico still flourishes.

know-how. A worldwide chain of TVA-type dams, from the Yangtze to the Danube, has been projected, and I can see no reason why it is not America's interest and duty to favor these dams and help build them. Any project which gives American engineers and American businessmen opportunity to work with other people will work toward an expanding world economy. Direct investments, which have been the stabler and more profitable part of our capital exports in the past, are another example. Some businessmen appear to have been buffaloed by the old "dollar diplomacy" cry on this score, and have already missed some rather obvious opportunities as a result. I repeat, there is no basis whatever for being afraid of the Molotov yowls. Direct investments increase the productivity of the nation where they are made, and it is only by increasing other people's productivity that we can balance our trade and permanently enrich the world. As Mr. Knox says, "You can't do business with a poorhouse." Yet in comparison with America, "poorhouse" is a very kind term for the economic condition of most of the world today.

I have mentioned two of the obstacles which American business faces as it sets forth on this new crusade. One of them is nationalism, which will make you feel unwelcome; the other is socialism, which will make you feel impatient, as though sophomores were running the world. The program I have outlined can undermine both these obstacles. Petty nationalism in undeveloped countries or in countries which have retrogressed stems from the lack of the very industry and capital we offer to bring them. Socialism, which is first cousin to nationalism, will seem increasingly sophomoric for the same and one other reason. The other reason is that if American businessmen go abroad as builders, as wealth-makers, as creators of productivity—in short, as good capitalists—they will be good salesmen for their system as well as for their country.

Our diplomats will tell you, and they are right, that America should not try to impose an economic system on any other country. But it is surely the best diplomacy to be honest about what we are, and not to pass ourselves off as socialists when we do business in a socialist country. The struggle for freedom will not be won by refusing to make converts to our cause as we go. It is true that economic systems are not final absolutes; but this applies to other systems as well as our own. The stakes of the effort are not merely the survival of capitalism; they are much greater, which is why I ask you to take this task so seriously. To raise the level of the world's prosperity is to give ourselves and the world another chance. It is to keep the door open to an expanding future in which the issues and choices will be all new and not even discernible to us here now. Our job here and now is to open that door.

8   ON COMMON SENSE

When the Republicans returned to the White House in 1953, the expansion of world trade and investment which Luce had begun to prophesy in 1946 was still dominated by government emergency programs such as the Economic Cooperation Administration. It was also held in check by trade and exchange controls in most countries. By 1959 all major Western currencies were to be convertible, other barriers were falling and world trade had indeed begun what Luce foresaw would be "one of the proudest [upward] curves on any chart." The following speech, delivered at the Franklin Award dinner in New York City on January 18, 1954, is one of Luce's contributions to that development.

For the first time in years, we live more or less free of national tragedy. We may laugh without the knowledge that Americans are dying in Korea. We may sleep without the serious fear of waking to disaster. We know, of course, that neither peace nor prosperity is guaranteed. We know that the world is full of mines which may explode at any time and that our enemies are as strong as ever. But we also know that our foreign policy is no longer like a fire engine rushing from alarm to alarm while leaving too much initiative to the arsonists. A new Administration, using what was good in past policy, has launched a vigorous program for fire prevention. There is what the diplomats call a *détente*—a relaxation of tension—not only in the world and in the nation, but in our hearts.

Well, let us thank God for that grace. But what do we do next?

Mightn't it be sensible to do nothing, or at least no more than absolutely necessary? Mightn't it be wise to hold onto the good life we have and not endanger it through any daring gesture—like the one which I mean to propose here tonight? Mightn't it be smart to adopt as a motto for these days the song "Sit down, you're rocking the boat"? Mightn't it be common sense?

Common sense—it seems to be that lately this has become a very popular ideal. No more crusades! Let's mind our own business! Well, this mood is easy to understand after twenty-five years of terrible depression, social revolution, war, cold war, treason at home, crisis and ambush on foreign shores. One can surely sympathize with this longing for a little rest. Perhaps taking a rest is only common sense.

I'd like to say a few words about common sense. And perhaps the best way to talk about it is to talk about Ben Franklin, who, as every schoolboy knows, practically invented it.

An eminent man of letters called Franklin "the only man in history who never bored anybody." I am sorry, but I must enter a small correction. He bored *me*. When I was first introduced to him at school by a very dull teacher, I was appalled by the narrow and thrifty maxims of *Poor Richard*. What did all that have to do with the glory of the American Revolution, or with the wonderful continent-spanning America to which we were born?

Later, of course, I learned that there was more to these little truths than I had realized, and more to Franklin than these little truths. I came to know the brilliant, versatile 18th-century mind, questing, restless and yet serene, the master of all trades—printer, editor, publisher, librarian, educator, diplomat, postmaster, politician, inventor, scientist, dabbler in medicine, letter writer, raconteur, joiner, ladies' man and—after his own relaxed fashion—Christian. I realized that, unlike Richard, he was more generous than thrifty, more courageous than prudent.

It took, of course, more than common sense—namely, guts—to face the powdered wigs of 18th-century Europe in a fur cap, to face the elegant swords of the aristocracy with a knobby stick. It took more than common sense—namely, intelligence, subtlety and humor—to be active in so many causes that over the years both atheists and believers, Whigs and Tories, Prohibitionists and Wets have claimed him as their own—the Wets pointing to his remarkable argument that God made the joints of the arm just long enough to carry a glass to the mouth without missing the mark.

It took more than common sense—namely, vision—to stand before the House of Commons and make a case for the fantastic proposition that thirteen relatively poor colonies could hold out against the might of the British Empire. The French statesman Turgot said of Franklin: "He snatched the thunderbolt from heaven and the scepter from tyrants."

And what we require *now* is more than common sense. That is to say, we need today, now, in this hour, that peculiar American mixture of common sense and uncommon courage, and vision, that teaming of the practical and the heroic. We need it in many fields. But it is most urgent in the field that is close to all of us who are, in one way or another, businessmen. I mean trade, world trade.

There is one specific thing which the United States must do about world trade. We must make a radical reduction in our tariffs. There is no substitute for that plain, simple act of economic statesmanship.

Does someone really believe in common sense? Then the reduction of tariffs is demanded by every canon of economic common sense. But you know perfectly well that it will never happen if it is left merely to the painless course of common sense. A radical reduction of the American tariff will only come about if a few political leaders will display some uncommon courage and if enough of us arouse ourselves to a feeling of urgency about this subject and if we give to it public-spirited effort beyond the call of ordinary civic duty. Here is a cause, squaring completely with common sense, which requires nevertheless some truly patriotic and even heroic action on the part of American businessmen. And surely the business leadership in this cause should come from this very island of Manhattan. New York *is* part of America, all suspicions to the contrary notwithstanding. And I know of no good reason why the influence of New York should be confined to the jukebox, the clown and the gag writer. There is a great business community in New York—the greatest in the world. The business leaders of New York should speak up, now, for free trade. What are they waiting for? What are they afraid of?

Every intelligent New Yorker knows that the American tariff ought to be radically reduced, and I will not presume to attempt a technical exposition of this problem. But let me try to put the subject in perspective and to show its relation to the whole of human destiny in this age.

Here in America we enjoy not only prosperity but, more important, we enjoy truly remarkable conditions of economic order—that is, efficient production with vast and rapid exchange and distribution. This is the kind of order which can only exist through freedom—this kind of order can never be created by tyranny, whether red or black. We have our anomalies, to be sure, such as paying huge subsidies to the richest farmers since Abraham. But by and large, the American scene is one which combines dynamic progress with a remarkable degree of rational order.

But what about the rest of the world? It is commonly said that the rest of the world is a poorhouse. And common sense says that Americans just can't go on very much longer living their life of prosperity in a worldwide poorhouse. The rest of the world is, in resources, just as rich as we are. Take oil. Is there any country in the world which hasn't got an ocean of oil beneath it? Maybe—but I don't know which one. I only know that there are lots of countries which are sitting on oil and haven't the whatever-it-takes to reach for it. Or take Brazil—by all physical yardsticks, it may be richer than the United States; why don't they find out? Or, more broadly, take technology—the United States hasn't got any patent on it. There are millions of good technicians of various grades in Europe. Why isn't Europe rich? Does Europe *like* being poor? There are enough technicians in Europe to make Europe and Africa rich— and enough technicians in Japan alone to make all of non-Communist Asia hum with industrial activity.

Then what, in the name of truth, is the matter?

The descriptive diagnosis is fairly simple. From a business or an economic point of view, the world as a whole is an appalling jungle of irrationality. The ubiquitous sign of this irrationality is restrictions, restrictions, restrictions. First of all, there are restrictions *within* countries. Bureaucrats and politicians dominate the life of nearly every country in the world. Businessmen come to terms— honorable or dishonorable—with this appalling worldwide political bureaucracy. Communism is only one form of this 20th-century bureaucracy. The curtains of economic restrictions crisscross the so-called free world. Restrictionism rises to monstrous heights of absurdity and evil—in restricted currency, restrictions of every kind on investment, to say nothing of tariffs, quotas, embargoes, rackets, blackmail, bribery, chiseling, and all manner of crookedness and every form of harassment to trade.

An almost utter irrationality in the world's economy: that's what we are up against. And if American leadership means anything, it means that we've got to take the lead to overcome some of this irrationality and try to bring about a little rational freedom in the economic life of mankind.

The American tariff in itself is only a very small item in the sum total of the world's economic irrationality. But it has an importance beyond its statistical weight—for a reason you all know: namely, that whenever the United States tries to induce other nations to move toward less arbitrary restrictions, they alibi themselves by pointing to our tariff, and set up a wail about the "dollar gap."

A radical reduction of the American tariff would be of some direct help to the rest of the world—and therefore to us, too. But the truly great good it would do is to set the example that a leading nation should properly set, and put us in a position to go on from there and work out with patient and firm diplomacy a world of economic common sense.

Surely, everyone knows, this is just common sense. But always and everywhere, it takes heroes to make common sense happen. I ask you tonight—some of you—to think about being the heroes of common sense, in this cause, now—to make evident to President Eisenhower that you will give him strong backing in a determined leadership for the radical reduction of the American tariff.

This action would galvanize the world. It would prove that we mean what we say about free enterprise and free trade. And it would enable us at last to tell our friends without the appearance of hypocrisy to cut out *their* restrictions, to wake up and live like free men in a modern world.

America paints in iron, and writes in steam, and makes music with the sound of its engines. But our greatness lies not merely in the marvels we have achieved—it lies in the fact that we achieved them not for the few but the many. Americans take pleasure, not in possessing but in creating; not in having, but in working. That is why they can be asked to show vision and faith in such a pedestrian matter as trade. The great poet Goethe, a contemporary of Franklin, gave us a memorable version of the Faust story, and a mirror of our character. The hero of Goethe's dramatic poem hungers for gold and knowledge and glory. He gets all these. And yet what does he wind up doing? What is his crowning achievement, the thing that finally brings him salvation? It is work, work for mankind—a thoroughly American solution which would have been appreciated by Franklin, who believed that serving God meant doing good to man.

Before he dies, Faust builds a dam to reclaim vast lands from the ocean. His words sum up the American faith of free human effort under God's grace, which is a very different thing from materialism. They sum up the heart of the American dream, the duty to the world and to ourselves which that dream imposes on us. Faust speaks—or is it an American settler on the frontier, or a progressive American businessman in New York or on a construction job on some other continent? Faust speaks:

> *I shall open up space for millions,*
> *Where they shall live, not secure, but free to work.*
> *Green will the fields be, and men and beasts*
> *Will be at home on the new land, daring and diligent. . . .*
> *For this is wisdom's ultimate conclusion:*
> *Only he deserves his liberty and life*
> *Who must conquer them each day anew. . . .*
> *Such is the turbulent scene I long to see,*
> *To stand on free soil among free people.*
> *Then to the fleeting moment I could say:*
> *Stay, you are good.*
> *The traces of my earthly days*
> *Then could not vanish in eternity.*

9   THE CHARACTER OF THE BUSINESSMAN

*In Paris, in June 1957, 1,200 businessmen from twenty-
seven countries came together under the auspices of the
International Congress of Scientific Management. Luce
spoke at the final session.*

Twenty-five years ago, Alfred North Whitehead gave a lecture
on "Foresight" at the Harvard Business School. In it he said: "A
great society is a society in which its men of business think greatly
of their functions."

If we are to have an Age of Abundance, the businessman must
be worthy of his great vocation. He must be worthy of this calling
in two senses: first, in the sense of his own personal character;
second, in the sense of the general character of the worldwide
fraternity of businessmen. You are responsible for yourself; you
are also your brother's keeper. Let me put the matter more bluntly.
In my judgment we shall win or lose the Age of Abundance to the
degree that the businessman exhibits two basic virtues. The first is
honesty—downright, old-fashioned truthtelling. The second is that
businessmen must have clear convictions about the kind of society,
the kind of system they want, and they must be willing to stand up
and fight for these convictions. The businessman must have courage—the courage of his convictions.

Before dealing with these two virtues in the modern application,
let us pause a moment to consider the character and reputation of
the businessman generally in history. Perhaps the first thing to be
said is that, at most times and places, the businessman has not been
an attractive figure. The word "bourgeois" springs to mind. I was
shocked the other day when I looked up the meaning of the word in
Webster's dictionary. Let me say that I consider myself a bourgeois. And here is what I read about myself in Webster's:

Bourgeois 1. Characteristic of the middle class. Hence: *a* Engrossed in material things; Philistine; often, conservative; hidebound. *b Colloq.* Common; boorish; stupid. *c* Capitalistic.

A shock indeed: to look into the mirror of a dictionary and find such an ugly face. In my dismay I rushed like a wounded child to the scholars. How could this be? I had been proud of my bourgeois ancestors. Was it not they who overthrew feudalism, formed the great nation-states of Europe under kings and emperors, and then overthrew the kings and emperors when kings and emperors stood in the way of human progress? Were not the burghers identified for 500 years—in France, in Holland and elsewhere—with the rise of the cities and their civilization, with parliamentary rule, with liberty under law, with exploration and discovery, with science and literacy?

The scholars came to my rescue—especially the Reverend Father R. L. Bruckberger,* a French Dominican who knows and loves both Europe and America. Father Bruckberger explained many things which I can but touch on here. For one thing he explained that it was Karl Marx and the *Communist Manifesto* that finally made "bourgeois" a dirty, stinking word. But what he was mainly concerned to explain was that in the word "bourgeois" you find just about the deepest difference between the experience of the Europeans and the experience of the Americans in the 300 years since my own ancestors crossed the sea. And, of course, in America we do not actually use the word "bourgeois"—except in little literary reviews; in America we say "middle class." We are a middle-class, that is to say a classless, country.

The businessman in America today enjoys a good enough position in our vast middle-class society—and it is, I think, important, even necessary, that the businessman in other countries should be respected and should feel at home in the nations that are everywhere being born or renewed.

But there is something else the businessman must realize: though generally in the past he has been associated with the rise of freedom and the progress of civilization, he has only a mediocre record in modern politics. Too many German businessmen were associated with Hitler. Too many businessmen were hand in glove

* Author of *One Sky to Share* (1956) and *Image of America* (1959).

with Fascism in Italy and elsewhere. Too many Japanese business-men took the way of the sword. Too many American businessmen were isolationists before the war. In the past decade too few businessmen have really fought against Communism. Perhaps the most sensational record of political stupidity was made by the businessmen of Shanghai; they thought it would make no differ-ence if Communists took over China. So now there aren't any Shanghai businessmen. No, the modern political record of busi-nessmen is not good.

Now, to be sure, it is not the businessmen who run the politics of their nation or the world; they have their own vast and onerous job to do. But I do plead that in the coming Age of Abundance the businessman must learn a little greater wisdom about politics.

The whole business of the businessman is changing, and he with it. His ranks are being strengthened, not only by new risk-takers in the direct bourgeois line, but by the rise of the industrial manager. This new man, native to the age of large corporations and high taxes, has merged his high standards of efficiency with the capital of ownership, in such a way that business today has many attrib-utes of a profession, and the businessman is or ought to be a respected servant of society well worthy of his hire. Owners and managers alike add luster to this new title of businessman.

I have said that I would speak of just two virtues. The first is honesty. This is an old-fashioned virtue—perhaps even a *bourgeois* virtue. We need it now more than ever—and in broader terms than ever before. As one travels around the world, or as one listens to businessmen speaking of doing business in various countries, one is appalled by the amount of dishonesty that infects the so-called free world. In so many places, bribery is taken for granted. In so many places, cheating on taxes is accepted as part of the way of life. I urge businessmen to stand against all this cheating. Of course, governments bear their heavy share of guilt for the dishonesty in the world. Historically it is governments that have been the great robbers of the people—through inflation and other forms of mis-government. The Soviet Government has just publicly enacted the biggest steal of the decade; by defaulting payments on Soviet bonds, it robbed a generation of Russian workers of their alleged savings. Governments rob by inflation and by expropriation, but also each and every government restriction in the field of econom-ics is an invitation to dishonesty. I ask businessmen to protest against all forms of corruption, legal corruption as well as illegal. I ask businessmen to refuse, even at personal cost, to participate in corruption.

The concept of honesty is necessarily broadened in our time. The radical doctrine I hold is that all business is invested with a public interest. Therefore all business must be open to public inspection. The annual reports of corporations should be models of candor even beyond the demands of legitimate public curiosity. The businessman's pride should lie in the fact that his every transaction can withstand the scrutiny of the law courts and the historians, and above all the daily scrutiny of his own conscience. The consequences of such open honesty will be so profound they cannot be exaggerated. For what the world needs today more than anything else is good faith and credence between man and man, between class and class (where classes exist), between nation and nation. Let us determine that we will so act as to establish, across all boundaries, one great web and frame of common honesty, openly demonstrated and proudly proclaimed.

I come now to the second great and immemorial virtue that the businessman is specially called on to display—the courage of his convictions. I assume all honest businessmen share a common belief in business—a belief, that is, that business is an honorable occupation, and that the best way to develop wealth and to spread it is through business. I suppose that most of us would agree that one great condition of healthy business is that our society should have a dependable currency, *sound* money. But do businessmen, even bankers, really fight for this absolute condition of our business economy? In my own country there are general cheers when the Federal Reserve Board relaxes credit. But when it tightens credit and thus tries to keep the boom under control, there is apt to be large outcry. Someone, it is said, is going to get *hurt*. Of course that is so. But, I submit, it is far better for a few people to get momentarily hurt through decent fiscal and credit policies than for everybody to get hurt through inflation and subsequent collapse.

In our time we businessmen have sought many ways to define the system we stand for. We have called it free enterprise or the people's capitalism. Permit me to suggest an older definition. What we must stand for and fight for is the *free market*—not just a free market for Europe, but a free market for the world.

For the market *is* the heart of our system, and let us be clear what we mean by it. Assuredly we do not mean a condition where businessmen can do just as they please. Nor do we mean that there is no room for social welfare. What we do mean is a system under which the overwhelming proportion of the world's goods and services are produced and distributed, not by government edict, but rather in response to choices freely made in the marketplace. We mean a system where the consumer, who is Everyman, is able to register *what* he wants, and we businessmen and entrepreneurs are *forced* in seeking our own gain to serve the public will.

The markets of the real world are quite a different place from the free market of classical economic theory. Many new but nonetheless legitimate interests—trade unions, pension funds, all kinds of social pressures—make their claims on these real markets, and these claims are seldom susceptible to slide-rule measurement. The role and scope of managerial judgment have become more challenging than anything known to Ricardo's entrepreneur.

On the other hand, the classical doctrines are very far from obsolete, for they contain abiding truth. Let me soberly recall to you that toward the very end of his life the most revolutionary economist of our day, the late Lord Keynes, who once wrote an essay called *The End of Laissez-Faire*, stood up in the House of Lords and admonished his countrymen "not to defeat, but to implement, the wisdom of Adam Smith." The virtues of what he called the "classical medicine" include good money, free pricing, free competition and trade, with the state acting as umpire and ground-rule keeper, not as master planner and economic dictator.

Of all economic systems, the free market is the one that makes the most demands on the intellect. It takes no more than the mentality of a ten-year-old child to see the plausibility of a planned economy. It takes intellect of a high order to appreciate the sensitive organity of the free market. We have been going through a period when, paradoxically, most "intellectuals" have been against the free market. That is partly a response to tragic circumstances; it is also partly because of the temperamental bias of intellectuals, but it is no credit to their intellects as such. I think we are now getting out of the period when intellectuals have been, unwittingly, enemies of economic progress. I think we can reasonably look forward to an era when the intellectual and the businessman can converse together in rational terms. This is what Whitehead foresaw when he said that it is our business as philosophers and practical men to work together to envision and to create a society "penetrated through and through with unflinching rationality."

10   BUSINESS AND THE GREAT SOCIETY

Luce had not only anticipated by many years Lyndon Johnson's use of the phrase "Great Society" (page 239), but he became a genuine enthusiast for the Ann Arbor speech in which Johnson announced that program, which was close enough to Luce's own hopes for building a great American civilization. The following is from a speech at the Harvard Business School on June 6, 1964.

The title of this conference is Business Leadership and National Policy Issues. To speak to that title, the first question to be asked is: what *are* the national issues? I have been tempted to say: there are no national issues. The American people today are not so much challenged by issues as they are confronted by problems. They have innumerable problems of day-to-day living—such as parking, commuting and smog. And they have problems rushing at them from the future, like what to do if you live to be 100, which you will. But none of these have turned into rousing issues like Prohibition or Woman's Suffrage or Sixteen-to-One or 54–40 or Fight.

"Problem" has become an overworked word in the American vocabulary. We shouldn't have to use the same word for the problem of poverty as we do for the problem of your golf swing. And problems ought either to go away or to shape up into arguable issues. But it does seem, for the moment at least, that problems multiply but issues linger.

Take, for example, the problem of The City. Our cities must be rebuilt, says President Johnson. And, in fact, some of them are being rebuilt—notably, Boston, where we are. But if we are to envision all or most of our cities being rebuilt—and on a scale even bigger than has yet been tried in Boston or Pittsburgh or Baltimore—then we need to have a much clearer idea of how they are to be rebuilt, so that in a decade or two they won't have to be built all over again. We will have to see more clearly than we do the problems of the future. And this will require much more than simply technological or utilitarian calculations. We will have to think about what cities are for—and when we say they are for people to live in, we have to go on and ask—for what kind of people to live in, and for what purposes they live, and even for what ideals.

Here we get into the now familiar paradoxes of the affluent society—and they are not one, but several. We are affluent, yet we cannot afford, either in our offices or in our homes, the high ceilings which lent some dignity to the environment of our forefathers. We have immense capacity to do things—and can't make up our minds what we want to do. The moon-shoot is the exception which proves the rule. Why go to the moon? Well, let's for the moment just say because it's there. How about rebuilding The City? Isn't The City there, too? No, it's not—the great and beautiful city of the future is not yet there in our imaginations and in our wills.

President Johnson made a remarkable speech at Ann Arbor two weeks ago. It is, I think, the first proclamation by a President of the United States that the goal of our efforts is the creation of a great American civilization.

He said: "For a century we labored to settle and subdue a continent. For half a century, we called upon unbounded invention and untiring industry to create an order of plenty for all of our people. The challenge of the next half-century is whether we have the wisdom to use that wealth to enrich and elevate our national life, and to advance the quality of American civilization." The name President Johnson gave to the American civilization of the future is the Great Society.

The American economic system is producing the material basis for the Great Society. We may expect that it will continue to do so. In fact, it will do more than that. The American economic system is already producing more than we know what to do with. This present and foreseeable flood of abundance is not only producing the means for a great civilization; it is forcing us to think in those terms.

But, beyond having forced the issue, how can business leadership help to shape the civilization which we are building—and which we must build? The answer, I suggest, may lie in that new, prestigious tool—R & D—the research-and-development department. Every self-respecting company has one today—even publishing companies have them. We have all become quite adept at internal corporate R & D—in sizing up the needs of our markets, in designing and producing our goods, in testing them and in selling them. And my suggestion is that R & D should be put to work to envision the alternative possibilities of the Great Society. My stress is on the word "alternative." Much of R & D is no doubt already at work on trying to foresee the shape of things to come, the markets of the future. But the future is not deterministic. At least, free men ought not to think so. Free men ought to think that there are alternatives and that we can choose.

Already, as I have noted, there have been some beginnings in the rebuilding of cities. And these beginnings will inspire more. But we cannot say that there is any real surge on the part of the people to launch this mighty task. Why not? Because they have not been inspired to do it. And they have not been inspired because they have not been shown alternatives. The public is full of complaints about the city, but they are far from seeing the city as something which they can and should recreate to their hearts' desire. They have not been shown how various kinds of cities can be built to combine convenience and interest and beauty and pride.

There are indeed city planners and there are organizations, governmental and nongovernmental, working on this problem. My suggestion is that their work should be supplemented by the quite independent efforts of the research-and-development departments of all major corporations. For there can hardly be a corporation whose future does not depend on how well we build the cities of the future.

I cannot predict what might happen if the R & D departments of fifty great corporations would address themselves to community projects, including entire cities. For this purpose, R & D departments might have to get the services not only of sociologists and economists, but also of philosophers and of political scientists and artists. It might also be appropriate for a number of R & D departments to cooperate with each other—and if they did, we could certainly demand that the antitrust boys keep out.

One objection to such blue-sky thinking bothers me: how could corporations hope to make any money out of such efforts? This brings up a very large question of the future—namely, the place of the profit system in the Great Society. We certainly want to maintain the profit system—because it is efficient, because it is necessary to the free society, because it spreads the risks of novelty, and for many other reasons. And yet more and more, what seems to need doing falls into what is called the "public sector." The "public sector" in our society is not only the government sector—we can use the term to include all nonprofit enterprises such as universities, hospitals, parks, art galleries, churches. To be sure, business profits from building and supplying such nonprofit institutions. But that does not make them business enterprises. Or take, for example, one of the most exciting of the new frontiers— oceanography, the mining and farming of the wealth of the seas. Will this become part of the "public sector," or will business enterprise be able to play a risk-taking and creative part in it?

The kind of R & D I have suggested might provide new and surprising answers to this kind of question and thereby provide navigational charts for the course of business enterprise in dealing with the present and the shaping of the future.

My plea, then, is that business leadership should engage itself, in the broadest sense, with the alternatives of the Great Society— alternatives of ideals and also alternatives of ways and means, of style and characteristics. This, it seems to me, would be, in every sense, the most rewarding task of business leadership in the years immediately ahead.

If I were to try to put in a sentence or two the difference between the task of my generation and the task of the generation now ready to take over, I think I would put it somewhat as follows:

The task of my generation was to prevent the overthrow of Western civilization; the task of the next generation is to build a finer civilization than the world, including the West, has ever known.

6

ART AND
ARCHITECTURE

The esthetic sense was not Luce's long suit, but he worked at it. It was characteristic of him that he even invoked a "will to beauty" (page 272). There was always a touch of the dutiful about his efforts to keep up with the beautiful. Also, the fine arts could be thieves of time. Yet in his magazines he did more to popularize art and architecture than any other man of his age.

He was a benefactor and for a while a director both of the Museum of Modern Art (1940–50) and of the Metropolitan Museum (1948 to his death) and was a conscientious member of the latter's purchasing committee. But he justified the time so spent less as a personal pleasure than as a form of civilization-building. As a spasmodic collector of Western painting, he felt secure only as far as the postimpressionists and was always inclined to trust his wife's judgment above his own. He did put together, con amore, a small but admirable collection of Oriental sculpture, ceramics and prints, now in the Phoenix Art Museum.

Luce seldom spoke of art except in a cultural or political context. He looked for the "meaning" in every work of art, whether the artist intended one or not. The gradual divorce between Western painting and "objective reality," which reached a climax with Jackson Pollock and the American school of abstract impressionism, gave Luce some painful moments. It came at a time when LIFE was leading the popularization of contemporary art in the "cultural explosion" of the 1940s and 1950s. Luce was urged and strongly tempted to take sides in the public controversy between the avant-garde and the cultural conservatives, some of whom claimed that abstract expressionists were either subverting sound American values or hoodwinking a fad-ridden art public. LIFE, *with Luce's encouragement, explored this controversy by sponsoring and publishing a round-table discussion (October 11, 1948), but did not take sides and continued to report the avant-garde sympathetically. Since Luce could not sell his own conservative tastes to his more eclectic editors, he refrained from imposing them.*

He was primarily a word man, but he was by no means "picture blind." He regarded all pictures as an important form of communication. He would spend hours, both on FORTUNE *and on* LIFE, *experimenting with picture choices, sizes, shapes and layouts. He once told a conference on photojournalism (at Coral Gables, Florida, in 1961) that a photograph should aspire to fit Robert Frost's definition of a poem: "something which begins in delight and ends in wisdom." "For delight," said Luce, "we may sometimes have to read 'shock'—the shock of horror or tragedy. But this too has the power to 'stab the spirit broad awake.' And whether a picture begins with pleasure or with shock, we would wish that it should always end in wisdom."*

Toward the end of World War II a dinner companion, joining Luce in the bar of the Union Club, found him staring intently at an English sporting print. It showed a race-day crowd with horses, grooms, jockeys and genteel spectators, all—at first glance—happily mingled in the paddock. But not at second glance. Said Luce to his guest: "That picture tells me something I'd almost forgotten: England is not a democracy."

Architecture was of special interest to him as the "social art" (Number 1 below), the outward and visible sign of the spirit of a civilization. His interest in architecture intensified after Time Inc. acquired the ARCHITECTURAL FORUM *in 1932. Luce took increasing pride in the leadership which the* FORUM, *chiefly under Publisher-Editor Howard Myers, gave to a then disunited, demoralized and under-employed profession, notably by crusading for better school buildings and by introducing Europe's "international" style to American taste. In 1935 he predicted an architectural revolution in America (Number 1); in 1957 he could salute it as complete*

(Number 6). The FORUM was its prophet and Luce its cheerleader and occasional monitor.

There is, however, a certain poignancy in his "extraordinary affirmation" (page 277) that "good architecture is good economics." At that time (1957) he was about to discover that there were limits on that affirmation, even for the largest stockholder in Time Inc. Before the present Time & Life Building in New York was planned, Luce envisioned a more smashing architectural pathbreaker than proved practical. For a while he and architect Eero Saarinen worked on schemes for a dreamy semirural campus near Valley Forge, Pennsylvania; but the psychic and other costs of uprooting Time Inc.'s staff, who had homes all over the metropolitan area, proved prohibitive. They also played around with an even more dramatic solution: a Moorish enclosure in upper Manhattan the size of Piazza San Marco in Venice. That dream also receded in the face of real-estate realities.

The actual Time & Life Building was one of the many compromises in Luce's life that nevertheless represented a net gain for the American cultural environment. It intruded Rockefeller Center into the commercial slums west of Sixth Avenue and broke a path for a dozen other imposing buildings, including Saarinen's for C.B.S. At the cornerstone ceremonies on June 23, 1959, Luce dedicated the Time & Life Building to the nonmonumental purpose that it admirably serves: "to work."

---

1   THE SOCIAL ART

The following is from a prospectus Luce wrote in 1935 to explain his hopes for the FORUM. It undoubtedly owed a great deal to conversations with Howard Myers and his staff.

To influence architecture is to influence life. The most widely accepted concept about architecture is that architecture is above all other arts the *social art*. Perhaps never before has it been so imperative and so possible to do something, by conscious thought and effort, about "designs for living."

The reason why it is imperative to do something is that, by general agreement, the existing order of life and thought is passing or has already passed—and unless chaos is to intervene, a new order must be more or less consciously created—and soon. "Architecture or revolution" is the famed phrase of Le Corbusier. The reason it is so possible to do something is that the physical materials of a new order lie so abundantly about us. These materials are not only steel and glass and their potentially enormous production, but they include also a wealth of scientifically accepted facts and notions such as hygiene (sunshine), physical culture (playgrounds), transportation (airports and weekend cruises), the mass enjoyment of leisure (cinemansions), education (small classrooms) and dozens of other concepts which have not yet been translated into anything like a satisfactory or coherent or universal pattern either of social life or of architectural construction. We do not yet know how to build a house for the new age. Much less can we yet visualize the relation between a house and an airport and a movie and a factory.

In recent decades, not only has no publication served architects in any significant or influential manner, but architects have not served society in any significant or influential manner. Indeed, architects have not in fact been the architects of even that form of civilization under which we have recently been living. Architects have had almost nothing to do with what is new and characteristic and disruptive or hopeful in our times. Airports were decreed by engineers and visionary promoters. Skyscrapers were decreed by engineers and realtors and prideful auto manufacturers or 5- and 10-cent-store merchants. Architects were called in for certain decorative services in connection with these technological dreams. A few of them, like Hood,* had some small influence on the result. But the vast majority of good architects—the ones you and I know —had no part in all this. The architect did nothing except to provide out of past ages a decorative costume for those who could afford it and who knew what they wanted. The famous ones †† provided Mr. Harkness and Yale with Gothic or Mr. Mellon and

* Raymond Hood (1881–1934), architect of the Daily News Building in New York City and a consulting architect for Rockefeller Center.

† James Gamble Rogers (1867–1947), designer of Yale's Harkness Memorial Quadrangle, and John Russell Pope (1874–1937), designer of Washington's National Gallery of Art.

Washington with Greek temples. The successful ones provided tycoons with English or French mansions on Long Island, and the rest—in Indianapolis and Seattle—made a living by providing lesser tycoons and Babbitts with lesser 18th-century mansions in the subdivisions of a thousand realtors. The middle or lower classes had neither architects nor architectural services.

But if the architect played no influential part in recent decades, is there any reason to suppose that he will play a part in the coming decades? The answer is that several thousands of *planners of structures* will play a vital and even a determining part in our immediate future. Some of the *planners of structures* will be men who now hold architectural diplomas. Some will not be. But whether or not they have degrees, those *planners of structures* are the architects of the next decades. And the big point is that these new architects cannot help being conscious planners to a vastly greater degree than were the architectural decorators of the recent past. The reason, to repeat, is that the materials of a new order lie so abundantly about us—and *in* us, in our minds. If an earthquake should demolish Mr. Mellon's Greek temples, they could not be rebuilt with casual complacency. If they were rebuilt at all, it would be only after a fury of debate and with deep misgivings on the part of the architect whom a Mr. Mellon might hire.

The fact seems inescapable that in the Twenties there occurred in America one of those unnecessary misfortunes of mistiming which often occur in history. The nation had the will and the power to build. But when it went to the planners of buildings, the mental and spiritual cupboards of those planners were bare. The men who should have had the convictions as to what ought to be built, and how, had neither ideas nor convictions. This was not because of any particular moral turpitude on their part. It was because the ideas which lay implicit in the rising tide of technology and the ideas which lay implicit in the new social trends and mores —these ideas had not anywhere been clarified or crystallized to any useful extent. With all the doubt and confusion which exist in the world today, these ideas, or some of them, are clearer today than a few years ago. They are clearer at least in this sense—that we feel the inevitability of their emergence, even if we cannot see their shape or color.

These ideas came too late to control the architecture of the Twenties. The perfect example of mistiming was the little fact of air conditioning. Air conditioning missed the boom—but completely, so that every one of the skyscrapers of the Twenties is already technically obsolete.

In some respects, then, we are better prepared to build today than we were ten years ago. We have an accumulation of technology which was not available then and we can see a little more intelligently into the 20th century. Basically, however, we are no wiser—except in one respect, namely, the consciousness of our unwisdom. We know that we must learn.

And precisely here is the opportunity for a magazine designed to *instruct the planners of structures.*

The magazine needed today is not one which, based on well-established, mandarin-like canons of taste and form, will hand down monthly dicta in accordance with the canon. The magazine needed today is one with sufficient courage, enterprise and elbow grease to instruct itself—to discover and correlate facts where there are facts, and to attempt bold if tentative conclusions where the needs of the hour call loudly for conclusions of one sort or another.

All professional men need postgraduate instruction. No one needs postgraduate instruction today more than do architects. Even the most ordinary architects have got to deal today with a far larger variety of facts than did Michelangelo or Sir Christopher Wren. Wren did not have to bother with oil burners or electric lights—and scarcely even with sewers. And only a very small part of what he has to know did any modern architect learn at school. Thus the architect needs instruction in the most literal sense of the word—instruction in simple facts, in elementary techniques.

Ten years ago the house included oil burners and electric lights and sewers. But now it has expanded ever further: a house now includes its own interior decoration. This was not so ten years ago; then the architect built a house complete with sewers, and then a female decorator, with Mr. Nast's * help, decorated. But functionalism has marched on. Today, and if not today, certainly five years from now, the first and fundamental question about a house will be: shall it be modern? If the answer is yes, then the architect has really become responsible for its decoration. Thus style (on top of technological paraphernalia) has become once again important. And the circle having gone round, Sir Christopher Wren would again be in command of the situation.

But the modern style, whatever that may turn out to be, is not

* Condé Nast (1874–1942), then publisher of *Vogue* and *House and Garden.*

the style which any architect learned at school. The architect who graduated last year and who may have worked almost exclusively in "modern"—he, too, has got to continue his studies because, of course, there is as yet no such thing as the modern style but only shifting intimations and adumbrations of it. It is a style which is becoming, not one which has become. Nor is the style-in-the-making necessarily a mass production of one or two patterns. Within modernism there may be—and this editor devoutly hopes there will be—a hundred styles—a style for Boston and one for New Orleans and another for France and another for Madras.

Driven by the new techniques and ideas, the architect must acquire a knowledge of fields of thought and action which he did not require in other times. For one thing, he has got to get into large-scale, collectivist building. Hitherto the architect has built homes for less than a third of the people. To build for the other two-thirds, he has still practically everything to learn—economics, city planning, social mores, etc.

The new ideas in the world make change inevitable, not only in houses but in a variety of other things such as theaters, airports, apartment-hotels, restaurants, beach cabins, schools, hospitals, zoos. The point is *not* that these have not already been built. The point is that they have got to be rebuilt. Those who pay for their replacement will demand the skilled application of the new ideas.

2   "OUR UNKEMPT COUNTRY"

On returning from a trip abroad, Luce customarily delivered an impressionistic report to his staff. The following excerpt is from such a report on June 22, 1938, after a three-week tour of Europe.

And here let me mention the countryside of Germany and indeed of all Europe. Europe is beautiful landscape. There is almost no place in Europe that is not beautiful. The actual factory district of an industrial town is perhaps no prettier in Europe than America. But half a league from the factory you are, in Europe, once again in a well-kept garden. In Europe you do not have to go to special scenic spots in order to see beautiful landscape. What an amazing contrast this is to our horribly unkempt country. It will take 500 years for America to become as pretty as Europe. We have 500 years of weeding, and sewing, and trimming and picking up to do. And I know no better reason for being optimistic about America. Today we have a people who do not care about their country—a people who do not *have* to care. We have been a nation of speculators and vulgarians. But surely our great-great-grandchildren—they will love their land as we do not. Surely America will not decline and decay until after its beauty has matured. But never forget this garden beauty of Europe. It is one reason why patriotism, even brutal patriotism, runs so high. No question but that Europeans enjoy nature, and take delight in nature, far more than we do.

Europe is divided into valleys, and every valley has its history and its local demons and its fairies. There is in Europe not only a *Zeitgeist* but also an *Ortgeist*, a place-spirit such as we do not know. Without this deep emotional attachment to place, you cannot have civilization. We must not be contemptuous of Europe because it has this spirit-of-place, this attachment to soil. We need much more of it in America. And then we must seek how this may be made compatible with modern conditions of life which tend to cancel dimensions of time and space. We do not want an undifferentiated robot world. We want a world of conscious men and women, each of whom belongs uniquely somewhere, and yet all of whom belong to the Federation of each other.

3   TO BEAUTIFY—TO BUILD

The first Time & Life Building, at 9 Rockefeller Plaza, New York, contained in its lobby Carl Milles' handsome "singing mural," a forest scene carved in wood. A horseman paused to listen to a clarino, or Mexican nightingale; the bird announced each hour by singing its (recorded) aria and flapping its wings. These were Luce's remarks at the Milles unveiling, on February 5, 1941.

Ten years ago the spot on which we stand was the site of a shabby, four-story, brownstone house. I remember as do most of you the months in which the buildings were being torn down to make way for Rockefeller Center. We remember those houses: brownstone stoops, brownstone façades, shabby and spiritless. We remember those days of 1931 when the world was slipping into an abyss: America moving toward the Bank Holiday, Berlin's black days, Japan moving into Manchukuo.

These winter evenings of 1941 I walk out the door of the Time & Life Building and look down at the figures of the skaters on the rink below and up to the blazing windows of the sky-reaching summits of the center. They are the windows of the only world city which today still shows light. Thinking thus, I remember that this thing has been done—that Rockefeller Center has been built—in ten of the most destructive years that any century has seen. I remember that there was nothing here but stagnation and decay before, but that men came here with a vision and built with courage at a time when half the world had lost its courage and the vision was gone.

It is thus doubly appropriate that we are met here today to honor a great artist of our age in this center of American industry, this great focal point of American communications. With half a world in darkness and ourselves girding to defend our way of life, it is doubly significant that so innocently happy a figure as that of Mr. Milles' forest rider should be brought into being—to typify that dream of beauty without which man's bread is dust.

It is strange to think that in such a time as this the song of the woodland bird will call out above the heads of the hurrying men and women coming here on all the matters of a troubled world. Yet it is a happy thing that the ageless beauty of song may reach us here at this crossroads of the troubled present.

To beautify—to build; in this is found the ultimate happiness of man.

---

4 BEAUTY AND UTILITY

After the war the "architectural revolution" went into its early Levittown phase, which helped solve the accumulated housing and school shortage but created new esthetic problems. During that phase Luce addressed the Chicago Producers' Council, a trade association of building-products manufacturers, on September 29, 1949.

Let us ask ourselves how much real pleasure, how much joy, how much inspiration democratic man derives from the buildings through which he is continually passing.

Take, for example, our schools and colleges and universities. Democracy means education. Public education sheds the idea of the private tutor on the one hand and the ignorant mob on the other —it introduces the idea of vast numbers of boys and girls, men and women congregating in places of education.

How much inspiration do our young people get from the buildings in which so many of their formative years are passed?

On a trip to Europe last May, I went over to Oxford, which I had not revisited in many years. Once again I stood in the great hall of Christ Church. You could not stand there for a minute, of course, without knowing how subtly and surely that magnificent building had molded the minds and manners of generations of the leaders of England, and especially the generations which spread over the earth and did so much to lay the foundations of this country in liberty and law. Aristocracy built the great hall of Christ Church. But shall not democracy also build for its sons buildings which ennoble the spirit and elevate the mind? Not the same buildings, of course; democracy must speak with its own voice, and wear proudly its own garments of steel and glass and scattered gold. But the buildings of democracy must be not less but more beautiful, more endearing, more ennobling than the buildings of any other dispensation. And of such buildings there must be many, many more than in any other age, for the sons and daughters of democracy are not few but multitudinous.

Democracy has grown up with a strong bias toward the merely useful—the utilitarian. It is this bias which continually needs to be corrected. There is no inherent conflict between utility and beauty. Granting all the claims of utility, I say that beauty must be sought and achieved for its own sake—in our school buildings and in all else. Is it too much to ask that our schools and colleges should be expressions of democratic idealism? To ask for less is to fail, at the very height of our adventure, to bring about the kind of society for which history waits.

John Ruskin, that great propagandist for better buildings, put the whole matter very simply: "We require from buildings, as from men, two kinds of goodness: first, doing their practical duty well; then that they be graceful and pleasing in doing it, which last is another form of duty."

The individual man seeks beauty and inspiration; must he no longer hope to find it when he, a democrat, enters the democratic throng? Will democracy accept the charge that it degrades the individual man? Certainly not. How, then, rebut that charge? Rebut it by action; rebut it in what we build.

There's a tide in the affairs of men that, taken at the flood, leads on to fortune. Gentlemen, your tide is in; you are bringing it in. You have a huge volume of business now. But your real future is not in that. Your real fortune—in dollars, in satisfaction—lies in the transformation of the whole American attitude toward building. Out of the huge demand now before you, every *better* building you can cause to be built, every beautiful building, will establish this industry in the hearts and minds of the American people.

Those who by the democratic process, including the process of free competitive enterprise—those who come into positions of leadership in a democracy in whatever sphere—have not only the right, they have the duty to lead democracy, to lead toward the highest and best that they know.

---

5 ART IN AMERICAN LIFE

This excerpt is from a speech delivered in Des Moines, Iowa, on October 13, 1955, to the American Federation of Arts, of which Luce's colleague, Daniel Longwell, former managing editor of LIFE, *was president.*

Perhaps there has never been a society of which it could be said that art, even in the broadest sense, was the central and unifying purpose. But there have been some great civilizations of which this was very nearly true.

We who are their distant and claimant heirs think first of all of Greece. The Greeks, until rather late in their story, were not so much interested in the making of a nation as in the perfection of the individual. The Greek ideal was *arete*, which we may translate as "excellence." *Arete*, the ideal of personal excellence or of personal honor, is achieved in personal conduct and in the pursuit of excellence in all the arts of war and peace. Given the ideal of excellence, beauty cannot be far behind. When we think of Greece we think of beauty.

But let us come to another great moment of our spiritual heritage: the Age of Faith in Christendom. Now I think it must be quite clear that art, or the love of formal beauty, was not a major impulse in the early Christian faith. The "beauty of holiness," perhaps, but not art as we understand it. Socially the task of the Christian community was to take over the bankruptcy of the Roman Empire and to keep some light of humanity shining for six or seven dark centuries. But in the 12th century, the darkness has passed: all Europe is pervaded by a new form of order and a new style of feeling, and the Age of Faith begins to express itself in the great cathedrals. There has never been a greater example of man's faith and feeling expressing themselves in an art form than the cathedrals. And along with the cathedrals, there were the 10,000 village bell towers, which even today seem to call us back to some lost Paradise.

Thus we remind ourselves that art and beauty in ceremonial form or in individual creation or group creation have been very nearly *the* purpose of other societies. And having done that, I think we must then be quite clear in our mind that art has not been, and is not, the dominant or unifying purpose of American life.

But I think it may become so. Certainly it ought to become so. Thus, I express my bias in favor of the "moral imperative"—a bias from which, in any case, few Americans can escape.

What Americans feel ought to be done, they usually manage to do. If this seems a little ponderous when speaking of art, let us remember the saying that the Kingdom of Heaven cometh not without violence. William James, typically American, speaks of the will to believe; may we not equally speak of the will to goodness or of the will to beauty? So I invoke for the American of the future a will to beauty.

The exaltation of beauty will not come as a sudden national mutation. It will come first, as we see it already, through interest in works of art—in painting, in sculpture. But the historian twenty-five or 100 years from now will be able to see how the love of beauty spread until it was felt everywhere—in our houses, in our schools and in public places, in entire cities and in our countryside, in all our forms and ceremonies—yes, in our football stadiums as well as in our churches. Yes, even on TV!

We have made a breakthrough from an economy of scarcity to an economy of abundance. Can we make the breakthrough from an economy of abundance to an economy of abundant beauty? I believe we will. A broad base for a new era has been laid in widespread art education and in the fact that art has become so important in the personal lives of individuals. Gradually—and perhaps sooner than we think—the personal love of art will manifest itself in our public life. Thus, every man and woman on a school board has a chance to make the next school building beautiful as well as efficient. Every director of a business corporation has a chance to make the next office building a little more beautiful, with a little more fun and joy in it, even if it adds 25 cents per square foot. And the extra 25 cents might even turn out to be a good investment. We shall not have become truly masters of our economy until we have taught it to serve also our ideals of beauty.

In years to come, there will be an American poet who will write not only of the love of the American land and not only of the making of a nation; that future poet will write of a people who love beauty and surround themselves with it and live in it. Today we are making some of the building blocks for that poem.

---

6 GOOD ARCHITECTURE IS GOOD GOVERNMENT

"Life is more than economics! And so is architecture!"
wrote Luce. The following speech, expressing his belief
that functional architecture would express the demo-
cratic dignity of American civilization, was delivered to
the American Institute of Architects in Washington on
May 16, 1957.

The major premise of my remarks tonight is that the 20th-century Revolution of Architecture has been accomplished. And it has been accomplished mainly in America—no matter how great our debt to European genius. The founding fathers of the Revolution in Architecture, the great and the colleagues of the great—many of them are in this room tonight. I salute you. If I should live to an old age and my grandchildren should ask me where I was and what I did during these earthshaking decades of the mid-20th century, I will tell them that on May 16, 1957, in Washington, D.C., there was celebrated the 100th anniversary of the American Institute of Architects. And I was there. If that doesn't sound as exciting to my grandchildren as might the mention of war or interplanetary travel, then I will explain to them that here, on this occasion, I shook hands with the men who gave the shape to their America, the men who raised the towers toward the sky, who stretched the roofs across the land, who formed the façade—the face—that their America presents to all the world. And, I am sure I will be able to add, these were the men who, in the fullness of time, made God's country a splendid habitation for God's most fortunate children.

Is this wishful thinking? Objective facts support my prophecy.

The American Revolution in Architecture has been accomplished at a providential moment. For it comes precisely at the moment when there is taking place, and is about to take place, the most staggering mass of building ever done on this planet.

A quarter of a century from now, only a small fraction of the houses which now stand will be tolerable to the Americans who in 1976 celebrate the 200th anniversary of this nation. And besides houses, there is everything else to build—factories, offices, stores, schools, churches, airports, sports arenas, parks, playgrounds, places of art and entertainment; the list is endless, as varied as American life itself. And let's by no means forget highways—a great symbol of a continental and democratic people. This moving of the earth and making the waters to flow—this is the picture of modern man, of the American, making a new dwelling place on earth.

Well within a decade this picture of a whole new physical environment for Americans will be in the imaginations of the people. It will even be in the algebra of politicians.

But, you may say, granted the hundreds of billions of dollars, granted the billions of tons of iron and concrete and glass that will be put in place, granted the billions of rivets that will hold the millions of girders, etc., etc., what guarantee is there that any appreciable part of all this will express good architecture? Does not a lot of evidence so far point to ugliness rather than beauty?

I must now take account of two things—the appalling amount of ugliness in the American scene at this moment and the degradation of democratic taste.

Nor do we have to go to our friends in Europe to hold a mirror to us and find ourselves to be monsters of bad taste. We find outraged critics right here at home. In fact, the most readable description of ugly America is to be found right in the

ARCHITECTURAL FORUM,* written by an esteemed colleague, Mary Mix Foley. In one sweeping phrase she speaks of "this mess that is man-made America." In her catalog of horrors she lists "19th-century buildings 'modernized' at street level with chrome, glass and neon—the restaurant in the derby hat, the candy-striped motel and the frozen-custard stand, dripping silvered, concrete icicles." "Probably never in the history of the human race," she continues, "has a culture equaled ours in the dreariness and corrupted fantasy of a major part of its building."

The whole story is even more appalling. For dreariness and ugliness were not thrust upon the American people; they chose it, they, the freest people in history. To quote Mrs. Foley once more: "In no previous culture have people in general been so free to choose what they like or do not like with so little deference to authority."

Here I am prophesying a splendid age of architecture on a continental scale. What chance is there for architecture if the will of the American people is for ugliness?

This cry of distress raises many questions—for one thing, the old question as to whether democracy is, after all, any good. None of the world's great architecture up to now, none of the architecture that American tourists go to see every year—none of it arose at the wave of the magic wand of democracy. Except Periclean Greece, you might say. But then you might also say the Parthenon, that wonder of light in the shining sun, is really a monument to the fall of Greek democracy, which was, in any case, a very short-lived affair. As for the Versailles of Louis XIV—*l'état, c'est moi;* as for the Taj Mahal; as for the Great Wall of China, so infinitely romantic; as for the Mayan temples; as for the stately homes of England—you go on with the list—nearly all of majesty or beauty in architecture springs from imperial autocracy or from Aristocracy with a very capital A.

Is then our choice between democracy and architecture? Is real political freedom incompatible with pervasive beauty?

These are big questions, even "ultimate questions." I shall not attempt ultimate answers. But there is one answer which can be given—an answer drawn from the experience and character of the American people.

My argument—and prophecy—is this. First, for 200 years, the

* February 1957.

American people have been faithful to one dominant purpose—namely, to the establishment of a form of government. Second, that purpose has now been fulfilled, and we are at present seized by a broader challenge, namely, the shaping of a civilization. Third, we will meet that broader challenge, too; we will succeed in creating the first modern, technological, humane, prosperous and reverent civilization. This creative response will be most vividly expressed in and by architecture.

After 200 years, here in this city of Washington, we can say that, to an extraordinary degree, we and our forefathers have carried out our tremendous purpose: a form of government which, while profoundly recognizing the frailty of human nature, should nevertheless seek the balance of liberty and justice, the balance of freedom and equality, the balance of individualism and social cooperation. Today our America is an amazing example of functioning law and order and of liberty. Of course, we must stay everlastingly vigilant to keep it so—and we will.

So here is the plateau we have reached after so long a struggle. And now what? Now we are not satisfied with the quality of American life. Millions of us are grateful, as we ought to be, for the blessings we enjoy. But divine discontent is at work everywhere. We must have more and better education, says this one. We must have more and better medicine, says another. And mental health. Yes, and though we go to church in tens of millions, we must seek deeper spirituality. All of this I have summarized by saying that we are challenged to build a civilization.

Today the American people are "sold" on education, as they always have been. They are sold on medicine, yes, and culture, too. Witness, in the last twenty years, the tremendous increase in the enjoyment of music, of the theater, of painting—from Giotto to Picasso to the Sunday painter. And now comes architecture. To use an American expression of elegant lineage, the American people are beginning "to get the word"—about architecture.

It's up to us to send out the word more vigorously. You have accomplished the American Revolution in Architecture. Now it's for the editors and good citizens to make known the news of that revolution.

Twenty years ago, the revolution was under way. But there weren't enough actual buildings to show it. And those that there were seemed odd. But now you've given us the buildings—enough of them. And to millions of Americans they don't seem queer; on the contrary, they seem right.

Furthermore, millions of Americans, not only the professionals, have begun to see that in our 20th century architecture is more than a building here and there, vitally important though each good building is. Architecture is a whole city. Architecture is the whole sweep of the American continent.

That is my answer to the nightmare doubts about the derby hat and the candy-striped motel. Not that all ugliness will be abolished. This is indeed a free country and a man must be free to sin against beauty just as he is free to sin against truth. We will not have a State with a capital S—*l'Etat, lo Stato, das Reich*—to decree our morals, our religion, our culture, our taste.

But we do work at these things—and they work on us. The ideal will not leave us be. It nags us, prods us, inspires us. The vision of the good, the true and, yes, of the beautiful is like our conscience —it catches up with us sooner or later.

The Revolution in Architecture is perhaps best defined in terms of an extraordinary affirmation: good architecture is good economics. Modern architecture did not grow up in the palaces of emperors or maharajas. It was not designed to proclaim pomp and glory —except the glory of a free and self-respecting people. Modern architecture, or at least a large part of it, grew up in response to the people's needs. It has had to meet an economic test, and its chance for freshness and vitality was in making use of the vast wealth of material and technology produced in a profit-and-loss economy.

To be sure, a great deal of bad building is being done, and people make money out of bad building. But the affirmation remains: good architecture is good economics.

Tonight in this capital city of Washington, let me make a further affirmation: good architecture is good government.

Good government in our age must meet the economic test. But government is more than economics. Government must *stand* for things, for principles, for ideals. Government must be a symbol. And architecture is, above all, the symbolizing art.

Will you be given the chance to transcend economics, the chance to express the more-than-economic character and aspirations of the American nation? That is what we must mainly strive for now—to get buildings, many of them, big and little, which point beyond themselves to the best in American life. The chance to express more than economics must be given you by the home builders of America, by the industrial corporations, by the universities—notably by government in all its many branches, federal and local.

The relation of government to architecture may be put under two heads. Most important, perhaps, there is the effect of government laws and policy on architecture. Government's influence for better or for worse is enormous in terms of urban renewal, city planning, housing policy, even the lowly local building codes. All Americans who wish to build a better America must learn how to teach politicians that bad architecture is bad politics. I believe this can and will be done. Let us try to develop a powerful lobby for architecture. Not for handouts, for favors, but for good architecture as such.

Government itself is a big builder. It is in its own buildings that government has the duty—and the right!—to symbolize what government stands for. We applaud the founders of this capital city because they laid out a magnificent city plan. But they did something else. They fixed on a style of architecture to symbolize the great American determination to establish a form of government. The choice of style was the classical Greco-Roman style—the natural and perfect choice for that time. To be sure, Rome did not symbolize democracy or liberty in our hard-won sense of those words. But it did symbolize good government—it symbolized order, law and equal justice under law.

What the Founding Fathers said and what Jacksonian democracy said was this: we *will* have a government of free men, we will even have a democracy, and we will prove that a democracy does not have to slide into chaos and tyranny. We will prove that you can have a democratic government which will be both honorable and honored. We will prove that a nation of free men can be dignified, maintaining self-respect at home and respect throughout the world.

That is what our forefathers said 150 years ago; they said it partly as fact, partly as bold aspiration. They said it symbolically.

Today, America has the same thing to say and more to say, new things to say—the determination to build a great civilization. We must say the old and the new in new language—your own language, the architectural language of the 20th century.

Some of the new American embassy buildings are triumphs of modern architecture. They are also great acts of statesmanship. The Department of State deserves, I think, an award from this institute, not only for the buildings themselves but for the magnificent directive * under which they are being built. The Department of State has written a Magna Carta of fresh, imaginative architecture—an architecture symbolizing the dignity of this republic and its profound concern for all mankind.

What we have done abroad we must do at home. We must do it here in Washington and down to every county courthouse and post office.

No one architect can tell another how to express, how to symbolize, a great virtue or a great aspiration. And certainly a layman cannot. This sort of expression is an act of inspiration. But the architect who touches government has a duty to steep himself in the meaning of America. The citizen has a duty to pray that out of the architect's profound understanding of America will come the inspiration to express what we want to say as a nation.

What is it that we want to say? Perhaps it could all be put in two words. We want to say "democracy" and we want to say "dignity."

Modern architecture can certainly express democracy. We say democracy by requiring that buildings meet an economic test—the test of wise, farsighted economics. We say democracy by buildings which are frank, open and unaffected. Our welcoming shopping centers, our cheerful new schools, our glass-front banks, all emphatically say democracy.

And what about dignity? I choose that word because in World War II and after, the phrase most commonly used to express what we fought for was the "dignity of man." It may not be your favorite phrase or mine, because it so readily reminds that most often man exhibits himself as a most undignified animal. Yet right there perhaps is the clue. Man is not a noble savage—and never was. He is a created creature having implanted in him the power to create nobility. He is a striving creature. We Americans are striving creatures. We have achieved magnificently. And now we have set out upon a magnificent adventure. To express, step by step, the

* In 1954 the Department set up an advisory group of top architects and decided that the design of new embassies should be modern but related to the culture and style of the host country.

progress of that adventure, to express it in fact and in aspiration—
so to do will be the fulfillment of the American Revolution of
Architecture.

In the dawning light of that fulfillment, I salute you in faith and
in hope. In reasoned faith in our own fellow Americans. In confident hope that the divine discontent which has led us to this hour
will abide with us now and forever.

7

CHRISTIAN AND OTHER TRUTHS

The selections in this chapter are mainly sermons and speeches to church or college groups and deal with higher-order abstractions like the nature of truth and the destiny of man. As Dr. Read said (page 7), Luce was a man of faith with his "roots in the world unseen," a faith he owed in the first instance to his parents.

He could preach a strict Calvinist theology when he felt like it, but he usually preferred to relate his faith to worldly problems, especially large historical problems like the probable fate of America and of Western civilization. Among his favorite themes was the question of whether, and in what sense, America is a Christian nation; another was the idea that America's main problems would stem from success rather than failure. Strongly grounded in the Old Testament, he well knew the temptations of idolatry, whether in the guise of nationalism, democracy, science or even the cause of peace ("Thou shalt have no other gods before Me"). He deplored the increasing secularization of American life without blinking it; "Americans have been mostly Christian and may still be," he would say. He thought the exclusion of the Bible from the public schools was bad constitutional law and could not see why the Supreme Court should forbid the state even "to tip its hat to God."

As these and other speeches make clear, Luce believed firmly in the religious base of American democracy and in its Providential purpose. He liked to find historical evidence that the American Revolution was largely Calvinist in inspiration. He believed that the U.S. may still be an instrument of God's will in history. See, for example, his remarks in speech Number 7.

1   THE WORLD'S NEED FOR THE CHURCH

Having heard lots of sermons, Luce tried preaching himself at the age of five to an admiring family. At Yale, as an active member of Dwight Hall, he preached to both gown and town audiences. As an active layman, he preached at his own and other churches. The sermon below was delivered on December 10, 1944, at the Immanuel Congregational Church in Hartford, Connecticut, the city in which his father had taught Chinese religion and culture at the Kennedy School of Missions (Hartford Seminary) from 1928 to 1935.

In thinking about the world's need for the Church in our time, it might be useful to stand for a moment in some quite other time and place, and see how another world of men needed the Church and found it.

Turning the dial of history, we might tune in for a moment on the seventh century in England. It is the year 627. A monk named Paulinus has come to the court of Edwin, King of Northumbria, and endeavors to persuade him to accept the Christian religion.* The king is of two minds about it, and one of his warriors addresses him in these words: "The present life of man upon earth, O King, seems to me, in comparison to the time which is unknown to us, like to the swift flight of a sparrow through that house wherein you sit at supper in winter with your caldormen and

---

* Paulinus had come to Edwin's court two years earlier in the retinue of the new queen, a Christian. St. Augustine of Canterbury, the first Christian missionary to England, arrived there in 597.

thegns, while the fire blazes in the midst, and the hall is warmed, but the wintry storms of rain or snow are raging abroad without. The sparrow, flying in at one door and immediately out at another, whilst he is within is safe from the wintry tempest; but after a short space of fair weather he immediately vanishes out of your sight, passing from winter into winter again. So this life of man appears for a little while, but of what is to follow or what went before we know nothing at all. If therefore this new doctrine tells us something more certain, it seems justly to deserve to be followed."

Thus was Edwin persuaded to receive baptism and to build the first York cathedral in a Christian North of England. And thus began the slow but miraculous growth of English civilization, not without its bloodshed and cruelty and evil, but yielding over and over again miraculous harvests of golden poetry and law and liberty.

That England of 627—so rude, so crude. Sparrows flew in and out of the king's house. Other men and women lived in caves and huts, their children familiar with the howl of the wolf. How great were the needs of those pre-Christian Englishmen! Everything we have—they needed. A monk came offering only to *tell* them something, "something more certain." And they became Christians and built a great and glorious Church.

Could it be that now in 1944, in this incredibly different world of ours, men need most of all and may even be waiting to hear "something more certain"?

There is a hunger in the world—and in America—which is not a hunger of the body. It is a hunger which the Church was commanded to assuage. In the grossly practical terms of the market, there is a pressing demand for a certain commodity. The name of that commodity is Truth.

Here, then, is the real challenge to the Church today. Does the Church possess any Truth? Can it supply—to those who hunger and thirst for it—any Truth?

I am not much concerned with whether you spell Truth with an absolute capital T or only with a relativistic lower-case t. Of course, we are bound to say that what people are looking for is not relativistic lower-case truth. They have a good deal of that—and it is all excellent in its way. Science has been flooding the market with a very reliable and highly consumable brand of relative truth.

Even we journalists hope that part of what we supply is at least relatively true. But the hope in men's hearts—a rather timid and bashful hope—is that the Church might perhaps have another kind of truth. Has it? Surely this is the question—and pretty nearly the whole question—regarding the Church in the modern world. In a world of an incalculable wealth of knowledge, and that wealth incalculably increasing, the increasing need is for truth. Who but the Church can supply it?

Historically, it is cause for angelic rejoicing when men come to the Church with their *minds* as well as with their bodily pains or emotional hurts. The Christmas pageant reminds us of a trinity: angels, humble shepherds and wise men, coming from afar, who first brought gifts to the Prince of Peace.

If it is now again truth which men deeply desire from the Church, it is a test which the angels themselves must welcome. For this hunger for truth presages the dawn of another Age of Faith.

The essential characteristic of the great Ages of Faith was not that faith was one thing and reason another. The characteristic of an Age of Faith is that faith and reason march together—march together against doubt and evil and disunity, march together to attack the most terribly practical problems, march together toward the highest aspirations of the soul.

The rude men of King Edwin's court of Northumbria were not very well trained in the stern disciplines of the mind. Still, what evidently concerned them was the elemental question of true-false. They gave themselves to that which was "more certain."

Yes, the great Ages of Faith began in serious inquiry. And a few centuries after Edwin, the foundations of England having been laid, there was a great Archbishop of Canterbury, St. Anselm. And thus he spoke: "Just as the right order of going requires that we should believe the deep things of God before we presume to discuss them by reason, so it seems to me negligence if, after we have been confirmed in the faith, we do not study to understand what we believe."

It is in our time the great and joyous privilege of the Church and of all her members to study more zealously than ever before— with all the wit and reason of modern man, to study "to understand what we believe." So may the knowledge of God return to the Church, where it always was, though sometimes it was repressed by anxious competition with modish fallacies. Again burning bright with the knowledge of God, the Church may in our children's time bring blessing and healing to the world.

---

2   THE FIRST AND GREAT COMMANDMENT

Luce addressed the Duke Divinity School Convocation at Durham, North Carolina, on February 12, 1946. He began by describing the "profound sense of optimism" that had pervaded America 100 years ago in "the American Age of Faith . . . faith in God, faith in man, faith in the future of America." He then spoke as follows:

If Christianity proves to be ineffective or irrelevant, it is unlikely that America in the next generation can find any other inspired guide to moral coherence. My argument is simply that the United States owes its existence as a nation, more than anything else, to the happy concurrence of a strong Christian faith and a brand of 18th-century enlightenment which, however anticlerical it may have been, was not hostile to Christian faith. Thomas Jefferson, the "deist," was able to join with the Calvinists of New England in knowing that all men are equal *because* God created them. But it is especially to be noted that this civil marriage, so abundantly blessed, between Christianity and enlightenment involved no slightest compromise in Christian doctrine or ethics. There was no feeble truce of tolerance between good and evil. On the contrary, with its human ups and downs of enthusiasm, the Church continued to be the Church Militant, retaining its power to bring human behavior under Christian judgment, to temper judgment with mercy, and to offer to all men the possibility of redemption from their sins.

History does not repeat itself in the same terms and accents. But surely the only Christian hope for our country is that there should once again occur, by God's grace, a dynamic tension between strong Christian faith and a society of political freedom.

I do not mean to exclude any American, of any faith or none, from his full share of responsibility for discovering again, by heart and head and hand, an adequate moral basis for American political activity. But my concern is necessarily for the responsibility of the Protestant Church. By what gifts of prophecy and guidance can the Church inspire men to the pursuit of just ends by just means?

If we may speak at all of a social demand upon the Church, what is now required of the Church is not many things, but one thing only. That is to give to the problems of our times the Christian answer. By the Christian answer I mean an answer which is so distinctively Christian that it cannot be confused with an economic answer or a sociological answer or a political or intellectual or Democratic or Republican or Socialist answer— though it would powerfully influence and correct all these other answers. By the Christian answer I mean one which could *not* be equally the Mohammedan or the Confucian or the Platonic or the Aristotelian or even the Jeffersonian answer. By the Christian answer I mean an answer so distinctive that it could only be given by the Christian Church, even if it might be assented to by any men of good will.

What is the Christian answer? Jesus summarized all the law and the prophets in two Commandments: "Thou shalt love the Lord thy God with all thy heart [and] thy neighbor as thyself."

Insofar as Protestantism has given the Christian answer in the last thirty or forty years, it has been the "social gospel" based on the second of Christ's Commandments. In itself this needs no apology. No one could estimate how much of the general good will which still pervades our society and keeps it together springs from earnest Christian effort to apply Our Lord's Second Commandment to modern civilization. The "social gospel" was undoubtedly a great, if somewhat laggard, ally of the social advance of the last 200 years. But today it is difficult for the layman to perceive wherein the so-called "social gospel" is both meaningful *and* distinctly Christian.

If Christian promulgation of the Second Commandment lacks power today, that can be for only one reason—namely, that the Second Commandment has lost its connection with the First. The brotherhood of man implies the Fatherhood of God. Liberal Protestantism has allowed the implication to become very obscure and tenuous. Modern Protestantism too often gives the impression of believing in everything except God. It must therefore be plain what assertion the Church needs now most of all to make: the Church must assert the Sovereign Majesty of God, the First Commandment.

And we may even need to begin to learn it, as the Boy Jesus did, in its original form: "Thou shalt have no other gods before Me . . . for I the Lord thy God am a jealous God."

It is hardly necessary to remind you of the many, many gods which men do now worship—worship so earnestly that the knowledge of *God* is almost wholly obscured from them. Nor are they merely the gods of materialism or lust or pleasure. They are gods —*good* gods—who obscure the knowledge of God. We have noted the "social gospel," now become for many a god in itself, though it has lost most of its identity in the greater god of sociology. There is also patriotism. Love of country is a very high-order virtue; let him who cries out against it take care that he has achieved some more responsible or some more selfless virtue. But yes, it is true that love of country can become in our time a barrier between the patriot and the love of God. The Stars and Stripes, which our fathers' fathers loved so much, partly because they loved God more, has become, because men are so confused, a competitor of God. "Thou shalt have no other gods before Me."

Lastly, to cite only one more example of a good god—there is the god of peace. Peace, peace, men cry—we *must* have peace. Our wise men, our scientists, now come with frantic cries: we must have world peace, absolutely sure-fire world peace; otherwise, they say, otherwise our whole world may be destroyed. Suppose it was. Thus saith the Lord: "Heaven and earth shall pass away, but my words shall not pass away." Is it conceivable that, for the Christian, it is more important to keep God's word than to keep this little planet physically intact? That would indeed be an exclusively Christian answer and it would lead on . . . well, let us try to see in a moment where it leads. There is no nobler work for men than to be the peacemakers. But: "Thou shalt have no other gods before Me."

Unless you do proclaim the primacy of the First Commandment, whatever else you proclaim may indeed be superfluous. The Church will not restore respect for the other nine Commandments —or for ninety-nine commandments—until it has effectively reminded men of the First.

The reinstatement of the First Commandment to its place of

primacy in the teaching of the Church would, needless to say, have mighty consequences in all the thought and life of the Church. First of all, it would free Protestantism from its excessive compromises with secularism. It would give to the Church a vigorous independence of thought and action which it has long lacked. In so doing, it would further clear the mind of the Church on many contemporary human problems. For it would restore to Christian thought its unique combination of urgency (love) and perspective (eternity)—a combination not to be found in any secular philosophy or politics.

Consider now again the direct relevance of the doctrine of the Sovereignty of God to our international relations. The relevance lies, of course, precisely in the word "sovereignty." We discovered a few years ago, when we Americans began thinking very earnestly and somewhat childishly about world peace, that the devil in the brew was the existence of sovereign nations. It is still the problem. For while in many respects our country is behaving as a pretty good internationalist, still, the basic fact of international life is symbolized by the veto in the U.N.—the symbol of the doctrine of the absolute Sovereignty of Great States.

Absolute sovereignty should not, in fact does not, exist anywhere short of the throne of God. The claim of any earthly king or any earthly government of any form to absolute sovereignty is, in the last analysis, blasphemy. And we Americans will understand our problem better—even more "realistically"—if we remind ourselves that our country was founded on no such blasphemy and by its nature is incapable of functioning as an absolute sovereign. Our government did not and does not undertake to be minister or special agent of the Sovereignty of God. But the basic characteristic of our form of government was and is its compatibility with the absolute Sovereignty of God.

This is, politically, a dangerous doctrine. As long as it has any power in the world, no tyranny anywhere is safe. And neither is any Christian. Not that Christians will seek the path of violence. On the one hand, they will go a long way to render unto the Caesars of this world the things that are theirs; and on the other hand, they will press continually for the development of the principles of justice, being thereby united with all those who seek to follow the only road to enduring peace, the difficult and thorny road, the road marked "Peace with Justice."

And finally, to speak of our own beloved land, we cannot but be aware of one supreme challenge which in this particular time of its history our country presents to the Christian faith. That challenge is not the possibility of national failure; a far greater challenge will be presented by a successful America. It can be met only by a very great love of God Himself.

European philosophers who prophesy the final collapse of Western civilization may be right. They may even be right to include America in their sphere of doom. But in that case I think the Church would know what to do. In the agony of a collapsing civilization, its heart of compassion would shine forth and it would gather the remnants of a stricken people and comfort them.

But suppose America does not fail! There is the greater and more baffling challenge to the Church. Suppose in the next few decades America makes good in a remarkable degree. And I expect her to—and so do you. Suppose we do produce on this continent a vast, and a not too unstable, prosperity. And suppose that we do exercise throughout the world a beneficently expedient influence. There is the challenge to the Church. How can it inform with Christian faith and Christian virtue so vast a prosperity and so great a power?

The point is not inconsistent with our belief that a civilization lacking in moral coherence will collapse. In the case of America, with its huge physical capacity, there may be enough moral capital to see us through for two or three decades of immensely successful activity. Indeed, there probably is.

But the problem—as I see it, the essential Christian problem for America—does not need to be cast into the future. Let us pose it in the present: how can we learn to write in meaningful letters across some of the vast arches of our American life the words "To the greater glory of God—*ad majorem Dei gloriam*"?

In all the earth there is no more beautiful sight than that which meets the eye of the traveler by air as he flies after sundown over a great American city, New York or Chicago or San Francisco: the dazzling beauty of multitudinous light, a cosmic jewel sparkling gaily and serenely on a planet's breast. The lights shine more warmly than the stars; and yet they give, like the stars, the sense of an ordered beauty. The traveler must believe, if only for a moment, as he descends, that here in the city of lovely light there is peace and harmony and no sounds but sweet music or gentle laughter.

Yet he knows it is not so. The electric lights are not the sign of the City of God. In a minute, the traveler is on the ground, in the city, harassed by its hard noise, hit by its violence, made wary. And when the traveler has made his way into the rooms of that great city? It is better there, people are human. But still in the whole urgent life of the city, nothing—or only a very little—says, sincerely and naturally, "To the greater glory of God—*ad majorem Dei gloriam*."

There perhaps is what I have wanted to say. *There* is the challenge of American life to the Church. It is not the poverty which is now the great challenge, but the wealth. Not the weakness, but the power. Not the illiteracy, but the literacy. Not the disease, but the health. Not the back-breaking toil, but the play and the pleasure. Not the squalor, but the lights. These are the great challenges—these American triumphs and achievements.

How to write across these achievements—not all of them, but some part of them: "To the glory of God"? We do not know. Surely the Church will tell us—but only a Church which has thought very deeply, and very exactly, about what God wants His American children to do with their American opportunities. For it is certain that we are commanded, both in the fall and in the rise of empires, always to consider, with St. Augustine, "whether the City of Man may approach to the ineffable goodness of the City of God." The signs of that approach will be known to the Christian pilgrim.

3   THE FLOCK AND THE HOST

Luce inherited from his father an interest in the Protestant ecumenical movement, the great effort to end "the scandal of disunity" among the churches. One sign of this effort was the annual banquet of the all-Protestant pastorate of the State of New York, which Luce addressed at Syracuse as follows on February 5, 1947.

As I think of you who are in this room, pastors of the great and greatly scattered flock of Christ, I cannot escape the feeling that in one respect this meeting is like a gathering of the early Church—in Jerusalem or Corinth or Ephesus or Rome: the task before you is impossible. Humanly speaking, your task is more impossible than theirs. The early Church expected the end of the world: its mission was no more than to save a remnant from the wrath to come. You also are faced, for the first time in centuries, with a prospect of the end of the world; yet you feel your divinely commanded mission is not merely to save a remnant, but somehow to save the world; or even to prevent that very end of the world which now, once again, after so many centuries, presents itself as threat or judgment.

Now, as Christians, we cannot be too much disturbed about the world's coming to an end. Someday we know it will. Our primary concern is not for the world's survival; it is for the kind of world that does survive! What kind of a world will it be? In all human probability, a spectacularly un-Christian world. Which is not to say an unsuccessful world. It is not difficult to imagine an un-Christian human race getting ever more powerful and proficient, and making venturous voyages to the moon and beyond, before it relapses toward extinction. I know of no law which puts a limit to the height of the Tower of Babel—short of Judgment Day! And while it obviously requires some sort of morality to keep the traffic of history moving without too much catastrophe, it is not, I think, demonstrable that civilizations must be Christian in order to survive and after their fashion to succeed.

The Christian pilgrim today contends with more hideously powerful forces than Bunyan knew. Merely to name their names is to suggest their size and horror: the Machine, Total War, Total Politics, Race Hatreds, Idolatrous Nationalism. These are names, outward signs, of powers more terrible than ever Roman legions were—and far more pitiless than Caligula or Nero.

And that is why I say that the task you meet to consider in these days is, humanly speaking, not less impossible than the miracle of salvation commanded to the early Christians. On the one hand your human resources are immeasurably greater, but so are the forces implacably against you. And your task, our task, is not to save a remnant only, but the world entire!

The Church of God today is *not* the early Church. It is the early

Church *plus* 2,000 years of tremendous history. Between us and Peter's flock is the obvious difference that we Christians have become a great thing in the world. *They* were the leaven in the lump—*we* have become the lump. In any case, we are no longer a handful. We Christians of all sorts, good, bad, and many of our friends, we number 600 million—yes, 600 million out of a total of 2,000 million people on earth. And it is not only what we are, it is what we have been. The Christian Church has *made* history—it has probably made most of all the human history that ever has been made. Science itself, with all its attendant wonders, is at least a grandchild of the Church, having come out of the European civilization which the Church largely created. And even today science and technology are greatest where Christians are most numerous—especially Protestants! Oh, we have been and we are a very great thing in the world! The consequence being what? The consequence being that we Christians have a responsibility for the world such as the Holy Spirit clearly did not impose, as an immediate obligation, on the Church of Pentecost.

If today the laws of human society are not in conformity with the will of God, we cannot say that it is because God has not given us enough votes! He has! Who disposes of the overwhelming economic and military power of the world today? Obviously, the so-called Christian nations and—count them, nose by nose, Christian individuals!

We have the votes that dispose of the power. It is an awesome thing. To have such power and not to use it is certainly to be wicked and unprofitable servants. To have this power and to use it is certainly to become involved in sinful corruptions. We modern Christians are evidently caught in an awesome dilemma. We cannot, as the early Christians did, separate ourselves from the world —we are the world, a very large part of it.

"Fear not, little flock," said Jesus; "God will give you the victory." And the little flock did not fear and it had the victory. Even on earth, the mustard seed grew into the vast tree of Christian civilization and all the birds of the air did sit on its branches. That is why we are here today. But now we are not a little flock. We are a great host. Will not Our Lord and Master all the more expect that we shall receive and implant upon the earth the victory He so desires to give?

4 CHRISTIANITY AND WAR

The ecumenical movement took a great forward step at Amsterdam in the summer of 1948, when representatives of 147 churches from all parts of the world formed the World Council of Churches. Luce attended the Amsterdam meeting and TIME *gave a somewhat critical account of it (September 13, 1948). Luce explained the personal consequences in this speech to the National Assembly of the United Council of Church Women at Milwaukee, on November 16, 1948, and then proceeded to discuss a problem common to most churches. The cold war had recently reached a menacing stage with the fall of Czechoslovakia, but NATO had not yet been formed.*

When I was a little boy, Mother could never manage to spank me properly. The difficulty was that we would both get to laughing before she got the old hairbrush really swinging. So she left that part of the business to Father. But a couple of months ago I really did catch it. That was after TIME's big story on Amsterdam. Oh yes, I had paid attention; TIME *did* have a big story on the World Council. Only, the editors of TIME, including me at the top of the list, didn't think that the World Council was quite as inspiring as it might have been. So I caught it. Mother was very sick. Her store of physical life was all but gone. But that didn't stop her from writing what she had to write. In a firm, clear hand she wrote me three tightly written pages, telling me what a bad editor I had been. If you thought you knew the trouble editors could get into—now you really know!

Fortunately, in that case it was possible to make some reparation —enough to seek and find the infinite forgiveness in a mother's heart. And I am glad to make further reparation here by reasserting my allegiance to the purposes of Amsterdam and to our great ecumenical leaders.

To me the greatest sign given at Amsterdam is that the Church, with all its human faults, is earnestly striving to pull itself together in order to be a united and responsible Church—to be responsible to the truth and therefore to society.

There is, of course, a reason why Church unity has hitherto seemed unimportant in this country. Our forefathers—and the Founding Fathers—assumed that America was and would be fundamentally Christian—and therefore diversities were diversities only within a Christian environment. We can assume that no longer.

Our forefathers did not assume that most Americans would be Christians. Far from it. But they did assume that the standards of right and wrong would be Christian. They did assume that everyone at least agreed with Emerson that the moral law rules the universe. To them, the Constitution made intellectual sense on the assumption that God lives and makes His will known effectively to men in history. But that interpretation, I am sure, has long since been rejected by the Harvard Law School as irrelevant and absurd. And, I'm sorry to say, I guess Yale would say the same thing. And Vassar, too.

There is another reason why our forefathers cared so little for Church unity. They felt little responsibility for the old world—except as they might give it an example of political freedom. But now we are called to great worldwide responsibilities. The Church is in the forefront of this vocation. And this is, at bottom, why American Christianity can no longer be content to be so quaintly local, so provincial and so divided. The challenge to American Christianity today is the challenge of universality.

Am I being wholly unrealistic in suggesting that America may play its part in history as a Christian nation? Very likely. But we think we have some responsibility to work for that purpose, don't we? I am going to try to serve that purpose tonight by tackling what is for modern American Christians the most difficult single problem in the relationship of Christianity to statesmanship. That, of course, is the problem of war.

In our church groups, war is almost never discussed. It is a very unpopular topic. You know what I mean. In church assemblies, war is denounced; war is condemned by resolutions—and that is the end of it.

But you also know that many of the same people who vote for these resolutions know that merely to condemn war is not the end of it either for themselves or for their children or for the Church. All statesmanship is involved with the risk of war. Faced by this reality, can the Church take any attitude except one of complete pacifism or complete evasion?

Consider, for example, the Marshall Plan. Great church convocations in America have nearly all endorsed and propagandized for the Marshall Plan. At the same time they have denounced every form of American military preparedness. Does that make sense? Not to any responsible statesman I know on either side of the Atlantic. Least of all, for example, to Prime Minister Attlee, who has said to me: "I assure you British Socialism owes far more to Christ than to Marx."

Very briefly, the essence of the Marshall Plan was that Western Europe might all too likely fall a prey to Soviet Communism unless its economic life was built up. In other words, without the Marshall Plan, Soviet Communism might take over all of Europe *without* war. But suppose today our government announced that under no circumstances would we fight with arms. That, to say the least, would be a considerable temptation to Soviet Russia to take by military means what it failed to get through economic collapse. Thus, in plain terms, the Marshall Plan increased the chances of war—unless the Marshall Plan is backed by the assurance that, under certain conditions, we will defend the Marshall Plan and its purposes by force of arms.

This illustrates the kind of basic dilemma which confronts the Church—when it sets out to give Christian guidance on public matters to modern man.

We shall not resolve the dilemma tonight. But we may understand it better if we put it in the perspective of 2,000 years of Christian experience. Let us glance over the long sweep of Christian history and see what we can learn.

First, then, there are the early Christians of the first and second centuries. They were undoubtedly the most attractive Christians that ever lived. They were full of tender kindness and joy! Through the vast Roman Empire, despite its splendors, its tolerance and its prosperity, the prevailing mood from top to bottom was one of pessimism. But the Christians—history writes of them that they were law-abiding, inoffensive, good workmen—and full of kindness and joy! They had, however, one other unfailing characteristic: they took absolutely no responsibility for society.

As Gibbon put it: "The Christians were not less averse to the business than to the pleasures of this world. . . . They cheerfully submitted to the authority of their Pagan governors. But . . . they refused to take any part in the civil administration or the military defense of the empire."

And, of course, we know why they were thus socially irresponsible: they believed in the imminent end of the world. So they campaigned for no social reforms—not even for the abolition of slavery. Leading lives of extraordinary purity and grace, the early Christians just went about their business of being Christian and attracting other people to be Christians and hoping in the Lord.

And so, as we move along through the third century, we find that there are more and more Christians while the Roman Empire gets sadder and sadder. And then suddenly something happens—a colossal milestone in Christian history. The Roman Emperor becomes a Christian. In the year 312, Constantine raises the glorious banner: *In Hoc Signo Vinces!*

But it was far more than that. It wasn't just that one man who happened to be Caesar became a Christian. The Christians had multiplied and had become the most effective political support for a tottering empire. In other words, it was Mr. and Mrs. Christian who became Caesar. That's what happened.

Well, now, how do you "render unto Caesar" when *Christian* is Caesar?

One answer is that Christian ought never to have become Caesar. I think that is a rather feeble answer. Maybe it was unfortunate for the Church and Christianity that Christian became Caesar just at the time that he did and in terms of empire. But something similar was bound to happen sometime—especially in democratic terms. Christians were bound to become responsible for the state: that's where we got to in 312 and that's where—with many changes—we are today.

And now let's stop in a millennium later at the 13th century, and catch a glimpse of a man writing and praying and praying and writing—St. Thomas Aquinas. The old Roman Empire has fallen long, long ago. The dark ages have come and gone. Under Christian inspiration and leadership a new civilization has risen—one which owes much to the classical age, but which has a new spirit, different from anything mankind has ever known. The new civilization is called Christendom.

At that point Christians had to think. They had to think responsibly about everything. They had to think about farm prices, labor relations, taxes, marriage, war. They came to be great thinkers. The greatest of all was Thomas Aquinas—perhaps the greatest and certainly the most monumental thinker of all time. Coming to the problem of war, St. Thomas worked out in prayer—he never worked out anything except in prayer—the "doctrine of the just war."

Today all serious Christian thinking about war starts with St. Thomas' systematic doctrine of the just war. Some may feel that this doctrine is inadequate to the vastly changed conditions of the modern world. But basic truths are there which we can, with repentant hearts, relearn. For example, St. Thomas lays it down that a just war can only be fought for clearly defined objectives. When the enemy is willing to yield on clearly defined conditions, then the war must stop. Surely that simple proposition must strike deeply into our Christian consciences. For in St. Thomas' doctrine it is unlawful to demand "unconditional surrender."

A few months before Hiroshima, I was with Admiral Halsey's Navy as it assaulted the coast of Japan. Two things seemed clear to me—as they did to many of the top fighting men I talked to: first, that Japan was beaten; second, that the Japanese knew it and were every day showing signs of increasing willingness to quit. If, instead of our doctrine of "unconditional surrender," we had all along made our conditions clear, I have little doubt that the war with Japan would have ended soon without the bomb explosion which so jarred the Christian conscience.

In any case, if we as Christians really want to be serious about this problem of war, we can nail one proposition to our conscience and fight for it. The United States must never again fight a war for "unconditional surrender."

One thing we can do to make war less likely, and, if it should occur, more nearly just, is to define clearly the reasons for which we will fight and the terms on which we will cease fire.

The men of the Middle Ages did not succeed in working out a

Christian society capable of solving all human problems and going on and on in a straight line toward the City of God. A century after St. Thomas, Christendom became rapidly more and more secular, worldly. There came the Renaissance, the long brilliant burst of human energy and pride, in whose gloomy twilight Europe now lives. Our Reformation was as much a revolt against this exciting worldliness as it was against the Catholic Church. And one of the strong tendencies of the Reformation was once again to reject all responsibility for secular affairs. In *Pilgrim's Progress*, from the day that Christian left the City of Destruction until he reached Heaven, he did not once confront, did not once consider, a single problem of social justice or public policy. The giants and monsters he fought were exclusively the giants and monsters of personal sin and doubt.

But historic Protestantism also took a different road—a road of extremely active concern for economics and government. We here tonight are proof of that. America is the proof of that. At the dawn of the 20th century, America, largely shaped by Protestant influences, had become a huge success. And, indeed, most of the world was feeling mighty successful—or hopeful. There could be no more dark ages. Progress was certain. Science and education were sure to bring to pass every good thing. So, of course, it was taken as axiomatic that the problem of war would soon be solved—i.e., eliminated almost any minute. Does that seem incredible?

Well, listen for a minute to a man who was an excellent example of the spirit of his age and his adopted country: Andrew Carnegie. Here is what he wrote in his letter of instructions to the Trustees of the Carnegie Endowment for International Peace: "When war is discarded as disgraceful to civilized men . . . the Trustees will please then consider what is the next most degrading evil or evils whose banishment would most advance the progress, elevation and happiness of man, and so on from century to century without end."

That was the high point in human optimism and human pride— an optimism and a pride which, furthermore, was thought to be Christian!

And what now? Now that in our lifetime we have seen more human suffering, more obscene human suffering, than in any period of history before us? Well, God is patient. He continues to teach us. He continues to raise up great teachers in our Church who do not despair, who have the courage to relearn the lessons of human nature and destiny. One such is Reinhold Niebuhr, one of the very great leaders at Amsterdam. Dr. Niebuhr has abundantly corrected the false presumption of modern Protestant optimism. But at the same time he does not despair, he does not teach us merely to escape from the world and all its folly.

A few weeks ago Dr. Niebuhr said * that if we are serious about protecting Western Europe from Soviet domination, we must take the *risk of war*. Now the average American probably knows that, but for a Christian leader to say it—that took courage—moral courage. That was real, honest facing up to Christian responsibility.

Andrew Carnegie and the spirit of his times badly needed correction. And history has given it. But there is one thing which both Mr. Carnegie and Dr. Niebuhr have in common with each other and most of us. They both—and we—reflect the historic Protestant tradition in this country—which is that the American Christian has the right and the duty to exert himself to influence the course of our nation's life in accordance with God's will. In setting up the separation of Church and State—along with the doctrine of a government of limited power—the last thing our forefathers ever wished or supposed was that the United States should not be guided by Christian principles. America has been an outstanding example of Christian creativity in building a state.

From these reflections on Christian history, we may come to at least a few conclusions as to the problem of Christianity and war.

First, the responsibility for the war-making power runs concurrently with the responsibility for the life of the nation in all other aspects: political, economic, legal, moral, cultural. When the Church feels generally responsible, the Church must be responsible for the principles which guide the use of the sword no less than of the ploughshare—or the tractor.

Second, I believe that once the Church has accepted its responsibility, it will be in a position to make its voice clear and strong so that the war-making power of our nation is put under Christian judgment, Christian restraint—*and* the courage of Christian conviction. With the courage of Christian conviction, the Church can have effective influence on the principles and policies for which this nation will fight. The Church can then go even further and lay down principles as to how we fight. In order to do this, I see—is it

* In an article in Life, September 20, 1948.

hopelessly visionary?—I see the great leaders of the Church sitting down with our top military men and viewing them, not as the enemies of society, but as men who as much as any laymen desire to do the right as God gives them to see the right.

The engulfing tide of barbarism cannot be turned back by armies ignorant of the Church. It cannot be turned back by armies abandoned by the Church. In my view it can be turned back only by a nation willing to be guided by Christian principles and whose willingness is tested by the courageous willingness of the Church to enter into the fiery depth of the problem of war and *there* to stand and *there* to guide.

And so we come finally to the basic question: Is America today a nation for which the Church can in fact have significant responsibility? From the bulk of available evidence, the answer is no. Civilization in America today is largely secular—that is, American civilization is concerned almost entirely with *this* world. In modern American life, how much actual concern can you find with the *next* world? That question defines what is meant by secular as radically opposed to Christian. And the question answers itself. The climate of American civilization is predominantly secular, both as a whole and as revealed in nearly all its parts—in our industry and commerce, our amusements, our art and literature, in our education, which largely excludes and rejects God—and, of course, in our press. This is the measure of the miserable ambiguity in which nearly all of us stand. And how do we get out of it? History may provide the answer—the Church may have to become once again the Christian of *Pilgrim's Progress*, making its way with the little flock of the faithful through a barbarous or at best worldly world with which it can have no useful communication.

But the leaders of our Church say no. They say that there can be a real Christian responsibility for America. I think they are right, and I wish, however lamely, to follow them. I believe they are right. I cannot prove it. But I know why I believe it. The roots of America are Christian, and despite the vast overgrowth of the un-Christian, we shall find more and more that we cannot live or breathe or even think except as we draw with a fierce hunger on those roots of Christian faith.

And above all there is a new sense of vision in the Church itself —the ecumenical vision and mission. This ecumenical mood and mission are, I believe, the great manifestation of God's will for His

Church in this historic situation, and especially in America. Only the united Church can be the responsible Church. In this chaotic and revolutionary age, only the responsible Church can point toward a just society and a righteous peace.

5 A CHRISTIAN SOLDIER

The cold war also explains the somber overtones of this speech, given at Washington and Lee University on December 10, 1948.

I have to thank you for one of the great personal experiences of my life. A few weeks ago I ran into a man whom most of you know but whom I have never met before—Robert E. Lee. He probably didn't notice the encounter. But for me it was a collision.

The fact that I had never met this gentleman before is not to be attributed to the eccentricities of a Yankee upbringing. In my youth, I must have consumed four or five boys' biographies of Stonewall Jackson. And that was *not* just because he became a Presbyterian. There was also a period—sophomore year, I think—when I was an ardent Calhoun man. That probably was because he *was* a Yale man. One way and another I early encountered many a rebel and knew that Lee was the noblest of them all. But the man himself I had hitherto caught sight of only distantly in the general history books, veiled by the smoking dust of complex battles, the leader of the world's hardest-to-beat army. And now I have met him—now.

I wish that all of you might meet him, as it were, for the first time, now—in 1948. Outstanding at any time in the gallery of heroes, why does he seem so especially extraordinary now? It is because Robert E. Lee was—is—a Christian. He was an able and active man, a career man—ambitious and brilliant—a leader of men —and a Christian. Do I mean that it is rare to find a public man today who is Christian? No. But let's see what kind of a Christian

Robert E. Lee was when he walked this troubled earth. I shall read
to you from the first volume of Mr. Freeman's biography: *

> His manners reflected his spiritual life. . . . He was a
> simple soul, humble, transparent, and believing. Increasingly
> through the years prior to that historic railway journey to
> Richmond, religion had become a part of his very being. . . .
> Reading daily his Bible and his prayer book, spending much
> time on his knees, he believed in a God who, in His wisdom,
> sent blessings beyond man's deserts, and visited him on occa-
> sions, with hardships and disaster for the chastening of the
> rebellious heart. . . . As Robert E. Lee viewed it, on the eve
> of his plunge into the bloody tragedy of a war among broth-
> ers, life was only a preparation for eternity. Whatever befell
> the faithful was the will of God, and whatever God willed
> was best.

Would we not be a little surprised if we were to read those
words in the obituary of any one of the many leading figures now
on this stage of the Western world who might die tonight? And yet
we say that we have fought and are fighting for Western civilization—for the American way of life. Does anyone truly feel that
Western civilization has much to do with the will of God? Is the
American way of life a "preparation for eternity"?

You see what I mean: it is startling to encounter suddenly in
1948 Robert E. Lee's *kind* of Christianity.

Now, of course, that kind of Christianity—which we may describe as humanly speaking a complete Christianity—is rare at any
time. Nevertheless, to our forefathers that kind of Christianity did
not seem to be strange; it did not seem foreign or alien to their time
and place, either in the South or in the North. And today surely it
does seem out of place, out of date, not only in the field of public
affairs—but also in the common life of men.

Already some of you are thinking that times change—change is
the first law of life—and that with changing times come changing
attitudes about everything, including religion. But we can hardly
dismiss Lee's Christianity quite so glibly. For the God whom Lee
worshiped every day of his life was, he thought, the same yesterday, today and forever. The point is that fundamentally Lee was
just plain right or plain wrong.

* *R. E. Lee*, by Douglas Southall Freeman (1934).

In the first week or so of my absorbing acquaintanceship with Lee, there was only wonder and awe and admiration that such a truly noble and lovable man could be. And then I ran into a profound puzzlement. Again, to put it oversimply: how could God lead a man who had such perfect trust in Him and who lived so nearly by that trust—how could God lead such a man into such bitter ambiguities of fate? I do not mean, of course, how could God let such a man fail in his greatest endeavor? That is never a problem, even to a secondhand Christian. Nor am I referring even to the general philosophical problem of evil. What I mean is this: Lee was devoted, proudly and passionately devoted, to the United States, and as for the rightness of the cause for which the South fought, he was, to put it mildly, very skeptical. When the terrible parting of the ways came, he had to guide him only an instinctive loyalty to Virginia and his kith and kin, plus a notion that somehow the North had behaved rather badly. When the enthusiastic rebel cries first went up that first Sunday morning in Alexandria, Lee's face was ashen still.

That men should get into deep trouble because they follow the desires and devices of their own hearts, that the pursuit of selfish aims leads to all sorts of personal ambiguities and public disasters —that is understandable. But if a man follows faithfully the path of duty and honor—is there not at least the guarantee that he will never be at war with himself or with what he holds most dear? That kind of conflict is the greatest of trials that can come to man. It is the pure essence of tragedy. The name for it is "conflict of loyalties"; conflict of deeply held allegiances. It is only the noblest men—Lee on the one side, Lincoln on the other—who experience the fullness of the tragedy of this conflict, because the loyalties of most men are, like themselves, only too easily compromised. And only the profoundly religious man survives the tragedy—Lee watching the momentous disaster of Gettysburg—"It is all my fault"—and yet never doubting God's will.

It is the popular fashion today to speak of the desirability of moral and spiritual "values." They are recommended as being almost on a par with economic or military assets. The implication is that if we increase our stock of these assets all will go well with us. What needs to be said perhaps is that religion, unlike prudent morality, is a very dangerous proposition—it leads men and nations into depths. The path of righteousness is not the path of comfort.

"I came not to bring peace but a sword. . . . My peace I give unto you, but not as the world gives."

Most Americans today have never known, in public affairs, any really serious conflict of loyalty. We have our political bickers—often very intense; and plenty of people have plenty of reason for not liking what goes on. Among these, include me. But deep conflicts such as between loyalty to home and country on the one hand and loyalty to the greatest good, to the best that a man knows—that kind of conflict has seemed to us for several generations almost unthinkable. We are a most fortunate nation—may God permit us long to remain so. But we know this is a time of really profound crisis in human affairs; if we understand anything by that, we must understand that the greatest issues of human destiny are now at stake, the kind of issues which are, humanly speaking, irreconcilable, and which do indeed set brother against brother as well as nation against nation. The fall of France in 1940, which made Frenchmen ashamed of themselves; the shameless horrors of a shameless Germany; the death of Jan Masaryk *—these are the signs of our times, and no nation can easily escape their portents.

America, almost naively innocent of the sense of tragedy, is destined to play a great part in this world crisis, but we shall surely fail except as our leaders—the leaders of the future represented here—achieve insight into the full height and depth of the human drama, with all its possibilities of evil and courage and redemption. Can American leadership achieve this depth of understanding before the worst happens? Perhaps not.

There is need for some pessimism in America—a highly unpopular commodity. We can do with less cynicism, we can get along without the wise guys—but we need to understand a little better than we do how great human disaster can be, to understand in Woodrow Wilson's words how the heart of the world can be broken.

Having spoken thus pessimistically, I can with better conscience regain my natural right as an American to speak with optimism. Can America overcome the crisis? Yes. Can we as individual Americans help to lead America, in tasks of leadership, great or small, to a triumph, under God, over the grave challenges of our

---

* Masaryk (1886–1948) was Foreign Minister in the postwar Czech Government. His death, by falling out of a window, was called a suicide by the Communists, but has more recently been ascribed to Soviet agents.

time? Yes. And what do we require for this general task and for the many, many tasks of leadership of which the whole is made? First of all we require, as at all times, the ancient virtues.

The other day General Omar Bradley * was telling me about the talk he used to give in the early days of the war to as many groups of officers as he could meet. It was a talk about leadership. It was General Bradley's observation that there are five or six essentials of leadership, that every great leader has all of them in some degree, and one or two of them in outstanding degree. The first essential is character—and to General Bradley the greatest example of character is—yes, Robert E. Lee. Character, human understanding (Lincoln), tenacity (Grant), professional competence—these are perennial qualities which make leaders.

We make our vision of the world out of the best we have. America is rich in traits of character, in social experience, in ideals and in actual achievements, of which this university is an immediate example. If Americans are optimistic, they have reason to be so, and our confidence in the future can in itself be a gift to the world—indeed, a necessary element in our vision. But anyone who tries seriously to construct a vision of the world comes sooner or later to the religious problem. The religious problem in our time is very curious. There is on the one hand a growing feeling of the lack of religion in our actual modern civilization and of the need for it, and there is also the feeling that no actual religion is true. There is, in short, a feeling that there must be somehow a new religion.

Obviously you cannot invent a new religion—not even with a billion-dollar Manhattan Project. But some say—and they are among the finest minds of our day—that we have available the materials of a new religion. And there's even at hand a name for the new religion. The other day one of our most famous men was asked if he was a religious man. "I certainly am," said he, "and my religion is democracy."

Can democracy be the religious principle of the coming world— or the equivalent of religion? Frankly, I do not think so. But I leave this question with you as the most serious question of your age. For myself, I believe that just the contrary is the case—namely, that what we call democracy cannot conceivably work except as it is inspired by an allegiance to a religion higher than itself.

* Leader of the U.S. First Army during the invasion of Europe.

What religion? The cry goes up—but what religion? Might it be, after all, the religion of Robert E. Lee? Might it be, after all, the true religion?

---

6   A SPECULATION ABOUT 1980

In 1955, FORTUNE *asked ten leading Americans to speak their hopes and prophecies for the next twenty-five years. After the distinguished scientists, lawyers, educators and others had had their say, Luce concluded the series on this most "speculative" of all the topics, the future of the human spirit. His enthusiasm of that year for the evolutionary vision of Pierre Lecomte du Noüy was to be superseded by his later discovery of Teilhard de Chardin (pages 327 and 332). The following is excerpted from the December 1955 issue of* FORTUNE.

One day a year or so ago Margaret Bourke-White, who in the last two decades has been roaming the ends of the earth for LIFE, asked to see me. That meant that she had some big and probably wild and expensive project to propose. I wondered what it could be, for it seemed to me she had already done everything, including the North Pole, to say nothing of the darkest depths of coal mines and of Africa. When she came into my office she proceeded in a matter-of-fact manner to register her request. She wanted a promise that it would be she and no other who would have the assignment to go to the moon. Taking her quite seriously, I said yes.

Naturally, we will be happy to have the trip to the moon in LIFE —and an analysis of its economic consequences in FORTUNE. But I began to ask myself in the following days: Do I myself want to go to the moon? I mean even after Miss Bourke-White has got back quite safely and regular service has been established and Pan Am is kicking up an awful fuss because the route has been allotted to an upstart? I have concluded that I do not really care about personally going to the moon. This conclusion has been a little disturbing to me, since up to now there has never been any place that I didn't want to go to. I have never had my fill of traveling this earth and visiting its inhabitants. Human destiny is here—is it not? —and it is this which has fired my curiosity and aroused my concern. But if men and women are soon to be tripping to the moon, that surely will radically change the whole outlook on the human adventure, which will have passed beyond any grasp I might have of its meaning and purpose.

But still, I further reflected, it will continue to be the *human* adventure. And if that adventure does, as I believe, have meaning and purpose; if it is true, as Lord Tennyson sang, that "through the ages one increasing purpose runs," then none of us will be alien in any new and vaster age. Occupationally obsolescent I may be; but not personally alien. So—on to the moon! In mental reach, if not in physical fact!

Furthermore, if Lord Tennyson is right, then going to the moon is significant (and it doesn't matter too much if it really is *not* so pretty as Hawaii or so splendid as the Alps). It is significant because man gets there by his own efforts, by the use of his God-given faculties. Second, it is significant because when man gets to the moon, it is because God may want him to get there to see what he has never seen before, to see everything in literally a new light.

How painful it is to see things in a new light! When only a few centuries ago the suspicion dawned with Copernicus that our earth was not the center and greater part of the universe, it was frightfully upsetting. Human life has never been the same since. And when, in our great-grandfathers' time, the Darwinian rumor ran, all too plausibly, that Adam and Eve were not created in B.C. 4004, and that we came from a long line of monkeys—that half-truth brought spiritual derangement to millions. Will God never let us alone for an eon or two to get used to enjoying the half-lights of the world we have? Evidently not.

With all these shocks of change, the wonder is that we—speaking especially of Americans—hold so firmly to the sense of purpose in human life. Why do we so stubbornly refuse to believe that life is meaningless? Science discloses no "meaning" or "purpose." Our artists and our novelists have disintegrated the human personality into the most miserable shreds of degradation. But we persist in talking of "human dignity." Is our talk a last collective shout in a cosmic graveyard? Twenty-five years from now, will men believe still that there is in life a "dignity" infinitely precious—that liberty wagered against death will win and is forever worth winning?

Such questions will never be answered with universal satisfaction. But these are the questions around the answers to which human life has always been organized. The long-gowned Scholar of China, the Christian Knight of Chivalry, the Brahman of India, the Russian Commissar, the Responsible Citizen of America—all of these have been living symbols of the types of organization which have embodied the meaning of life in every civilization.

It is the premise of this article that as the world rushes into ever vaster and more complex organization, the ultimate questions of human destiny, far from being left behind like children's questions about the stork, are likely to become more than ever the primary stuff of human conversation and controversy.

To the ultimate question of whether there is actually any purpose in human life—or any "meaning" beyond the pleasure-pain calculus—there are only two respectable or noble answers, one of which must be false. One answer is: Yes, there is a purpose in human life, and it is God-given. The other answer is: No, there really isn't except as man invents his own purpose and upholds it.

The first answer is the Christian or Tennysonian answer generally accepted by Americans A.D. 1955. Our acceptance of the Christian answer is apt to be careless, shallow and ignorant, both in theory and in practice; but it is the one we are used to; it is the one which, despite our quarrels and uproars, has given to American life and politics a remarkable *consensus*.

The second answer is less familiar to us; it is chilling and even frightening. Americans rarely face up to it; it is contrary to the American ethos. In Europe the skeptical or atheist position is much more at home. Noble expression has been given to it by the lively eighty-three-year-old mathematician-philosopher Bertrand Russell. Here is one of his many eloquent passages:

> Brief and powerless is Man's life; on him and all of his race the slow sure doom falls pitiless and dark. Blind to good and evil, reckless of destruction, omnipotent Matter rolls on its relentless way; for Man, condemned today to lose his dearest, tomorrow himself to pass through the gate of darkness, it

remains only to cherish, ere yet the blow falls, the lofty thoughts that ennoble his little day; disdaining the coward terrors of the slave of Fate, to worship at the shrine that his own hands have built; undismayed by the empire of chance, to preserve a mind free from the wanton tyranny that rules his outward life; proudly defiant of the irresistible forces that tolerate, for a moment, his knowledge and his condemnation, to sustain alone, a weary but unyielding Atlas, the world that his own ideals have fashioned despite the trampling march of unconscious power.

Lord Russell's stoic view has never sustained any process of civilization. However, if ever there could be a time when the Atlas-Prometheus faith could provide the *consensus* for a civilization, it is the age on which the sun of knowledge and power is now rising so high. By 1980, the whole outlook on life will have so radically changed that there might emerge, for the first time on this planet, an elite capable of sustaining a magnificent civilization (probably global) on the basis of the noble lord's noble and Promethean philosophy.

Whatever may be the purpose of human life, if any, one thing is clear: that in all past experience human purpose has had to be worked out primarily within the limits of an unbreakable economic equation. That equation was stated in the third chapter of Genesis in terms of a divine command: "In the sweat of thy face shalt thou eat bread."

In our time this "sweat-of-brow" equation has been radically altered. The equation was shattered by *pre-atomic means*. It was apparent more than 100 years ago that it would be. It was the dear little old steam engine and the Du Pont chemistry of 1925 vintage and the simple electricity of those quaint old utility tycoons—these simple, straightforward Newtonian tools were enough to change utterly the physical condition of life on earth.

And now comes the atom. In a previous article in this FORTUNE series (June), Dr. John Von Neumann of the Atomic Energy Commission summarized the whole thing in one stroke: in a few decades all energy (electric, atomic, solar) is likely to be virtually costless. In Von Neumann's vivid phrase, energy may be "free—just like the unmetered air."

Now faced with the superabundance of atomic technology, we

Americans have just barely experienced the pre-atomic abundance. Having not yet had time to learn how to live and think in one new economic world, we are already walking into another, newer, stranger, greater.

The Calvinist cosmology put a high spiritual value on productive (economically valuable) work, work being not only salutary in the sense that idleness leads to sin, but more profoundly in the sense that through work man can exercise his personal responsibility, can, in St. Paul's phrase, "work out his own salvation." This ethos—this deep belief in the moral imperative of work and of personal responsibility—is still a driving force in America. What will happen to America when work seems not to be the gyroscope of morality? Oldsters have been shaking their heads about this for a long time.

Meanwhile, now, at this moment, we are in a transition stage between the Calvinist work-imperative and the Von Neumann "free energy." And we have pretty well matured our social ideal for this pre-atomic age of abundance. We call it "a decent life for all." It is a balanced compound of work (production) and pleasure (consumption). Specifically, our social ideal has this bill of fare: enough food and clothes and housing for everyone to live healthfully (with plenty of medical care), and *also* a full diet of education and culture. Why not?

This "decent life for all"—and culture, too—is a magnificent thing, more splendid perhaps than all the cathedrals ever built. It is the realization of the hopes of all the thousands of the servants and lovers of mankind who for the last 200 years have given their lives to free mankind from its misery, to make forever untrue Hobbes's famous definition of human life as being "solitary, poor, nasty, brutish and short." Let the heroes rejoice that their warfare has been successful, that their goal is in sight. And let us give thanks that we have inherited their victories, far beyond our own deserving.

But—and there is a but—there is a wonder and doubt whether this ideal of "a decent life for all" is good enough. Why the doubt? The truth is that *no conceivable utopia on earth will satisfy man.* However profoundly compelling is the urge to overcome whatever misery and brutality there is, and to substitute for it a man-conceived utopia of workless prosperity and global peace—no such utopia will satisfy, even in the imagination, much less in the realization.

So, I speculate that a consequence of the abundance which now is—and even more of superabundance to come—may be that men and women will experience a more direct confrontation with the ultimate questions concerning the meaning of human life and its purpose. If prosperity and security will not satisfy, what on earth will? Answer: nothing.

What, then, *is* the purpose of life? Trips to the moon will not abate the naked urgency of this question: they will only confront man all the more with the meaning of his existence in the whole light-year cosmos. The confrontation is predictable; whether men in 1980 will have the grace and intellectuality to cope with it is unpredictable.

"If God did not exist," said Voltaire, "it would be necessary to invent Him." Then another brilliant Frenchman, Auguste Comte, an idol of his age, proclaimed that God was no longer necessary because in fact man *had* invented Him. Surveying the amazing triumphs of intellect and science even 100 years ago, when there were hardly any railroads (and no plumbing, but much filth and lice), Comte was in an ecstasy of joy over the final victory of man. Man had himself conceived the good, the true and the beautiful, and now that man had at last fashioned the key to truth, namely science, it was only a matter of a short while before a universal utopia of the good, the true and the beautiful would envelop the world. In token whereof Comte generously elected Moses, Homer, Aristotle and various other well-known characters to a universal Hall of Fame—but not Jesus, whom he disliked.

In the lifetime of many of us now living, H. G. Wells was a lively and attractive prophet of the same utopia. Alas, Wells died at the age of eighty, confessing most pitiably his utter disillusion and despair. Somehow, he confessed, he had been quite wrong about the nature of things, including human nature. The world, instead of coming under the rule of Wellsian scientist-kings, had lapsed into what Churchill designated as history's most terrible and most unnecessary war.

In 1955 there is still, as we say, a lot to be done and, in America, plenty of will to do it. First of all, we seem wonderfully united in a determination to keep going, to maintain the tremendous economy we have. Furthermore, the economy of abundance does not yet include everyone. There are slums to tear down and cities to rebuild. Furthermore, even the American who is part of the economy of abundance, and knows it, feels that he could do with a bit more: ask the budget-conscious housewife. As for the rest of the world, the job of creating abundance has hardly begun. So, even without going beyond the realm of economics, there is no lack of "challenges" demanding purposeful "responses."

But as we Americans stand now, emerging from the age of work-imperative and entering an imaginable age of "free energy," the question must be asked whether the sense of purpose which spurred the achievements of the past century or two will also incite the next generation to perform the vast work which has yet to be done.

To be sure, we can always count on a full quota of "selfish" motivations. Indeed, never in history has the desire for material goods and even for sheer survival been so appealed to as in our time. The modern potency of "selfish" motivation (including survival, the most "selfish" of all) seems to make irrelevant any concern with ideal purposes.

But I argue that men are not moved solely or even primarily by materialistic motives of gross self-interest. Certainly the history of the last hundred or two hundred years in the West cannot be read in materialistic terms. If the economic progress of the 19th century rested heavily on the dynamism of individualistic "selfish" interests, it was accompanied all along the line by the greatest display the world has ever seen of the altruistic, of humanitarian ideals in action. It was not simply that Carnegie and Rockefeller ended up as philanthropists; the point is that even as the rugged individualists pursued their rugged ways, thousands of other Victorians and post-Victorians devoted their lives to the "social gospel" and achieved every kind of humanitarian reform, from the abolition of slavery to the forty-hour week and hospitals and free education. What we have been seeing in America and partially elsewhere—a phenomenon without historical precedent—is the merging of the gospel of work ("free enterprise") and the social gospel ("humanitarianism"). The merging of these two vast rivers with the third river of science has made the sea of abundance around which the Western world now lives.

Paul Henri Spaak, the great socialist, said in one of his most eloquent speeches that no political party in Europe could claim a monopoly of the Christian tradition. He wanted to claim a fair share of it for himself and for his anticlerical and even atheistic socialists. It is not necessary to claim that Christianity uniquely inspired the ideals of humanity and liberty, but one must be stubbornly blind not to see the Sign of the Cross above the victories of the social gospel and of political freedom. One must be blind indeed not to see Communism as a Christian (not a Buddhist or Hindu) heresy. One must be blind indeed not to see that the godless French Revolution could have happened only within Christendom; and in fact nowhere have "liberty, equality and fraternity" been proclaimed save where the Gospel light has shone. So, even in the heresies which have so nearly destroyed it, the power of the Christian faith is revealed in history.

The question is whether the Christian faith, which has so much inspired and guided us, will still inspire and guide us in those greater works that must be done. The simple Christian answer knows that the faith will endure till the end of time, but it does not know how effective it will be in shaping history in any particular period; Christianity may become once again the mustard seed hidden in the catacomb of civilization. This is the simple and ineffable answer. But there is another, more complex, answer which more narrowly concerns us, namely, that the Christian gospel must be preached in every tongue, that is to say *it must be preached in the different language of every different age.* How may it be preached and apprehended in 1980? Or even now, in 1955?

Efforts to "restate" the Christian faith have been going on for decades. In the social field, these reformulations, both Catholic and Protestant, have had their victories. In the political field there is some partial success: the Christian Democratic movement tries to recreate in Europe a consensus of Christian humanism; and in America, President Eisenhower and Secretary Dulles assert the moral basis of foreign policy, though the effort to relate politics to the moral law is widely opposed, resisted and sneered at.

But the crucial area is neither politics nor sociology; the crucial area is in men's sense of total reality. The "restatement" of Christian faith most urgently needed is in terms of the new kind of universe, which science has been revealing and which even the "common man" apprehends as reality as he steps on his accelerator or flicks his dial.

The conflict of science and religion, which so agitated our parents, is no longer a major topic in America. Another Scopes trial is hardly a possibility. Today the Scopeses, and the Bryans and Darrows, too, understand that they do not have to make a choice between knowing the age of rocks and the Rock of Ages. We have come to the realization that science and religion are two distinct worlds, in which different "affairs" go on. The two worlds are not in substantial conflict. Border incidents crop up from time to time, but the general atmosphere is one of peace. Perhaps "armistice" would be a better word than "peace." For, while we have got science and religion fairly well distinguished from one another, we have not yet got them cooperating with one another. Where there should be only distinction, there is separation. The two affairs go on unrelatedly, whereas they should go on unitedly. The result is a certain impoverishment of both the religious and the scientific enterprise. The man of faith fails to know the full truth about this terrestrial universe, which is the concern of science. Conversely, the man of science fails to know the full truth about the destiny of man, which is the concern of religion. Yet man himself—whether he be savant or simple—pursues his destiny within the horizons of this terrestrial universe. And if the two knowledges proper to the two worlds of science and religion are completely divorced, man will lack the kind of picture of himself-within-the-universe that can unite his mind, his hope and his conscience in the service of some intelligible, confident and lawful purpose, place him at home in a harmonious universe of truth, and assure him that all his terrestrial tasks have their final consecration from the fact that they further a destiny that is not terrestrial.

Such a picture of man is by no means unimaginable; and there are already notes and sketches for it in our age. One such was glimpsed in 1947 by the great French scientist Lecomte du Noüy, author of *Human Destiny*. There is in this closely reasoned book an almost maternal urgency to recall the lost children of Christendom to their proper spiritual home. Science, he said, which had undermined religion, must now be invoked to restore religion to its rightful place and man to his rightful dignity. Reason does not "prove" God any more than beauty or goodness does. But reason testifies to God; and without God, reason becomes madness.

Du Noüy takes evolution as the framework of his argument. First of all he demonstrates that evolution could not "have just happened." The mathematical chances are billions to one against that. Evolution was a response to the divine will. Man arises from within the evolutionary process, and at a certain moment, say the

Cro-Magnon age, 30,000 B.C., man became truly man by a *mutation*, when God breathed into him a "free will," a capacity and duty to choose between "good" and "evil," that is to say, a conscience. Human dignity, says du Noüy, rests on a new mechanism born with conscience—namely, free will—*which orients evolution in a spiritual direction*. Then, surveying all the vastitudes of time and space, du Noüy is able to see man's place and purpose in precisely *that* universe. He says: "The respect of human personality is based on the recognition of man's dignity as a worker for evolution, as a collaborator with God. . . . Not only his own fate, but the fate of evolution is in his hands."

Collaboration with God in the whole of evolution—this is a vision so new that it may even be regarded as dangerous in its sweep. For it is nothing less than at last to Christianize Atlas, to unchain Prometheus on his own recognizance, to create a greater Renaissance which shall not become pagan, and to suffuse Lord Russell's dark, icy cosmology with the light and warmth of Christian love and sacrifice and hope.

Some facts about the present condition of man, even about the present *nature* of man, are quite as striking as the facts of science. One is the fact that man in our time, and especially in America, has become cooperative man. Foreign writers on America, whatever their other insights, all agree on the spirit of cooperativeness that pervades American life. Tocqueville, in a famous passage, noted this long ago; just the other day, in a French business magazine, another observer exclaimed, "They train them, they educate them to cooperate!" The habit and spirit of voluntary cooperation form the ideal base for organization. Today, to a degree never before known, man is Organized Man.

To be sure, organization of some sort is essential to all forms of society. The naturalist reveals to us the wonder of the ants and the bees. The anthropologist entrances us with his reports on a thousand forms of organization from tribal cannibals to poetic Mayans. But the organization of *homo Americanus* makes all previous types of organization, including the Roman Empire, appear simple and naive.

The Roman Empire in its prime organized about 50 million people, scattered from the Caspian to Britain; perhaps a third of them were slaves, and all but a fraction were poor, ignorant and short-lived. The American organization is not only vastly more complex, abundant and humane, but also incomparably more free. Americans believe—and nothing has proved us wrong—that organization with freedom, however untidy, is in every way superior to organization by tyranny, however benevolent. This choice was made long ago and has been vindicated by our faith and by our experience.

The American business corporation typifies (though it by no means exhausts) the American capacity for high organization. Having organized production and distribution as the ninth wonder of the world, the modern corporation now finds a new subject for its organizational prowess: itself. It is now organizing itself, quite self-consciously, as a responsible social unit. It is publicly and even noisily concerned about its responsibility to its employees, its customers, its stockholders, the city or cities it dwells in, its "public relations," its share in the support of education, culture, patriotism. It subscribes to the symphony and helps its executives' wives get their kids into college. Whereas the old "soulless corporation" used to proclaim its own honesty and legality, and let it go at that, today it accepts responsibility for every aspect of the social environment on which it impinges. That is a large order, largely self-imposed.

Is it too large an order for the corporation? If so—if the corporation is checked in its career of unlimited altruism—then other forms of high organization will snatch the torch. They are already in the field. Visualize, for example, not only vast bureaucracies (state, federal and local) and labor unions, but also universal education and the *organized concern* for education and for mental health and a thousand other matters, and indeed for "cultural" advancement generally.

But the degree and breadth of high organization we now see are nothing to what we will see. Even today, Dr. Von Neumann tells us, the main problem facing technology is this: it hasn't enough room on earth for its own appropriate organization of products and services. The largest nation, perhaps even the whole world, is too small a staging area for the demonstration of what science can really do with nature.

The future of organization, then, must be at least a world-spanning future, perhaps involving the moon and several planets as well. In other words, the vast, complex, subtle, flexible and efficient organization of men and means in America today must become still more vast, complex, subtle, flexible, efficient and interrelated.

This is a horrifying prospect to many sensitive people. The worry is not only about civil rights, but about the dangerous leveling of thought and standardization of feeling; about the effects of a mass press, mass entertainment, and mass-advertised ways of living, of which TV is only the most recent example. The same wise and sensitive people who yesterday preached social consciousness to the individual are today trying to rescue individuality from a too-well-organized social conscience. Poets and thinkers who earlier wooed the embrace of the downtrodden masses now flee the tread of the organized crowd.

In any case, we've got it—social consciousness organized on a scale never attempted before. And before we flee or condemn it, let us appreciate what we've got. We have made a turn in the development of human nature. We have brought to birth that cooperative society, or a reasonable facsimile thereof, which Kropotkin * foresaw in his answer to Darwin. Unless calamity comes, we can surely call its virtues an achieved characteristic of our civilization.

But still there is the question: What about the individual? And first let it be said, there is no reason to assume that abundance, safety, comfort and wide cultural opportunities will of themselves crush the individual in the society of 1980. There will be conflict between society and the individual, as there always has been, and it will not be resolved. But the anarchy that kept the cavemen from venturing out without a club, or even Dr. Johnson from walking the unlit streets of 18th-century London unarmed, is surely not more propitious for the development of the individual than the social order I am forecasting. Secure in his person, his larder, and his opportunities, the individual of 1980 can start his private quest from a higher plateau of earthly human achievement. His quest will lie upward still.

President Whitney Griswold of Yale spoke a few years ago of "man's immemorial effort to find his place as an individual in a world that seems to recognize him only as a species." "Since that moment, lost in the mists of time," said Griswold, "when man first looked upon himself and saw the image of God, he has struggled against all the powers of nature and the supernatural, and against all the tyrannies of his fellowman, to fulfill the promise in that image. He has lived to the full, in pleasure and pain, the gregarious life to which half of his instincts and appetites committed him.

* Prince Peter Kropotkin (1842–1921), the great Russian anarchist, argued that nature teems with examples of mutual aid.

And in response to the other half, he has striven in every element on earth, in the skies above the earth and in the waters under the earth, to express himself as an individual."

It was the inspired individual—*his* dreams, *his* indignations, *his* inventions—who created our present society, just as past society helped shape him. And just as all biological mutations must start in some unforeseeable organism, so the mutations in human nature that mark the evolution of man must start with one or a few individuals, who in a manner beyond our understanding become possessed of and by the ideal to be proclaimed, the new vision of the eternal logos. Dante was no mere cock crowing at some "inevitable" dawn of the Renaissance; he was a shaper of the Renaissance; he did help make that sun rise; he was a collaborator with God.

But he was not the only collaborator then or before or after. For then as now and in the future, there is not only the inspired individual, there is also the humble servant of truth, the individual servant of charity. And the gifts of the spirit are various: there is foresight and imagination; there is also duty and tradition. For if, as we believe, the spirit is at work in the race of man, then the work of the spirit is done not only in the atom of the individual but also through the generations of men and in traditions and in treasured wisdom and in the moral law slowly apprehended and in the beloved community and in the Church.

While we indeed require individuals who are, as we say, "ahead of their time," we may also liken the hosts of the spirit to an army having its advance scouts but also its main body of faithful and even, importantly, its rear guard, guarding against backsliding, guarding what has been won at such cost. With this simile, may we not also say that at any given moment—in 1980, say—all the elements of the army have a common sense of where they are despite the continuous cacophony of argument? In 1980 we have suggested that the sense of spiritual geography may be characterized by a wider consciousness of responsibility for the spiritual evolution of that special creation into whom was breathed ages ago the meaning of these very words: responsibility, spirit.

That creation was taught and learned to pray both together and alone, at the altar and in the chamber. In one of mankind's books of common prayer, this is prescribed for priest and for congregation at morning service and evensong:

Minister: *O God, make clean our hearts within us.*
Answer: *And take not thy Holy Spirit from us.*

As long as that prayer continues to go up and continues to be answered, we need never fear the greatest triumphs nor the most amazing victories.

---

7 GOD OF OUR FATHERS

This speech, given at the centennial of Lake Forest College in Illinois, on March 25, 1957, is an example of how the Protestant ecumenical movement, which Luce supported, nevertheless stimulated him to reassert the special values of the Presbyterian tradition. It includes a good version of his Christian interpretation of history.

There is a difficulty in the way of our talking to each other just as Presbyterians. For many decades now it has been increasingly fashionable—in the good sense—not to stress denominational differences. We identify ourselves rather as Christians than as Presbyterians. Or perhaps we say we are Protestants. But even so, we urge the ideal of tolerance, we say we respect all religions, not only our fellow Christians, the Roman Catholics, but also those of Jewish faith—and now that we are more and more related to the whole world, we wish to grow in sympathy for other religions. In short, we say there are many roads to God. So indeed there may be. But the question I would like to raise in this family gathering is whether we know as clearly as we should the road to God which you and I are on. If you and I are on any road to God, it is the Presbyterian road. Let us remind ourselves tonight of what that road is. It is a very special road. There is nothing vague or meandering about it. The Presbyterian road is marked out very clearly with tremendous signposts.

What, then, are some of the distinguishing marks of our Calvinist or Presbyterian faith? What are the marks not only of our faith but of our works, our behavior? For one of the marks of the Presbyterian is that he is an activist. What he believes he shows quickly in what he does. On the historical record, we Presbyterians are not famous for mysticism. We are not pacifists nor quietists. We are famous for what we have done—and also perhaps infamous. For example, Presbyterians are credited with the invention of modern capitalism—and if we accept the credit, as we might as well, we are accountable for the horrible sins of capitalism as well as for the revolutionary advance of human productivity and physical well-being.

A distinguishing mark of Calvinism, which we meet to honor tonight, is its historic faith in education. Scotland was probably the first country in the world to become a literate nation. In the story of our own America, the mark of the Presbyterians was that they established schools. Calvinists founded not only Princeton but also Harvard and Yale. As they crossed the Allegheny Mountains, as they opened up the Mississippi Valley and passed on to Oregon— everywhere, it was Presbyterians who built a school as soon as they had built a church. We rejoice to celebrate the centennial of Lake Forest College—a sign and symbol of 400 years of Presbyterian faith in education.

If today we are challenged by a gigantic problem of providing schoolrooms and teachers for all Americans—we Presbyterians have primarily ourselves to blame. It was largely our idea to begin with.

Of course, American education has long since got out of Presbyterian control. That, we might say, is a pity. And it is a very serious matter for this country that education, public education, is dominated by secular thought and is no longer under Christian auspices and inspiration. The generation of Americans 100 years ago who launched our great system of universal education had not the slightest intention of divorcing education from religion. Of course, they did not intend that the public schools should be dominated by church or sect. But neither did they intend that the boy or girl at school should be made a captive in a world which knows no God.

The fact that today American education is dominantly secular and agnostic is one of the profoundest problems facing responsible Christians. The Roman Catholics have their answer—one which compels our respect. We are baffled by the problem. We do not know what to do about it on a broad national scale. But one thing we can do. We can make sure that we give full support to institutions like Lake Forest College, where sound learning and the pursuit of truth are carried on in the light of faith.

But *the* distinguishing mark of Presbyterianism is something quite other—and far greater—than any temporal matter. The first article of our faith has nothing to do with us. For it is about God. It is a blinding light. It is a voice in that radiance which says, "Be still, and know that the Lord, He is *God*." We Presbyterians assert, first of all, not ourselves, not who we are, not what we can do; we assert, first of all, the sovereignty and the majesty of God.

The first emphasis in the Presbyterian faith is that the God we worship is the Lord of All—the sovereign ruler of the starry universe and sovereign ruler, too, of human history on this planet.

The part of that emphasis which I want to emphasize tonight is that God is the ruler of human history. To believe that God is the ruler of the infinity of the physical universe is not too difficult. Indeed, in the present chapter of our scientific age, as the wonders of the universe become daily more wonderful, there seems to be a natural turning to the idea of God as ruler of the universe.

But that God should be *operative* in human history—that seems much more difficult to believe. Does God fight in the wars we fight? Does he participate in our elections—is He a Republican or a Democrat? Can we even be sure God is an anti-Communist? If so, why didn't He send His legions—or somebody's legions—to help the Hungarians in their fight for freedom?

Yes, it seems easier to believe that God controls the galaxies of stars and the myriad flights of neutrons and protons—a lot easier to believe in that, than that He is with us in our daily problems and as we confront what seems to us a supreme crisis in human history.

But, someone may say, if God is the God of history, then He's a God I don't like. What is so good about history? A panoramic survey of history shows wars, cruelties, slaveries, treacheries, vileness and evil of every sort. So indeed it does. We will not try to cope tonight with the problem of evil—a problem no philosophy has ever coped with successfully. Christianity takes its stand on Christian realism and says: There *is* evil, mighty and monstrous. Do not think that it's only a matter of time before man will pull himself unto utopia by his own scientific or other bootstraps. He won't. But don't get gloomy, either. Praise the Lord! For it is precisely into the evil of history, where man lives, that God has come—and works. The light shines in the darkness. Our minds are enlightened—our knowledge grows, greater than any imaginable miracle. Yes, and our compassion grows—a sense of compassion has spread through the world, unknown before the coming of Christ. And freedom, political freedom, dawned only a few centuries ago—and here are we, living in a land where the promises of freedom have been so abundantly fulfilled.

Christianity is a historic faith in the literal sense that it is first of all a series of happenings. God works in history. God is busy in the world He created. This particular knowledge about God marks Christianity off from all other great religions, except Judaism.

Consider the Old Testament. It begins with the story of Creation—cosmology, if you like. But that is only stage-setting. The story really begins with Abraham, who obeyed God's command to leave Ur of the Chaldees and lead his people into a new land, far away. For centuries thereafter, the Jews converse with God and God deals with Israel. They praise him—the God of their fathers—and they rebel against him. They are enslaved in Egypt; they conquer Canaan; they are taken captive to Babylon. At last, through the twists and turns of imperial politics, God leads the Jews back again to Jerusalem and they rebuild the temple. As they build they pause for an hour every day to recite the doings of God. Blessed be the Lord, the God of our fathers!

And now what of the God of *our* fathers?—of our Presbyterian fathers during the last 400 years? It is not presumptuous to say that the story of the God of *our* fathers is every bit as extraordinary and tremendous as the story of the God of Abraham and Isaac and Jacob and Moses.

Look at the hand of Providence in *our* Presbyterian history. Two things happened simultaneously—the discovery of the New World and the Reformation. John Calvin organized the reformed faith in the mid-1500s. That gave just a short 100 years for the reformed faith to spread through Western Europe before America was ready to be colonized. Everywhere that the reformed faith took hold—notably in Scotland, in England, in Holland—it laid the foundation for representative government; for a government of free men under law. This was the Presbyterian form of government. In the fullness of time, the Pilgrim Fathers set forth across the sea with their faith in God, and their form of government.

During the next 150 years, our new world began to get some

people in it. All kinds of people—many of them adventurers, fugitives from justice, godless. But at the time of the American Revolution two-thirds of the people were Calvinists. The numbers are important, but even more important was the extraordinary quality of leadership which was developed in the thirteen colonies. The more time passes, the clearer it becomes that the Founding Fathers were the most remarkable group of men ever assembled for the founding of a nation—for the making of the American Constitution. Not all were Calvinists—but Calvinism was a mighty force. Who arranged it so? The God of *our* fathers.

We need not exaggerate the dominance of Calvinist influence in the founding of the United States. Enough to say that Presbyterians played an immense part in it—and without the Calvinist influence, the American form of government and the American ethos are inconceivable. Historian after historian attests this truth. John Lothrop Motley says: "To Calvinists more than to any other class of men, the political liberties of England, Holland and America are due." And here is a Catholic statesman-historian—Emilio Castelar y Ripoll of the University of Madrid: "It was necessary for the republican movement of America that there should come a morality more austere than Luther's, the morality of Calvin, and a church more democratic than the German, the church of Geneva." The historian Leopold von Ranke calls John Calvin "the virtual founder of America."

But of all the tributes to the role of Presbyterianism in the making of America, I like best the comment of Horace Walpole, the man of the world, the man-about-London-town. He is speaking of the Reverend John Witherspoon, president of Princeton, the only clergyman to sign the Declaration of Independence. This is how Walpole is said to have described the American Revolution: "The Colonies have run away after a Presbyterian parson."

God moves in a mysterious way. Who would have thought that He would have dedicated the New World, the new hope of mankind, to freedom, by the means of such ornery people as us Presbyterians? But the record is there—facts are facts.

Who, then, should know better than we that the God we worship is indeed the Sovereign Lord of History? Through the latest and greatest chapters of human history, He has been, He is, the God of our fathers. If there is any difficulty in our believing it, it is only because it is such an awesome fact. It is too great for us. We shrink from the glory of it.

If we had all night we could go on showing how in scores of ways God has laid His hand on this country—in our trials and tribulations no less than in our triumphs, in our sin and in our weakness no less than in our nobler moments and in our strength. And now in a short period of less than 200 years—in the twinkling of an eye—this nation has come to its greatest epoch of historical influence. And again how glorious and how solemn is the scene before us. The first moment when America has world influence is also the first moment of world history—the first moment when the destiny of mankind is one. Who arranged it so? Dare we think that it is the Lord of history—the God of our fathers? Or shall we dare *not* to think so?

When God commanded Joshua to take up where Moses left, and to lead the people into the promised land, Joshua, like Moses before him, felt dismayed by the greatness of the task. And God said to him: "Fear not. . . . Only be thou strong and very courageous. For the Lord thy God is with thee whithersoever thou goest."

We Americans, in relation to the future, stand about where Joshua stood. Before humanity lies a magnificent future. Before it lie appalling dangers. It is for America today to have and to exercise both wisdom and moral courage. Fear not! Fear not the consequences of doing right. Fear not that right and wrong cannot be distinguished. Fear not—"for the Lord thy God will be with thee whithersoever thou goest."

8　SCIENCE AND THE RELIGION OF THE FUTURE

Luce's parallel interests in Protestant theology and in the metaphysics of science, which he was characteristically determined to reconcile, led to this commencement speech at the Princeton Theological Seminary on

June 4, 1962. He had attended the Third Assembly of the World Council of Churches at New Delhi the previous winter.

At one of the big section meetings in New Delhi, a lively disputation broke out between the laymen and the ecclesiastics. The laymen attacked the churchmen for being too theological, for using language which laymen do not understand. After enduring quite a lot of this kind of talk, one churchman finally replied that it was high time laymen made some effort to get on speaking terms with theology. Mentally I said, "Hurray for him." For on this point I have long agreed with what the churchman said. Indeed, I have gone further and complained that most educated Protestants are theologically illiterate. Thus, I am in favor of stronger theology —if you like, tougher theology—and tough theology more widely communicated to all the people.

The question of more theology raises the whole question of mass culture and of democracy itself. In the field of secular education we seem to have made up our minds that, having embarked on the democratic adventure, there is nothing to do but go on through with it—that is, to make all men as educated as possible. In the case of religion confronted by democracy, this strategy has not been adopted. Perhaps for good reason.

Among my neighbors in Arizona is a lady born and brought up a French Catholic. She married an American Episcopalian with several children. Their family custom was to go on alternate Sundays to the Episcopal Church and to the Catholic.

The Sunday before Trinity they were at the Episcopal Church and the rector gave an extended explanation of the Holy Trinity. The children fidgeted almost beyond control, which was the only thing that kept the parents awake.

Next Sunday, Catholic Church. And thus spoke the pastor: "My friends, this is Trinity Sunday, but I'm not going to tell you about the doctrine of the Trinity because you couldn't understand it. But don't let that bother you—the Church understands it. Now, about the new parking lot which hasn't been paid for yet."

The priesthood of all believers is all very well, but there may be something to be said for relieving truck drivers and housewives and editors of the burden of theological truth.

Science is all around us; we take it for granted, bursting in the skies and ventilating this room. Surely, you will hope, it is not the conflict of Science and Religion which your speaker is going to take up; he can't be quite so old hat as all that. Well, it *is* the conflict of science and religion that I am going to take up, and however seriously this was coped with thirty or fifty or 100 years ago, I will submit, as a prediction, that in the decade beginning now, you will have to cope with it more seriously and on a grander scale than ever before.

Now it does indeed seem that, in recent years, the relation of science and religion has entered into a new phase of peaceful coexistence. Instead of conflict, there is felt to be reciprocity, a desire for accommodation and even for mutual support. There is very little overt attack on religion. Scientists are among those who tell you cheerfully that religion is a good thing. Religion supports ethical values which are seen to be necessary on this shaky planet. Indeed, it is a fairly typical attitude of science—and you must allow me to use some such corporative term—that some scientists are eager to show that science advances the cause of religion because science helped to create higher ethical values. I cite as an example the distinguished dean of science at M.I.T., Dr. George Russell Harrison. In a very readable book for laymen, *What Man May Be*, some of Dean Harrison's characteristic statements are as follows:

"The technological progress that results from science, important to the world as it is, is far less important than the intellectual and spiritual progress that science can help to accelerate."

And again: "The slow accumulation of human experience results in an uneven but progressive increase in those spiritual qualities which . . . have great survival value to the race—love, integrity, humility, sympathy and hope."

That is what I would call a theology of optimism. What happens now to neo-orthodoxy? What happens now to Christian pessimism? And if it is Christian hope you would prefer to accent, what have you got to offer in competition with Dean Harrison? Not that the dean has any least desire to start a quarrel. I am afraid it is I who am the disturber of the peace.

My generalization is this: that there exists a happy concordat between science and religion, but that the dialogue is not serious. I get the impression that religious leaders are not paying strict attention to what scientists are saying, and that scientists are making up their own versions of religion and, even when they call themselves Christians, are politely ignoring all of the decisive propositions of the Christian faith.

Let me try to test this generalization at a higher level than that of popular moralizing. I bring in evidence Teilhard de Chardin's *The Phenomenon of Man*. Those of you who have read it know that this book by a Jesuit is not at all a work of Christian apologetics; it is the work of a paleontologist who develops an evolutionary spiritual cosmology rooted in scientific knowledge and probabilities. This book made a great impression on me—perhaps a greater impression than any book since Niebuhr's *The Nature and Destiny of Man*.

A year or so ago I spoke to President Van Dusen * about it. And it was almost with impatience that he said to me, "Emergent evolution—we had that thirty years ago." Nevertheless, there are a number of things that need saying on this subject that could not have been said thirty years ago.

Let me remind you of the fantastic rate of advance in scientific knowledge—and of mathematical speculation. Let me remind you of that chart, that graph as big as this wall, which you have all seen in one form or another. Down in that corner is the beginning of *homo sapiens*, and the line running along the floor shows man's discoveries and inventions, beginning, say, with fire and the wheel. The line begins down there and then for 50,000 years or so it runs along the floor, creeping upward a few inches every yard. Then, look over toward the opposite corner: we are in the 17th or 18th century A.D., and the line starts curving dramatically up, up. And now in the mid-20th century the line rises like a jet rocket up the side of the wall, and it goes up, up, right through the roof.

The point of reminding you of the explosive rate of advance of science is simply this—that jet airplanes and atomic bombs are simply the crude outward and visible signs of far more amazing discoveries and guesses which are invisible to scientific ignoramuses like me and most of you. I give you but one example from my dimness of comprehension. Four dimensions, including time, are about all you and I can get along with. But it seems that won't do at all for protons and neutrons. If a physicist is to express how a proton gets from here to there, it seems he needs fourteen dimensions, if not forty. And furthermore, as to causation, it is not simply

* Henry Pitney Van Dusen, then president of the Union Theological Seminary.

the past that pushes things into the present: things are pulled into the present by the future, however contingent. *Sursum corda.* We have at least recovered a teleological God.

As is evident, it is easy to get intoxicated from the heady fumes of modern science. Indeed, we hear of young scientists who are so completely absorbed in their trade that they have no interest in anything else—not even family and friends. Is it the modern beatific vision?

But back to the challenge of emergent evolution. I put now in evidence a quite different book, *The Humanist Frame.* In this book, Sir Julian Huxley is evidently setting out to found a new religion. I mean literally that— a complete religion—for I suppose religion can be quite amply defined as a cosmology plus a demand on all men for service and duty. For the purpose of founding this religion, Sir Julian has procured scriptures in the form of brilliant essays from twenty-five scientists and other kinds of thinkers. They all write in extraordinary harmony, leaving few problems of exegesis; and all seem to agree that the name of their religion is Evolutionary Humanism.

What is new for me and, I think, for most people is this proposition: that, in modern lingo, there has occurred a decisive breakthrough of human consciousness, so that the race of man can from approximately now on control man's future development and, not only that, but can also control all forms of life on this planet and perhaps throughout the solar system.

At school we used to hear about what a shock it was for man in the 16th century or thereabouts to discover that he was not the center of the universe. Well, medieval man and postmedieval man did not think he was the center; he thought God was. But now you see it is discovered that man really is the center—and not in any trivial geographic or astronomical sense, but in the profound sense of being the center of power, the center of directive purpose.

And there is more. Not only can man control his multimillennial future; he will control his future in an ever upward spiral of moral goodness and spiritual power. That is the new, scientifically based, gospel.

Perhaps you will not take the Huxley scriptures seriously. But let me try a few quotes from among the twenty-five evangelists. I choose Oliver Reiser, chairman of the department of philosophy at the University of Pittsburgh. He recognizes that the task of organizing and propagandizing evolutionary humanism is, quote, "stupendous"—so stupendous that "mental isolationists"—that might include you—will shrink from the task. Nevertheless, Professor Reiser says:

> Indeed, it is only a question of time before peoples everywhere, reduced to a common destiny by the coercions of science and technology (e.g., controlled thermonuclear power, automation in industry, the conquest of outer space), *and guided into cooperation through the overwhelming pressures of integrative psychosocial aspirations*, will accept the general ideology ("humanist frame") as the architectonic for an emerging planetary democracy.

Note especially the word "psychosocial." I quote now Sir Russell Brain, president of the Royal College of Physicians. Heartily approving Teilhard's term "noosphere," * Sir Russell says that now for the first time science sees "mind" as a dominant factor in evolution. And, psychosocial evolution is "the matrix for the development . . . of 'spiritual' values, ethics and artistic creativeness." Comes now C. H. Waddington, professor of animal genetics at Edinburgh University. In more detail, he expounds the marvel of the transmission of knowledge from generation to generation in the animal kingdom, and not wholly through the genes. And he says, "Man, alone among animals, has developed this extra-genetic mode of transmission to a state where it rivals and indeed exceeds the genetic mode in importance." And so instead of "psychosocial," Waddington prefers "sociogenetic" to describe the suprabiological modes of transmission of knowledge and values. And so he concludes that it is man's duty not only to mankind but to the whole living world to carry on evolution in the direction of the good and the beautiful. This is man's destiny—and he has no choice but to do his duty because, evolution having made its great breakthrough, the very mode and means of evolution respond to moral imperatives. I take it that what Brain and Waddington and others are saying is that conscience has become a sort of pituitary gland of the whole evolutionary process. No longer survival by tooth and claw, but guidance ever upward by the still small voice.

Now surely this is a challenging proposition. Many things come together here—one might say all the dominant phenomena and

* See page 333.

glories of our time. First of all, and basic, you have the vast structure of scientifically reliable truth and ever more sophisticated mathematical speculations. Along with that, naturally, you have the immeasurable technical power now in human hands. And along with that, also naturally, you have, for the first time, one world— humanity more and more aware of itself as a whole yesterday, today and forever more.

Nor can we say that the new religion will be automatically discredited by the chaotic and perilous world situation. Christian preaching may make a grave tactical blunder if it continues to assume that the world picture will be one of ever imminent disaster. For thirty years we have indeed been living in a time of massive crises and upheaval. But in my view the next thirty years may pass without catastrophic upheaval.

Pragmatically, you may be saying that not many of your ordinary pew-members will desert you and follow after this new religion. I wouldn't be so sure. As the years go by and you look down from your pulpit, you may find the well-known bodies in the pew—but their faith may be elsewhere.

And how about young people, as the years go by? As this world-minded, humanity-loving religion is more and more effectively uttered, as it is more and more inspired and made potent by amazing discoveries, cannot this new religion have a profound and self-evident attraction for the idealistic and for the millions of educated men and women of today and tomorrow?

Not so long ago what we had to deal with was agnosticism. The scientist said he was an agnostic—he knew about protons or about butterflies; he just didn't know about God; God was not his affair. Today we are not confronted with agnostics but with believers.

Scientific humanism is a religion of concern, of responsibility, of fraternity, of democracy, of honored truth and of cosmic hope.

What is the Christian answer?

We are not concerned in this brief hour to dismantle the new religion dialectically—to test its psychology and find it weak; to test its pragmatics and find them naive. We are concerned only to assert the truth that men can most truly live by, and that we ought to live by. For of course there is a tremendous Christian answer— an answer to be theologically expounded, but first of all to be seen as that Light of the World whose blaze of love and glory makes all other lights, however lovely, broken lights and pale reflections.

That Light is the Cosmic Christ—who has always been there and known to theology no less than to the songs of praise.

There were many splendid sermons in New Delhi. But the one that seemed to speak most truly to the whole human condition today was the sermon preached by Professor Joseph Sittler. "The way forward," he said, "is from Christology expanded to its cosmic dimensions, made passionate by the pathos of this threatened earth, and made ethical by the love and the wrath of God." I will not try further to summarize it. Enough simply to read to you again Professor Sittler's text—the longest text I ever heard a preacher use: Colossians 1:15–20.

> He is the image of the invisible God, the first born of all creation; for in Him all things were created, in heaven and on earth, visible and invisible, whether thrones or dominions or principalities or authorities—all things were created through Him and for Him. He is before all things, and in Him all things hold together. He is the head of the body, the church; He is the beginning, the first born from the dead, that in everything He might be preeminent. For in Him all the fullness of God was pleased to dwell, and through Him to reconcile to Himself all things, whether on earth or in heaven, making peace by the blood of His cross.

After these words, there is nothing more to say. But let me attempt a little following after. May we not say that God comes into the world in three ways, that there are three Immanuels?

First—not chronologically, but only because I cannot speak and you cannot hear three things at once—first, God comes to the individual human being, to the lost sheep, to the prodigal son, to Nathanael under the fig tree, to the man who fell among thieves, to the woman who had lost her penny and didn't know where to find it.

Second, God comes into history and comes as the Lord of History, and this is what we in this century have some awareness of. This is the social gospel, this is the question of democracy, this is Armageddon and this is the atomic end of Armageddons.

Third, God comes into his own creation to taste the beauty of the lilies and the music of the spheres and, yes, to have a look at His tiger tiger burning bright, and to speak with man, His coworker in all this cosmic enterprise.

And so, finally, about the Church. Is it not first of all to men and women in the Church that the humanity of Christ speaks, saying, "This is my Father's world"?

Therefore it is about the whole world, the whole of creation, that the Church is commissioned to speak and to act. The message of personal redemption and the Church's prophetic office in history both find their completion in a "Christology" expanded to its cosmic dimension.

9   THE ESSENCE OF TEILHARD

As indicated above (page 327), Luce allowed the kind of Christian hope expounded by Teilhard de Chardin to qualify the lesson of Christian pessimism expounded by Reinhold Niebuhr and by so much 20th-century history. This summary of Teilhard's thought appeared in LIFE, *October 16, 1964.*

Very few people had ever heard of Pierre Teilhard de Chardin when he died in New York on Easter Sunday, 1955. He was revered by his personal acquaintances, deeply respected by his scientific colleagues. But his writings had been kept in delicate obscurity by his superiors, who forbade publication of his non-technical treatises during his lifetime.

Today the name of Teilhard de Chardin is known to millions, and some people rank him as the greatest thinker-prophet of the 20th century. As one reviewer has put it, Teilhard "has become an inescapable intellectual presence of the age." His master work, entitled *The Phenomenon of Man*, was published in the U.S. in 1959. It is very difficult reading, for therein he lays out in elaborate detail his systematic account of evolution.

By contrast *The Future of Man*, a collection of his reflections and essays published in this country this month, is very readable. Moreover, it will bring to the reader most of Teilhard's essential notions and conclusions as well as his style of thought and feeling. One of its earliest chapters was written on a scientific journey in China in the 1920s, many others in Paris after World War II, the last of them in New York, where he lived out his final years.

He deals with many topics—heredity and evolutionary progress, the prospects for world peace, the essence of the democratic idea, the spiritual repercussions of the atomic bomb. Throughout them all, using the same luminous mixture of scientific method and philosophic mysticism, the same central theme recurs: a world-wide evolution, through education and Christian love, toward a "final maturing and ecstasy of mankind"—a metamorphosis toward a supreme synthesis, a spiritual and inward escape from this planet.

What Teilhard has mainly to say to us might be summed up in one word—Joy.

With all the scientific knowledge at his command, Teilhard paints a vast panorama of all creation, and it delights him—every bit of it, from the atom to the stars, from the amoeba to man. What delights him most is Life, a word he always capitalizes. And what brings even more than delight, what brings him an inexpressible joy, is that through all of time and space, Teilhard finds an intense driving purpose. That purpose, first seen in primordial gas and molten rock, is toward life and toward yet more life. That purposeful drive toward life reaches its center and climax in man.

In man, life is most intensely concentrated. But the story of man has only just begun. At this very moment, the pressures in human life are building up to such an explosive point that quite soon man must make a breakthrough, resulting in what amounts to a new order of mankind.

The entire universe makes progress. Man is the uniquely important result of that progress and man is now endowed with the power and the duty to shape his own evolution toward far greater heights of intellectual and spiritual being. This view of the *future of man* puts Teilhard de Chardin dramatically against all the pessimisms, despairs and nihilisms which crowd the literary and academic stage of our day.

One key to all of Teilhard's vision of reality is a concept for which he had to invent a word—*noosphere* (pronounced *new sphere*). For those who are not yet at home in Teilhard's cosmos, I will attempt here a very simple description of *noosphere*—with all apologies to the experts.

Thinking only of our planet earth, it is possible to speak of a *barysphere*—the mass of fiery metal way down under. Then there is the *lithosphere*—the hard rock surface of earth, on which lie the oceans and the lakes—the *hydrosphere*. Out of the waters came life, and so Teilhard shows to us all living creatures as forming the *biosphere*. And then comes his special vision. Just as the earth is covered with a biosphere of flora and fauna, so it is also, now at last, covered with a layer of mind, emanating from man—the *noosphere* (*noos* in Greek means mind or thought).

This noosphere is not simply "inside" the minds of men. A great part of the noosphere is the total complex of all the tools and machines which man has made. Thus the noosphere is composed of, among other things, practically everything listed in the Sears, Roebuck catalog plus railroads, steamboats, automobiles, jet airplanes, telephones, TV stations, atom bombs, etc.

All of man's tools and machines constitute not only a mechanism for use and action; they also constitute an incredibly vast and intricate thinking machine. And that was even before computers. Add more and bigger computers and you have an even more incredibly vast man-made, man-used global thinking machine.

But of course the noosphere is not composed simply of machines. Even more important, the noosphere is composed of all the thoughts in men's minds and all the poetry and music in their souls.

So man must be seen today as living and operating not only in the biosphere, of which he is both painfully and gloriously a part; he lives and operates with even more freedom and power in the noosphere, which has evolved out of his biological brain.

There is one more thing to say about the noosphere, and that has to do with heredity. It is fundamental to Teilhard's vision of reality that, in man, heredity does not proceed only through his genes and chromosomes. Man is shaped by his social environment. What we in fact are we owe quite as much to our cultural heritage as to our genes. And this will be even more true of our children's children.

And the reason why man is due for a great breakthrough to another order of mankind is that the noosphere (with atomic fission and other things) has become so full of knowledge piled on knowledge and of ideas piled on ideas that, all intercommunicating, it is bound to explode into some new kind of being.

To imagine the future, consider the past. Here's a kind of time-table of man and the noosphere:

300,000,000 years ago is when life began on this planet.

100,000 years ago—the first "man"—cf., Peking Man, whom Teilhard helped to discover.

30,000 years ago—the first *homo sapiens*.

10,000 years ago—the first social man.

200 years ago—the scientific revolution.

The point of this timetable is that most of our amazing noosphere (remember, it means everything from your Chevrolet to the Einstein equation) has been created in the past 200 years. Suppose it goes on developing that fast or faster? What happens in another 200 years? Or even in fifty? Or . . . in another million years?

Well, what? What will be the "Future of Man"? Teilhard does not know, of course. But he is utterly convinced of his vision—on scientific grounds and on logic—insofar as science and logic can provide or sustain a vision. That vision is of the unique importance of man in all the universe, of the destiny of man to rise toward spiritual perfection, until at last a united humanity is united with God, who draws all men unto Him.

There is nothing new about the end of the vision. What is new about Teilhard de Chardin is that he makes it applicable to today —to the human crises of today and tomorrow. And not only applicable, but urgent, for Teilhard says that man will make that breakthrough, which is pressing on us, only if we understand in what direction we ought to move, in what direction we should apply the cosmic powers we possess.

But how are we to understand aright? And how can we direct our wills to do the right even if we see it? These questions remain. Teilhard de Chardin does not drive us by moral imperatives. He draws us by the splendor and joy of his vision.

8

PEOPLE, PLACES AND EPISODES

This chapter is a miscellany of vignettes, judgments, descriptions and reports of conversations. Luce was a tireless interviewer and reporter as well as editor, with a thirst for arresting trivia as well as for inside dope. He was more gregarious than most editors and deliberately cultivated a wide acquaintance with important people here and abroad. "It is a fine thing for a journalist to dine out. It is a finer thing for a journalist not to dine out," he once advised his colleagues; but he himself preferred the risks of dining out. The firsthand impressions and bits of partial information he thus acquired might have been a source of prejudice in a less self-critical editor. With Luce, every fact and observation had its value and deserved recording, but it was also to be weighed, compared with others, and probably discounted before it saw print.

Most of the observations in this chapter did not see print, and some he would doubtless have revised. Some of them could as well appear in Chapter 2, for however dispassionate his foreground reporting, a political issue was usually in the background. In any case, these selections illustrate the open-eyed yet discriminating zest with which he savored the people and places, sights and sounds, memories and insights that thronged his busy life.

1   HERBERT HOOVER

*In a speech in Rochester, New York, in March 1928
some months before the national conventions, Luce reviewed the leading presidential possibilities. (He was to
vote for Alfred E. Smith.) The following is an excerpt.*

Mr. Hoover can administer. Mr. Hoover has an engineer's vision. The bigger the job, the better is Mr. Hoover. But the bigger
the issue, the worse is Mr. Hoover. Politically indifferent, he asks
for the highest office of political leadership in the world. Dull in
public speech, he asks for a White House chair which has rightly
been called the most influential pulpit in the land. Asking to be
chiefly responsible for our infinitely difficult foreign relations, he
has expressed no clear views on foreign policy since he ceased to
be an endorser of the League of Nations. Honest without doubt,
he evidently expects that the dishonesty of his party shall be
regarded as irrelevant to him. There are two other things to
say about Mr. Hoover. First, Mr. Hoover deserves the Presidency. But it is almost the ultimate in the degradation of politics to
make a man President simply because he deserves it. The White
House ought not to be regarded as a mausoleum. Second, Mr. Hoover's nomination would represent a widespread popular preference,
and as such should be regarded as a joyful noise unto the Lord.
Here the paradox reaches its climax. So despairing are we of
finding great politicians that we feel forced to oppose bad politicians by clamoring for a poor politician.

2   CALVIN COOLIDGE

*This vignette is from a speech on "Indispensable Men"
at the University of Chicago, April 19, 1933.*

Mr. Coolidge, a very perfect symbol of the American people, had as great an opportunity to promote what I conceive to be the welfare and the purposes of this nation and of the world as has ever been given to any man anywhere in history. And nothing that he did will appear to be of the slightest importance ten years hence except the fact that he did nothing.

I want to make this point as something larger than a fragmentary list of his omissions. They are not his omissions. Mr. Coolidge got great applause, perhaps the greatest applause of his life, for vetoing the bonus bill. But he did not stop the bonus evil, nor did he prevent that evil from growing. He did not settle the war-debt question. He said: "They hired the money, didn't they?" He did nothing about Prohibition. He reduced the tax rate, but he did nothing effectively to prevent a fantastic increase in the rate of public expenditures throughout the nation. He was warned about tariffs, and he did nothing except raise them and permit his party to grow ever more conscienceless about them. He vetoed one or two farm bills. Did he solve the farm problem?

But let us not be unjust to Mr. Coolidge. If he had tried to do anything more than he did, if he had forbidden the railroads to pile up totally uneconomic debts, if he had put all banks in the Reserve System, if he had forced Mr. Ripley's * advice on the Stock Exchange, if he had curbed either the tariffs or the foreign investments, if he had made peace with Japan by a couple of harmless amendments to the Immigration Act, if he had undertaken to abolish the largest slums in the civilized world—some of which were in

* William Z. Ripley (1867–1941), Harvard political economist, author of *Main Street and Wall Street* (1927).

his own backyard; if he had abolished child labor and if he had exhibited just enough interest in unemployment to find out how many unemployed there were, if he had done any ten of a thousand things he might have done—well, the answer is we wouldn't have stood for it, we would have howled him down. Mr. Coolidge's genius was that he realized this. In a decade of utterly astounding changes—in everything from lipstick to cigarettes to dynamos and Communism—he sat tight.

3   ENGLISHMEN IN '34

From a report on a European trip in July 1934.

If the world steps into another era of "progress," I fear England will be left placidly behind. England is living on her capital. It is a tremendous capital. Even greater than its vast money and material capital is its capital of character and laws and customs. But a rot has set into this character. I feel that now, just as I did in 1921. And the most *specific* instance of it is homosexuality. So far as I know, no figures exist on this subject. But a certain man having been recommended to me as TIME's correspondent and I having later learned he was a fairy, I taxed the recommender with this and she (a very brilliant she) said: "Ah, but that goes without saying —there isn't a clever man in England who is not homosexual." I asked whether that meant the end of England. She said, "Yes, of course."

The fairy business in England is not like Berlin. The casual tourist doesn't see it.

But quite aside from all this, you don't feel any vitality in England. You simply feel the peace and comfort of a well-ordered place in a disruptive world. And you are aware also of very calm and clever bankers making money by their intelligent observation of the world scene.

4   EUROPE BEFORE MUNICH

These three items are from Luce's notes on a "quick jaunt through Europe" in May and June 1938, four months before the Munich agreement between London, Paris and Hitler. Of his unlucky prediction that the Czechs would fight, Luce said a year later: "I still say I was right in a totally unpredictable world. The Czechs never had a chance to fight."

Berlin. We returned to the Adlon and spent a comfortable night. But this once most luxurious of Berlin hotels is no longer really luxurious. The servants are nice and polite. The waiters run around in tailcoats. But the tailcoats of waiters are the only tailcoats to be seen in the Adlon or anywhere else in Germany. The menu was very limited. The water in the bath was muddy. The taps did not work. The toilet paper is the worst I have encountered in years. There is no luxury in Germany. There is some extremely comfortable upper-bourgeois life, but the luxury and swank to be found in any Statler hotel is greater than any in Germany.

The great apologetic slogan in Germany is "Everyone has enough—no one has too much." Of course to my old liberal-capitalistic mind, it is extremely doubtful if everyone can have enough unless some lucky (or unlucky) bastards have too much—but that's their story and they stick to it, and it would take more than a week's whirl through Germany to prove they aren't right.

We had tea with the British Ambassador, Sir Nevile Henderson, a suave bachelor diplomat in tweeds who, of course, was quite pleased with the success of his diplomatic démarche * the week before, but since he has a low opinion of the popular press he was inclined to deprecate all dramatizations of the Czech crisis. Sir Nevile said that on several occasions Hitler had flown into a violent

* On May 20 and 21, there were reports of German troop movements near the Czech border. Henderson registered the official British protest.

fit of temper with him. Sir Nevile confirmed the growing popularity of Goering. That very day Goering's daughter was born, and
Sir Nevile thought that it would tend further to soften the rough-
ness of Goering's character. Also I gathered from Sir Nevile that
the kind of people he met socially, especially ladies, did not feel at
all afraid to indulge in a certain amount of grumbling against the
regime—and later I gathered that oral grumbling is not forbidden
in Germany. Indeed, it would appear that at least on Saturday
nights every German is entitled to grumble into his beer just as he
has always done—the grumbling is not usually about matters of
high politics, but rather about the particular grievances which he
has against his own local bureaucratic bosses.

That night we went to the Winter Garden—a vast vaudeville
place where you eat. There was almost no humor in the whole
show. There was not much sex, and what there was was crude and
badly done. It was mostly acrobatics. The act that got by far the
biggest cheers was an old, old sentimental German song called
Little Rose, Little Rose, Little Rose on the Meadow.

Vienna. The story of Vienna is "how it used to be," the gaiety,
the elegance, the charm, etc.—before the war, and even again
before Hitler. In London I met the aristocrat who had been Austria's ambassador for many years and who is now somewhat of a
pet in English society.* He wanted to prepare me for my visit to
Vienna but when he got down to it he didn't know what to say
except, "If you had only known Vienna before . . ." One night I
saw him at a great ball given by the Duchess of Rutland. He wore
the stars and ribbons and crosses of many a great order of knight-
hood. I watched him dance a waltz with my wife. He danced
beautifully—and that, I think, was his story.

Czechoslovakia. The first thing that strikes you about Prague is
that it is really far away from America because you can't read any
of the signs. It is a Slavic country—the language has no connection
with the languages we learned in school. But the second impression is that it is somehow a free country. This feeling may arise
entirely from pathetic fallacy—but anyway it is there. For one
thing, we knew, after all the fuss and feathers about money in
Germany, that we were once again in a land where we could get
money by the ordinary process of free international capitalistic
exchange.

We were met by a Dr. Kubka, a very fat fellow of the Foreign

* Baron Georg Franckenstein, Austrian minister in London 1920–38.

Office. He took us several miles out of the city to a great terraced restaurant perched high on a hill above the Vltava River. This river flows into the Elbe and down to Hamburg and thus it is that all the foreign trade of busy, industrious, honest Czechoslovakia must flow through Germany. On the terrace we immediately began talking politics. That conversation I shall always remember, because I knew not from words but from the fire in the eyes of the fat man that I was talking with a man who would fight—a man indeed who, for all his proper gloves and polite speech, had reconciled himself to individual death for the sake of his country and of freedom. Next day President Beneš * in his great white palace said to me: "Ask anybody—anybody you meet in the street—he will tell you he will fight." I hardly needed Beneš' words. We saw tens of thousands of good stolid Bohemians going about their business, and Dr. Kubka had already caused me to look at all of them as men—*and* women—who would fight and die for country and for liberty. It was a thrill—I confess it—to touch, however briefly, such a people.

The most interesting thing in my conversation with Beneš was his relatively optimistic view as to the development of a kind of democracy in Russia. When he spoke of "three nondemocratic powers" I asked, "Which three?" He said: "Germany, Italy and Japan." I said, "What about Russia?" And he then said, first, that Russia was not antidemocratic, and second, that Russia was tending toward a democratic development. I am confused.

Next day President Beneš talked to me for over an hour. I asked him whether it was any longer possible to hope for the creation of a relatively peaceful epoch in Europe, and if so, along what lines that hope could be pursued now that the whole idea of collective security through the League of Nations had broken down, etc. His reply was that an ultimate European solution must rest on democracy—that is, on the general acceptance of democratic principles by all countries. At the moment, of course, various countries are definitely antidemocratic. So, at this period, the only end which could be pursued was the avoidance of war. He believed war *can* be avoided. If a general war is avoided during the next five or ten years, he believes the totalitarian systems will collapse and that democratic systems will again triumph in Germany, Italy, etc. And

* Eduard Beneš (1884–1948) was President of Czechoslovakia, 1935–38 and 1946–48.

that as soon as democracy is once again prevalent in the world, we will begin again the effort to establish peace on a democratic and lawful spirit within nations and between them. We have failed once, says he, but there is nothing surer in the world than that we shall try again. The ideals (of the League of Nations, etc.) are, he said, true—and truth will rise again. I challenged him on the collapse of the totalitarian regimes, and he said they would go broke—in fact, that they are already broke. He pulled out pencil and paper and began doing simple arithmetic in connection with Italy. In contrast, he explained with pride, conviction and satisfaction the financial achievements of Czechoslovakia—its heavy expenditures all paid for by the free will of the people, etc.

The little man's faith in democracy, in the truth of arithmetic, in the truth of truth, was very convincing—especially, as I have said, as he backed it up with the assurance that the average man in the street far down below his gleaming palace was ready and willing that very moment to fight for country and for liberty. There is no question but that Czechoslovakia sets a lot of store by her fellow Slav ally, Russia, and hence would like her fellow democrats to think as well as possible of her fellow Slav.

Beneš talks English much better than when I saw him years ago. He talks very precisely, loves to say: "For four reasons: first: . . ." and loves to write figures on a paper.

---

5   ENGLISHMEN IN '39

Luce made another visit to Europe in July 1939. The following is from his account of that trip.

Said a young Polish banker: "Two million British spinsters, who have no adequate function in peace, are morally mobilized for war. When the British spinster gets excited, the British lion roars."

England is today all one family. In the family, however, is an oldest brother who is one of those oldest brothers who take themselves and their responsibilities too seriously; everyone, including Papa and Mamma, wishes he would take a dose of castor oil. Oldest Brother is compounded of Chamberlain and three other old men—Simon, Halifax, Hoare.* But the news is that Halifax has broken away, is deciding to be Foreign Minister in his own right. The only man who can cause the fall of the Chamberlain government right now is Halifax. The fighting Foreign Office feels it has captured its chief, and is therefore much happier.

* Sir John Simon (1873–1954), Lord Halifax (1881–1959) and Sir Samuel Hoare (1880–1959) were Tory cabinet members identified with Chamberlain's appeasement policy. Halifax later so dissociated himself from the Munich pact he helped negotiate that Churchill named him Ambassador to the U.S. in 1941. See page 350.

6   CHINA AT WAR

In May 1941, the Luces flew to Chungking, then under daily Japanese bombing, and visited Chiang's troops on the northern front. The following extracts are from Luce's description of this trip in LIFE, *June 30, 1941.*

At 2:30 A.M. we are routed out of our beds in a Hong Kong hotel and driven to an airport. By the strange light which lights all baggage rooms and places of departure, we shake hands with our pilot, an American, tough, hearty, clean-cut. He and five other Americans run the most dangerous passenger airline in the world. Their four Douglas DC-2s and two DC-3s are one of only two connecting threads between Free China and the outside world. The other is the Burma Road, still new and inefficient.

At 3 A.M. we take off on our five-hour flight in complete darkness—no lights in the plane and no smoking allowed. Pilot Macdonald zooms the ship up through the intricate hills of the harbor of Hong Kong, where the lights of an imperial city still twinkle in rows. Soon all is black and we are over Japanese-occupied territory. We pass to the right of Canton, the graveyard city where Japanese pursuit planes are concentrated. As the sun comes up and the clouds clear, we look down upon a land of intricate and fairy-like beauty. It is the land of thousands and thousands of hills, each hill a separate thing, rising with surprising steepness and falling off quickly to make room for the valley and the next hill, and each hill terraced nearly to its top with rice paddies of infinitely varied shapes, some square, some round, but mostly like the sliver shape of the new moon, shapes within shapes until all but the wooded hill or mountaintop is full. It is the landscape which might have been dreamed by a child of pure imagination. The hills in Chinese paintings which seem quite fantastic are representative of those hills.

An hour passes. The hills become higher and broader-sloped, a great vastness of beautiful acreage of rice. We are in Szechwan, the province which has been an empire in itself. The fields are very wet. We are glad to see this. People in Washington have been praying for rain in Szechwan.

Suddenly we see a place where two great rivers turn and twist in great circles, cutting the hills and coming together and flowing on, one river through the mountains to the sea. At their juncture is an old, old city—Chungking.

At ten o'clock Teddy White * and I were at the home of Foreign Minister Wang for a purely protocol call. At ten-thirty we were on our way back, our car tooting its way through the bustling thoroughfare. Suddenly Teddy said: "There's an air raid." I had noticed nothing, but he had noted that a few people on the sidewalks had begun to run. Then presently I noticed that everybody was walking fast and that the open fronts of the little shops were being boarded up. When we got back home, everything was calm, but the houseboys were in our rooms packing our suitcases.

As soon as possible we got into the streets again. By this time the whole town was trekking. Everybody had a bundle. Lots of bundles were babies. Bigger children walked along quite serenely. As we turned the corner we came to a place where an orderly stream of humanity was pouring down a hillside. Horns tooted. Trucks and crowded buses churned up the dust.

By this time the first siren was blowing, meaning that the enemy planes, having left Hankow an hour before, were now entering

* See page 190.

Szechwan province. They might or might not come to Chungking: that would not be known until the second siren in another half hour or more. We had an appointment for lunch at the American Embassy across the river. One of Dr. Kung's * secretaries who was assigned to us wanted us to go straight to a dugout. He would lose enormous face if anything happened to us. Nevertheless, White knew we had plenty of time and so we made our way circuitously down to the ferry on the riverbank.

At the embassy, way up the hill, Ambassador Nelson Johnson and the embassy staff greeted us, and we went to the terrace wall and looked out over the river at Chungking. The sun was high and hot, and the whole scene now lay in an amazing stillness. No creature could be seen. No sound could be heard. All the junks were tethered to the shore and no air stirred. The Ambassador chatted about previous raids—how that section over there—"See it, the big empty patch on the hillside"—had been cleaned out by fire. The majors pulled out their watches, looked up into the dazzling sky and listened expertly. May 3 and 4, 1939, were the unforgettable days—the first big raids. At least 5,000 people had been killed and untold thousands wounded. Thousands more had been killed that year and in 1940. But now the people of Chungking know what to do. They just fold up their town, boarding up their shops, storing away their valuables and themselves into the caves. Not more than 100 would be killed today—not unless a very bad fire was started.

"There they come!" I could hear nothing nor see anything except the blazing sky. Then: "Corrump, corrump, corrump, corrump." And again: "Corrump, corrump, CORRUMP." And then a mighty wall of smoke a mile long burst up from just behind the crest of the long city-hill. The majors were pointing into the sky and then I saw, *flick, flick, flick*, the little shiny flicks of silver mackerel scales. The majors said there were forty-two airplanes.

When we got back to the city, we wanted to see what damage had been done. Along the main road we saw a small house or shop knocked out here and there and people already busy in the mess of bricks, putting the bricks in piles and salvaging wrecked pieces of furniture. The columns of air-raid wardens, which we had seen marching to work three hours before, were now marching back through crowded streets. Presently we turned into the spacious

* H. H. Kung was head of China's civil government.

compound of the Methodist Mission, and there, right in the exact center of its biggest open field, was a huge new crater.

We went over the field to the hospital. The capable-looking Chinese doctor said he had received twelve cases. One old man was expiring up in the ward. Total casualties that day were forty dead and as many more wounded. There is not much sympathy for the victims now, because it is felt it is mostly their own fault for not going into the dugouts. But it was a bad day for precious automobiles, for which there are not yet quite enough dugouts.

* * *

That day we had our big appointment—tea with Madame Chiang and, possibly, The Man Himself. The Madame in the flesh is an even more exciting personality than all the glamorous descriptions of her. After her striking entrance into her large, dim-lighted living room, we were in almost no time at all talking 100 per cent American faster than I have ever heard it talked. Talk flowed on, and then a door opened and a man came, unnoticeably, into the room. For a moment or two the talk continued. And then, suddenly, you got the feeling that there was no person in the room except the man who had just entered it so quietly. We stood up. A slim wraithlike figure in khaki moved through the shadow, and there were a few distinct grunts of encouragement: "*How* . . . *How* . . ." ("Good . . . Good . . .") The Madame introduced us. Now there was pleasure and hospitality in the grunts—and a smile on the thin mouth: "*How* . . . *How* . . . *How* . . ." He went and stood before his armchair, next to where I had been carefully placed. "*How* . . . *How*," he said, motioning us to be seated.

He inquired about our journey, expressed his gratitude that we should have come so far to see his people. I showed him a portfolio of photographs of himself and Madame and leading personalities of his government. He grinned from ear to ear and was as pleased as a boy with the pictures of himself and Madame. He looked at each photograph very quickly, but the pictures of men in his government who were not really important, he passed without looking.

7   WASHINGTON AT WAR

These four vignettes are from a Luce memo summarizing a dozen-odd interviews in Washington, February 1–3, 1943. His chief errand was to get a line on official government thinking about the postwar world. The Time Inc. "Postwar Department," which he set up right after Pearl Harbor, had already published one set of recommendations and was planning others (the FORTUNE *memos referred to below).*

Cordell Hull, Secretary of State. The old man launched immediately into his standard speech about his twenty-year battle against "isolationism," which had "worn him threadbare." As he sat in his high swivel chair, half-turned from a desk piled high with papers, his arms gestured in a swooping movement like the wings of a graceful bird. Occasionally as his arms moved through the air he would snap his fingers, as when he explained how he and the President had always "clicked" on foreign policy—just like that, *snap, snap, snap.* For thirty uninterruptable minutes he reviewed the ten-year history of the State Department *v.* Congress (neglecting to mention that Congress was overwhelmingly controlled by his own party). Whenever he came to the surface of the present, it was to assert his fear that the U.S. would again revert to isolationism. The tenor of his sagacity was that in order to avoid this, it was necessary to be extremely cautious about any internationalist proposals.

He felt that the next few months were crucial. Nonisolationists must hang together or they would hang separately—but when he was asked what platform they must hang together on, Mr. Hull was not communicative. When it was suggested that something concretely constructive—something to be proud of—might be done about Anglo-American unity, he had no suggestion as to what that might be.

The old man has a statesmanly grace and charm, and presents a romantic picture of an old Simeon waiting to see the dawn of internationalism before he says, at last, *nunc dimittis*.

Sumner Welles, Under Secretary of State. Sumner Welles is an extremely satisfactory man to interview. His mind is clear and precise. He has not the slightest hesitancy in telling you exactly what he thinks—or at any rate, what he says he thinks. He never hurries you, but you feel you should not waste a minute of the time of a man who wastes so little himself.

I began by asking for his very general guidance on FORTUNE's forthcoming memo on postwar Europe. If there were two broad alternatives, (1) something new, big and different for Europe or (2) the status quo and the same old stuff—what were the chances for something new and big and really different? "Not good," said Mr. Welles; "about one out of three, maybe." A United States of Europe is impossible. What is possible is regional federations based on economic unities. A test case is an Eastern European Federation (from the Baltic to the Aegean)—and the trouble is Russia. Russia will not stand for it, unless it is dominated by Russia.

Russia, then, is the key to unity in regard to Europe and the world. Yes. But, said I, if Russia won't come in with us (and Great Britain) on a world order, wouldn't it be best to recognize that fact of life now and get on with our strategy as best we can on the basis of a Russia which prefers "isolation"? "Perhaps," said Welles, "but first it is essential to have a look at Russia's hand." That means that it is essential that F.D.R. talk with Joe Stalin—and he must absolutely do it before June 1, 1943.* Churchill was the wrong man to talk to Stalin. Roosevelt is the one man who might be able to bring Joe into the family of nations.

The situation, thus, is that there is absolutely no fundamental diplomatic or political accord at the moment, between us and Russia—and there has got to be such an accord within a very few months or else we've got to get busy on a wholly different basis—or else get badly left at the post with no real strategy at all.

Henry Wallace, Vice President. Wallace began, in a mood of very great friendliness, by saying how much he liked—and agreed with—the FORTUNE memo on domestic economy. And then very soon he said: "Have you been thinking very much about Russia?"

* Roosevelt did not meet Stalin until the Teheran Conference, November 28, 1943.

"What a coincidence that you should ask," said I, "since that is the one topic above all I wanted to discuss with you." I put to him the case for accepting Russia's isolationism. But Wallace would have none of it. It is vital to work toward full collaboration with Russia. The highway plus air route from California to Moscow via Alaska is the kind of thing we must get on with. "You and I," said Molotov to Wallace, "will live to see the day."

The wooing of Russia is the Number 1 problem, said Wallace. And then corrected himself—Russia is the Number 1 long-range problem. The immediate problems are (1) the submarine; (2) the opening of a real Burma offensive.

Wallace's recognition of the vital importance of the Burma campaign is enough almost in itself to indicate to me that in some respects he has a better grasp of the world situation than Roosevelt. And despite his political prejudices ("the Republicans are inevitably isolationist") often cleverly disguised in humanitarian bloviation, I am bound to like Wallace better than F.D.R. and to have a far greater respect for his integrity.

Lord Halifax, Ambassador of Great Britain. I like very much to talk to him. I talk too much, but he doesn't seem to mind too much. I expounded to him about American history—he at least pretended it was mostly news to him.

But about the world of today and tomorrow. We-ell, now, here's how Halifax hopes it might be: The world to be run by the British Empire, the U.S., Russia, China. In the family of nations, all the lesser nations are stockholders, but the Big Four are the directors who from time to time report to the stockholders. Director Russia and Director China more or less confine themselves to matters in their own vast bailiwicks. The U.S. and the British Empire attend to their spheres, in which happens to be most of the rest of the world, since it is the sea. (And the air? Halifax didn't mention this in his sketchy dream.) Well, there you are, and why not? If everybody were as nice and as honorable as Halifax, you could do worse. However, I felt it necessary to mumble a little incoherently and apologetically about how this seemed to force us into an American imperialism—you know, what they say Luce is sometimes—tut tut.

The above is *not* to be taken seriously as the limit of Halifaxian statesmanship. What is to be taken damned seriously is this: that if the governments of the world have any serious intention of creating any new internationalism (other than big-power politics) Lord Halifax is totally unaware of same.

Like a good Christian and servant of the King, he is therefore plugging along at making the best of what is. He sees hope in Anglo-American policing of the world.

---

8   F.D.R.'S "LEADERSHIP"

This memo, dated September 26, 1944, was Luce's reaction to the first draft of a LIFE editorial on the imminent election. The offending line was removed from the editorial.

In the first draft there is one item which it is particularly hard for me to swallow. That is where you give Roosevelt credit for being a leader of public opinion from 1937 to 1941, preparing "America for taking sides sooner and more effectively than we had any right to expect."

I am quite ready to admit that one reason it has been so hard for me to swallow this is a personal one. I was there, brother—or at any rate, I imagined I was. That is to say I was (or thought I was) in the public-opinion fight to prepare America for taking sides. And *at the time* (let alone since) far from feeling gratitude to my alleged *Führer* in that cause, I felt that no President (who was not deeply isolationist) could possibly have moved more cautiously and slowly or with more ambiguity in this field.

I could give you chapter and verse of a good many specific things I was specifically involved with (rightly or wrongly), such as (1) the fifty old destroyers; * (2) scrap iron to Japan; (3) initiation of the idea of the draft; (4) rearmament at various stages —to say nothing of various open propaganda groups, such as the

---

* In August 1940 the U.S. transferred 50 overage destroyers to Great Britain in return for the use of British bases in the West Indies and Bermuda.

William Allen White Committee.*

Now of course Bob Sherwood † and a number (not too many) of other New Dealers were also "there." And they don't tell the story as I do. They tell—and believe—the story you accept, that "considering the popular lethargy" Roosevelt did a wonderful job. Perhaps I can claim that there was no one in the warmongering groups who was so professionally involved as I was in "public opinion"—aware both of its "lethargy" and of the possibility of change under certain circumstances and with proper leadership. And my story is, and I stick to it, that no President could conceivably have done *less* than Roosevelt, or done it more slowly. If he deserves any credit for his pre-Pearl Harbor performance, it is for his ambiguity. That perhaps no other President could have matched.

So much for my personal story. Unfortunately I cannot take a completely dispassionate view of how Armageddon was or was not faced up to.

But I think my story can also be substantiated by historical research. In the first place, look at the dates you use—"1937 to 1941." You go back to 1937, I presume, because in that year Mr. Roosevelt used the word "quarantine." Yes, he did—he used, to "lead public opinion," just one phrase in one sentence in one speech—and then he dropped it like a hot brick, and you heard no more about even negative interventionism until the late summer or fall of 1939. The Neutrality Act—the most isolationist statute ever written into the laws of any country—remained the law of the land under Roosevelt and an overwhelmingly Democratic Congress.

Nothing more until 1939. And what did he say then? On September 3, 1939, Roosevelt said: "Let no man or woman thoughtlessly or falsely talk of America sending its armies to European fields. . . . The nation will remain a neutral nation." (Of course the laugh is on Hitler, but I must say I can almost feel sorry for the old bastard in not understanding that the President could lie as well as he could. Or wasn't the President lying?) And so it went—up to and including the "again and again and again."

I am willing to say that all of us who were involved in positions

---

* The Committee to Defend America by Aiding the Allies, formed by White in 1939.

† Robert E. Sherwood (1896–1955), the playwright, was a speech writer for F.D.R.

of leadership, high or low, in this crisis fumbled the ball in various ways and in about the same degree. But the idea that Roosevelt alone did *his* job with anything more than average courage or average efficiency is a proposition which even my tin-lined stomach can't quite digest.

---

9   THE FIGHTING LADY

After F.D.R.'s death removed the sole obstacle (page 17), Luce finally got to the Pacific front in June 1945 and to Chungking in October. The following is his bread-and-butter speech to the officers and men of Admiral Radford's flagship, the U.S.S. Yorktown, *in June.*

I am happy to have this opportunity to say "thank you" to the officers and men of the *Fighting Lady*. We who have been your guests for the past ten days have so much to be grateful for that it would take all the wavelengths of your radar to cover all the angles. First of all, of course, we are grateful for what this ship has done for our country. In that, we are no different from millions of other Americans.

But the "thank you" which I want to say today is a personal kind of thank you for all that we have learned aboard ship. I don't think I have ever learned so much about so many things concerning which I was previously so ignorant. For example, *I* never knew before that a man could eat a full meal of soup, meat and potatoes, ice cream and all the extras, in three and a half minutes flat. The C.P.O. mess taught me that. *I* never knew before that a man could sleep on a piece of iron with a 2,000-horsepower engine cooling each of his eardrums. But I've seen a hundred of you doing it—quiet as a baby.

And I have learned about hospitality. Many famous cities boast of their hospitality, but never have I been in an environment of such natural hospitality as here in this great oceangoing city. Hospitality is made up of little things, of individual kindnesses and courtesies. Here are a few of my individual "thank yous."

Thank you, Lieutenant Wiezerek, for taking me up in your bomber and showing me the prettiest seascape in the world—a carrier group of the U.S. Fleet.

Thank you, Boatswain Michaud, and your crew, for bringing me over from a can on a rope without getting my feet wet.

Thank you, Gunner's Mate De Martini, for operating the best coffee shop west of Seventh Avenue.

Thank you, Signal Officer Lee Spaulding, for putting on the most absorbing act ever seen, day or night, on any stage.

Thank you, Lieutenant Allen, for letting me think for a few minutes that I had a chance to win that chess game.

Thank you, Chief Electrician's Mate Hay, for teaching me acey-deucy—especially for how to roll an acey-deucy when you need one.

Thank you, Chief Aviation Storekeeper Score, for inspiring me to crack out all the answers to all the national and international problems which I never did get quite figured out back in the old Time & Life Building.

Thank you, Chaplain Moody and Chaplain Wright, because, in the hard reality of war, you have found the deepest evidence of the goodness of men. You have passed the word to us in a very human way, and it renews our faith in each other and in the Lord and Father of us all.

Thank you, Admiral Radford and Captain Boone, because we civilians can sit up on your bridge and talk to you as equals—equals under the Constitution of the United States. You talk to us, free and easy, as you would talk to *any* American who is not under the great and honorable compulsion of military discipline. Thus you prove to us—and to all who serve under you—that America's greatest fighting men are also great civilians—true lovers of that human liberty for which they fight. This was the spirit in which George Washington fought for and won our conclusive victory at Yorktown in 1781. You have carried that spirit and the name of Yorktown unsullied across half the world.

10   CHINA IN '45

*The following are excerpts from Luce's private account
of his visit to Chungking in October 1945.*

October 8. The high point of this day was a big party given
by General Chang Chih-chung in honor of Mao Tse-tung.* I was
the only foreigner present. The dinner—a buffet affair—was held in
the one big hall in Chungking—the National Defense hall or some
such thing. The hall was filled with big tables covered with food.
The host on greeting me said the food was no good but the stage
entertainment afterward would be swell. When the 300 guests had
assembled, General Chang began to speak over the mike. Speaking
with great earnestness in fast-paced, high-pitched Hunanese, he
insisted that China must have thirty or forty years of peace, that the
negotiations with Communists had achieved about 70 per cent
agreement, etc. Then it came Mao's time to step to the mike. His
face is heavier and more peasantlike than that of most national
officers. His sloppy blue denim garment contrasted sharply with
his host's snappy be-ribboned uniform. He started slowly, with a
slight clearing of the throat after nearly every phrase, but he built
up gradually to a full-voiced shout at the end. He said about what
Chang had said, plus: that the 30 per cent of the problem which
remained to be settled "will be settled by discussion *and by no
other means*" (great applause) and that China must find "unity
under Chiang Kai-shek."

I had also talked briefly with Mao Tse-tung. I told him we had
several mutual friends. He was surprised to see me there and gazed
at me with an intense but not unfriendly curiosity. His remarks:
polite grunts.

October 11. It's a long, bumpy road to Chengtu, but I am

* Mao, chairman of the Communist party in China, had worked in uneasy alliance with the Kuomintang during the war.

entirely content watching the fields and little towns and main streets going by. Then suddenly the Jeep breaks down—carburetor trouble. Presently a truckload of G.I.s comes by and they take Bailey * and me aboard. This isn't so pleasant. I sit on the floor of the truck. The G.I.s (mostly sergeants) offer the minimum of hospitality. As my tail is being beaten by the bumps and my eyes watch the retreating Szechwan landscape, I listen to the chatter of the sergeants. Sitting near me is one of those typical Americans who speak slowly and deliberately, repeating guidebook facts with what appears to be deadly accuracy. Most of the facts he recites are unflattering to China, though he maintains an air of ruthless scholarship. Up ahead there is the loudmouthed wisecracker. He leads what would be a chorus of anti-Chinese-ism except that the rest of the bunch doesn't happen to be in a good mood to play chorus. We pass a battalion of Chinese soldiers carrying guns. The loudmouth yells out, "The war's over, so now you're going to fight." He seizes two or three opportunities to make this crack. The scholarly fellow points out an airplane here and there parked under trees a little way from the road. He says there are a great many of these planes, which the Chinese kept completely hidden in reserve while all the time they were yelling for more airplanes to be brought over the Hump. As we enter the town the scholarly fellow explains about Chengtu to the others, who have mostly never been to town. It's not a bad town, says he. It's famous for its silverware—to be found on Silver Street—not bad stuff. Also there is an interesting Silk Street. There are two whorehouses, he says, one for 200 and one for 700 (China dollars or something). Yes, the girls will stay with you for quite a decent while. And so we are dumped off at the former Chinese Officers Club, which has been turned over to the G.I.s—but the G.I.s aren't thanking anybody for anything.

* Wesley Bailey was Luce's assistant.

11 NUREMBERG

Before Luce went to Nuremberg in April 1946, LIFE *and* FORTUNE *had already taken the position (also espoused by Senator Robert Taft) that a trial of vanquished by victors would ill serve the Western cause of international law. Luce was deeply anti-Nazi and therefore dubious about his editors' anti-Nuremberg line. These doubts were largely resolved when he saw Soviet judges, representing another totalitarian state, on the same bench with British and American judges. The following is an excerpt from a report of his trip.*

I am glad they took us to Nuremberg. There we looked at Hermann Goering and his fellow criminals in the dock. There we saw the films of the concentration camps, the lifeless facts more hideous than the evilest imagination. A bulldozer (the driver's hand to his nose) shoves a rolling mass of naked male and female corpses across the field into the big ditch.

In this 20th century, all our reckoning of the human situation must take as one of its starting points a hideous organized bestiality of which no beasts are capable.

That evening we dined magnificently with Justice Robert Jackson.* The champagne was of good quality. Mr. Jackson spoke well, defending the course of his trial against all possible lines of criticism. His best point—and one which I had not previously seen stated—was that a trial-at-law did not necessarily require that the relevant law should have been previously enacted. For, obviously, in the history of human society there were tribunals before there were legislatures. It is indeed dangerous to depart from the rule

* Jackson (1892–1954), on leave from the Supreme Court, was the U.S. chief counsel at Nuremberg.

against "ex post facto," but when civilization has broken down, the rule cannot be regarded as absolute.

Now one of the things which is on trial at Nuremberg—the most important thing—is a modern form of autocracy which we call totalitarianism. Jackson told us that Hermann Goering (cured by Americans of his dope addiction and revealing a keen intelligence) had made the classic case for totalitarianism.

If you are going to have totalitarianism (of any breed in any country), then, said Goering with remorseless logic, the following things are necessary:

First, obviously, you must suppress all *organized opposition.*

Second, you must suppress all *individual opposition,* since individual opposition leads to organized opposition.

Then, third, you must suppress *individual expression,* since this is a form of individual opposition.

Fourth, in order to achieve the above, it is necessary to have a secret police—a nationwide spy system—and the secret police must have an untrammeled power to arrest. The secret police does not spring from sadism or sadistic motives; it is simply that you can't have any form of totalitarianism without it.

Fifth, the people arrested cannot be tried by judges under habeas corpus, etc., because people must be imprisoned not merely for crimes they have committed but also for crimes which it may be presumed they may commit.

Finally, therefore, in a totalitarian state there is no means by which the government may be overthrown except revolution.

Now this Goering classic is by no means of merely historical interest; it states what is still the one great political issue of our time. For, of course, everything Goering said applies, without a hair's breadth difference, to Soviet Russia.

Concentration camps? Averell Harriman * states that it is of course impossible to know how many people are in concentration camps in Soviet Russia. But of purely political prisoners the lowest estimate he ever got was five million.

I have thus put at the beginning of these notes the two great realities of contemporary Europe and Eurasia: the hideousness of defeated Nazi Germany and the similar hideousness of victorious Soviet Russia. All the problems of Europe revolve around these two terrible realities.

* U.S. Ambassador to the U.S.S.R., 1943–46.

12   OSWALDO ARANHA

The following is from a report on Luce's trip to Brazil in May-June 1947. As a young man (thirty-six), Aranha had participated in the revolt that brought Getulio Vargas to power in 1930. From then until his death in 1960, Aranha served Brazil in many capacities: four times a cabinet minister, Ambassador to the U.S., and President of the U.N. General Assembly (1947). He received the hero's welcome here described for his handling of the U.N. special session on Palestine.

Oswaldo Aranha is one of the greatest and most irresistible personalities I have ever encountered. He is a sort of combination of Wendell Willkie and Franklin Roosevelt—with the forthright, belligerent honesty of Willkie, and the easy charm of Roosevelt, the inexhaustible animal energy of both, plus a love of beauty and philosophy which neither of the American democrats possessed.

Traveling with him on a special Brazilian plane down to Rio from New York, we came over the mountains into the skies above the famous Bay of Rio in the early afternoon of a cloudless day. Oswaldo commanded the ship to make a circle of this breathlessly beautiful spot of earth while, with an enthusiasm half-boyish, half-connoisseur, he poured out a stream of comment on the spectacular scene. At last he permitted the ship to land. A crowd of several thousand jammed every part of the airport. As soon as he had passed through the line of official greeters, he was swallowed up in a multitude of excited fellow citizens who seemed determined to squeeze him to death with their hugs and kisses. The American Ambassador * and I retreated well to the side of the crowd, where, presently, by standing on boxes, we could see the white head of the

* William D. Pawley.

returning hero delivering a speech which he had written a few hours before on the plane. In this speech he quoted the Frenchman Lamartine, who, when he entered Parliament, was asked whether he would be on the left or the right, and replied: "I shall fix my course neither to the right nor to the left, but by the stars above!"

During the next two weeks, I saw Aranha nearly every day, and was with him many hours, going about the city of Rio, jaunting out to Petrópolis, touring the city and state of São Paulo, attending receptions, and even once playing chess. (P.S. I won—Aranha was too rash.) Everywhere we went (except at the chess game) people would come up to him, throw their arms about him and receive from him the joyous gift of friendship. When Pawley had about forty of the top U.S. businessmen at his embassy, it seemed to me that at least half of them greeted Aranha like a long-lost brother. In going about with me, Aranha never for an instant tired of telling me about the wonders of his country and of what ought to be done to realize its possibilities. Aranha's consuming hobby—his vocation and avocation—is Brazil.

Aranha comes from a very upper-class family from Rio Grande do Sul. This province contains very little Negro blood. It was a ranchers' land and claims to have originated the *gaucho*. The name Aranha means "spider," but this apparently carries no unpleasant connotation in Brazil. Oswaldo Aranha's mother, Dona Luiza, who is still living, had, I think, fifteen or more children, and Oswaldo has literally hundreds of known cousins. The old lady was devout (as Oswaldo is not) and was tremendously respected. When the Congress passed a law to permit divorce, Vargas said, "I will sign the law only if it is approved by the Cardinal and Dona Luiza." (What happened, I don't know.*) All of Oswaldo's cousins, as well as his immediate family, seem to be as passionately and vociferously devoted to him as most of the literate populace.

Oswaldo Aranha is the great Independent in Brazilian politics. He is like Willkie in his passionate need for personal independence. Time and time again I thought I must be listening to Wendell as Oswaldo would cry out to me that he would not be bound by partisan politics, nor by the dull formalities of high society. (Aranha is a captivating figure in a drawing room, but he is far livelier out on the street or with a group of men clustered about him to promote schemes for the greater glory and prosperity of Brazil.)

* Vargas did not sign. Brazilian law still does not allow divorce.

Aranha became conspicuous in politics in 1930, when he was a leader of a revolution. But evidently Oswaldo was not the kind of man to boss a party; Vargas was, and so presently Vargas became boss of Brazil—with Oswaldo as his independent, most distinguished, best-looking, most outstanding cabinet minister. As we bounced about Brazil, it seemed that wherever a modern school or agricultural institute or a good road came in view, Oswaldo was able to say, with boyish enthusiasm, "I started that—I gave them the money."

The great fact of Aranha's career is, of course, that he brought Brazil into the war (and into the preceding "war effort") on our side and prevented Brazil going, actually, if not formally, against us. Vargas and practically *all the intelligent and influential people* of Brazil thought that Germany could win and that it would be folly to be found on the anti-German side. Aranha's achievement was against terrific odds—and is tremendously significant of the love of freedom which animates him. For Aranha, of course, had no "objective" reasons for supposing that Nazi Germany would not win; he only knew, because he is a deeply civilized man, that Nazi Germany *must not* win.

13   ENGLAND IN '52

The following are excerpts from a report on a trip in February.

This was my first visit to the new House of Commons building. It is almost exactly the same size as the old, and otherwise quite similar. The size of the House is very important. It is not big enough to provide a seat for every Member of Parliament at the same time. The two sides of the House face each other across a very narrow aisle.

There had been those who hoped that the new House would be built big enough to seat all the members—a logical enough idea—

and in general on more spacious and convenient lines. But Mr. Churchill would hear nothing of such heretical ideas. And he was and is undoubtedly right. What happens in a House too small for comfort and with opposing parties facing each other at such close quarters is that in the House actual men talk to actual men—which is a radically different thing from a politician making a speech to the press. Here is government by *communication*, by real debate.

Of course, the physical size of the House is not the only reason for this phenomenon—so rare in modern times. All the rules and customs and manners of the House, carefully developed over centuries, have produced this supreme example of government by real man-to-man discussions or debate. The wonder—and almost miracle—is that it is still there.

The key word about the House of Commons is "communicate." In the House, men communicate with each other. Great Britain is in significant degree ruled by their rational debate.

*   *   *

At the Midland Hotel in Manchester about ten people assembled as our guests for lunch. They were rather a mixed bag. They included the Dean of Manchester (rank of bishop), the High Master of the best local school, three or four businessmen of the second rank, *and* one Dickensian character named Sir Robert Catterall.

Actually, the King's sword has not yet touched the shoulder of this 20th-century cavalier, but, *D.V.*, it will do so in Buckingham Palace come February 27. The to-be Sir Robert is a seventy-year-old, hornyhanded son of toil who all his life has been a Tory; so, to prove that they can cross class lines, the Tories are making him, in his old age, a knight.

Sir Robert has a tough, ruddy face, quite whiskery. His appearance was made even more dramatic by his having his left arm done up in a sling with a lot of white bandages. This, however, did not prevent him from gesticulating vigorously with his right arm whenever he spoke, which he often did in the most emphatic and dogmatic manner.

Sir Robert's *Weltanschauung* can only be described as reactionary in the extreme—far more reactionary than any one would be apt to encounter at White's or Brooks's. His general view is that the English character has been steadily deteriorating since, sixty years ago, he set out to earn his living at the age of ten—his only alternative to starving. This deterioration of character was proved by the alarming increase in juvenile delinquency and was, of course, caused by pernicious socialist propaganda.

All these views were kept tolerably suppressed during lunch, while Sir Robert sat on my left, guzzling manfully; but by good luck, soon after the coffee was passed, I managed to get him involved in a dispute with the High Master, and the result of this was that for an hour there was a most un-English hubbub around the table, everybody joining in the fray.

The High Master was a very fine example of our finest people in America and England today—the liberal humanist. He was very intelligent and well able to hold up his end of the argument against anybody like me. But when Sir Robert got at him—"most teachers are Communist"—his arsenal of liberal-humanist arguments became a little confused. And everybody helped. The Bishop, for example, was also a liberal, but also one who took Christianity quite seriously. And therefore the Bishop, liberal and upper class though he was, had to dissent from some of the latitudinarian views of his fellow intellectual, the High Master. The businessmen rushed in, one almost inadroitly on Sir Robert's side, another on the High Master's side, and every man for himself.

Well, it was a terrific conversation, and nobody wanted to leave at three o'clock. In order to calm things down at the end, I put my hand on old Sir Robert's knee and told him if he really wanted to see a socialist country he had better come to America. This was apropos of the question of school-leaving age. I was actually a bit shocked to learn that in England's welfare state, 80 per cent of the boys and girls leave school at fourteen to earn a living, and, putting it on a bit, I told Sir Robert that in the U.S.A. we wouldn't think of asking a boy or girl to go out into the hard, hard world before they were twenty-two.

In general, the conversation had turned on the question of the British character. The High Master had said—and very persuasively—the boys (and girls) now at school would turn out to be better human beings than previous generations. And more generally imbued with Christian ethics.

On my return to London I had a letter from the most intelligent businessman at this lunch. Said he: "It was a great experience to hear some of my fellow countrymen exposing their souls in a way which would have been unlikely without an overseas interlocutor."

I was quite clear that I did *not* want to see Aneurin Bevan and equally clear that I *did* want to see Dick Crossman.* I didn't want to be burdened by the great Bevan personality—that subject I would take on faith from others. I wanted to see Crossman in order to get the pure poison of left-wing anti-Americanism, etc., without the complication of personality. But, of course, Crossman is a personality, too.

When I went up the steps of Crossman's little house, I expected to listen, with bland politeness, to the Crossman case. When, two hours later, I walked down the steps, I said to Andre † that if I had stayed in there another hour, I might have become a Bevanite. In any case, it was a fascinating conversation, at all times seemingly rational, good-natured, well-informed, and presided over deftly by a very nice Mrs. Crossman.

I flattered myself on one point—that I managed to depth-charge Mr. Crossman into exposing the real basis of his foreign policy. With great persuasiveness this is the thesis he put forward (toward the end):

The 20th century, now far gone, is quite clearly the century of totalitarianism. There is no possibility that within the next fifty— or even perhaps 150—years a "tolerably decent world" (my phrase) can be reconstituted. The only hope—and the hope that must be fought for by brains and muscles—is that some islands of liberty (or civilization) shall be maintained through this Totalitarian Age so that in the 21st or 22nd century the liberal progress of mankind may be resumed. These islands would be Great Britain, North America, perhaps some parts of Western Europe, and one or two other spots. That, said he, was the true or realistic basis of policy. Nevertheless, said he, America is bound to take another view—the view that a tolerably decent world can be reconstituted in a reasonably short time. This is the view he would take if he were an American. This, of course, made his thesis very appealing to an American.

A few nights later I was talking with Wyatt, ‡ and he said that Crossman had quite evidently—and quite typically—dreamed up

* Bevan (1897–1960) led the left wing of the Labor party. At the time of Luce's visit Richard Crossman, also a Labor M.P., was one of Bevan's strong supporters.

† Andre Laguerre was then TIME's bureau chief in London.

‡ Woodrow Wyatt, Parliamentary Under Secretary of State in the War Office in 1951.

the above thesis on the spur of the moment for my benefit. Admittedly, Crossman is an extremely clever fellow. But, says Wyatt, he is completely without personal influence, even in the Bevanite wing of the party, because of his lack of intellectual depth or whatever it might be called.

But on first encounter he is not only a brilliant but a beguiling personality.

14   THE PACIFIC TREK

Luce wrote an article for LIFE, *February 23, 1953, called* "America and Asia," *setting forth our special relationship with Japan, Korea, China and Southeast Asia as he saw it. The following is the conclusion as he wrote it, though it was omitted from the magazine article either for space or for tactical reasons.*

There is one more word to say about American relations with Asia—and that word is the Pacific, meaning the ocean itself of 70 million square miles and innumerable islands, the tiny ones hardly on any map a few years ago, and now famous—Kwajalein and Eniwetok and Truk and Saipan and Iwo Jima. The Pacific Ocean is now our ocean. It never before was anybody's, since the earth was formed. The Chinese of the great Central Kingdom never came down to the sea—they never built any ports, let alone ever set out across the stormy deeps. The British may have held a kind of sway as part of their Rule Britannia. The Japanese, with ferocious industry, pretty nearly held it commercially and made, as we recall, a bid to establish their imperial sun in all its skies, but they were doomed to fail because of the United States. Now the Pacific is America's. This is the kind of truth which may never perhaps be said and may not be moral to say. Yet it remains a fact.

Flying home over the Pacific from the last battles of the war, I wrote to my mother that I did not know what would be the future relations of America and China—did not know whether they would realize that constructive friendliness which my father had so desired to see. I said I only knew that the United States had planted its flag and buried its dead in Okinawa; so far west America in World War II had really, in fact and in spirit, gone, and from there it would never retreat.

And this fact caused me to reflect upon the nature of American expansion. America has expanded contiguously—the East Coast, and then the Mississippi Valley and then Salt Lake and then Oregon. And then on our Pacific coast we stopped for a long, long while, even intelligent Americans refusing to believe that Hawaii was American. (It took Pearl Harbor to get the Americans to recognize this possession of Hawaii.) As for the Philippines, everybody knew that they, of course, were a strange exception to the proper order of things.

It was as late as 1943 that Admiral King * grimly set the course for a colossal American trek across the Pacific. Admiral King, Admiral Nimitz, Admiral Halsey, Admirals Spruance and Kinkaid, and many another sea lord made their logistically colossal march across the middle of the mighty waters—while MacArthur paced them along the southern island coasts. The American fleet in Ulithi (never heard of before or hardly since) was one of the greatest spectacles ever presented to the human eye.

As the ships marched each island became a measured jewel, and every cresting wave saluted the first masters of the Pacific.

Now, America, your task of contiguous conquest is done. Henceforth your warfare is not with forest and desert and mountains or jungle and wave. Henceforth you struggle with principalities and powers, with good and evil, not in nations only, but in yourself and in all men. But for this you are also prepared. Go forward, bravely, straightforwardly, gently.

* Ernest J. King (1878–1956), Fleet Admiral and chief of U.S. naval operations during the war.

15 JOHN F. KENNEDY

In the book of political recollections which he left unfinished at his death, Luce devoted this chapter to the late President.

The Democratic National Convention of 1960 was held in Los Angeles. It opened on a Monday. On Tuesday, in New York, I had a telephone call from Joseph P. Kennedy, "Old Joe," "the Founding Father." He said he was going to be in New York Friday on his way to Europe and could I see him? We made a date for five o'clock at my apartment at the Waldorf. It did not occur to me that that meant that Joe would be leaving Los Angeles before the convention was over.

Five o'clock came but no Joe. Seven o'clock and still no Joe. My son Henry was with me, having come to dinner. Soon after seven, the phone rang and, with a typical burst of expletives, Joe told me his plane had been delayed. I asked him whether he would like to come to dinner. He would. Half an hour later he was there—ruddily hale, hearty and happy. He consumed a couple of lobsters while we exchanged small talk about the convention and the nomination of his forty-three-year-old son for the presidency of the United States.

Jack Kennedy was scheduled to make his acceptance speech at ten o'clock our time. How come Joe had not stayed in Los Angeles to hear the bands play? When we adjourned to the living room after dinner, Joe still showed no signs of getting down to business. So I opened up. I said my attitude (as editor-in-chief of Time Inc. publications) toward Jack could be very simply stated. Let us divide the question into two parts: domestic policy, foreign policy.

As for domestic policy, naturally it was to be assumed that Jack would adopt a "liberal" policy. Old Joe broke in with blazing blue eyes and many a goddamn. He said: "Harry, you know goddamn well no son of mine could ever be a goddamn liberal."

I told Joe to hush. It was the nature of American politics that in order to win, a Democratic candidate for the presidency had to take a liberal position (while, of course, retaining the automatic support of the Solid South) and that we would not hold that against him. "But," I said, "if Jack shows any signs of going soft on Communism (in foreign policy)—then we would clobber him."

Joe said, "Well, you don't have to worry about that."

Then the TV came on and there was John Fitzgerald Kennedy with voice and gesture and face and figure that would soon become imperishable in the world's vision.

What must have been the emotions of that father watching and listening to that son? Mission accomplished—almost, for there was still the election. Life fulfilled beyond all the hazards of chance. It would take a very great dramatist-novelist to portray Joseph Patrick Kennedy's emotions—to mix the rhythm of earthy selfishness and higher loyalties.

When the speech was done, we chatted for a while, and then Joe got up to leave. At the doorway, he turned to me, took my hand again and said: "I want you to know that we are truly grateful for all that you have done for Jack."

It was a moment after the door had closed before my inner ear took in these words. I was touched, of course, but what had I done? Had I ever done too much?

In no sense were President Kennedy and I close friends. Yet, as I look back, it seems to me we were in constant communication. This was partly by way of third parties—mainly through Joseph Patrick, but also through others. Most important, the President and I were in constant communication because he was an instant reader of TIME—and kept a close eye on our other publications. TIME had to be delivered to President Kennedy personally every Sunday evening by special messenger from the printer—usually before I got it.

One Sunday evening, as he landed at a Washington airport on his way back from Hyannis Port, he was met by Larry O'Brien, his chief political operator. "All right, all right, let's have it," he said. That was a slightly unusual occasion, because that week O'Brien was on the cover * and it might be expected that TIME would be a little rough with the political operator. Kennedy read

* TIME, September 1, 1961.

the story on his way to the White House and concluded, "Well, Larry—not too bad, not too bad."

How do I know this? I knew this or its equivalent every week. For on Monday, or by latest, Tuesday, either the President himself or one or more of his many White House staffers told John Steele, chief of our Washington bureau, or Hugh Sidey, our round-the-clock White House correspondent, just what the President and the various staffers had thought about the handling of this, that and the other story in TIME. Our marks varied from A-minus to very bad.

The fact that Kennedy was a TIME reader naturally biased me in his favor, for after all, the chief desire of an editor is that he should be read.

Kennedy was a great reader of history and of politics. A few weeks after his nomination, candidate Kennedy came to lunch with my editorial colleagues in the Time & Life Building in New York. Before the general conversation got going, I said to Jack, apropos of something: "Of course, you haven't read it, but you may have heard of the new 600-page biography * of McKinley."

Jack broke in: "What makes you think I haven't read it?"

I said: "You just couldn't have had time."

Jack: "You forget the kind of life I've been leading—traveling on airplanes."

That left me even more amazed. After campaigning for fifteen hours a day he climbs bone-tired into an airplane—and settles down with 600 pages on McKinley!

During his three years in office, I was received by the President ten or twelve times, usually alone. The first important occasion was in May 1961, about five weeks after the Bay of Pigs. But it also happened to be the day on which Kennedy addressed the Congress, proposing that the U.S. should aim to land on the moon by 1970 and that to that end $7 billion to $9 billion should immediately be voted to beef up the space program begun by Eisenhower. I heard the speech at the Capitol, went to the White House and waited for half an hour. I met the President as he stepped out of the White House elevator. He pulled some papers out of his pocket and handed them to me with a look of utter disgust. They were memoranda from the Joint Chiefs of Staff about the Bay of Pigs and other matters. The cause of the President's disgust was that

---

* *In the Days of McKinley,* by Margaret Leech (1959).

they were so wishy-washy. So we went in to lunch. I couldn't think of anything much to say about the Bay of Pigs and so I began by complimenting him on his space speech. I confess that I myself was not sure that space required all that priority, but Kennedy's speech had made a good and even inspiring case for it.

Inevitably, however, the ghost of the Bay of Pigs returned, and led to the wider problem of the threat of Communism in South America. What would I do, the President asked. I replied that, for one thing, I would, with due diplomatic preparation, make a firm reaffirmation of the Monroe Doctrine. The President thought it was a little out of date in a world of global politics. Perhaps he was right. I think all the signs point to a world of global politics, but I also think that at this stage there is much realism and virtue in "regional" arrangements.

The next time I was at lunch in the White House, the President had something specifically on his mind for me to do. It was about China. He wanted me to make a restudy of the problem of admitting Red China into the U.N. I took it as a command performance. The President argued that we couldn't keep on winning this point in the U.N. indefinitely. Since I was widely credited with being a leader of opposition to Red China, the President properly assumed that if, on the basis of study, I were to modify my views, that would be helpful to a change of China policy. I took the assignment seriously. I did restudy the matter. And I sent the President a longish memorandum * saying that if immediately he would command his people to get busy on the China matter, the U.N. would once again vote decisively against admission of Red China. My prognostication proved to be correct—and I think the President was quite content to have it so.

I thoroughly enjoyed all my conversations with the President— except one. The bad half-hour was when he criticized me bitterly for TIME's story † on the renewed attempt of his brother-in-law Prince Radziwill to get an annulment out of the Vatican. Our story did no violence to journalistic ethics. Nevertheless, the President was bitter as he pointed out the hurt feelings that would be caused by this story. Like other laymen when their own feelings are hurt, the President had no conception of what masses of material most of

---

* It was prepared with considerable help from Henry Cabot Lodge, at that time a Time Inc. consultant.

† TIME, September 14, 1962.

the press throws into the wastebasket because of our editors' judgment that feelings will be hurt without adequate journalistic reason. But even this bad half-hour was somehow got out of— thanks to the President's urbanity.

Talking to the President, at least for me, had always the aspect of fencing, of thrust and counterthrust. He would, in modern idiom, give me the needle, and the question then was just how sharp a needle I could, with due deference, return. One of his gambits was to exaggerate my Republicanism and leave me with the alternative of defending Republican stupidity or seeming to desert that unhappy party.

The last time I saw the President there was no fun whatever. It was a solemn, even an awesome, occasion. It was the Wednesday after the Monday [October 22, 1962] on which he had delivered his ultimatum to Khrushchev on the missiles in Cuba.

The Monday speech to the nation, I had heard on a huge TV screen. The next noon I was told that the President of the United States was calling me. It was arranged for me and the managing editor of TIME, Otto Fuerbringer, to be in the White House Wednesday. My recollection of the forty minutes when the three of us sat together is that hardly a word was said. That, of course, was not the case. Words were spoken. Mostly they were in contemplation of that cloud that hangs over our century—atomic war. At that moment there was no intellectual analysis. It was just the unknown that had to be faced. Otto and I could only convey, low key, our empathy for the President. Finally he said he wanted us to go over and see Robert McNamara.

The Secretary of Defense took us into a big room where at least 100 photographs, some three feet square in size, were laid out on tables and easels. They were reconnaissance photographs of Cuba over a period of thirty or forty days. They showed how extremely difficult it was to spot the first beginnings of the building of missile sites in the heavily timbered hills. Bad weather for ten days had further complicated the procedure. One reason the President had wanted us to see these photographs was to show that the Administration had not been sure until October 22 that the Russians had been up to outrageous international deviltry.

A number of arguable points exist about the Cuban confrontation. Weeks before the President's ultimatum, Senator Kenneth Keating had warned that the Russians were installing missiles in

Cuba. Why was our ground intelligence not able to pick up the scent even if air reconnaissance failed? To be sure, the President had, the week before, called in the Russian Foreign Minister, Gromyko, and Gromyko had lied as only the Russians can lie. The more serious question has to do with the conclusion of the matter. Why did Kennedy give up his requirement that there must be international inspection to make sure that all Russian missiles and men had departed? Why did he allow many Russian military to remain in Cuba? The argument goes round. My judgment is that Kennedy did well, that he taught the Russians and the world the lesson he wanted to teach—namely, that he himself was a man of courage and that the United States could not be made a victim of fear or frightfulness.

The time has come to stand off at some distance and give an estimate of Kennedy in terms of history. My estimate will be largely in accord with that of most contemporary observers.

Style! That is the word. It is almost as if John Fitzgerald Kennedy had appropriated that word to himself. The word will still go on being used for oratory and clothes and other things, but when it comes to speaking of a man, it will not be possible to use the word for many years without evoking the image of President Kennedy.

The picture in your mind may be of the tall, lithe young man with the heavy crop of hair, his hand fiddling with the second button of his carelessly stylish jacket. But remember him, too, in white tie and tails. The tailors of the 19th century must have invented the dress suit precisely for President Kennedy.

The Style presented itself in many other ways. It presented itself in manner of public speaking and at press conferences—in the art of understatement, in the dry throw-away humor, and, when the occasion called for it, the burst of oratory or the carefully structured essay on poetry or John Adams.

The Kennedy Style was precisely what Americans needed. Besides being a thing of beauty in itself, it exemplified much that needed to be exemplified, and also, it had important consequences. It exemplified the desire for something called "excellence" which had just become a widespread aspiration. It exemplified the new emphasis on education, higher education and the arts. The President's own knowledge of such things as painting and music was not extensive, but as a man of his generation he appreciated their relevance. The President also loved parties—he was a fun man after hours. Despite the atom bomb America was becoming, again, a fun country. Kennedy was a little too old to have the new, new beat—but he was close to it.

The important consequence of the Kennedy Style was that it gave a lift to Americans' pride in their country. This it did in many quite different ways. Thus, it attracted "youth"—a large and increasingly self-conscious category. It appealed to the academicians or intellectuals among whom it was not fashionable to find much to like, much less to love, in America. And it appealed, perhaps most subtly of all, to the great majority of the people who had been immigrants of the last 100 years. Kennedy was a Catholic; many Catholics had not wanted him to be the first President of their faith, but it is a fair bet that in the secrecy of the voting booth, most of the disapproving nuns voted for him. But Kennedy was also Irish—of the fourth U.S. generation. The majority of Americans could identify with him as a non-WASP. Provided, of course, that he was a man you could genuinely be proud of. And he was.

Thus, in various ways, mostly unspoken, Kennedy united the country. He did this, not by any proclaimed consensus—and not by dedication to any particular cause—except America.

The pride in Kennedy, and hence in America, was most vivid when he went to Europe. What style! The dress suit descending the stairs with de Gaulle, but also the tousled head at the Berlin wall: *"Ich bin ein Berliner!"*

Not that Eisenhower had not been a tremendous success abroad. In crowded India he drew the biggest crowd ever assembled in that teeming land. But Eisenhower was the gentleman-hero of a receding past. In Kennedy, a new star had been born.

A man ought to love his country even when he cannot be proud of it—as witness the famous photograph of the Frenchman weeping at the Arc de Triomphe after the unspeakably shameful fall of France in 1940. But there does seem to be some relationship between pride in one's country and patriotism.

Patriotism had by no means waned in this country in the postwar years as it had in the 1930s. But the country had become perhaps a little bored with its own achievements—most people a little indifferent and anesthetizing themselves with TV, others a little oversophisticated and displaying what Professor Frankel *

* Charles Frankel, professor of philosophy at Columbia University.

diagnosed as "cosmic hypochondria." Kennedy woke them up. Vigor was the word. And the New Frontier. Joy in the present— and on with space.

And so—the greatest consequence of the Kennedy Style was that it could speak acceptably the words of patriotism.

Kennedy did not actually accomplish much in a specific sense during his three years in the White House. He brought a new atmosphere to Washington. At home there was indeed forward motion in civil rights, and perhaps it was a tribute to Kennedy that President Johnson's first State of the Union Message gave decisive priority to the Negro problem. The American economy, never as badly off as Kennedy tried to make out in his campaign, moved up. The Peace Corps was a brilliant stroke—highly responsive to the needs of "youth" in an affluent and secular society. Yes, of course, there are constructive items to his credit. It remains true that what was important about President Kennedy was not what he did, but who he was. In this period of the American Century what millions of can-do Americans needed was not so much the capacity to do as the courage to be.

9

AMONG FRIENDS

Luce was especially willing to speak to members of Time Inc., to students or alumni of Yale, and to other groups with whom he felt close personal ties. Sometimes his remarks to such groups were impromptu, rambling and verbose; sometimes they were as carefully prepared as his more public speeches. In either case, the content of these more private utterances was not very different from that of his public speeches. This chapter contains three prepared speeches which are representative of his more intimate style and are also revelatory of his personal philosophy.

The Columbus speech of 1962 (Number 3) was by no means his last but it was in some ways the ultimate statement of his lifelong optimism. Nothing happened between then and his death to change his expectation of a decade "of relative calm." His last trip abroad was with a Time Inc. junket of leading businessmen to the capitals of Eastern Europe in October 1966. Like almost all his companions, he returned confirmed in the opinion that Communism as an ideological force was dead or dying in those countries, that they wanted to resume their ancient ties with the West, that "bridge-building" was the right U.S. policy, and that the cold war was receding into the past.

1   AN AMERICAN STORY

The so-called "Senior Group" of Time Inc. editors, executives and writers (set up in 1939) was supposed, said Luce, "to be made up of those who had the main call on the jackpot"—i.e., a bonus plan—but also of "responsible men, responsible each to our own job and responsible to each other and perhaps responsible to some greater causes." Luce spoke as follows to its members on May 4, 1950, at the Waldorf in New York City.

I want to tell you tonight the story of one American—my story. Each of you has his own story of being an American—a story with its own special accents and meanings. I am telling my story, not because it is a particularly extraordinary one, but because it is my story. And while I am telling it, you might be reflecting upon yours. And then, when I am through, you may know better how to judge what is valid in my story, and what to select out of all our varied experiences that will give us the consciousness of being Americans.

I was born in Tengchow, a small but very ancient seaport town on the Shantung promontory that juts out into the Yellow Sea. Long years ago, poets lived there. On the rocky point above the port a temple stands, a really proper temple with bells and glazed blue tiles. From the temple court you could look out over a summer sea and trace on the near horizon a necklace of islands.

Sometime after I was born I was baptized in a Christian church in the name of the Father and of the Son and of the Holy Ghost. Then sometime after that my parents had a chance to go to Chefoo, another port across the hills of the promontory, fifty miles and a two-day journey away. Chefoo was now well known and progressive because it had become a treaty port where the white man had special rights. There was an American consul there, and as soon as they could my parents went to him to tell him and to tell Uncle

Sam the fact that they had a son—me.

Years later, when I got to the Hotchkiss School, one of the first charges brought against me by the boys of the Lower Middle Form was that I could never be President of the U.S. Naturally, it was necessary for me to correct in my fellows their shallow understanding of the American Constitution. That was quickly done. It took me somewhat longer to shake off the nickname Chink.

This, then, is the prelude to my story—*civis Americanus sum.* The rest I will tell in three scenes.

A few years after I was born we moved inland to a bigger city, near the center of the province. Actually we lived a mile or two outside of the walled city, in the middle of a great plain where grain grew—winter wheat and millet and sorghum fifteen feet high. We lived in what is called a compound—only this was a very big compound, because it included a little college as well as a boys' school, girls' school, hospital and church. All the work of the missionaries, both teachers and itinerant preachers, was done, of course, with the Chinese, and much of their lives were lived with them. But there was one day in the year when we Americans, old and young, withdrew from China and the Chinese. That was the Fourth of July. That day we Americans kept to ourselves.

I remember a Fourth of July when I was nine or ten at Mrs. Frank Chalfant's. She had a lovely lawn with shade trees and the sweet fragrance of lilacs along the wall. Forty or fifty Americans, old men and children, assembled there in the hot afternoon. The children were gay in red, white and blue paper dresses and suits, and everybody had a flag. There were plenty of firecrackers. Dr. Roys kept popping them off, scaring the ladies. Presently came the eats—especially ice cream, made, of course, in our ice-cream freezers, brought from America. And strawberries from our lovingly tended patches. Ice cream and strawberries and chocolate cake. Then the babies were taken home, and slow summer twilight began —it was time now for the fancy fireworks. They burst and whirled above us. And then again the hush of eventide and we sang our song:

> *My country, 'tis of thee . . .*
> *Long may our land be bright*
> *With freedom's holy light,*
> *Protect us by Thy might*
> *Great God, our King.*

Then the handclasps all round, and then, through the darkness, each to his own home, each with his lantern.

Scene Two is a boarding school in the port town of Chefoo I mentioned a moment ago. There is a great deal I could say apropos of that school. I hated it and loved it. I was terribly homesick. When I didn't have a bloody nose or a skinned knee, my face and hands were swollen with chilblains. The school was very religious and very rough and tough. It had never heard of any of the pedagogical ideas taught at Columbia. Yet, after Chefoo, the getting of A's at Hotchkiss and Yale was for me a rather pleasantly soporific pastime. If scholarship in America had not been so soft, I might be an educated man today.

But in the story of an American the Chefoo school is important because it was British. About one-fifth of the 120 or 130 boys were American. We were a strong, conspicuous, successful minority. The British code—flogging and fagging and toadying—violated every American instinct. No wonder that hardly an hour passed— in classroom or on football field—that the Americans didn't have to run up the flag. For example, a master insists that Ohio is pronounced O-hee-ho. What are you going to do? Will you agree? The American can't agree; it would betray every other American. So first your knuckles are rapped, then you get your face slapped—by the master—then you are publicly caned. By this time you are crying, but still you can't say O-hee-ho.

Shall I draw the moral from this? My Anglo-Americanism is deeper than any words. Indeed, it is written in the blood of that shameful, futile, endless two hours one Saturday afternoon when I rolled around the unspeakably dirty floor of the main schoolroom with a little British bastard who had insulted my country. You see, I know the British *intimately*. I knew them long before I went to Oxford. I can recite the list of English kings. I have read much of their poetry. The best they have—a very great best—is bred into me as much as anything can be bred in me. I love the beauty of Britain and the power and the strength, the grace of ritual on cricket field or Aldershot Tattoo. I would be utterly not-me without it. But I know the British. They are not me; they are not American.

Scene Three is short and simple. It is the scene of summer vacation. The place is Tsingtao, which, to my biased eyes, seems even now to be the most beautiful of all places on this earth where the mountains come down to the sea. Kaiser Wilhelm II called it the fairest jewel in his crown. It was the last grab of European imperialism in Asia.* When I first knew it, forty years ago, the well-ordered Germans had built a neat little colonial town in a corner of the great bay and were reforesting the surrounding hills and building roads. My father and his friends built the first little summer cottages on a point called Iltus Huk, which later became one of the swank resorts of the China coast. On summer afternoons we could sit on our porch and see way out on the ocean white moving targets and the splashing foam of high-explosive shells as they hit short or long. The shells came right over our cottage from gun emplacements in the hills behind.

Then early in the morning, while we dozed, we could hear from across a little valley behind us the heavy tramp of German soldiers and the songs they sang, the German *Lieder*, as they marched from barracks to manoeuvres. "*O Wandern, Wandern, meine Lust . . .*" It was all, to be sure, a little militaristic, but also very remote from our real lives as missionaries or as young Americans.

We liked the German town—the clean streets, the good music and bands, even the beer, which my mother shockingly insisted was no sin for her to drink. But we learned about the Germans. We learned about Germans in relation to Chinese rickshaw coolies. Germans beat rickshaw coolies. They beat them over the bare back with their sticks. Britishers, on the other hand, never beat coolies; Britishers were simply mean and nasty. After a long pull they would give the coolies only a minimum fare or less and walk haughtily away. The American didn't beat coolies; they didn't know how to be mean, and they always overpaid. If an American did lose his temper, that was a lucky break for the coolie—because it meant he got twice as big a tip.

And shall I spell out the moral of this? It's quite simple. When Secretary of State Dean Acheson—or Owen Lattimore †—says that the United States cannot intervene strongly in Asia for fear of being "imperialistic," he is talking just plain unadulterated bosh and drivel. You remember when Wendell Willkie came back from his world tour and spoke of the vast reservoir of American good will in Asia, which he said was leaking. There was still plenty of

---

* Following China's defeat by Japan in 1894–95, Germany got a ninety-nine-year lease on Kiaochow Bay and the port of Tsingtao.
† Lattimore, the eminent Sinologist, was then at Johns Hopkins.

that good will in 1945 when I revisited Tsingtao. It was all I could do to prevent the mayor from declaring a city-wide holiday, complete with parade, to celebrate the return of their American boy. But all I wanted was to swim on the beaches of the bay. And I did. And I took with me the finest swimmer in the United States Marine Corps, Major General Shepherd.* I tell you very solemnly, if American affairs had been entrusted to Major General Shepherd and to me, China would not now be Communist.

Well, there is the story of one American's boyhood as an American. In some ways that background endowed me with special qualifications to be editor-in-chief of great American publications in this critical period of history. In some ways it disqualified me. Each of you will have your own opinion of what was lucky and unlucky for me—and for you, in that story. Your opinion as a jury will be far more right than mine, but let me try to make a few points of assessment.

First of all, I probably gained a too romantic, too idealistic view of America. This was not simply because America looked better at a distance. And it had nothing whatever to do with America being an Eldorado—the typical European immigrant's dream. Indeed, I was brought up to think that if anything was wrong in America it was that too many people were too rich and rich people were apt to be more sinful than other people. My ancestors in America for 300 years had always been solvent, sometimes distinguished, but never rich. The idealistic view of America came from the fact that the Americans I grew up with—all of them—were good people. Oh, missionaries have their faults, but their faults are comparatively trivial. I had no experience of evil in terms of Americans. I knew Chinese of all sorts—good, bad, very bad and indifferent. My favorite Chinese was our cook, who smoked opium. In the countryside, in the villages and in the crowded cities I saw, even with a boy's eyes, plenty of evil and wickedness, plenty of cruelty and squalor—among the Chinese—as well as much goodness and good humor and artistry and gentleness. But the Americans I knew, they were all, all, good Christian people. Put along with that the idea that America was a wonderful country, with opportunity and freedom and justice for all, and you get not only an idealistic, but a

---

* General Lemuel Shepherd, who received the surrender of the Japanese forces at Tsingtao in October 1945, later became commandant of the Marine Corps.

romantic, view—a profoundly false romantic view. Such a view implies that *inherently* there is no problem of evil; that it is possible, even natural, for men to be all at the same time good, well to do, educated, energetic, ambitious, generous, practical, spiritual and happy.

I never went through any special period of disillusionment with America. It marks, I think, some grave fault in me that I did not. I was never disillusioned with or by America, but I was, from my earliest manhood, dissatisfied with America. America was not being as great and as good as I knew she could be, as I believed with every nerve and fiber God Himself had intended her to be.

There is a great deal more I should like to say about America and me, but I will cite just one more point. You could never guess what I have most missed having in my life. It is the fact that I have never had—and cannot have—a hometown, an American hometown. "Where do you come from? Where were you born and raised?" That is a basic American question. Few learned anthropologists have pointed out the deep and special significance of that question to and in America. The other day Vice President Barkley got himself off the hook for not being a teetotaler by saying that he came from Kentucky. You see an American can always explain himself satisfactorily by citing where he comes from—be it the sidewalks of New York or the farmlands of Illinois, or Houston, Texas.

"Where do you come from?" I would give anything if I could say, simply and casually, "Oskaloosa, Iowa." *

A verdict on me as an American might be that I am too much the American-in-general and not enough the American-in-particular. The ideals conflict in me—and perhaps in every American. The ideal of hero (Washington) and saint (Lincoln) on the one hand, and, on the other, the ideal of being a regular guy. Perhaps these are the two conflicting ideals that run through all of mankind. But they are, I think, peculiarly American-ideals-in-conflict. Nowhere is the sweet compulsion to be a regular guy so strong as in America. Yet nowhere I think do so many people have so great a yearning to rise above the commonplace and identify themselves with their country in its aspect of nobility. That, I think, has an application to journalism, and to us in particular.

* This wish was reported in a *Saturday Evening Post* article about Luce in 1965, after which Oskaloosa made him an honorary citizen.

Obviously, the editor, the publisher, has got to be, to a considerable extent, a regular guy. The figures about our audience become more and more fantastic. Every week you present your ideas to thousands and millions of people in this country who are part of the TIME and LIFE audience.

Over and above the desire, there is here a very deep and very serious purpose to serve your country and serve it not only as a nation that we happen to belong to, but to serve it in the belief that it represents and that it somehow serves the highest and the best that we know.

So while I criticize the overidealistic or falsely romantic view of America I cling to, I hold also to the basic thing which was taught me long years ago. And today I believe that a great fact is a feeling on the part of our fellow citizens that they too should be good Americans, should serve America for this very reason.

Thank God I can be with you, because I know what, in your work in these last many years, this sense of purpose has accomplished, and I think it has borne great fruit. Probably you are stuck with me for quite a long while; and for my part, I am very glad I am stuck with you.

What I have tried to bring out tonight is my notion about this country and what it means—much more than a great state. I believe it is expected to play a great part in history today.

All of us, I guess, remember Wordsworth's "Ode on Intimations of Immortality." Let me read a passage of that poem, not in this case having to do with the subject of mortality, but your and my notion about America long years ago. Wordsworth gives praise and thanks for those first affections:

> *Those shadowy recollections,*
> *Which, be they what they may,*
> *Are yet the fountain-light of all our day,*
> *Are yet a master-light of all our seeing;*
> *Uphold us, cherish, and have power to make*
> *Our noisy years seem moments in the being*
> *Of the eternal Silence: truths that wake,*
> *To perish never;*
> *Which neither listlessness, nor mad endeavor,*
> *Nor man nor boy,*
> *Nor all that is at enmity with joy,*
> *Can utterly abolish or destroy!*

Well, far from being abolished or destroyed, this love of America, this belief in it as a nation destined for good, lives in me and lives in your hearts.

I have a faithful belief that the America that we work for will win in this time and age, if we do our part. You remember the phrase, "Pray as if everything depended on God; work as if everything depended on you"—because, in a sense, everything does depend on you.

There will come in the lifetime of many here present, not the peace of God, but certainly the truce of God won by American fortitude, energy, generosity and ideals. I hope to be with you when that day comes. Meanwhile, I am proud and happy and indeed grateful to be with you—regular guys and pursuers of the American creed.

2 THE IDEA OF YALE

This was Luce's major speech to a strictly Yale audience, an alumni dinner in Cleveland on May 1, 1954. Yale's then President A. Whitney Griswold was present.

To be asked to speak for Yale in a great gathering of the clan is a milestone in any man's life. Yet when was a Yale man ever satisfied with any other Yale man's speech on Yale?

Homer himself never dared to describe the beauty of Helen of Troy. He described her only in her effects—the face that launched a thousand ships. And he tells how the old men of Troy, sitting at the gate when Helen passed by, made noises like the sound of many cicadas in the summertime. So it is with the splendor of Yale —old Yale men make noises which are both more and less than speech when the vision of Alma Mater passes through the gates of recollection.

My theme tonight is the right and the propriety and the duty of every Yale man to represent Yale wherever he is and in whatever he does. There was a time when any such a preachment would have seemed quite superfluous. Yale men were Yale men, unmistakably so. But a few decades ago, the unmistakability of Yale men began to give offense to some of our fellow citizens. It also became a subject of jest and ridicule. It is wrong to give needless offense, and it is unpleasant to be the object of a joke. The tendency therefore grew for Yale men to conceal their identification—to conceal it even to the point of losing it. Perhaps, too, this seemed to be democratic in an age of mounting democracy.

But things have changed in the last few years. We have grown up with democracy and our democracy has grown up. In many respects, if not all, America is more tolerant. A man is no longer regarded as a second-class citizen just because his ancestors came over on the Mayflower or just because his papa built a railroad. As for American nationhood, it, too, has come of age. Today Americans, as members of a vast continental fraternity, rejoice in every good thing America produces—whether it is meat in Chicago, oil in Texas, stars in Hollywood, bishops in Ohio Wesleyan or, as has sometimes been said, men at Yale.

In his definitive history of Yale, the Yaleness of Yale and of Yale men is plainly set forth by George Wilson Pierson, a most careful historian. He begins by showing that when Yale was still hardly more than a small college, it was already a great American legend, like Daniel Boone or Paul Bunyan.

In 1892—that happened to be the year my father was graduated —in 1892, the most brilliant young man on the Harvard faculty set out to examine this legend, this extraordinary phenomenon called Yale. He was George Santayana, the most beautiful of all American philosophers—and a Harvard man. No one could have been less likely to be taken in by the Yale legend. Yet Santayana came to the conclusion that the legend was no fiction; Yale had a character of its own, authentic, valid. The Yale spirit was a ponderable reality. And what were the distinguishing marks of that character? They were, said Santayana, two. Yale believes. Yale is patriotic. "No wonder," he cried, "that all America loves Yale, where American traditions are vigorous, American instincts are unchecked, and young men are trained and made eager for the keen struggles of American life."

What is it, therefore, that Yale men are to represent everywhere and always? First, Yale believes. Second, Yale is patriotic. Third, today, Yale is a university. It is the idea of a university which we

Yale men are especially called upon to represent.

President Griswold sometimes sounds as if he felt that he ought not to have to spend so much time and energy justifying the basic idea of a university. Throughout the academic world today, professors and other intellectuals speak as if they were unreasonably put upon. They seem to be saying that they ought to be allowed to go about their business without having continually to justify it.

I am reminded of the attitude of the business world in the 1920s before the crash, at the time when it occurred to me that business, being so large a part of American life, was a proper field for serious journalistic inquiry. Some businessmen at that time were not averse to having blurbs written about them, but anything faintly resembling an honest analysis of business was regarded as vulgar or Communistic or both. The attitude then, under King Calvin Coolidge, was that something called private business as then organized was the God-given order of the universe. Not perhaps immaculate—but certainly immutable. No gentleman would think of questioning it. The only people who questioned it were wild-eyed radicals or bums. Editors are easily assigned to either category.

Then came the crash. Then confidence in the whole American system seemed to collapse. The shock, the trauma, more devastating than any war we ever fought. The New Deal. Class warfare. World War II.

Today it is considered a natural part of the business process to be continually justifying itself. Perhaps to the point of boredom. But what do we have? We have not only a national economy fantastically great, but along with this, immense prosperity, and, as its greatest guarantee, a wider, more critical understanding of free enterprise than has ever been known anywhere in the world.

President Griswold, you will not object, I hope, too violently to the obvious moral. Relying on my seniority in age in the Yale family, I would suggest to you that the need to justify the university idea is not an irrational imposition. Quite the contrary. To you and to your colleagues in university leadership, this is a golden opportunity. Now you can implant and establish in America, as it has never been established before in any great democracy, the idea of a university. And you should have, among 60,000 Yale alumni, the willing evangelists of the gospel as you expound and elucidate it.

There is, of course, a difference between the university and business in the hierarchical scale of values. The university outranks business or "economy." Men do not live to eat; they eat to live. And the university is life—it is the light of life: *Lux et Veritas*.

Five hundred years ago, Gutenburg invented movable type. That invention changed the world. A few years ago, the atomic bomb blasted a great gulf between us and all previous ages. But long before either of these two inventions, there was another invention, or discovery, greater and more radical than either, from which has resulted both the printing press and the bomb, and nearly everything else we know. That was the discovery of reason by the Greeks—critical reason and objective truth. We cannot couple with that discovery an exact date or name. But it was about 600 B.C. And among the names are Heraclitus, who noted that you can never step into the same river twice, and Thales, who, as I recall it, fell down a well and saw so many stars that he came up with astronomy. And then there are Anaximander, Anaxagoras, Parmenides and all the others in that first *Who's Who* of intellectual man. But though the date is inexact and the names various, I think of the discovery of reason as just as definite an occurrence as the printing press or the bomb or Christopher Columbus.

It is to that event, Mr. President, that, I take it, you appeal in claiming for the university—and for the free mind—an autonomous imperative. The true charter of a university comes not from a king nor from a transient government of politicians, but from the discovery of Reason. Politicians can neither make nor unmake truth, although they can and do torture it, cripple it and humiliate it. What is required of kings and politicians and majorities and mobs is that they should respect truth and support its servants.

For the discovery of critical reason was the discovery, too, that there is Truth with a capital T—and that men, by critical reason may search for it and may actually find it, bit by bit, each bit being real, being a bit of the whole of objective truth, which is, as a whole, unknowable, yet real, because God is real. And the bits are real. The bits are tested, refined, put together, partially discarded, put together again in a larger pattern. Reality is real. That is the consequence of the discovery of critical reason. That is the rock of our Western civilization, and there is no civilization like unto it. For the Buddhist reality is not real; for the Confucian it is merely pragmatic; for the Hindu it is merely deplorable; for the Taoist, merely contingent. But in the West, reality is real, and so we have marched forward across many a valley and plain and across the high mountain ranges of vision, discovering not only science, but also freedom itself and, incidentally, America and the nebulae racing to the curvature of infinity.

The condition of human life has been radically changed. Politics and economics and society will radically change. But reason remains—critical reason links us with all the glorious and brave and humble searchers and finders of truth. And this will abide forever, through triumph and disaster, until the end of time.

Charles Malik, the great philosopher-statesman, has said, remove the church and the university from the Western tradition and you have nothing distinctive left. God has so arranged matters that even He Himself must be continually justified to man. So also the university must be justified. Of course. For the university, like the church, in its concrete realization falls short, from age to age, of the sublime idea. After 2,000 years of Christianity, why do we live in conflict and anxiety? By the same token, after 2,500 years of reason, why are we not all philosopher-kings—and democrats, too? The tradition of the university is not without its shameful and errant moments. The German universities—the sign of their crime was that they proved capable of little or no heroism against the monstrous wickedness of Hitler—indeed, German intellectualism is one of the progenitors of that monstrosity. Oxford and Cambridge have had their disgraceful periods. All have fallen short. In this country, the characteristic error of the universities has been their neglect of philosophy. But since the mind, no less than nature, abhors a vacuum—into the philosophical vacuum of our academies rushed seven devils labeled materialism, positivism, etc. Our intelligentsia, and all of us more or less, became bewitched, entranced by the charm of the amazing facts of physical science and psychology and anthropology and archaeology and other lore. In love with the bits of truth, many were indifferent to Truth itself.

Meanwhile, however, American intellectuals have got in the habit of viewing with alarm something they call a wave of anti-intellectualism. And we can hardly blame them. For certainly there is on the American scene an appalling amount of vulgarity and claptrap and dangerous demagoguery. And yet the intellectuals are only half right. The noises they hear disturbing the academic calm are only partly the war whoops of the witch-hunting, book-burning Philistines and their sadistic Goliaths. The other part of the noise is the murmur of millions of earnest and decent people who are asking not for less intellectualism, but for a better intellectualism. And that, by God's grace, is, I think, what we are getting.

Now, of course, whatever may have been the failings of the university at any time, we Yale men ought never to have failed in our appreciation of the great idea itself—or in our allegiance to it. If you and I are even a little bit civilized, if we are only a little different from cannibalistic savages, we owe it in great part to the discovery of reason, to the liberal tradition of the university, and to Yale in particular. And we ought never to forget to whom we owe it. Who of us could have been at Yale even most carelessly without having caught a glimpse of what civilization is and of what it means to be civilized? There, under "Visigoth" Mitchell * or some other one, we saw the meaningful pageantry of history. There, however deaf, we heard the great music of Shakespeare—"flights of angels sing thee to thy rest." There we glimpsed the prophetic atom and wandered at least once through the stacks of the library, treasures greater than all the gold of Fort Knox. This was our privilege, and forever after it is the obligation of our privilege to represent in the life of America the blessed sight and sound of truth, and of beauty. Those who attack the freedom and the autonomy of truth and beauty—let no Yale man be of their company. If any of us have ever at any time become confused and got mixed up with the witch-hunters, with the ruffians, with the enemies of civilization—and perhaps all of us have in some degree—let us confess our fault and resolve hereafter to be what we are: men of Yale, men of the university, men of the great tradition of reason and reasonableness. Let us represent as best we can, and better than we have, the idea of the university. So we represent most of what is good in us.

* Sydney Knox Mitchell (1875–1948) was a professor of history described in Pierson's history of Yale as "a great, burly, bearish man with the face of a Visigoth king."

3   WE ARE SUCH STUFF . . .

John M. Vorys, a lawyer and former U.S. Congressman
of Columbus, Ohio, was a Yale friend of Luce's who in
1961 was president of the Kit-Kat Club of Columbus,
home of Ohio State University. The Kit-Kat is a small
literary sodality, half town and half gown, modeled on
the 18th-century London club adorned by Addison and
Steele. Invited by Vorys, Luce read this paper to the
Kit-Kat on May 15, 1962. The members and their
wives were invited to ask questions afterward, but none
did because (said one member) nobody wanted to break
the spell.

John Vorys gave me to understand that at the Kit-Kat Club it
doesn't matter in the slightest what the speaker says. Nor even
how he says it. My indoctrination is that the Kit-Kat Club is a very
exclusive society of superior souls—so superior that they can afford
to meet every now and again for no weighty purpose at all, and
that they can allow even the speaker to share in this happy hour of
irresponsibility.

Irresponsibility! That was the lure that fetched me here. The
chance to be irresponsible—that at least was the lure which, as an
editor deep in the murky waters of the world's events, I read into
the glittering trout fly which, months ago, John dangled on the
bright surface of the future.

We editors stand for the free press. That was enough in Jefferson's day—and even in Hearst's. But, in my time, all journalists
feel compelled to announce themselves as the free and *responsible*
press. We would no more go around without our cloak of responsibility than a lady would be caught without her mink. It is not my
purpose tonight to attempt a striptease act—being, in a number of
ways, disqualified. But I do propose to indulge in irresponsibility.

The general corpus of my remarks must necessarily be the state of the world. The proper, responsible thing to say is that the world is in a terrible jam and going to hell in a handbasket. And not, mind you, simply because of the hydrogen bomb. No, there are deeper reasons—moral decadence, creeping socialism and the population explosion of bugs and other night life. These are the challenges we must meet. These are the things that must be said, boldly and clearly.

Tonight I want to say something else—almost the exact opposite. I want to say—and by Kit-Kat! I am going to say it—that the world situation over all is good and is likely to continue to be good for a good long while. This is what I say, having left that heavy cloak of responsibility back on the other side of the Alleghenies. Does that mean you should not take me seriously, that I do not intend to be sincere? There's a natural confusion here which I must quickly clear up. From now on, I shall be meaning, very sincerely, what I say. It is simply that I shall be indulging myself in the freedom of your hospitality to say, in a free manner, what I think. *In vino veritas*. So also it can be that in a friendly atmosphere of irresponsibility one's truth comes to the surface.

The last sentence of the lead story in TIME of May 4 read as follows:

> As summer beckoned, the relaxation of tensions for once did not seem to be merely the calm before another storm. It almost seemed like calm.

I did not dictate that sentence. I was in Arizona when I read it on a Monday morning. By coincidence, the evening before, I had been saying the same thing to a friend—only more. For with great hesitation, I had been saying that perhaps the world was in for a relatively long period (like ten years) of relative calm. To make this kind of prediction is, of course, dangerous. For in the nature of human affairs almost anything can happen any time. Generally speaking, it is safer to be pessimistic than optimistic. For thirty years good journalists have seen trouble ahead, and while I know of some bad things that loomed but didn't happen, most of the bad things did happen.

For over thirty years, the world has been in a state of crisis. The Great Depression of the early 1930s. The rise of Hitler. The Japanese attack on China in the early and mid-1930s. World War

II and its aftermath. The atom bomb. The danger and horror of
Soviet Communism. The take-over of China. And the general revolutionary sweep of things culminating in Africa. Thus for thirty
years the true picture of human affairs has been one of great crises
together with innumerable "little crises," any one of which, it was
thought, could trigger larger crises.

But this has not always been the condition of human affairs.
Along about 1878, to take the date of the Congress of Berlin, it
was felt, and more or less rightly felt, that the "world situation"
was under control—mostly under control of the European Concert
of Powers. This international political stability, *plus* amazing advances in science and technology, led to the generally optimistic
view of human affairs which, in the 20th century, has been so
roundly condemned, theologically and otherwise. And the effort in
1907 to establish Permanent Peace at the Hague, however naive
it sounds to us now, was expressive of much of the temper of the
times. Permanent Peace seemed both reasonable and possible.

One of the things that was overlooked by many in the era of
Victorian optimism was the seriousness of the "social problem"—
the rise of socialism, the labor movement, anarchism, and ultimately Communism. At the turn of the century it was not thought
that the "social problem" would upset the world applecart. And in
fact, by itself it didn't. It had little to do with the outbreak of
World War I—though a major consequence of World War I was
the coming to power of Communism and socialism.

Western man in the last 200 years has been much more his-
tory-minded than men in other times. We might say that the reality
of current happenings has been more existentially real than in past
ages—with very few exceptions, notably the case of the Old Testament Israelites. This existential reality of current happenings has
been due to (1) the size and scale of events, (2) the communica-
bility of them—and also to an insistence by such people as ourselves that people owe it to themselves and to society to "keep
informed" on current events. A revolution in Patagonia may affect
your pocketbook! In any case, your status will be affected if you
venture forth to a cocktail party without adequate briefing on
Patagonia!

Desirable or not, a state of relative well-informedness *is* the state
of mankind today—or anyway, of Americans. Then: what *is* the
proper evaluation of the present world situation? I would say that

the situation is good. Some of the big and obvious good factors are as follows:

(1) The strength of the U.S. militarily and otherwise.

(2) The "success" of Europe.

(3) The very great weakness of China.

(4) The economic difficulties of Russia—and, to whatever extent it exists, the "liberal" thaw.

(5) The fact that the obvious trouble areas, considerable though they may be—such as Africa or South America—do not seriously threaten world dislocation.

To these broad geographical categories, I would add some qualitative categories, *viz.*:

(1) The idea and practice of constitutional government (generally "democratic") seem to be more widely and firmly established than in any previous epoch.

(2) As a concomitant of constitutional government, the idea and practice of "market" economy seem to be ditto. If someone wants to argue that, at the height of the 19th century, market economy dominated the world more than now, I might agree. But in the last few years our sort of market-conscious mixed economy has gained notably in prestige over socialist or Communist economics.

(3) Third, if it is hazardous to attempt global evaluations of politics and economics, it is a kind of folly to attempt a moral or spiritual balance sheet. Nevertheless, it is a folly which must be attempted—otherwise you would have *Hamlet* without Hamlet. And I would say that while the doctrine of Original Sin has not been repealed and is not likely to be, the moral condition of mankind is relatively good. Several years ago, Toynbee wrote a piece about Japan, in which he noted how little attraction Christianity had for the Japanese. But, said Toynbee, what he observed in that dynamic country was an increasingly widespread acceptance of the Christian ethic. I would say that the moral condition of mankind is good because there is an intelligible, worldwide dialogue on right and wrong. There is a feeling among scientists and other "nonreligious" people that ethical standards are essential and that religion is on the whole a "good thing" because it contributes to the maintenance of ethical standards. All of this might be subsumed under the head of "democratic idealism"—with its various slogans, such as "dignity of man." From a seriously religious

point of view, this ethical culturism may be deplored as standing in
the way of truth—but, for the moment, that may be called another
matter. Syncretism may be bad for true religion, but it is good,
short term at least, for the development of a worldwide moral
community.

Here, then, is my case for an optimistic appraisal of the present
and foreseeable future—an appraisal drawn largely from the data
of journalism, from the march of events. But actually, of course,
any view of man's fate must depend on an appraisal of the nature
of man himself. "What is man," cries the Psalmist, "that Thou art
mindful of him?" And exuberantly he replies, "Thou hast made
him but little lower than the angels, and hast crowned him with
glory and honor. Thou hast made him to have dominion over the
works of Thy hands; Thou hast put all things under his feet."

Well, the Psalmist's view of man has by no means been typical
of man's estimate of man over the ages. Even in the optimistic
19th century a gloomy view of human affairs was not lacking. The
lady in the Victorian novel, horrified by some lapse in manners,
was continually asking, "What's the world coming to?" Christian
hymns sighed about this vale of tears and notified the Lord that
"change and *decay* in all around I see." Or take Mark Twain—he
was a misanthrope and would characteristically say, "There are
times when one would like to hang the whole human race, and
finish the farce."

In our time, churchmen have made prolific use of the A-bomb or
H-bomb to prove the perversity and moral turpitude of mankind.
But it only goes to prove the persistent determination of man to
think the worst of himself and his future. Ample evidence seems
always available.

Centuries before the bomb, the most bilious view of man had
been expressed in the most brutal terms. Hobbes, the political
philosopher who stands at the beginning of modern times, justified
the Absolute State on the basis of human depravity. The anthology
of man's disgusted view of man is a fat one. Let's have just a little
more fun with it.

Here is a saint, Saint Bernard, telling us that "man is nothing
else than . . . a sack of dung, the food of worms." And like unto
the saint is Leonardo da Vinci, the artistic and scientific genius of
the optimistic high Renaissance. "Man and the animals," says he,
"are merely a passage and channel for food, a tomb for other

animals . . . a coffer full of corruption."

Job is more poetical: "Man is born unto trouble, as the sparks fly upward."

And finally, Homer, in the heroic age, when you might have thought it was a joy to be alive—Homer says: "Of all the creatures that creep and breathe on earth, there is none more wretched than man."

Well, it's time to sweep all this biliousness aside—no matter how prestigious the owners of the upset stomachs were. As for da Vinci, Hobbes and a thousand others—either I have unpardonably quoted them out of context, which I haven't entirely, or else even they, at times, should have had their mouths washed out with soap and been sent to bed without any supper. And the genius who can most quickly get all the bad taste out of our mouths is, of course, the supreme and immortal bard, Shakespeare.

It is not only that his Rosalind is so gay and his Juliet so tender and his Falstaff so irresistible, and his kings and warriors so brave and his statesmen so patriotic—it is rather that all the pageantry of Shakespeare's humanity is so real that with eager pride all of us gladly claim to belong to Shakespeare's human race. And yet we must be cautious with old Will: he's a sly one. "What a piece of work is a man!" Now watch it—is Shakespeare kidding?

> *What a piece of work is a man! how noble in reason! how infinite in faculty! in form, in moving, how express and admirable! in action how like an angel! in apprehension how like a god!*

Yes, of course, Shakespeare is laying it on a bit thick there. Yet whether through deepest tragedy or highest comedy, Shakespeare sends us on our way with a throb of Elizabethan glory in our veins and a joy in our humanity. And—one haunting doubt. Not any miserable doubt about the worth and savor of life—but only a doubt as to whether it is of ultimate importance under the aspect of infinity.

> *We are such stuff as dreams are made on*

and

> *And, like the baseless fabric of this vision,*
>   *The cloud-capp'd towers, the gorgeous palaces,*

The solemn temples, the great globe itself,
Yea, all which it inherit shall dissolve;
And, like this insubstantial pageant faded,
Leave not a rack behind.

Under the aspect of eternity. *Sub specie aeternitas.* "What is man that Thou art mindful of him?"

How will you answer that question? Santayana, for all that he lived his life in the uplands of reason and of beauty, never quite found the answer. Wistfully he admires Columbus—

Columbus found a world, and had no chart,
Save one that faith deciphered in the skies;
To trust the soul's invincible surmise
Was all his science and his only art.

Shall we, too, trust the soul's invincible surmise?

How will you answer that question? I, for my part, will make affirmation with the Psalmist—that we are here and that we venture forth from day to day by the decree and by the intention and toward the faithful promise of the Eternal. And what I have said to you in reasonable hope about the present moment of history rests, ultimately, on that affirmation.

But for the resolution of your own doubts, whatever they may be, I give you a word spoken by a great artist to us in our time—a word spoken by Thornton Wilder, whom John Vorys and I are proud to claim as a friend of our youth.

The Skin of Our Teeth was produced in the bloodiest year of World War II. It was a strange allegory which had critics quite confused. Adam and Eve are mixed up with Mr. and Mrs. Antrobus of Excelsior, New Jersey. The Ice Age was coming—had already shattered Boston—but on the other hand the wheel had just been invented, an invention announced by a Western Union boy. The New Jersey house harbored all sorts of odd characters, including a dinosaur and a mammoth. All quite mixed up. Yet ordinary people loved the play and if you read it or see it today, it is all quite clear.

When the worst has providentially failed to happen and when, in New Jersey, all has returned to a sort of family normalcy, Mr. Antrobus makes to Mrs. Antrobus his big speech, as follows:

"All I ask is the chance to build new worlds and God has always given us that second chance, and has given us voices to guide us; and the memory of our mistakes to warn us. Maggie, you and I will remember in peacetime all the resolves that were so clear to us in the days of war. Maggie, we've come a long ways. We've learned. We're learning. And the steps of our journey are marked for us here."

"All I ask is the chance to build new worlds." We, all of us, build new worlds every day. Without expecting any radical change in human nature, let us learn from the past. Without expecting to achieve the wisdom of angels, let us rejoice in the new knowledge and the new power that flood in us. The moment has come again, I think, for mighty deeds of human progress through the great globe entire. That is the view I express to you in this hour of freedom which you have granted me. And this vision will not be wholly extinguished when the magic doors of the Kit-Kat Club close for the night and we return, each of us, to the world of responsibility.

Thank you—and good night!

INDEX

JOHN K. JESSUP

John K. Jessup's long career with Time Inc. has included major editorial posts on three of its magazines. He started with FORTUNE as a writer in 1935, and the following year he became an editor of that magazine. In 1940 he was transferred to TIME, where he became a senior editor in charge of the Business section. When Time Inc. formed a committee in 1942 to study and report on the postwar outlook, Mr. Jessup was appointed its chairman; he was responsible for the preparation of reports on this subject which were published periodically as a supplement to FORTUNE. In 1944 he became Chief Editorial Writer for LIFE, a post which he held until he was called upon in 1948 to head FORTUNE's Board of Editors. Three years later he returned to LIFE, where he was Chief Editorial Writer until 1969. A graduate of Yale, Mr. Jessup was born in Rochester, New York, in 1907, and now lives in Wilton, Connecticut.